# ADVOCACY RESEARCH IN LITERACY EDUCATION
## SEEKING HIGHER GROUND

# ADVOCACY RESEARCH IN LITERACY EDUCATION
## *SEEKING HIGHER GROUND*

**Meredith Rogers Cherland**
*University of Regina, Canada*

**Helen Harper**
*University of Nevada*

LAWRENCE ERLBAUM ASSOCIATES, PUBLISHERS
2007     Mahwah, New Jersey                    London

KH

Lawrence Erlbaum Associates, Inc., Publishers
10 Industrial Avenue
Mahwah, NJ 07430
www.erlbaum.com

Cover design by Tomai Maridou

**Library of Congress Cataloging-in-Publication Data**

Cherland, Meredith Rogers, 1947–
Advocacy research in literacy education : seeking higher
ground / by Meredith Cherland, Helen Harper.
    p. cm.

Includes bibliographical references and index.

ISBN 978-0-8058-5056-2 (cloth)
ISBN 978-0-8058-5057-0 (pbk.)
ISBN 978-1-4106-1544-8 (e book)

1. Literacy—Social aspects—Research. 2. Critical pedagogy.
3. Social advocacy. I. Harper, Helen J., 1957– II. Title.

LC149.C456  2007
302.2'244072—dc22                           2006017398
                                             CIP

Books published by Lawrence Erlbaum Associates are printed on
acid-free paper, and their bindings are chosen for strength and
durability.

Printed in the United States of America
10  9  8  7  6  5  4  3  2  1

7/09/08

# Contents

# Preface

This book is a project that we hope may offer some small measure of energy and focus for the future of research in our field. We have written it for those who work or soon will work in literacy education. We have also written it for ourselves, as a response to our own struggles in literacy education and our own despair over the conditions and circumstances of 21st-century life inside and outside of the classroom in these most conservative of times. This book is a review of what we are calling *advocacy research* in literacy education. It assesses just what educational researchers who are working for social justice (we count ourselves among them) have accomplished, describes current challenges, and outlines future possibilities.

The book has two purposes: to categorize and describe advocacy research, and to explore ideas about literacy and justice. Chapters 1–5 survey the terrain of advocacy research in literacy education. Advocacy research includes scholarship that explicitly addresses issues of social justice, equity, and democracy with the explicit purpose of social transformation. Although there are many studies that could have been included here, and many ways of mapping advocacy work, we have chosen to group this large and expanding body of research into four categories: (a) critical literacy(ies), (b) radical counternarratives in literacy research, (c) literacy as social practice, and (d) linguistic studies. Each category is outlined in its own chapter; two chapters in the case of Radical Counternarratives. Each chapter describes the research area, traces its history, provides example studies, and assesses the contributions of research to advocacy work now and potentially in the future.

Chapters 6–8 explore ideas about literacy and justice. These chapters provide a deeper consideration of challenges to the field of advocacy research, and suggests future directions for advocacy research and scholarship. It reflects the need to complicate and trouble the terms and relations between and among social justice, ethics, democracy, freedom, and literacy. We argue that these terms and relations need to be reconceptualized to ground advocacy work against the current popular understandings of literacy education which limit the efficacy of advocacy work. Moreover, we will be examining the psychological investments, the dreams, desires, and utopian visions that seem to underpin and at times constrain possible work in the field. In discussing challenges and future directions, we will address the materiality of bodies and the actual labor involved in doing advocacy research as well as theory. This book is an attempt to seek firmer, dare we say higher, ground on which to situate, secure, and effect advocacy work in our field in these troubled times.

And these *are* troubled times. The proliferation of standardized testing, teacher testing, scripted lessons, and programs, along with the privileging of particular forms of "scientific" research are destroying the gains made by radical and progressive educators over the last three decades in the literacy education of all children, particularly those marginalized by poverty and other forms of social difference. Treading deeply in the waters of a burgeoning conservative backlash, it is difficult for an advocacy worker because teachers, teacher educators, and the poor themselves are blamed for social and economic failings of society. We believe it is time to strengthen and intensify our efforts as advocacy workers in promoting the most principled, the most effective literacy education for democratic life. We hope this book contributes to such efforts.

Who are we to undertake such work? We are researchers produced by the discourses of our times. One of us was schooled in postmodern theory, the other in critical theory and sociolinguistics. We both believe that knowledge and truth are produced in many locations, and from many perspectives. We believe that who we are is a shifting question. That identity is dynamic, plural, and discursively constructed, but that there are material structures and circumstances that contain or restrain the "floating signifier" of selfhood. We both speak from positions of material privilege, from within family histories of upward mobility. In our individual and collective histories within advocacy work, we have been positioned at various moments as outsiders and, at times simultaneously, as insiders, as women, as Canadians, as feminists, as whites, as middle class, as heterosexuals. These various positions produce and push up against our performances of and our efficacy in advocacy research.

As English Studies educators and former schoolteachers, we are positioned in particular ways regarding advocacy and literacy work. We are highly invested in language and literacy. We have lived with the power of story, and have come to see that language is where the world gets constructed and produced. We believe in the power of learning to read and reread the word in the world. So, although despair may have inspired us to write this book, we find hope in our critical beliefs in education, in literacy work, and in the future of the advocacy research we are about to critique.

## AN INVITATION

We will close this preface by inviting our readers to think critically about what we offer in the chapters that follow. Bear in mind that we are presenting *our* reading of advocacy research in literacy education. We produced our categories and subcategories by reading widely and discussing them with each other and with other colleagues in the field. The studies described in the text are chosen from those we found or were directed to in the research literature. Knowledge is always partial (Kumashiro, 2002), in that it is never complete and always depends on where you stand (Harding, 1996). Also it is certainly likely that despite our best efforts, we have failed to include important studies that could qualify as advocacy research in literacy education. Therefore, we invite our readers' critical participation in this enterprise by commenting on the categorization, and by adding to the lists of advocacy studies contained in this text.

Every effort has been made to choose studies that meet the criteria we ourselves have set for advocacy research, and which we will describe in the introduction that follows. Of course our project, like all others, is doomed to shortcomings, but we think that what we have done is practical and necessary for understanding the field, assessing its accomplishments, and pointing to its possible futures. We hope our readers will agree and that they will find the book useful in forwarding advocacy work in literacy education, in all our efforts to secure a profoundly democratic life.

## ACKNOWLEDGMENTS

We would like to thank Barbara Comber, Carole Edelsky, Carol Schick, Naomi Silverman, Dennis Sumara, and Michael Tymchak for their responses to earlier drafts of this book; and Bettie St. Pierre for pointing us in the direction of so much wonderful scholarship.

Meredith would like to thank Joel Taxel and the Department of Language Education at the University of Georgia for welcoming her as a Visiting Scholar during the 2002–2003 academic year, and the University of Regina for the past 28 years of intellectual space and material sustenance. She also thanks Carole Edelsky for inspiring her by example to think and write for feminism and for social justice, and Carl Cherland for more than 30 years of tolerance, companionship, and support.

Helen would like to thank her former colleagues from the Faculty of Education, University of Western Ontario, in particular Rebecca Coulter, Michael Kehler, and Suzanne Majhanovich, for their ongoing support, and her new American colleagues and students in the College of Education, University of Nevada, Las Vegas, for welcoming her to the daunting adventures in literacy education that constitute their world. She remains forever indebted to her early mentors, Dr. John Willinsky and Dr. Roger Simon; and, of course, to Tom Bean, without whom nothing would seem meaningful.

—Meredith Cherland

—Helen Harper

# Introduction: Advocacy, Research, and Education

*All of us have "dangerous memories" that can disturb the comfortable and comfort the disturbed in us, can challenge complacency and renew commitments … When we return to them, they challenge our compromises with the status quo, help us to remember what we should not forget, and inspire recommitment to whom we ought to be—they revitalize.*

(Thomas Groome, 1998)

*Qualitative research that frames its purpose in the context of critical theoretical concerns still produces, in our view, undeniably dangerous knowledge, the kind of information and insight that upsets institutions and threatens to overturn sovereign regimes of truth.*

(Joe Kincheloe & Peter McLaren, 2000)

*I believe too much in truth not to suppose that there are different truths and different ways of speaking the truth.*

(Michel Foucault, 1988/1984)

## LITERACY AND POLITICS IN THE TWENTY-FIRST CENTURY

We began thinking about this book in the months that followed the events of September 11, 2001, and writing it in the shadow of the U.S. war against Iraq, a war that has drawn in and affected all of us on this

1

planet. The world at the beginning of the 21st century has become, for us and perhaps for many of you, a much more frightening place.

We believe that the current state of education in the United States, Canada, and Australia, and perhaps elsewhere, is firmly connected to the discursive organization and the material effects of September 11 in that both are products of a right-wing, neo-liberal agenda that has come to dominate our lives in and outside of schools. Like many of you, we are angry and alarmed at the discourses that continue to name and condition our world and our schools as individualistic, competitive, and militaristic spaces. We despair that the radical politics, progressive teaching, and research of the late 20th century seem to have had so little lasting effect in our classrooms. Our anger, alarm, despair, and at times our guilt crystallize around particular moments and events that for us have become disruptive and dangerous memories that demand critical reflection and action. September 11 is an event that unsettled us, but there are also other personal memories connected more directly with our work as educators and researchers that have been and continue to be disruptive. We will share two:

Meredith: Gloria Steinem says that most women suffer from "terminal guilt." I know I do. I feel guilty about many things: I feel guilty about being wealthy enough to have another woman clean my house, about being addicted to coffee and sweets, about having been a working mother. I use my intellect to see where my guilt comes from, to see the societal and cultural forces that position me as guilty, and then I am able to live with it. But there is one package of guilt that I have carried with me for the past 15 years that I can't explain away. Fifteen years ago I did my doctoral research in a small town for one full year. I constructed a critical ethnography of the literacy practices of seven sixth grade girls, their parents and their teachers. That study benefited my career greatly, but it did nothing for the people I studied. They never understood it, or learned from it, or benefited from it in any way that I can see.

Helen: I remember a difficult moment when Meredith was telling me about one of her graduate students who had just recently completed a study of girls in school—a study that confirmed once again, *once again*, the marginalized status of young women in school contexts. It was, of course, just another study in the long history of feminist studies in education, reiterating a story with which I am all too familiar. But this was a *recent* study, conducted in a place and time that I had so wanted to believe was better. All of my professional life, nearly twenty years as a teacher and a professor, has been focused on understanding and challenging the ways in which femininity is understood, organized and normalized in schools. Meredith's story left me wondering what if any difference any of our work has made. I still wonder.

There are many events and many moments in educational contexts today, where the most suitable response may well be despair, anger, or guilt. In Ontario, as in many parts of the United States, high-stakes testing of primary, elementary, and secondary students has been deemed necessary. Streaming (tracking) has been affirmed as a practice and the number of streams has been significantly increased. The province has recently established a literacy test that high school students must pass to graduate. Not surprisingly, English as a second language (ESL) students, minority students, working-class students, and the disheartened, unfortunate enough not to find themselves in the university, bound-for-glory streams, are failing this test in large numbers. More generally, we despair at the seeming ineffectiveness of the literacy and language research and scholarship that has characterized progressive and radical education across the continent and the globe for the last 30 years. It seems to us that, as literacy practices become ever more complex in an increasingly global, technological, and dangerously inequitable world, critical research and scholarship seem to be losing their momentum at the very moment they are most needed.

## ADVOCACY RESEARCH: A HISTORY OF THE TERM

Advocacy researchers are people who are working for social justice. But that doesn't say much. There are many discourses of social justice circulating among educational researchers today, many meanings for social justice. And there are many forms of educational research, informed by different theories of the world. Advocacy research is not tied to any one form of research. In our view, it can appear in almost any research paradigm and make use of any method. What distinguishes advocacy research from other educational research is the intent of the researcher and the explicitness of that intention. *Advocacy research* is explicitly transformative, and so explicitly political. It is research and scholarship *for* transformation, and a more compassionate and equitable world.

More than 20 years ago Bogdan and Biklen (1982) used the terms "advocacy research" and "action research" interchangeably, saying that advocacy (or action) research was done for the benefit of someone, and that it sometimes involved collaboration with the community of those who were to benefit from the research. Bogdan and Biklen (1982) explained that qualitative research methods came into use in the early 20th century, a time of social turbulence when people were facing major problems caused by industrialization. Researchers in a number of fields began to collect data so that people would act to stop water pollution, or urban slum expansion, or the tracking of the poor in school. Ethnographers especially used their research to reveal the depths of poverty and despair, and to call for social change that would allow the poor to lead better lives.

In 1982, when Bogdan and Biklen were mapping methods for qualitative research in education, *advocacy* research was also called *action* research, which they defined as the systematic collection of information designed to bring about social change. This research was meant to be applied. The researcher was actively involved in the cause for which the research was conducted, and acted as an advocate for the people studied. Even when the people studied collaborated with the researcher, it was the researcher's job to represent their views, to help those with power understand a problem, and to convince them to act to remedy it. In 1982, advocacy research was one small subcategory of qualitative research in education.

By 1992, when the first *Handbook of Qualitative Research in Education* was published, the term *action* research was used more frequently, but it was still sometimes called *advocacy research* or *advocacy planning* (Schensul & Schensul, 1992, p. 171). Included in the chapter entitled "Collaborative Research: Methods of Inquiry for Social Change," action (or advocacy) research was presented as one kind of *collaborative* research. Schensul and Schensul explained that collaborative research involves educational researchers with members of the community or group under study (people who do not usually engage in research) in inquiries intended to benefit them. Either side can initiate this research. Often the community seeks the assistance of the researcher for advocacy. The collaborative research that results is viewed as a tool for the empowerment of groups with limited access to research data and the research methods that produce it: women, ethnic minority groups, and the poor (Schensul & Schensul, 1992, p. 195). This work is informed by an ethic that links research with service and advocacy, engaged in "for the common good" (p. 164).

In the same 1992 volume, Linda Grant and Gary Fine provided a chapter entitled "Sociology Unleashed: Creative Directions in Classical Ethnography." Grant and Fine (1992) counted "action research" as one of those creative directions. In their view of action research the researcher forms and acknowledges a specific commitment to individuals or groups involved in a social relationship, frequently to a "have not," less powerful, or stigmatized group. The research is organized at least partially according to the needs of the group to which the researcher has partisan ties, but it is not necessarily collaborative. The authors comment that researchers inevitably have partisan ties that they ought to acknowledge. When researchers do not acknowledge or, more fundamentally, do not consider their political commitments, Grant and Fine suggest, they most often unintentionally serve the interests of elite groups (1992, p. 443).

At a time when collaborative approaches and single researcher approaches to action research were both labeled "advocacy research," Patti Lather (1992) discussed the ways in which research "paradigms" were being posted and articulated. She categorized some research as belonging to an "advocacy" *paradigm*, using that term to name the many approaches to qualitative research that were openly value based. At a time of "methodological ferment in empirical research in education," when refuting positivism seemed to be on every qualitative researcher's mind, feminist researchers, neo-Marxist critical ethnographers, community-based collaborative action researchers, and some of those exploring the uses of postmodern approaches in educational research, all belonged to an "advocacy" research paradigm which acknowledged social inquiry as value laden. Lather (1992) pointed out that this advocacy research was openly ideological, and made use of change-enhancing advocacy approaches to inquiry, which were for the purpose of "enabling" social change and the redistribution of social power. Such work, Lather argued, was not more or less ideological than mainstream research that failed to make visible and acknowledge its political commitments. In short, advocacy research made an epistemological break from the positivist insistence on researcher neutrality and objectivity. More than a decade later, this definition remains compelling and useful.

But by the year 2000, the discourse had changed again. In the second edition of the *Handbook of Qualitative Research in Education,* Kemmis and McTaggart (2000) provided a chapter on "Participatory Action Research," which distinguishes between *participatory research*, which is often associated with social transformation in the Third World, and which has roots in liberation theology and neo-Marxist approaches to community development, and *critical action research*, which makes a commitment to bring together broad social analyses and the study of power in a local setting, for the purpose of improving people's lives. Both are committed to the participants. But where *critical action research* sets out to reveal the disempowerment and injustice created in industrialized societies, *participatory action research* may include varieties of action research that do not. Both emerged as forms of resistance to conventional research practices that colonized, by imposing research agendas on local groups from central agencies far removed from local concerns and interests. Both require participants to take the construction and reconstruction of their social reality into their own hands. Both enable people to make change thoughtfully, after reflection. But it is *critical* action research that studies practice as *socially and historically* constituted and reconstituted, and which includes theorizing for collective political action.

At this point in the history of the term "advocacy research," we want to claim it and redefine it, at least provisionally, for ourselves and our purposes. For us, *advocacy* research (which includes scholarship that is not necessarily empirical and field-based) is research that stands in solidarity with oppressed peoples and communities, and works to improve their material, economic, and political circumstances. But in understanding and challenging such circumstances, advocacy research also serves to improve conditions for *all* of us, including those who are in privileged positions. As we use the term, advocacy research looks to humanize us all, to open spaces for social and personal possibility (Simon, 1992). Thus, advocacy research is not something done *for* others. Instead it is work intended to create global community(ies) in which material, social, and individual needs are met, where human dignity is assured, and where human possibility is continually nurtured. Advocacy research names this vision and pushes for action.

This book will concern only the advocacy research in the field of literacy education. This is, of course, only one small part of the *advocacy* research, and only one small segment of the *literacy* research of our times. We have chosen to engage in this work for our own purposes, to consolidate, support, and strengthen our own efforts in the field. We hope to help to discursively construct *advocacy research in literacy education* as a field, much as Tate (1997) once constructed *critical race theory* as a field by bringing together a number of studies and explaining their cohesion around a common purpose (see Lather, 1999). In this effort we hope to inspire a new sense of purpose and direction in ourselves and perhaps in others. At the very least it is important to see what has been accomplished, to celebrate some of the brilliant work being done, to acknowledge the challenges and limitations that constrain this kind of work, and, most importantly, to consider new directions.

Lather (1999) said that any review of educational research does not simply provide a mirror for a field. It *constructs* a field in situated and partial ways. A review is a gatekeeping device that polices and excludes. It is also a productive device that frames and interprets from an invested positionality. Our investments in knowledge-producing practices, and our sense of what constitutes worthwhile research are obvious in this text. We are (or attempt to be) ever vigilant of our own categories, our own social, psychological, and intellectual investments, our own "will to power." At the end of the day, we want research in literacy education to advocate more powerfully for marginalized "Others," and indeed for all of us in an increasingly troubled world.

## MORE ABOUT ADVOCACY

*What will he call his dominant instinct, assuming that he needs a word for it? No doubt about the answer: This sovereign man calls it his conscience …*

Friedrich Nietzsche, 1887

Nietzsche, in tracing the historical evolution of concepts like morality, guilt, conscience, responsibility, law, and justice, argued that ethics and politics were and always would be linked. Masculinist translations aside, he envisioned possibilities for overcoming the nihilism he had described in his earlier work, the nihilism for which he is perhaps best remembered. Nietzsche's later work views nihilism as a pathological transition stage that humanity must pass through while old values and ideals are being revalued and new ones created (Ansell-Pearson, 1994).

If ethics and politics are linked, then it can be inferred that people who experience guilt will do so because they feel a sense of responsibility for something, and a responsibility to act. Keenan (1997) pointed out, however, that in postmodern times the "fable of responsibility" poses a predicament. There are no grounds for an ethic of responsibility, no rules, no foundations, no certainties that can guide our human lives and actions. How can researchers then assume responsibility for others, and act to advocate? This is a very good question for researchers who struggle to take account of poststructural theories of the self and the other, of knowledge and power, of truth and the impossibility of justice. Poststructural theories do not call researchers to social action. But Caputo (1993) argued that deconstruction offers no excuse not to act. At this historical moment it is not easy to find or create an ethic for justice and advocacy. But there are those who are doing that work, those who are working for and from an ethic of responsibility for the other.

## MORE ABOUT RESEARCH

*While those with power and resources have access to the media and can shape perceptions to their own benefit, the same is not available to the poor. Thus, giving voice to those who are not often heard or seen is a distinct contribution of qualitative research.*

Ray Rist, 2000

In 1970 Ray Rist published a groundbreaking article in the *Harvard Educational Review*, in which he described how, for one class of children he observed, their public school (and specifically their reading lessons) mirrored the class system of the society at large and actively contributed to maintaining it. In that research he used a qualitative design and methodology, arguing that education was a social process that could not be reduced to numbers and test scores, and that only qualitative research could do justice to education's complexities. Thirty years later, Rist (2000) still pointed to the value of qualitative research, which gives voice to those who are often not heard or seen; which provides a window into the actual lives and views of others, conveying information in powerful ways and creating new awareness; and which brings the views and beliefs of those who are marginalized to those who are at the centre of social and political power.

Almost all of the empirical advocacy research we will review in this book (apart from the theoretical scholarship that advocates in a different way) is qualitative research. But all this qualitative advocacy research does not proceed from the same set of assumptions or from the same worldview. Patti Lather (1991), extending the work of Habermas (1971), listed four categories or "paradigms" of research: positivist, interpretive, critical, and poststructuralist. Each is a category of human interest that leads to certain knowledge claims. Each offers a different approach to generating and legitimating knowledge. Lather (and Habermas) explain,

> Prediction is the purpose of positivist research.
>
> Understanding is the purpose of interpretive research.
>
> Emancipation is the purpose of critical research.
>
> Deconstruction is the purpose of (and a method for doing) poststructural research.

Because each paradigm has a different ontology and epistemology, each paradigm offers different views of knowledge and power, of justice and injustice, and of how injustice can be remedied. Inevitably, each paradigm has different goals or purposes for advocacy research in literacy education. The chart that follows provides a limited summary of these assumptions.

Most of the "advocacy research in literacy education" described in this book is qualitative research inspired by the premises of the last two categories, critical research and poststructural research. Positivist research rarely advocates, although some positivist premises occasionally find their way into the three kinds of linguistic research we describe in chapter 5. Interpretive research can rarely go beyond presenting what participants

TABLE I-1

| | Truth | Knowledge | Power | Justice | Self | Goals for advocacy research |
|---|---|---|---|---|---|---|
| Positivist | There is universal Truth, external to human beings, which is immutable, objective, and reliable. | Knowledge requires the discovery of what is true. It uncovers Nature's laws. It is neutral, and exists outside of human history. It leads to progress. | Knowledge can serve Power without distortion of the Truth. | Justice is the rule of Truth, universal, and transcendent. It requires administration by a wise authority, who applies predictable laws and rules by the right use of Reason, and requires retribution without mercy. | The human self is stable, coherent, and pre-existing. | Advocacy is called for when Truth and Justice are not being served. Researchers who uncover the laws of nature and find the Truth will contribute to progress and the possibility of justice. |
| Interpretive | Reality is a social construction. | Knowledge is socially constructed, human and contextual. | Power is something individuals may hold and use, but there is also power in the collective, which can choose to act. | Justice is also a social construction, locally situated, informed by cultural norms. Injustice occurs when social realities conflict, and human suffering results. Compassionate justice is possible. | The self exists in relation to other people, and is at least partly socially produced. | Research seeks to understand participants' meanings. Advocacy research seeks to listen, and to hear participants' voices, so that suffering can be eased. |

| | | | | | | |
|---|---|---|---|---|---|---|
| Critical | Reality is a social construction, and can be changed. Social realities are reproduced over time. | Knowledge is varied, and is produced and reproduced to serve different vested interests. What counts as knowledge is political, tied to power and privilege. | Power results from the unequal distribution of wealth and resources and social privilege, according to categories like race, gender, and class. | Justice requires the equitable distribution of resources (distributive justice), and an end to exclusion and oppression. | The self and the social order are mutually constituted. The self is historically and politically defined according to race, class, gender, religion, sexual orientation, etc. | Advocacy research can help to emancipate. By revealing the workings of privilege, and power, and empowering people to act against privilege, it can shatter systems of inequity and change the world. |
| Post-structural | Reality and Truth are multiple, produced in and through language and discourse. | There are many forms of knowledge, all partial, all historically and socially contingent. The world is unknowable, and we must look beyond the known. | Knowledge is an effect of power. Power can be positive and productive. | Justice is complex and an unstable concept. Whatever direction we take, some voices will be silenced; some interests will not be served. | The self is unstable, shifting, always in flux. The self is produced and performed. Through crisis and resistance, the self is resignified. | It is productive to disrupt Truth, to de-construct, to unsettle, to examine our cherished attachments to see how they limit us. Research can disrupt the way things are. |

think and feel. But critical theory, which works to change the world by exposing and shattering systems of privilege and power, has inspired and is still inspiring advocacy research in literacy education. And poststructural theory, which seeks to disrupt "truth," and unsettle the ways things are, is proving useful in other approaches to advocacy research.

## MORE ABOUT LITERACY

Literacy has long been associated with advocacy work. The scholarship of historians of literacy like Harvey Graff (1987) reveals that literacy education has always been imbued with moral and political agendas, more specifically, with a powerful and at times dangerous desire to refashion society. Certainly at various times in history teaching African American slaves, women, and/or the working class to decode print was a controversial if not illegal practice. More recently, highly illegal efforts to provide literacy education for the women of Afghanistan under the Taliban have been dangerous life-threatening acts, and demonstrate all too well the importance and the passion that underlie literacy work.

Literacy has been and continues to be widely studied. Researchers and teachers know more about encoding and decoding print, more about reading processes, more about the wide and increasing range of texts and textual modalities, and more about the sociology of reading the word and the word critically and politically than ever before. Yet for all this knowledge there seems less clarity about literacy. The term literacy is now applied to so many areas of human endeavour that some have argued the word is fast becoming meaningless (Wysocki & Johnson-Eilola, 1999). There are at least 197 different kinds of literacy listed in ERIC databases, including forms such as media literacy, workplace literacy, computer literacy, and visual literacy, but also Christian literacy, museum literacy, risk literacy, somatic literacy, ecoliteracy, and post-literacy. The complexity, and we would argue the murkiness, in the naming of literacy speaks to a need to determine what is meant or produced when the term is invoked. Of necessity, this book will review (through descriptions of specific studies) how literacy has been defined in advocacy work.

Moje and O'Brien (2001) take a different approach. They have offered four compelling metaphors for literacy, each one linked to a different goal for research. These metaphors can enrich our understanding of the differences in the ways literacy researchers understand literacy education and engage in advocacy through it. Moje and O'Brien (2001) explained that when the goal of literacy researchers is to predict, they are inclined to envision literacy as a *pattern*. When their goal is to interpret, they are inclined to envision literacy as *experience*. When their goal is to reform or emancipate, researchers are likely to envision literacy as *power*. And when their goal is to interrupt, they are likely to see literacy as *turbulence*. We find the last two metaphors for literacy (*power* and *turbulence*) at work informing most of the advocacy research reviewed in this book.

The critical literacy research we cite in chapter 1; the research studies using sociolinguistic analysis and critical discourse analysis reviewed in chapter 5; and many of the studies of literacy as social practice all assume that literacy is a form of *power* and that the systems of privilege and dominance through which the world operates are there in literacy and in literacy education. Assuming that literacy is power, these studies assume that literacy education has power to maintain those systems and to challenge them. This is a critical view.

The literacy research we describe in chapters 2, 3, 7, and 8, however, is more inclined to assume that literacy is *turbulence*, chaotic, to various degrees uncontrollable and unpredictable. It seeks to reveal and interrupt the power relations in literacy practices that create literacy as a seemingly stable and normalized practice. This research and scholarship works to disrupt, to keep systems in play, and to fight the tendency for categories to congeal (Lather, 1992). These researchers remind us of the need to fight the tidiness evident in any account of literacy research, to consider the leakiness of categories and rubrics, and to question authority in any construction; more particularly, to continually challenge our own discursive practices as we write (Davis & Sumara, in press; Richardson, 2000). This is a poststructural view.

Another important view of literacy comes from Linda Brodkey. Her 1991 classic essay on literacy as a social *trope* described the ways in which nations (and literacy researchers) use literacy to justify or to rectify social inequity. She explained that all official definitions of literacy project both a *literate self* and an *illiterate other* and are therefore implicated in the construction of the political and cultural terms on which groups of people live with each other. Brodkey (1991) pointed out that definitions of functional adult literacy are changed over time, to serve the interests of those who have the resources and power to make certain people (the illiterate) a social problem, to make illiteracy an explanation for the society's ills, and to promote literacy as the solution to social and economic problems. Literacy is then seen as the sole difference between "us" and "them," and the ways in which the value of literacy is confounded by race, class, and gender are ignored. Brodkey quoted Michelle Fine (1986), who has said that "Targeting schools as the site for social change and the hope for the next generation deflects attention and resources, critique and anger from insidious and economic inequities" (p. 407). Brodkey then pointed out that this literacy trope, which constructs the illiterate other as one who cannot *read,* excludes *writing* from definitions of literacy. She says that when literacy means *writing* as well as reading (as it did in the Cuban literacy campaign of 1961), the illiterate other can be constructed as someone who might "talk back," and the literacy trope becomes one of liberation and a means for social change. The relationship between the literate self and the illiterate other becomes one of reciprocity. Brodkey argued that a Freirean critical literacy curriculum for adult education in the United States would serve the interests of the poor by teaching them to read the political and social world, and to "write back." She pointed out that a functional literacy curriculum teaches the poor only to read what *we* (those in positions of dominance) write. Brodkey's (1991) explanations of literacy as social trope remain useful and compelling in efforts to understand the present neoconservative American government's literacy policies, and more generally, the current climate for literacy research in the United States, Canada, and elsewhere.

## MORE ABOUT EDUCATION

It seems to us that, in the past 10 years, literacy educators and researchers have had more to say about education in general. Carole Edelsky's (1994) essay "Education for Democracy," for example, has been widely read and cited. Teachers have formed study groups to consider her message, and to work at teaching for democracy (see Allen, 1999). Edelsky (1994) argued that education ought to be for the purpose of bringing about democracy, a political system that emphasizes participation among equals, and that does not privilege the rights and interests of the wealthy over those of other people. Education *for* democracy would be education aimed at ending the systems of dominance that create the conditions under which we live now, conditions of unequal influence over who gets what. Education for democracy would be aimed at helping people to *see* those systems of dominance, and then to take action against them. Education for democracy would teach critique. It would actively tie language to power. It would require the teaching of a critical literacy that would enable people to use reading and writing to undermine and counter systems of dominance and unequal social and political power. It would take literacy learning beyond the personal and the individual, to put the act of challenging systems of privilege at the center of the curriculum. This is a critical view of education, in which both teaching and research would work to bring an end to systemic privilege and domination, and to create a climate where people could have a significant say in what affects their lives. These are views of the purposes of education that inform much of the advocacy research described in this book.

But there are other advocates for justice who speak of education in a different way. Kevin Kumashiro (2003), for example, described possibilities for using education to disrupt common sense. Kumashiro (2001, 2003) offered examples of teaching for transformation that come from several different subject areas, including math, social studies, science, and English studies. Kumashiro viewed education as a site for making common sense visible, and for contesting it. He examined curriculum as a common sense discourse that needs to be challenged and disrupted. He described teaching that brings to light students' unconscious and unstated assumptions about the world and makes visible the discursive practices that work to disadvantage some people. The educative enterprise for Kumashiro (1999) requires interrupting repetitions of unjust practices and challenging harmful readings of the world. Literacy education in this view involves teaching students to understand the harmful lenses that color their readings of the world. Kumashiro uses his scholarship to present a view of education, not so much as an enterprise for revealing structural and ideological oppression, but rather as a means for interrupting and refusing them.

Here we have two views of education as an arena for transforming the world: one informed by critical educational theories; the other by poststructural theories. But their separation is not neat or complete. Both allow for and support certain forms of advocacy research in literacy education and the studies described in this book. Both views of education will appear in the chapters that follow. In chapter 8 in particular, both critical *and* poststructural views of education can be seen to inform the discourses surrounding democracy, citizenship, literacy, and freedom.

## ADVOCACY RESEARCH IN LITERACY EDUCATION

Advocacy research is not easy to describe. It does not stand still to have its portrait painted. Nor does it lend itself to any easy categorization. The discourses described earlier are some of those that surround advocacy, research, literacy, and education. They circulate, interact, and work to shape what is being done and what will be done, as well as how we understand past efforts. There is a long and dramatic history of advocacy research and scholarship in education and more particularly in literacy education. This book will concentrate on the last 30 years, beginning in the 1970s with the work of Paulo Freire and his conception of critical literacy. Freire's legacy is powerful. Much of the research described in this text could easily fall under the category of "critical literacy." But advocacy work in literacy education is also rooted in the ongoing research and activism emanating from feminist, postcolonial, queer, Black, indigenous, and minority studies and from the interdisciplinary field of cultural studies. These areas expand the ways and means through which literacy in advocacy work can be articulated. These fields share common ground with critical literacy in a focus on power relations, but differ in emphasis, in methods, and in theories of knowledge, truth, and justice.

As envisioned here "advocacy research in literacy education" is an umbrella term intended to capture research and scholarship that is concerned with explaining, both theoretically and practically, the explicit connections between linguistic and discursive practices, and social power and pedagogy. This includes work that resonates broadly within the sociology of education. It can be situated within the politics of feminism, antiracism and critical multiculturalism, postcolonialism, queer studies, and neo-Marxism. It is research that is explicitly committed to social justice and equity, working toward the radical transformation of our global society.

But the divisions among categories are not always clear. This book provides examples of the ways in which qualitative research informed by critical theory has begun to take account of poststructural theory (Kincheloe & McLaren, 2000), and has benefited in the process. Certainly, critical scholars have been expressing impatience with the ways in which the "linguistic turn" of postmodernity has led researchers to stress ambiguity and indeterminacy, so that the word "critical" may no longer be counted on to quickly and easily name a view of the world that recognizes systems of dominance and privilege (Edelsky & Cherland, 2005; McLaren & Gutierrez, 1996). Postmodern debates over essentialism, social constructivism, and the politics of deconstruction have in this view deflected attention away from the analysis of capitalism and global economic shifts (McLaren & Gutierrez, 1996), and research that focuses only on textual exegesis (it is argued) has turned attention away from present conditions in the schools. But critical researchers have had to respond to accusations that their very efforts to "liberate" have perpetuated relations of dominance by ignoring or repressing differences in identity and power (Ellsworth, 1992). And in spite of their impatience, many critical researchers have responded to poststructural theories in positive ways. Most have turned away from the economic reductionism of Marxism and have found new hope for emancipatory forms of social research in poststructuralist theories of discourse, knowledge, and human agency.

Kincheloe and McLaren (2000) argued that research grounded in critical theory has been "reconceptualized" to include studies of privilege that concern not only class, but also race, gender, sexuality, and other forms of social difference; to expose the discursive forces that prevent people from shaping the decisions that affect their lives; to critique technical rationality; to take account of the impact of desire on emancipatory projects; to respond to the centrality of language and discourse in the construction of hegemony and ideology; and to focus on the relationships among culture, power, and dominance. Literacy research grounded in critical theory has been enriched by poststructural theory and some of that research has been included in this book.

This book will also provide examples of new literacy research and scholarship informed by poststructural theory, research that has begun to follow critical theorists and researchers in looking at its own implications for classroom practice (McLaren & Gutierrez, 1996). Postmodernist discourses have been accused of "political uselessness and [of having] debilitating effects" on educational research (Rikowski & McLaren, 2002). But lately poststructural theories of subjectivity have been used to explore the ways in which identity is constructed and negotiated in literacy lessons, and also the ways in which teachers can act to interrupt these constructions that result in unequal power relations. Queer theory, for example, has been used to inform classroom teaching that destabilizes identities and power relations and unsettles the common sense assumptions of classroom life (Britzman, 1998; Kumashiro, 1999; Sumara & Davis, 1999). Poststructural theories have taken account of some critical theory, moving educational researchers far beyond textual exegesis to a more critical engagement with pedagogy and classroom constructions of power. And critical theories have taken account of poststructural theories of discourse, knowledge, and power, moving literacy researchers beyond structural analysis to a greater engagement with identity and difference. Jennifer Gore's (1992) comment on how critical theories and poststructural theories might work together in our research comes to mind: "I believe academics must continue the kinds of political struggles which are the concern of critical and feminist pedagogies, but should do so while constantly questioning the 'truth' of their/our own thought and selves." (p. 69)

## AN OVERVIEW OF THE CHAPTERS

In light of the tensions and difficulties in describing advocacy research and the perspectives that inform it, we close this introduction with a theoretical overview of the chapters of this book.

In chapter 1 Helen discusses Paulo Freire's life and work and "the Freirean legacy" (Slater, Fain, & Rossato, 2002). She presents us with an overview of Freire's life history and his writings, to deepen our understandings of the beauty, depth, and influence of Freire's work in this world. Included as well are some of the feminist and poststructural critiques of Freire's philosophies that trouble the transparency and the inevitability of his theories and his political projects. The chapter also offers reviews of some of the advocacy research in literacy education that has grown out of a Freirean tradition, research that speaks openly of differential power and the effects of the politics of exclusion that many people experience every day. Much of the research and scholarship cited expands the kinds of power relations it deals with, without ever neglecting the capitalist materialities that organize and disorganize the society in which literacy education exists. In effect, the chapter lays before us Freire's legacy. Like Michael Apple (2002), we see a twofold Freirean legacy: Freire has shown educationists how to accept critique and change in response to it, and he has provided a model of how to act to interrupt multiple forms of dominance, inside and outside of education. Freire's legacy begins this book for good reason: His thinking continues to inspire "the long revolution" (Williams, 1961).

Chapters 2 and 3 extend the critical legacy of Freire in educational research by exploring four theoretical orientations to research that complicate Freire's sometimes modernist views of literacy education and his ways of working for social transformation and social justice. In chapter 2, Helen presents literacy research informed by feminist theory and Meredith presents literacy research informed by queer theory. In chapter 3 Meredith addresses postcolonial theory and critical race theory in relation to literacy education. All four theoretical counternarratives (feminist, queer, postcolonial, and critical race theory) can and do inform thoughtful, reflective advocacy research that works for justice. The contrast between this kind of research and Freirean critical literacy research is not always obvious. Perhaps it is that the research described in chapters 2 and 3 takes an understanding of subjectivity beyond Freire's concept of *conscientization* and complicates his notions of the sources and effects of power.

In chapter 4 Meredith presents advocacy research informed by a view of literacy as social practice. This kind of research comes from researchers educated in the discipline of anthropology or sociology who know how to use the research tools of ethnography to good effect. But each kind of literacy research reviewed in chapter 4 goes beyond concerns for laying bare the unstated norms of a culture. Although all this research does see literacy as social practice, each subcategory approaches literacy in a different way. The *situated literacies* research Meredith reviews demonstrates that literacy is different in every place and time and context, and it also begins to tie literacy to social power. *Multiliteracies* research explores a wide variety of emerging representational resources for "literacy" (visual, audio, spatial, multimodal) and advocates by concerning itself with how educators might use these resources to redesign social futures for and with those who are "at risk." The *adolescent literacies* research Meredith reviews advocates for an age group, attending to power inequities and working to improve the literacy education and the material lives of teens by pointing to possible social action. And the advocacy research inspired by *activity theory* uses cultural–histori-cal theories of the human mind in society to demonstrate the intelligence of bilingual children whose education is being restricted and curtailed by racist antibilingual education policies in conservative times. Inclined to be critical of systems of privilege and dominance, much of this research on literacy as social practice also complicates identity and the cultural discourses that work to shape it.

In chapter 5 Meredith presents literacy research inspired by the field of linguistics, reviewing work in three major areas: sociolinguistics, psycholinguistics, and critical discourse analysis. This is research en-gaged in by those who have knowledge of the "science" of language, but who refuse to analyze language without attending to its social con-text and to issues of power. Pennycook (2001) has pointed out that lan-guage is central in human life, and that language is fundamentally tied up with the cultural politics of the everyday. In chapter 5 socio-linguistic advocacy research in literacy education is shown to reveal the cultural politics of the everyday, as it demonstrates the ways in which the systematic failure of working-class and minority children is accomplished in schools. Critical discourse analysis too works at high-lighting the social injustices language accomplishes, by demonstrat-ing connections between language in use and larger societal systems of privilege and power. Both sociolinguistic advocacy research and criti-cal discourse analysis (CDA) take a critical stance, and both seem to be influenced by poststructural theories of language as the location for the construction of meaning.

Psycholinguistic advocacy research works differently, however. It uses a theory of reading grounded in linguistics (in its theories of lan-guage acquisition and the psychological construction of tacit language rule systems that are implicated in reading) to confront government pol-icies that use literacy education to control teachers and limit the poten-tial of poor children through education. Even though it is often grounded in a discourse of "right" and "wrong" theories of literacy ac-quisition, psycholinguistic advocacy research engages energetically in political battles by working to discredit the conservative legislation of basal reader programs and strict phonics instruction, and by tying these to a neoconservative political agenda and to corporate power. Lately psycholinguistic advocacy research has turned its attention to revisiting critical literacy and whole language instruction, bringing them together in ways that are better suited to teaching.

In chapter 6 Meredith looks back to reflect on the views of social justice and of ethics represented in the advocacy research in literacy education presented in the first five chapters of this book. She highlights the fact that advocacy research in literacy education is coming from a number of different disciplines (psychology, linguistics, sociology, philosophy, and literary theory) and from a variety of theoretical orientations within those fields. There are many views of how to do research for social justice and many visions for achieving social justice. Chapter 6 presents a number of constructions of the nature of social justice that have found their way into advocacy research and it reflects on the ethics that inform them. In postmodern times, without grand narratives that legitimize and direct their actions, advocacy researchers must work without guarantees and without clear guidelines. Without agreed-on meanings for knowledge, truth, and power, advocacy researchers must find an ethic that allows them (and requires them) to act. And they do. Meredith names the ethic that informs advocacy research today as an ethic of responsibility for the Other. Chapter 6 concludes with six challenges that we see for the future of the advocacy research in literacy education.

In chapter 7 Helen picks up on one of those challenges by reviewing psychoanalytic and feminist poststructural scholarship about the body, scholarship that addresses literacy education. This is scholarship that insists that researchers attend to the materiality of bodies in teaching and in advocacy work. In part this means acknowledging that advocacy is not simply the work of the mind, it is also the work of the body. Moreover Helen argued that attention must be paid not only to the body's physicality but also its relation to desire, pleasure, fantasy, and the irrational in the reinscription of literacy practices in and out of school. The chapter draws on discourses of the body as flesh and the body as text; moreover, the transgressive and erotic body; the body as governed and schooled; as stylized; and as a machine: *the cyborg body*.

In the concluding chapter Helen presents scholarship that reflects on the connections that relate literacy, democracy, and freedom. Instilling literacy (or literacies) through education is a goal that has remained firmly attached to public schooling. The mandate of public schooling, whatever else it may be, is to produce literate citizens. Democracy, freedom, and literacy in Western societies are tightly bound in a triad that continues to sustain the role and value of public education. Often literacy within this triad has referred to providing individuals with the ability to decode and encode print independently, so that they might participate fully and freely as rational and informed citizens in democratic practices. But the research and scholarship of advocacy work expand this notion of literacy and add the concept of social justice to the mix. This book concludes with an exploration of advocacy research that examines and critiques the relationship of literacy to the concepts of social justice, freedom and responsibility within democratic communities.

## A CAVEAT

*Change-oriented researchers who interrupt turbulence*
*continually interrogate discursive practices,*
*including their own.*
                              Elizabeth Moje and David O'Brien, 2001

We are, of course, well aware that naming and constructing a research field is a representation, one of many possible, and there are difficulties inherent in any effort to represent a field: Categories inevitably leak; details are obscured, oversimplied or exaggerated, or simply missing. More to the point there is, as Foucault insisted, no "natural taxonomy" here or anywhere. Our definitions, our maps, are constructions—fictions—but we hope that they are useful ones.

In addition it is important to note that, though extensive, our text is not comprehensive. It was never intended to be so. We are reviewing the general directions of the field of advocacy work in literacy education and considering the future. Inevitably some fine research and researchers will be marginalized or excluded by our particular purposes, by practical necessity, and/or by the limits of our own knowledge and perspectives. We regret this.

Ultimately, it is our hope that readers will refuse this book as a way to firmly secure their understandings of research and instead accept this book as a way to claim space for advocacy research, as a way to act on an ethic of responsibility for self and other. In the end we hope the book serves as a site of possibility for researchers, for literacy educators, and ultimately for their students.

# 1

# Paulo Freire
# and Critical Literacy(ies)

*It is impossible to carry out my literacy work*
*or to understand literacy ...*
*by divorcing the reading of the word*
*from the reading of world*

Paulo Freire, 1987, p. 49

## INTRODUCTION: CRITICAL LITERACIES

As stated in the introductory chapter, much of the research and scholarship we will be tracing in the first section of this text might be said to fall under the rubric of "critical literacy." Even those studies that do not reference the term directly are largely informed by critical literacy and the legacy of Paulo Freire. However beyond the confines of this text in the larger world of school, academic, and popular discourse, the connection between critical literacy and advocacy cannot be readily assumed. Unfortunately, critical literacy has come to be deployed in such a wide range of educational discourses and practices that some of what is done in the name critical literacy may well lie outside the nature and purpose of advocacy research.

In part this may be due to a fuzzy notion of what constitutes "critical," and the linking of critical literacy with "critical thinking," "critical awareness," and the more closely aligned term "critical pedagogy"

**23**

(Lankshear, 1997). According to Colin Lankshear (1997) the descriptor "critical" "suffers from having too little meaning or from having too much," and notes further that the calls for teachers to become more critical, "come from quite disparate theoretical positions—or from no discernible theoretical position at all" (p. 40). As an example, Lankshear noted how the development of students' "critical" thinking has been touted as the answer to improving the economy, on one hand; on the other, a "critical" literacy is widely advocated as a means to making learners more powerful language users. In both cases critical is rarely described or theorized. Certainly we agree critical is often inserted into educational discourse with much hope but without much meaning.

Another difficulty is that the explicit, often unsettling politics underwriting critical literacy and its insistent demands for social change has often been diluted with a softer, more liberal discourse. In the opinion of many advocacy scholars such a discourse has allowed wider but often highly problematic usage. Donaldo Macedo (in Freire, 2000) noted that some "critical" educators either overindulge and exoticize the voices of learners or "refuse to link experiences [of learners] to the politics of culture and critical democracy, thus reducing their pedagogy to a form of middle-class narcissism" (p. 18).

In addition the notion of what constitutes critical literacy even among advocacy researchers and activists is shifting and changing. Ongoing research and scholarship have extended, modified, and challenged what critical literacy has traditionally referenced. As will be outlined in this text, postmodern, postcolonial, and feminist theories, along with critical discourse analysis and the emerging field of cultural studies, have expanded and challenged the politics and possibilities of critical literacy. Indeed at this time it may be more appropriate to speak of "critical literacies" to capture the scope and complexity of approaches, practices, and theory that constitute the field (cf. Muspratt, Luke, & Freebody, 1997). In the end it may be that, as Barbara Comber (in press) reminds us, "[w]hat constitutes critical literacy and/or democratic education needs to be negotiated in particular places at particular times and to be informed by our personal and professional histories." For advocacy researchers and educators such ongoing negotiations demand a careful analysis and evaluation of the power of critical literacy(ies) to name and support their work in literacy education.

At this time we consider research and scholarship in critical literacy(ies) as that which engages and challenges the relationship between textual practices and sociopolitical conditions—between the word and the world as suggested by Paulo Freire at the outset of this chapter—in efforts to create a more compassionate, equitable, and democratic world. In this there can be no reading or teaching of the word that isn't also a reading or teaching of the world. Moreover, to acknowledge and challenge the reading of the word–world is to connect critical literacy education to the possibility of radical social reform. Such a definition is narrower in meaning and more explicitly political then might well appear in conventional discourse, but such a naming does not eliminate negotiation, and indeed, as will be discussed in this text, complex questions and issues remain. Certainly critical literacy(ies) does not reference a unitary approach or practice even among those doing advocacy work. Offering a useful definition in this regard, Allan Luke and Peter Freebody (1997) suggested that critical literacy "marks out a coalition of educational interests committed to engaging with the possibilities that the technologies of writing and other modes of inscription offer for social change, cultural diversity, economic equity, and political enfranchisement" (p. 1). This coalition shares commonalities, one of which is a practical, and theoretic, if not spiritual, indebtness to the life and work of Paulo Freire.

## A BRIEF HISTORY: PAULO FREIRE: A PEDAGOGY OF FREEDOM, HOPE, AND THE HEART

Through the 1970s, 1980s, and 1990s, Paulo Freire has been the name most strongly associated with critical literacy. It was Freire, a Brazilian teacher and scholar, who captured the attention—if not the hearts—of left-wing educationalists in the United States, Canada, and elsewhere with his classic text *Pedagogy of the Oppressed* (1970), now in its 30th edition. Literacy education, according to Freire, demands attention to the material consequences of selective traditions and practices of literacy. In this he, among others, argue that the contexts of schooling and literacy are not politically neutral sites where all learners gain comparable access to linguistic and social resources, and the futures such resources promise. Instead, schools, like other institutional sites, are constituted by discursive and material practices that organize and legitimate power and knowledge in particular ways. In control ways of naming and living these institutions, and society more generally, groups are able to ensure that their interests are met. But the control is not absolute; transformation of the social and political world can occur. Drawing on Freire, and Marx, Eric Weiner (2001) wrote, "[t]he transformation of social formations as well as our individual and collective consciousness entails that 'we know ourselves to be conditioned but not determined'" (p. 204). As in all advocacy work, critical literacy projects are fueled by a belief that change can occur and by the desire to ameliorate social and educational inequities, and in particular the school faiiures of significant groups of students, particularly those of lower socioeconomic status, those from ethnic and/or linguistic minority communities, and those otherwise marginalized.

Literacy education according to Freire is viewed not as a set of skills to be learned to secure one's place in the status quo, but rather as the vehicle for promoting social change. Critical literacy is "a continuing process of reading the word and the world within the context of a commitment to the expansion of human and democratic opportunities for all people" (Freire, Fraser, Macedo, McKinnon, & Stokes, 1997, p. xii). For Freire the challenge is to enter the social fray as a subject rather than an object of history and in doing so to become more human and more ethical beings in a more democratic society.

Freire was certainly not the first educator to connect literacy with social and political transformation. It was only in the 20th century that the social and political aims and intents of literacy education were largely rendered invisible. Nor was Freire the first to bring a revolutionary practice to the oppressed and marginalized; as bell hooks (1988) reminds us her teacher Miss Moore was a teacher dedicated to a pedagogy of liberation:

> Passionate in her teaching, confident that her work in life was a pedagogy of liberation (words she would not have used but lived instinctively), one that would address and confront our realities as black children growing up in the segregated South, black children growing up within a white-supremacist culture. Miss Moore knew that if we were to be fully self-realized, then her work, and the work of all our progressive teachers, was not to teach us solely the knowledge in books, but to teach us an oppositional world view—different from that of our exploiters and oppressors. (p. 49)

Nameless teachers and scholars in America and elsewhere have educated against the status quo, at times risking their careers, and some, their lives, for a literacy that would transform conditions of oppression (e.g., the teaching of American slaves and freemen, pre- and post-civil war, the teaching of young women and girls during the time of the Taliban in Afghanistan). Certainly there are controversial and marginalized educationalists who have offered programs and philosophies before (e.g., Miles Horton, Sylvia Ashton Warren). But it is Paulo Freire who attained global prominence at the end of the 20th century at a time when progressive and radical educationalists, facing a conservative agenda that has only intensified, were in need of a new language, a more comprehensive philosophy, and a stronger and more viable means to secure and inspire liberal and racial school reform. It was Freire who articulated more fully the relationship between education, literacy, politics, and liberation. His ideas may not have been original but he wove them together and inspired a generation of radical and progressive education scholars.

As with many saints (we tease) his origins were humble. Paulo Reglus Neves Freire was born in 1921 in the city of Recife in Northeastern state of Brazil.[1] His family was middle class but a series of economic and family crises left them in reduced circumstances and secured for Freire a lifelong identification with working classes and other marginalized people. As a scholarship student, he completed secondary education and eventually attained a law degree. But almost immediately he abandoned law to pursue a long-held interest in education and literacy. After working in various educational institutions, holding a number of governmental posts, and finishing a doctorate, Freire became a professor in the history and philosophy of education at the University of Recife. In 1961, on the invitation of the mayor of Recife, Freire began developing a literacy program for the many illiterates in the city. In developing his program Freire drew heavily on his activities in the Catholic Action Movement and Catholic collectivism, and ongoing his reading of Marx and Hegel, most obviously, as well as a host of other philosophers including Lukas, Memmi, Fromm, Gramsci, Marcuse, Hursserl, Sartre, Fanon, Cabral, and Merleau-Ponty. These philosophers remained foundational to his thinking through his life (A. Freire & Macedo, 1998). Freire's literacy program was designed for workers and peasants and proved highly successful. The program expanded. One of his most noted achievements occurred in 1962 when Freire's literacy program helped 300 rural farm workers to read and write in a mere 45 days.

Freire's program grounded reading and writing lessons in the lived experiences of the learners. Teachers lived communally with learners and generated words and themes evident in the economic and social conditions of the learners' everyday life. Words were analyzed phonetically and semantically. Themes from these words were codified and decodified politically by workers and teachers, participating collectively in what was called "cultural circles." In learning to read, then, learners developed what Freire refers to as "conscientizacao," that is, a critical consciousness that allowed them to become active collective agents of social and political change. Peter McLaren (2000a) described Freirean pedagogy as "antiauthoritarian, dialogical, and interactive, putting power into the hands of students and workers. Most important Freirean pedagogy put the social and political analysis of everyday life at the centre of the curriculum" (p. 7). Lankshear and McLaren (1993) described the intent of this curriculum to make

> possible a more adequate and accurate "reading" of the world, on the basis of which, as Freire and others put it, people can enter into "rewriting" the world into a formation in which their interests, identities and legitimate aspirations are more fully present and are present more equally. (p. xviiii)

Freire's program gained national attention and by 1964 his programs were assisting nearly two million Brazilian illiterates, organized in some 24,000 cultural circles (McLaren, 2000b). However a military coup interrupted these programs. Freire himself was arrested and imprisoned as a subversive. Eventually released, he soon left the country for a self-imposed exile that would last 16 years. During his exile Freire assisted a number of countries in southern and Central American, and in Africa with their literacy programs and other educational projects. For a time he was a consultant to the Office of Education of the World Council of Churches in Geneva, Switzerland. Both during and after his exile, Freire made frequent visits to the United States and Canada. For a time he taught at Harvard University. In 1980 with the assurance of an amnesty, he returned to Brazil and continued to promote and to expand his educational philosophy and practice, while living and working in the city of São Paulo. He had a marked influence on that city's school system as an administrator and continued to teach and write until his death in 1997.

Freire published many books during his lifetime. His early works include *Education as a Practice of Freedom* (1970), *Education for Critical Consciousness* (1973), and the one he is best known for, *Pedagogy of the Oppressed* (1970/2003), later updated in *Pedagogy of Hope: Reliving "Pedagogy of the Oppressed"* (1994). Among his many subsequent books are *Pedagogy in Process: The Letters to Guinea-Bissau* (1978); with D. Macedo, *Literacy: Reading the Word and the World* (1987); with A. Faundez, *Learning to Question: A Pedagogy of Liberation* (1989); *Pedagogy of the City* (1993); *Teachers as Cultural Workers: Letters to Those who Dare to Teach* (1998b, 2005); *Pedagogy of Freedom: Ethics, Democracy and Civic Courage* (1998a); and finally, *Pedagogy of the Heart* (1997), written shortly before his death.

Although his books were highly influential, he was equally remarkable in person. Clearly those who met him and heard him speak were deeply affected by his strong message and gentle words. Kathleen Weiler (2001) described her response: "For many of us who heard him speak, Freire was like an imagined, idealized father—loving, kind, just, communicating a kind of inner peace and joy in living that seemed a model of a more humane way of being in the world. Like many others, I was deeply moved by Freire, although I met him only briefly" (p. 74).

Although considered controversial by educational establishments, most notably by Harvard Graduate School of Education,[2] Freire garnered an almost mythic stature among educators across the globe, teachers and students alike, and among the leading names in progressive and radical education in academe. Stanley Aronowitz, Henry Giroux, bell hooks, Pepi Leistyana, Joe Kinchloe, Shirley Steinberg, Peter McLaren, Donaldo Macedo, and Ira Shor, brought Freire, his person, and his scholarship to North America and continued to commune with him during his lifetime. Scholars from across the globe have written about Freire, elaborating his critical literacy/critical pedagogy from their own contexts, including Barbara Comber and Helen Nixon (1999, 2005), Hiliary Janks (2003), Colin Lankshear (1997), Allen Luke (2000), Peter Mayo (1997, 1999), Chris Searle (1993, 1998), Daniel Schugurensky

(1998), Carlos Alberto Torres (1993, 1998), and many others. Recent writings from Antonia Darder, *Reinventing Paulo Freire: A Pedagogy of Love* (2002), Batodamo and Torres, *The Critical Pedagogy Reader* (2003), and perhaps the most recently Peter Mayo's 2004 text *Liberating Praxis: Paulo Freire's Legacy for Radical Education and Politics* continue to promote Freire's work, as does the ongoing efforts of his widow, Ana Maria Araujo Freire.

From Freire's writing comes a philosophical approach to schooling and to literacy education rather than a specific pedagogical strategy or method. Attention to pedagogical method, although frequently demanded by North American audiences, was not the contribution Freire wanted to make, nor the one that his followers have drawn on in their own research and scholarship. Indeed he refused to give "prescriptive advice" (Shor, 1987, p. 211). Nonetheless in our reading of Freire and of those who write of him, there would appear to be four key pivotal points[3] that he repeats in his books and his interviews, most of which were addressed directly to educators:

1. Education is political—As stated earlier, for Freire, education was not a neutral enterprise but a deeply political and social endeavor. He connected classrooms to the social order; as noted by McLaren, Freire, "was able to foreground the means by which the pedagogical (the localized pedagogical encounter between teacher and student) is implicated in the political (the social relations of production within the global capitalist economy)" (2006, p. 160).

Obviously such a position has enormous implications for teachers. In an often-cited quote, Freire comments, "This is a great discovery, education is politics!" and insisted, "[T]he teacher has to ask, what kind of politics am I doing in the classroom? That is, in favor of whom am I being a teacher?" (Freire & Faundez, 1989, p. 46). These are crucial questions that need to be asked of every generation of new educators, and repeatedly over the span of their careers by those who stay in the profession. In a letter to North American teachers, Freire (in Shor, 1987) states, "Since education is by nature social, historical, and political, there is no way we can talk about some universal, unchanging role for the teacher ... It is my basic conviction that a teacher must be fully cognizant of the political nature of his/her practice and assume responsibility for this rather than denying it" (p. 211).

As Freire saw it, traditional methods and approaches to schooling ensured the continued marginalization of oppressed peoples. Throughout his life, he contrasted traditional education, what he called the "banking concept of education," with his own dialogic education with its focus on problem-posing and critical dialogue. In banking education,

> knowledge is a gift bestowed by those who consider themselves knowledgeable upon those whom they consider to know nothing ... The more students work at storing the deposits entrusted to them, the less they develop the critical consciousness ... the more completely they accept the passive role imposed on them, the more they tend simply to adapt to the world as it is and the fragmented view of reality deposited in them ... The capability of banking education to minimize or annul the students' creative power and to stimulate their credulity serves the interests of the oppressors, who care neither to have the world revealed nor to see it transformed. (Freire, 1970, pp. 58–60)

By contrast liberation education of the kind promoted by Freire (1970) consisted "in acts of cognition, not transferrals of information ... it poses the problems of human beings in their relations with the world" (p. 66). Later he was to write, "to teach is not to transfer knowledge but to create the possibilities for the production or construction of knowledge" (1998a, p. 30). Much like John Dewey, Freire's teaching begins with learners and, as indicated earlier, with the words and themes of their everyday lives. From there pedagogy is organized to develop a social–political analysis whereby learners and teachers in the process of learning are activated, that is, "experience their potency"[5] to know and transform society and themselves. In such a process, "it is absolutely necessary to surmount the limit-situations in which men [sic] are reduced to things" (Freire, 1970, p. 93). As the oppressed take "more control over their own history, they assimilate more rapidly into society but on their own terms" (McLaren, 2000a, p. 8). Evident in Freire's writing, the education required to name and surmount the ways in which people are marginalized and dehumanized is premised on particular assumptions about knowledge, society, the self, and other.

2. Authentic knowledge of the self and the world are interconnected and situated—For Freire there exists a dialectic between subject and object, the world and the self, the self and others, and that it is in this dialectic that authentic (accurate) knowledge is produced. This is in direct contrast with traditional education and the banking method of teaching, which assumes the world and individuals are separated: "Implicit in the banking concept is the assumption of a dichotomy between human beings and the world: a person is merely in the world, not with the world or with others; the individual is a spectator; not re-creator" (Freire, 1970, p. 62). But for Freire history is not separate from the individual, nor is the individual alone in creating or recreating the world. He elaborated,

> Education as the practice of freedom—as opposed to education as the practice of domination—denies that man is abstract, isolated, independent and unattached to the world; it also denies the world exists as a reality apart from people. Authentic reflection demands neither abstract man nor the world without people, but people in their relations with the world. In these relations consciousness and world are simultaneous, consciousness neither precedes the world nor follows it. (1970, p. 69)

Together the world and the self can be known and can be changed, for there was nothing deterministic about Freire understanding of history or of society. Hope and change are always possible. As noted by Lankshear and McLaren (1993), Freire insisted that "[t]he historical and cultural world must be approached as a created, transformable reality, which like humans themselves, is constantly in the process of being shaped and made by human deeds in accordance with ideological presentations of reality" (p. 162).

3. Teachers and learners as critical, ethical collaborators in expanding democratic life—The teacher, according to Freire, does not transfer information nor facilitate learning but engages and creates conditions for learning in the local and historical circumstance of the learner, and together with the learner seeks to name,

understand, and challenge the social and economic patterns of society linked to their circumstances. Both are transformed in the process; both learn and teach in the pedagogical encounter. Freire (1998a) writes,

> although the teachers or students are not the same, the person in charge of education is being formed or re-formed as he/she teachers, and the person who is being taught forms him/herself in this process ... whoever teaches learns in the act of teaching, and whoever learns teaches in the act of learning. (p. 31)

Critical dialogue between teachers and learners is necessary for social and personal transformation. For this dialogue to occur it is important to hear the oppressed:

> One of the necessary virtues of a democratic educators ... is to know how to listen ... the educator must be immersed in the real historic and concrete experience of the students, but never paternalistically immersed so as to begin to speak for them rather than truly listen to them. (Freire, 1997, p. 306)

Again like John Dewy, Freire insisted that this did not mean dispensing with teacher authority. Freire states,

> The teacher's authority ... is indispensable to the development of the learner's freedom. What may frustrate the process is the abuse of authority by the teacher, which makes him or her authoritarian, or the emptying of authority, which leads to permissiveness ... we need neither authoritarianism nor permissiveness, but democratic substance. (1997, p. xv)

Democracy and "democratic substance" featured prominently in Freire's later writings, most notably in *Pedagogy of Freedom* (1998a) and in *Pedagogy of the Heart* (1997). According to Freire, although teachers and students work toward greater equity, freedom, and participation in society, they do so in a rigorous but respectful and ethical way, challenging and exploring the world in ways that humanize and democratize society. Freire, in speaking about Brazilian efforts to democratize, writes, "A democratic style of doing politics, especially in societies with strong authoritarian traditions, requires concretely acquiring a taste for freedom, for commitment to the rights of others, and for tolerance as a life-guiding rule" (A. Freire & Macedo, 1998, p. 266).

In his later works, Freire would draw attention to teacher preparation programs, suggesting, "it is essential to create a situation where future teachers can engage in a meaningful discussion about the ethics of education," and he considered it unethical not to include such discussion in times when "human beings are becoming more and more dehumanized by the priorities of the market" (1997, pp. 312–314). Teachers are, for Freire at the forefront of democracy, able to defend their practice and thinking on ethical grounds against what he saw as the danger and narrowness of neoliberal pragmatics.

In short Freire greatly enhanced the role and importance of the teacher. As McLaren states Freire, "gave the word 'educator' a new meaning, broadly inflecting the term so that it arches across numerous disciplinary fields, embracing multiple perspectives: border intellectual, social activist, critical researcher, moral agent, insurgent Catholic worker, radical philosopher, political revolutionary" (2000b, p. 147). In turn the learner is not a passive recipient of knowledge, but an active co-investigator, bringing knowledge the teacher cannot know, and should not underestimate. Freire (1998a) writes,

> It is impossible to talk of respect for students ... without taking into consideration the conditions in which they are living and the importance of the knowledge derived from life experience, which they bring with them to school. I can in no way underestimate such knowledge. Or what is worse, ridicule it. (p. 62)

At the same time, Freire insisted that the learner required the care of the teacher and insisted that critical dialogue and the entire process of liberatory education needed to be infused with love.

4. Love and commitment to others—Throughout his life Freire reiterated the importance of love and a commitment to humanity in the struggle for critical education and critical literacy. In *Pedagogy*

*of the Oppressed* (1970), he named such struggle as "an act of love" and commented that the dialogue necessary for critical literacy could not exist "in the absence of a profound love for the world and for men [*sic*]. The naming of the world, which is an act of creation and re-creation, is not possible if it is not infused with love" (p. 77). In 1993 he wrote that process of critical dialogue could not exist "in the absence of a profound love for the world and for people" (p. 70). In *Teachers as cultural workers: Letters to those who dare to teach* (1997), Freire states, "It is impossible to teach without the courage to love, without the courage to try a thousand times before giving in. In short it is impossible to teach without a forged, invented, and well-thought-out capacity to love" (p. 3). For Freire, such love was distinguished from sentimentality, and false generosity, that is, love "as a pretext for manipulation, and domination as the pathology of love" (Gaztambide-Fernandez, 2003).

In general Freire insisted that emotions were important to the production of knowledge: "it is necessary to overcome the false separation between serious teaching and the expression of feeling … affectivity is not necessarily an enemy of knowledge or of the process of knowing" (1998a, p. 125). Similarly, he (1998a) noted

> how much pedagogical experience itself is capable of awakening, stimulating, and developing in us a taste for caring and for joy, without which educative practice has no meaning at all, [but] … that feeling and joy does not preclude serious, scientific education and a clear-sighted political consciousness on the part of teachers. (p. 126)

Critical literacy, for Paulo Freire, speaks to the social, political, and affective character of literacy education and to the centrality of education and particularly literacy, and thus of teachers and learners, in the project of social transformation.

## Challenges and Critical Response To Freire

According to Ira Shor (1993), the values that underlie Freire's pedagogy could be best be described in the words *participatory, situated, critical,* democratic, dialogic, desocialization, multicultural, research-oriented, activist, and *affective* (pp. 33–34). It is difficult to argue with such values, and certainly Freire's message can be easily embraced. As Peter McLaren (2000a) noted, "Liberal progressives are drawn to Freire's humanism; Marxists and neo-Marxists to his revolutionary praxis and his history of working with revolutionary political regimes; left liberals are drawn to his critical utopianism; and even conservatives begrudgingly respect his stress on ethics" (p. 13). The early reception of his work in America focused on the inspiration and on intellectual armor Freire provided in challenging conservative school agendas. Freire's work supported, some would say provided, the inaugural efforts in creating an oppositional critical pedagogy.

Many took his words to heart and together with other academic scholarship fashioned a critical pedagogy–literacy in their own disciplines and contexts. In literacy education, Freire's work was used though the 1980s to critique of traditional skills, cultural literacy and personal voice approaches (e.g., Lankshear & McLaren, 1993). Others have expanded Freire approach by reading along side postcolonial theory, postmodern theory, and and/or against particular scholars. Henry Giroux (1993) for example, in a chapter entitled "Paulo Freire and the Politics of Postcolonialism," argued that Freire's work must be read as a postcolonial text. McLaren and Lankshear expanded and elaborated Freire's work in relation to postmodern theory (McLaren, 2000b). Peter Mayo (1999) and Peter Leonard (1993) related Freire work to Antonio Gramsci; and James Gee (1997) examined Freire and Plato with an emphasis on literacy. The latest work of Peter McLaren together with Ramin Farahmanpur (2005) link theories of globalization and neoimperialism with a reinvigorated Marxism to contemporary renderings of Freire's work. More generally Barbara Comber, Helen Nixon, et al. (Comber, Nixon, Ashmore, Wells, & Trimboli, 2005) are using spatial theory in their research on children and the development of their critical literacies, as is D. Gruenewald's (2003) concern with a critical pedagogy of place.

Paulo Freire's scholarship has been and continues to carry influential in critical literacy education; however his work is not without criticism from both inside and outside the advocacy community. In part Freire himself encouraged discussion and debate about his ideas, and texts such as *Politics of Liberation: Paths from Freire* (McLaren & Lankshear, 1994), *Constructing Critical Literacies* (Muspratt et al., 1997), and *Mentoring the Mentor: A Critical Dialogue with Paulo Freire* (Stokes, 1997) include radical scholarship quite critical of his work. Some of the criticism of Freire's work has been justified, as some of his most staunch supporters have begun to admit. However, in some instances the criticism has concerned pivotal points foundational to his work, and though acknowledged, they cannot be undone without collapsing the entire project. As noted by Peter McLaren (2000b), some critics decry Freire's educational approach for its idealistic vision of social transformation. Certainly Freire's vision was idealistic. He dreamed of a better world and better education, and he believed wholeheartedly in people and their abilities to rework the present for a better future: "Within an understanding of history as possibility, tomorrow is problematic. For it to come, it is necessary that we build it through transforming today. Different tomorrows are possible … It is necessary to reinvent the future. Education is indispensable for this reinvention" (Freire, 1997, p. 55).

Underpinning Freire's early work was the Marxist notion of a widespread revolution instigated by liberatory education that awakens the masses to critical reflection and action, but in his later writing Freire shifted his rhetoric. Stanley Aronowitz (1993) noted that Freire was always an "open Marxist" but aligned himself more with Antonio Gramsci and, in his later writing, was less revolutionary, more cautionary in his words. In his last book, *Pedagogy of the Heart,* Freire spoke of the careful need to secure "tolerance in reconciling differing comprehensions of political action by party members," that a leftist party "cannot engage in a dialogue with the popular classes using an outdated language," and he warned that "in search of renewal, a leftist party must lose any old trace of avant-gardism … lose any trace of any leadership that decrees itself as the edge, as the final word, one who defines and enlightens" (A. Freire & Macedo, 1998, pp. 272–273). Although Freire continued to profess his belief that the oppressed could reread and rewrite the world, that is, transform the world, he used "oppressed" and "oppressor" less often and spoke in more nuanced terms. Wendy Morgan (1997) and others have suggested the need for rhetorical change:

> In the post industrial contexts of this world, the older revolutionary rhetoric still evident in the writings of Giroux, Aronowitz, McLaren, and others might need to be replaced by a less melodramatic agenda for social equality, "in the programmatic terms of stubborn advocacy, continuing conversation, and small gains" (Knoblach & Brannon, 1993). (in Morgan, 1997, p. 9)

Talk of "stubborn advocacy, continuing conversation and small gains" may be the best way to name and strategize advocacy efforts at the level of everyday practice and policy reform.

But the fear mentioned at the outset of this chapter, remains, that is that efforts to promote critical literacy more widely will reduce it to student-centred learning, devoid of social critique, which would be a gross misinterpretation and misappropriation of Freire's teachings. Such fear might be understandable. As indicated earlier, Freire's writing somewhat rigidly names "oppressors" and the "oppressed," good and evil if you will; and good and evil education, that is, liberatory pedagogy verses banking education. Similarly, Ira Shor spoke of two great rivers of reform: "the top-down river has been the voice of authority proposing conservative agendas that support inequality and traditional teaching; the bottom-up flow contains multicultural voices speaking for social justice and alternative methods" (Shor & Pari, 1999, p. vii). He iterates the need for educators to "take sides," reminding us that "Freire insisted that critical teachers have a special responsibility to align classroom practice with democratic theory, to make the learning process reflect egalitarian ideas" (Shor & Pari, 2000, p. 1). It is not surprising that educators and policymakers might indeed want to align themselves with what is described as good, ethical, egalitarian, and democratic. Furthermore, considering that Freire discussions of the teacher as a good listener, respectful, loving, generous, and antiauthoritarian, it is quite possible that many educators and policymakers might see themselves and their teaching practices as Freirean in this way, albeit passing the radical politics and critique demanded by critical literacy. It is also possible that strategically educators might well, in these most conservative of times, soft sell the radical edge of critical literacy to secure some semblance of the approach in school curriculum. Freire's idealism, his radical language, and revolutionary politics, which have inspired so many, may create in these times strategic problems in the promotion of his work in North American schools.

Another criticism of Freire's concerns the abstract nature of ideas and the related generalities that punctuate his writing. The lack of specific detail has frustrated many. McLaren (2000a) noted, for example, that few accounts are provided as to how teachers are to move from critical thought to critical practice. The desire for more explicit discussions of practice, and Freire's adamant refusal to spell out specifics, has proved difficult for teachers, and tiring to those defending his work. A disgusted Stanley Aronowitz (1993) has spoken about the North American "fetish for method," a term reiterated by Ana Maria Araujo Freire and Donald Macedo (1998). Such a fetish may be read as a form of resistance to engaging practically in Freire's work or simply the effects of long entrenched intellectual passivity. Whatever the reason, Freire indicated clearly that he wanted teachers to apply his ideas to their own contexts, rewriting them in the process. In speaking to Donaldo Macedo, Freire states, "I don't want to be imported or exported. It is impossible to export pedagogical practices without reinventing them. Please tell your fellow American educators not to import me. Ask them to re-create and rewrite my ideas" (in A. Freire & Macedo, 1998, p. x).

Despite Freire's request there remains a lingering question of whether his approach developed in and for the third world can be recreated and rewritten in first-world contexts by educators, who, in America, generally come from the privileged classes. Supporters like Ira Shor have been highly involved with the issue of transferability and the rewriting of Freire's philosophy in North American contexts. After he and Freire authored "A Pedagogy for Liberation," Shor edited three texts that reporting on teachers' sometimes difficult but inevitably successful attempts to incorporate Freirean pedagogy in North American classrooms. These texts include *Freire for the Classroom: A Sourcebook for Liberatory Teaching* published in 1987 and later, as a tribute to Freire, *Education is Politics: Critical Teaching Across Differences, K–12* (1999); and the companion text, *Educational is Politics; Critical teaching across differences, Postsecondary* (2000), both edited with Caroline Pari. The educators featured in these texts "honor the legacy of Freire" in presenting practical examples of Freirean-based classroom curriculum. As described by Shor, the "projects use diverse themes and practices that question the status quo, connect the academic to the social and the personal, and offer positive orientations to making change" (Shor & Pari, 1999, p. 11). Addressed to North American teachers and professors these texts demonstrate critical projects in social studies, mathematics, literature and language, classes in music and media literacy, disability education, health education, early childhood education, and queer studies. The second text also features a number of chapters from and about feminist pedagogy.

In addition to these texts, Stanley Steiner's 2000 *Freirean Pedagogy, Praxis and Possibilities: Projects for the new Millennium* contains innovative efforts by educators deploying Freire's critical education in their own contexts. Antonia Darder's 2002 book, *Reinventing Paulo Freire*, features the testimonials of eight teachers, reflecting on the implementation of Freire's ideas in their own teaching practice, and *Pocket of Hope: How Students and Teachers Change the World* (2003), by Eileen de los Reyes and Patricia Gozemba, offer six case studies of educational sites where teachers, drawing on the work of Freire, link their classrooms to projects of social change.

These efforts, coming some 30 years after the publication of *Pedagogy of the Oppressed*, may have a more wide spread effect on local classrooms, but Freire's ideas by and large have not been adopted widely, as Ricky Lee Allen (2002) noted:

> For the last three decades, critical pedagogues have struggled to extend the discourse of critical pedagogy into the United States educational system. Building on the work of Paulo Freire, they have primarily relied upon the paradigms of critical theory to guide their praxis. Although his work has been very influential in some United States contexts, it has had limited effects on a larger scale. (p. 122)

Shor reminds us of the obstacles for teachers and students in securing a critical education: (a) our prolonged exposure to one-way lectures and other unilateral authority in education, and to male and White supremacy in school and society that interferes with efforts to create critical spaces; and (b) schooling and all other institutional matters are controlled by power groups at the top of the social hierarchy. Such power groups have reasserted more traditional practices informed by neoconservative and neoliberal agendas.

It is also possible that, unbeknownst to the rest of us, many teachers might well be working within a Freirean perspective but are too busy or too careful in these most conservative of times to promote their work in academe or to the general public. Barbara Comber (in press; Comber & Nixon, 1999; Comber & Simpson, 2001) has spent much of her career promoting and profiling the efforts of those "critical practical educators," providing "good news stories" much like those provided by Shor and Pari, de los Reyes and Gozemba, and Darder, mentioned earlier. Despite these efforts, Freirean pedagogy has not been widely accepted and does not appear explicitly in school curriculum in the United States and Canada. Outside of the United States, those few who have worked in school leadership or educational policy positions to bring a form of Freirean pedagogy or for that matter a progressive philosophy to school boards and districts have faced daunting challenges (Church, 1999; Luke, 2000). Freire's critical literacy remains a tough sell these days.

The idealism and abstract nature of Freirean thought aside, perhaps the most challenging criticism leveled at Freire comes from feminist scholars and activists and from scholars of color who suggest that he fails to engage other forms of oppression, besides social class, in delineating his position. Most of the texts on Freire written by his supporters speak to this criticism, although often times defending Freire rather than engaging the criticism. Antonia Darder (2002) went to some lengths to describe the criticism Freire endured, suggesting that for three decades feminists across the United States "fiercely critiqued" him, that Marxist scholars "criticized him brutally," that many scholars, educators, and organizers of color were "dismayed" by his work (p. 43).

The criticism suggested that Freire's Marxism with its rigid categories and class-based analysis, as well as the abstract nature of his writing, ignored important social differences such as race and gender in understanding and challenging oppression. Although quick to defend Freire, Shor listed the criticism leveled toward him: the universal images of teachers and students found in his work, the abstractness of the language used, the lack of gender analysis including his use of only the masculine pronoun, in general, "the one-dimensionality in Freire's call for liberation (class-based only) and his undifferentiated reference to 'the oppressed' as a unitary rather than as a contradictory and diverse population" (Shor & Pari, 2000, p. 3). McLaren (2000a), in his account of Freire's work, also acknowledged that powerful critiques had been made. Drawing on the work of Kathleen Weiler (1996), he noted that

> Freire was a vociferous critic of racism and sexism but he did not suffi-
> ciently problematize his conceptualization of liberation and the op-
> pressed in terms of his own male experience and when Freire did
> address this issue he often retreated into mystical abstractions,
> thereby discounting the deep significance of patriarchy as a practice of
> oppression. (p. 14)

McLaren (2000a) acknowledged that indeed Freire used only a limited range of narratives to construct his praxis of hope and transformation; that he failed to articulate fully his position on Christianity; that the male bias in his literacy method rarely addressed the ways that oppression formed on the basis of ethnicity, class, and sexual orientation are intermingled; and that he failed to fully engage the issue of White male privilege and the interest and agency of African-Americans apart from a wider movement of emancipatory practices (p. 14).

Freire was not oblivious to these criticisms. Michael Apple (2002) recalled Freire's efforts to rework his ideas:

> In response to the criticisms that have been made of his work by femi-
> nists, he [Freire] set about to incorporate a number of their criticisms.
> His rethinking of his theoretical, political, and educational positions—
> without giving up the immense power of his original insights and argu-
> ments—provided a model for many of the other critical educators
> who were struggling to expand the kinds of power relations they dealt
> with, without forgetting the capitalist materialities that organized and
> disorganized the societies in which they live. (p. ix)

Freire insisted throughout his career that class analysis was critical in understanding the conditions of oppression and stated late in his life that attention needed to be paid to the manner in which "class factor is hidden within both sexual and racial discrimination" (Freire, 1997, p. 87). He warned about the dangers of divisive identity politics and according to Antonio Darder "insisted that the struggle against oppression was a human struggle in which we had to build solidarity across our differences, if we were to change a world engulfed by capitalism" (2003, p. 501). Freire (1997) also indicated that he saw the concept of oppressor and oppressed and the social positioning of teacher and student in more complex terms than criticism suggested: "In the first place these issues of layered and multiple identities always preoccupied me and I always thought about them. In my political and pedagogical experience I confronted many situations of profound ambiguities" (p. 311). And he suggested that it was important to know "how to position oneself—ethically—vis-à-vis the layered and multiple identities engineered by the history of oppression that is needed" (1997, p. 312).

More recent criticism has focused on the role of the critical teacher in the liberation of the learner more specifically in the dependency of the learner–oppressed on the critical teacher–intellectual suggested or implied by Freirean pedagogy. As Gerard Huiskamp (2002) suggested,

> for people to regain self-recognition of their humanity and dignity—that is, to assert themselves as 'subjects' active in making their own history, as opposed to passive bystanders to the cultural assertions of others—they must be assisted in developing and honing the critical and reflective capacities that are constitutive of that humanity. (p. 77)

This gives the intellectual something to do for the revolution. But Michael Foucault (1977) suggested otherwise:

> Intellectuals are no longer needed by the masses to gain knowledge: the masses know perfectly well, without illusion; they know far better than the intellectual and they are certainly capable of expressing themselves. But there exists a system of power that blocks, prohibits, and invalidates this discourse and this knowledge, a power not only found in manifest authority of censorship, but one that profoundly and subtly penetrates an entire societal network. Intellectuals are themselves agents of this system of power: the idea of their responsibility for "consciousness" and discourse forms part of the system. (cited in Steiner, 2000, p. 101)

Questions remain, and no doubt debate on the limits and possibilities in Freire's ideas will continue long into the future. We do know, however, that whatever direction advocacy research and scholarship in literacy education take, Freire's name will be invoked. He remains at the heart of the work and in the heart of advocacy workers. James Fraser (1997) commented, "in other times and traditions, Paulo Freire would been as not only a great teacher but also a spiritual guide" (p. 175). More profusely, Peter McLaren (2000a) stated, "Just as Whitehead was to pronounce that all philosophy was a series of footnotes on Plato, some educators will undoubtedly make the claim that all critical endeavors in education owe their greatest debt to Freire" (p. 10). Though Freire might reject such a thought in that he named his own pedagogical role as "the Vagabond or Pilgrim of the Obvious," the legacy of Paulo Freire is powerful and will continue to support advocacy research in literacy education now and in the future.

### Critical Literacy After Freire

*We can stay with Freire or against Freire*
*but not without Freire*

Carlos Alberta Torres, 1993

Critical literacy is an ongoing and developing set of discourse(s) organized in dynamic relations with other discourses emerging both during and after the lifetime of Paulo Freire. As mentioned at the outset of this chapter, the term has not stood still as educators extend critical literacy to new contexts and incorporate emerging theory. Although the work of Paulo Freire may be organized as a starting point for much of the scholarship in critical literacy, and although some current lines of research remain tightly aligned with his work, there are other lines that, though they have a less direct connection, may still be considered within the category "critical literacy(ies)." In what follows in this chapter, we will discuss four area sites where energies and interests have emerged and converged in the ongoing development of critical literacy(ies). These sites include (a) progressive education, (b) cultural studies, (c) historical scholarship, and (d) primary and elementary education.

## PROGRESSIVE EDUCATION

Though traditional or transmission education and the "the banking method of teaching" has remained the other to critical literacy, progressive education is another important discourse against which critical literacy has come to be produced. However, some of those working within the context of whole language, a pedagogical orientation that embraces progressive ideals, have sought to claim or reclaim a more radical and critical edge to their work. Sibel Boran and Barbara Comber in the introduction to their edited text *Critiquing Whole Language and Classroom Inquiry* (2001) wrote,

> Progressive movements in education, including whole language and inquiry, have reached a point where they must interrogate their own claims about and effects on the educational outcomes of diverse groups of students. It is no longer enough to assert a radical politics in comparison with proponents of transmission models of teaching. If these theories and associated forms of practice are to remain powerful and credible for educators, we must address their limitations, and where, necessary, reinvent them to be able to demonstrate real learning improvements for socioeconomically and culturally diverse young people. (p. vii)

Critics of progressive education claim that, despite best intentions of promoting student "voice" and empowerment in a context of creating natural and open learning environments, progressive education fails to engage the larger social and political contexts of classrooms and community. In particular the effort to develop students' free inquiry, exploration, and expression fails to acknowledge that "the discourses students and teachers bring to school are inscribed with differing amounts of cultural and economic capital, privileging some and silencing others" (Shannon & Shannon, 2001, p. 124). The effect of this is to reproduce a stratified classroom under the guise of a free market of ideas in the progressive classroom.

The works of Australians Marnie O'Neill (1992) and Pam Gilbert (1991) and American Timothy Lensmire (2001), among others, have been instrumental in speaking to a more critical notion of student "voice" and textual analysis. Part of the critique of progressive education concerns the humanistic notion of self that underlies much of its practice. Rather than conceiving the self as a central, unified, ahistoric, that is, as an essentialized phenomenon, radical educators informed by postmodern theory consider the self as an ongoing product of history and context—fragmented, plural, conflicted, gaining coherence in the moment of interpellation in discourse. Such an understanding draws away form the discovery of a unique individual to how texts name and position readers and their worlds: a key point in understanding how the text can be analyzed and resisted. Critique of progressive education also demands that critical educators acknowledges the political nature of their work and, most importantly, that value not only students' culture and intellects but "also their civic leadership and social agency" in projects located squarely in the specificity of their communities (Shannon & Shannon, 2001, p. 137).

Such efforts to rename whole language with such politics can be found in the chapters by teachers and researchers in Carole Edelsky's 1999 edited text, *Making Justice Our Project; Teachers Working toward Critical Whole Language Practice*. This work, described in greater detail later in this text, promotes the efforts of those in the field to develop what is being called "critical" whole language by re-theorizing and reestablishing the critical and political nature of their work. In doing so, such efforts work to bring together whole language and critical literacy, two fields that, as Patrick Shannon (1990) documents, have had a relatively long history of separation. In these hard times, left-leaning allies are important, thus "Whole language must become part of a larger educational effort to transform education and society" (Altwerger & Saavedra, 1999, p. x). The efforts of Carole Edelsky and others suggested that more radical progressive education and "critical" whole language may be at hand, expanding and supporting critical literacy(ies) in literacy education.

## Cultural Studies

Progressivism is not the only discourse that critical literacy has been defined with and against. Barbara Comber (in press) noted that, in the Australian context, critical literacy has been informed not only by feminist and critical stances to progressive pedagogies but "has also drawn upon critical discourse analysis (Fairclough, 1992a, 1992b; Janks, 1993; Luke, 2000), poststructuralist feminist analysis (Mellor, Patterson, & O'Neill, 1991), and new ways of theorizing literacy (Freebody & Luke, 1990; Green, 1988)." These new theories and forms of analysis, discussed in the chapters that follow, broadened and deepen the work of those committed to critical literacy with greater specificity to language and discourse. Discourse refers here not simply to linguistic practices but to ways and forms of being in the world that integrate words, acts, values, beliefs, attitudes, and social identities (Endres, 2001). Moreover, such "ways of being" can be articulated–performed in a variety of modalities extending far beyond the printed page. Despite the ongoing privileging of "the book" by educators, adolescents and children are embracing new communication and media technologies, including computers, DVD, videos, cell phones, e-mail, text messaging, and so on (Alvermann, 2002; Evans, 2005; Lankshear & Knobel, 2003; Luke & Luke, 2001). This emphasis on a broader notion of discourse and on the new and emerging forms of communication is extending the traditional focus on print literacy in critical literacy education. In doing so critical literacy has come to include much of the research and scholarship in the field of cultural studies.

Cultural studies has been linked with critical literacy for at least the last 15 years. In North American this connection was initially forged largely, though not exclusively, in the work of educationalists Henry Giroux, Colin Lankshear, Roger Simon, and, at least for a time, Peter McLaren. *Counternarratives: Cultural Studies and Critical Pedagogies in Postmodern Spaces,* a 1996 text edited by Giroux, Lankshear, McLaren, and Michael Peters, exemplifies this connection. Chapters in this text directly addressed the relationship or possible relationship between cultural studies and critical literacy education; for example, Giroux's chapter explicitly asked, "Is there a Place for Cultural Studies in colleges of Education?" and then concerned the implications of cultural studies for critical practice in teacher education programs. In their 1994 edited text *Between Borders: Pedagogy and the politics of Cultural Studies,* Giroux and McLaren brought together a number of scholars "whose work attempts not only to address the importance of cultural studies as a pedagogical practice but also to rework the political grounds on which the content and context of pedagogy define the meaning of cultural studies" (p. xi). Among other topics, chapters focused on the media, sports celebrities, and art and performance in the production of cultural memories. Dedicated to the memory of Paulo Freire, Giroux and Patrick Shannon's (1997) edited text *Education and Cultural Studies: Toward a performative practice* again drew together a group of scholars

> to analyze how the intersection of the language of the pedagogical and performative might provide cultural-studies theorists and educators alike an opportunity to address the effectiveness of pedagogical practices that are not only interdisciplinary, transgressive, and oppositional but also connected to a wider public project to increase the scope of racial, economic and social justice while expanding and deepening the imperatives of a radical democracy. (pp. 2–3)

The linking of cultural studies and critical literacy (and the broader term *critical pedagogy*) is also evident in the work of new generation of academics. Eric Weiner's 2003 piece "Beyond 'Doing' Cultural Studies: Towards a Cultural Studies of Critical Pedagogy" is explicit in this regard. Weiner reminds us that "a concentration on the pedagogical aspects of popular culture without denying the political and cultural aspects of pedagogy brings us closer to developing pedagogical strategies that encourage social engagement and fuse affective and intellectual dimensions of learning" (p. 130). Jeffrey M. R. Duncan-Andrade and Ernest Morrell (2005) argued for "the critical teaching of popular culture as a viable strategy to increase academic and critical literacies in urban secondary classrooms" (n.d.), drawing specific attention to the use of hip-hop music and popular film in the classroom.

A connection is easily forged between these two areas because both critical literacy and cultural studies are radical in their perspectives, intent on understanding and intervening in issues of power; and in doing so both draw on Marxism and Neomarxist theory. In addition, cultural studies, like critical literacy, began with a focus on the literacy education of adult learners. As pointed out by Lawrence Grossberg (1994), "All of the founding figures of cultural studies (including Richard Hoggart, Raymond Williams, E. P. Thomson, and Stuart Hall) started their careers and their intellectual projects, in the field of education, outside the university, in extramural departments and adult working-class courses" (p. 3). According to Grossberg, the discipline of education as early as the 1970s was one of the only places in the United States to give cultural studies a home (p. 4). In the 1970s and 1980s, critical educators included in their reading the text *Learning to Labor: How Working Class Kids get Working class jobs* (1977), by Paul Willis, a standard text in cultural studies. By the 1990s many critical educators and researchers were incorporating cultural studies into their work

However, cultural studies has always had a broader focus than critical literacy, and has addressed a vastly different academic audience. Moreover it has been argued by many that scholarship in cultural studies, despite its early involvement in education, has tended to marginalize pedagogy (Giroux, 1994; Grossberg, 1994, 1997; Weiner, 2005). Of concern to advocacy workers, cultural studies, it is said, fails to embrace not only pedagogy but also its explicit link to the political. Henry Giroux (1994) commented,

> There are few attempts on the part of many of the theorists in the fields of cultural studies and literary studies to link their own work as intellectuals to larger social and political movements. Hence, there is no broader sense of the relationship between the pedagogical and political in much theoretical writing. (p. 123)

But though cultural studies may not be attentive to education, or the politics of pedagogy, research, and scholarship, critical literacy/pedagogy has increasingly incorporated cultural studies, in particular the study of popular culture, media, and technology, into its fold. For example, Douglas Kellner in his chapter "Multiple Literacies and Critical Pedagogies: New Paradigms" argues, "transformations in pedagogy must be as radical as the technological transformations that are taking place. Critical pedagogy must thus rethink the concepts of literacy and the very nature of education in a high-tech and rapidly evolving society" (2000, p. 196). Colin Lankshear, Michael Peters, and Michele Knobel (1996) are consumed by this rethinking and in various ways are working to consider what becomes of critical perspectives in a time of new and emerging technologies. They argue that the modernist elements of critical education, with its attention to the enclosed space of the book, needs to be rethought in light of the more fluid and dynamic postmodern space offered in cyberspace, with its decoupling of the body and subject, open virtual communities, and widely and easily accessible information networks (Lankshear & Knobel, 2003; Lankshear et al., 1996). As the title suggests, scholars represented in Janet Evans' 2005 text *Literacy Moves On: Popular culture, new technologies and critical literacy in the elementary classroom* speak to the need to engage in the critical literacy in the contemporary lives of children, which means an emphasis on the new technologies these children are embracing. Vivian Vasquez's chapter, "Creating Opportunities for Critical Literacy with Young Children," reminds us that the "everyday texts" and "everyday issues" of children bring together texts of all sorts including those that are digitally produced, as well as to the social issues that are a part of the everyday lives of children. Kellner, Lankshear and Knobel, Evans, Vasquez, and many, many others are demanding a critical and engaged literacy open to and reorganized by the rapidly changing technological and social lives of contemporary learners and their teachers.

**Historical Scholarship**

In addition to to contemporary cultural studies, there is a line of ongoing sociohistorical research and political analysis concerning literacy and literacy education that has been integral in supporting and expanding critical literacy(ies). It too bears some attention in this chapter. In North American contexts, Henry Giroux and Peter McLaren, among others, continue to offer cogent radical analysis of the political landscape with reference to education; however, it has been the extensive scholarship of Patrick Shannon that has focused most particularly on the politics of literacy education. In his 2001 edited text *Becoming Political, Too: New Readings and Writings on the Politics of Literacy Education*, Shannon's many chapters address the political history of reform in American literacy education and the response to social difference within literacy education. In his chapter "Turn, Turn, Turn: Language Education, politics and freedom at the Turn of Three Centuries," he outlines the social and political circumstances of American life at the turn of the 18th, 19th, and 20th centuries and the nature and role that literacy education was accorded to answer what was understood at the time to be the needs of the nation and the naming of American identity. In his chapter "What's My Name?: A Politics of Literacy in the Latter Half of the 20th Century in America," Shannon frames the responses to social difference and the "politics of recognition" within conservative, neoconservative, neoliberal, liberal, and radical politics. Shannon then documents what each of these perspectives means in relation to literacy education. In a similar way he has framed the ways in which poverty has been named and understood from, for example, conservative, neoconservative, and liberal perspectives, as well as the implications for reading education that each perspective assumes (Shannon, 2000). Similar to the work of Harvey Graff (1987) and Suzanne de Castell, Allen Luke, and Kieran Egan (1986), among others, Shannon's work reiterates the fact that literacy education has never been politically neutral nor will it ever be. In making visible the history and politics of literacy education, Shannon provides a space to consider how equality, freedom, and democratic life can be expanded for all in literacy education. In arguing for a radical democratic vision, Shannon fits within and supports the coalition of interests committed to critical literacy.

Joel Taxel also offers critical educators sociopolitical readings of literacy education, more specifically of children's literature. In his 2002 article "Children's Literature at the Turn of the Century: Toward a Political Economy of the Publishing Industry," Taxel makes visible the often taken-for-granted workings of the children's literature publishers and their effect on school literacy education through the 20th century and on into this age of fast capitalism. He suggests that not only does the publishing industry exert tremendous influence over what can be read at school, but also what can be read in society at large, thus understanding the complex processes that determine that publication "is crucial to the future of both education and democratic society" (p. 145). The historical analysis presented by Taxel, Shannon, and others provides those who work under the rubric of critical literacy(ies) alterative readings of the past and present, creating the means of reenvisioning not only the past and present, but also the future in literacy education. Moreover the emphasis on democratic life in this work helps advocacy researchers and educators to defend their commitment critical literacy(ies) in public schools.

## CRITICAL LITERACY IN PRIMARY
## AND ELEMENTARY EDUCATION

Finally, it would be incumbent on us to mention that, over the last decade critical literacy has found a particularly productive place in the research and scholarship concerning primary and elementary education. An exciting body of literature has been quietly accumulating (Comber, in press; Comber et al., 2005; Comber & Nixon, 2005; Comber & Simpson, 2001; Evans, 2005; Knobel & Healy, 1998; O'Brien, 1994, 2001; Vasquez, 2005, 2004). It will remain to be seen whether this work will continue to flourish in American contexts where elementary education is feeling the effects of President Bush's "No Child Left Behind Act," but nonetheless work to date in Australia and across the globe has been amazing. Collectively this body of research is demonstrating quite aptly that critical literacy has indeed a place in primary and elementary classrooms, that "powerful and pleasurable" critical literacies will not steal young children's childhoods away; that popular culture and new technologies are a part of children's lives and are mediating both critical literacies and the traditional school literacies; that young students have sophisticated out-of-school literacies; and most importantly that even young children are quite capable of developing critical consciousness.

To highlight some of this research, we conclude this chapter with three examples of studies that reflect this recent emphasis on primary and elementary classrooms, as well as the more general theoretical shifts that are now encompassing the work in critical literacies.

### Three Example Studies

Vivian Vasquez's research and scholarship has been focused on developing critical literacy with kindergarten and primary school children (2004, 2005). As mentioned previously, Vasquez insists that critical literacy is best developed using the contemporary texts that children bring to school and the immediate social and cultural issues they face. In her 2005 chapter "Creating Opportunities for Critical Literacy with Young Children: Using Everyday Issues and Everyday Texts," she specifically examines the ways in which a group of American and Canadian children, 4 to 7 years old, engage in forms of textual analysis and textual redesign in a curriculum that integrates critical literacy and the use of texts such as food wrappers and toy packaging. In describing how teachers can build both critical literacies with their students, Vasquez indicates that in creating opportunities for students to engage critically in the popular discourses and everyday texts of their lives, educators should not be co-opting their interests and energies in these texts, turning what was fun into dreary, tightly bound schoolwork that serves only the interests of the teacher. To avoid this Vasquez suggests that teachers must listen carefully to students and capitalize on their interests, issues, and literacies they bring to school to create a meaningful, critical curriculum. Such a curriculum "will make visible a range of language options as a way of giving children an opportunity to become critical readings of the word and the world" (2005, p. 89). In documenting the conversation with children about toy packaging, and specifically with merchandising of Pokemon cards, clothing, and other artifacts, Vasquez noted that issues of gender were evident in children's talk. In analyzing and redesigning the Pokemon artifacts, students were able to see how texts worked in ideological ways. Vasquez concludes the chapter with questions intended to draw attention to the discursive practices that currently construct children as literate in school contexts and the need to consider the literacies and resources that students bring to the class. She suggests that teachers use popular culture artifacts in the classroom, and look for opportunities to work critically with these artifacts and texts.

Barbara Comber and Helen Nixon (2005) offered a description of how two groups of elementary students were able to engage in reading as a cultural practice, by rereading and rewriting texts related to their neighbourhoods and their identities. One group, 8- to 10-year-olds from a community experiencing attempts at urban renewal, authored a local alphabet book entitled "A is for Arndale." Children rewrote the traditional alphabet book using their own local sites and experiences. ("Arndale," for example, is a local shopping mall.) In doing so, they redesigned the traditional alphabet book from one representing somebody else's life to one that represented their lives. In doing so, they created "an inclusive, multivocal, contemporary text inviting conversation about their lives, cultures and times" (2005, p. 143).

The other group of students was a mixed age (8- to 13-year-olds) class of recent immigrants to Australia. These students produced a magazine-style film entitled *Cooking Afghani Style*. The film imitated popular lifestyle cooking shows but in their version used Afghani food prepared by the students themselves. The film also included a student-lead tour of their local neighbourhood. In producing this film, students offered a counternarrative to the dominant stories about Afghani immigrants and culture, rewriting the representation of themselves and their community.

As Comber and Nixon suggest, critical literacy has only recently emerged in the practice and policy of primary school literacy programs. From those primary school teachers attempting to implement critical literacy, Comber and Nixon noted in their study a set of principles and practices that characterize teachers' pedagogy. The pedagogy involved (a) engaging with local realities; (b) researching and analyzing language-power relationships, practices, and effects, including how power is exercised and by whom; (c) mobilizing children's knowledge and practices with a focus on children's use of local cultural texts; (d) (re)designing texts with political and social intent and real-world use; and (e) subverting taken-for-granted "school" texts (2005, pp. 130–131). Based on this study, Comber and Nixon recommend that teachers do a critical audit of the kinds of texts produced in the classroom, incorporate place-based activities in the literacy curriculum, and develop a critical literacy approach to the reading and production of all texts.

As one final example, Barbara Comber, working in collaboration with Helen Nixon and Louise Ashmore from the University of South Australia, along with elementary school teachers Marg Wells and Ruth Trimboli, have offered an initial report on an extensive project in which children were involved in the redevelopment of their school grounds in an area listed for urban renewal. This is the same group of students that were involved in the alphabet book described in study 2. The project, discussed in a 2005 AERA paper, "Urban renewal form the inside out: Spatial and critical literacies in a low socioeconomic school community," brought elementary school children, their teachers, university academics, and architectural undergraduate students together to redesign the school grounds with the goal of assisting "young people to assemble productive social practices and discursive resources that could translate into social action in their neighbourhood" (Comber, Nixon, Ashmore, Wells, & Timboli, 2005, p. 2). During the project, researchers collected various forms of data. They videotaped key events, interviewed teachers and students, and archived students' various artifacts in efforts to determine to what extent children would appropriate critical literacies and what Comer et al. call "spatial literacies" through their participation in the project. The researchers located their study within the legacy of Freire but incorporate it with new theory and themes. They write, "In a broad sense this project is informed by a Freirean sense of literacy as concerned with reading the word and the world" (2005, p. 6), but in addition their work reflects perspectives in "new literacies" and "multiliteracies" (that in this text we will be outlining in chapter 4) together with emerging theories and themes of place, time, and spatiality. In designing the schoolyard, the children in the study developed a critical language of design and a critical awareness of the needs of those who use the space so that it becomes a place where they "can actually belong." This was accomplished through a variety of strategies, including expressive and reflective writing, drawings, interviews, discussion, modeling, computer use, visits with architects, and local field trips, all focused on spaces and places and people.

Although the project is ongoing, to date the researchers have found that the children now understand that buildings have been designed by people or by a group of people as part of a design process involving consultation and negotiation and factors of use, materials, space, and time. Understanding that power and authority are key in imposing a vision on space, students can and do insist on their ongoing involvement with the project. Although set in local and immediate circumstances, students have critically assembled a set of material and conceptual resources that may result in durable literacies that transcend the project; as the researchers write, "we hope that the spatial, documentary and critical literacies associated with this project will contribute to building their [the children's] dispositions towards action and social justice in their future places" (2005, p. 15).

## Other Studies of Note

The following offers a brief list of studies that further represent the current work being done in critical literacies.

**Duncan-Andrade, J. (2004).** Your best friend or your worst enemy: Youth popular culture, pedagogy, and curriculum in urban classrooms. *The Review of Education, Pedagogy and Cultural Studies, 26,* 313–337.

Jeffrey Andrade-Duncan argues for the use of popular culture in urban classrooms, drawing on interview data with minority youth. In discussing the students comments Andrade-Duncan carefully notes the link between the use of popular culture, its affective investment, and the development of a critical literacy. He advocates for the use of popular film and music as legitimate academic texts, and for critical dialogue with youth about their various literacies.

**Hoechsmann, M. (2004).** Reading youth writing: Grazing in the pastures of Cultural Studies and education. *The review of education, pedagogy and cultural studies, 26,* 193–210.

Michael Hoechsmann describes the efforts of *Young People's Press,* a news service for, about, and by adolescents. Hoeschmann, drawing on cultural studies and critical pedagogy, describes the ways in which youth represented themselves and the issues of importance to them and how they and their copy were in turn represented by and ultimately rejected by the largest daily newspaper in Canada. He argued for a stronger emphasis in cultural studies on situated pedagogy and on the experience of young people.

**McLaren, P., & Farahmanpur, R. (2005).** Critical revolutionary pedagogy at ground zero: Renewing the educational left after September 11. In their text *Teaching Against Global Capitalism and the New Imperialism.* Lanham, MD: Rowman and Littlefield.

In this chapter, the authors provide a number of intellectual tools and pedagogical strategies teachers might use in approaching discussions about terrorism in the world, post 9–11. In this, they repeat a common theme running through critical literacy and critical pedagogy, that students need to develop "a language of critique" in this instance to collectively analyze and reflect on the social and historical construction of terrorism and patriotism, as well as the contradictions between patriotism and consumerism, between patriotism and democracy, and between patriotism and Americanism in media. They offer a reading of recent American foreign policy and of the economic and social globalization reread as American imperialism.

**Weiner, E. (2004).** Beyond Remediation: Toward ideological literacies of learning. *Journal of Adolescent and Adult Literacy, 46,* 150–168.

Eric Weiner describes his work with university remedial reading students and his efforts to redevelop their program. His efforts shift the curriculum from one based on literacy as a singular skill that can be mastered through specific pedagogical methods and high-stakes testing of decontextualized generic material to one that embraces critical literacy. He creates projects and contexts that teach the ideological literacies of learning that provided the tools to "read to learn" and transform the world.

As we go to press there are a number of texts forthcoming that we have not yet reviewed but that look interesting and indicate the ongoing and, dare we hope, increasing attention given critical literacies. These include (a) Vivian Vasquez and Jerry Harste (in press), *Keynoting Critical Literacies.* Newark, DE: International Reading Association; and (b) Robert White and Karyn Cooper (in press), *The Practical Critical Educator.* The Netherlands: Kluwer.

The chapters that follow in our text trace advocacy research in literacy education that is related to and but might be said to lie outside of the category of critical literacy. The next two chapters address the radical counterdiscourses of feminism, queer theory, postcolonial studies, and critical race theory as they apply to advocacy work in literacy education.

# 2

## Radical CounterNarratives in Literacy Research I: Feminist and Queer Theory(ies)

*Hope resides at the margins*

David G. Smith[1]

The next two chapters address research and scholarship in feminist, postcolonial, queer, and critical race theory in relation to advocacy work in literacy education. These areas have had direct impact, or have had important implications on much of, though certainly not all of, the work being done in literacy research. Other fields might have been included and/or the fields organized differently, but in our estimation these are the areas that have changed and are changing literacy research and pedagogy in ways that dramatically promote and support issues of social justice and democracy. Moreover we believe they are sites of hope for future literacy research. These chapters will briefly describe the characteristics and history of scholarship in each area, outline its most salient contributions, and outline its challenges to advocacy work in literacy. Each section includes several examples of literacy research that fall under the rubric of feminist, postcolonial, queer, or critical race studies. In this chapter literacy education will be examined in relation to feminist and queer theory(ies) and research.

## FEMINIST THEORY AND RESEARCH IN ADVOCACY
## RESEARCH IN LITERACY EDUCATION

*What does Paulo Freire mean for those of us who define ourselves as feminist educators? How can feminist educators imagine ourselves as actors in the Freirean world?*

Kathleen Weiler. 2001, p. 67

*How was the creativity of the black woman kept alive, year after year and century after century when for most of the years black people have been in America it was a punishable crime for a black person to read and write?*

Alice Walker in Cameron, 1998, p. 5

*If literacy is about "empowerment" through acquisition and critical awareness of "the word," and if women are subjugated through our sexualization—that is, the manipulation of our desire to be "feminine subjects" who are, by definition, not independent, intelligent and educated—and if the boundaries of education are set so that literacy and sexuality shall never meet, then what does literacy as empowerment for women mean?*

Kathleen Rockhill, 1993, p. 337

Feminist philosophical thought and political action has a relatively long and dynamic history. There have been numerous campaigns throughout recorded history to improve the status and living conditions of women and to increase their participation in public life. In the context of 20th-century North America, and the west more generally, feminist thought and action is divided into three general eras or waves. First-wave feminism is associated with the suffragettes of the late 19th and early 20th century who, drawing on and reworking liberal philosophical thought, sought to improve women's lives in part by securing the franchise and more generally by extending notions of citizenship, personhood, and public sphere to women.

Established in response to left-wing student organizations and a civil rights movement that seemed unable or unwilling to consider gender within its radical political agendas, the Women's Liberation Movement of the 1960s constitutes second-wave feminism. Second-wave feminism has been instrumental in effecting widespread social and political change through grassroots consciousness-raising, intense, and wide-ranging political activism and theorization. Informed by liberal humanism, Marxism, and psychosexual developmental theory, second-wave feminists sought to develop critical analysis of the structural features of patriarchy that work to secure greater economic and social power for men. In response to the assumption of sameness (or White sisterhood), third-wave feminism of the 1990s has emphasized differences among women and how women's oppression interacts with and is shaped by race, sexuality, social class, ethnicity, physical ability, and other forms of social difference. Third-wave feminist's focus on difference seeks to counter the assumption of sameness, invoked to fight male bias, in second-wave feminism that served to make invisible differences and more particularly inequalities among women (Stone, 1994). In addition feminist scholarship in third-wave feminism has engaged more diverse and complex theory, including elements of postmodern, poststructural, psychoanalytic, and postcolonial thought.

The legacy of third-wave feminism has been profound. There are now a multitude of feminist political and philosophical positions, including cultural feminism, radical feminism, liberal feminism, postcolonial, and poststructural feminism. Moreover, it has become common over the last decade to speak of feminisms and postfeminism, and impossible for any knowledgeable feminist scholar or activist to suggest or imply an essentialized female experience.

But as feminist thought and political action have become considerably more sophisticated over the century, and more accepted in the academe, its very success in the social, political, and personal arenas has invoked considerable backlash over the last decades of the twentieth century (Faludi, 1991). It is in these troubled and very conservative times that feminists of the 21st century continue to analyze and challenge gendered and other forms of oppression.

Although feminist studies is a dynamic area both theoretically and politically, there are a number of general characteristics or premises of scholarship in this area:

- Feminist research is overtly political. It seeks to understand and challenge gendered power relations and the ways in which race, class, ethnicity, sexuality, and other forms of social difference shape these relations.

- Like critical pedagogy, feminist research is concerned with equity and social justice. It assumes that knowledge and culture are imbedded in relations of power.
- Feminist research focuses on the experiences of girls and women, seeking to correct the invisibility and the distortion or to counter the reading of women's experiences in research.
- Theory occupies a central place in feminist work
- Research is designed to serve women's interests and questions.

In education, liberal, second-wave feminism has had the most impact. Research has focused on the myriad of ways in which school practices have been structured in ways that disadvantage girls and young women (see, for example, The AAUW Report, 1995; Sadker & Sadker, 1994). Research in the 1980s and 1990s revealed how teacher behavior, school polices, and practices, including access to courses and programs, as well as specific content, teaching strategies, and school climate more generally, placed girls at a disadvantage in securing, utilizing, and optimizing cultural capital in school and in life. In comparison to schooling of the 1960s, there has been considerable change and there continues to be efforts, uneven as they may be, to ensure equality if not equity in school opportunity. Such efforts are often aimed at girls' access, particularly in the areas of science, math, and technology.

**Feminist Theory(ies) and Advocacy Work in Literacy**

Early feminist research indicated some of the complexity in providing access to schooling and more particularly to literacy programs and courses. Providing access did not guarantee female participation let alone success. It was apparent that the failure to seize educational opportunities could not be explained by a lack of motivation or interest among women and girls. Studies by Kathleen Rockhill (1987, 1991, 1993) and Jenny Horsman (1990, 2000) were particularly powerful. In these studies Rockhill and later Horsman examined the experiences of illiterate women enrolled in adult literacy and upgrading classes. Participants in Rockhill's study were working-class Hispanic women living in California. In Horsman's study the women were working-class White women living in Eastern Canada. Both of these early ethnographic studies showed how literacy education was the site of hopes, dreams, and desires for a better life for women students. Interviews in Rockhill's study indicated the ways in which the hopes and dreams attached to English language literacy created conflict with traditional, patriarchal notions of marriage. It was evident that wives' increasing literacy posed a serious threat to husbands' own sense of themselves and their position in the family. Although women did most of the literacy work of the household, English literacy education became, according to Rockhill, caught up in the power dynamic between men and women, such "that literacy is 'lived' as women's work but not as women's right" (1987, p. 153).

Horsman's study found similar findings and, like Rockhill, also documented considerable domestic violence in the lives of the women in the study such that literacy education was experienced both as a threat and desire. Both researchers spoke to the danger of overemphasizing the "dream of literacy":

> The violence of these women's lives is frequently obscured by the illusion that illiteracy creates women's problems—that it is illiteracy that "disables" women or "chains" them in prison. In that way our attention is focussed not on the disorganizations of women's lives but on women's failure to become literate. (Horsman, 1990, p. 86)

Rockhill (1993) suggested that the literacy dream, cocreated by educators, policymakers, and employers, and taken on by women students, is read as "become literate, become educated and your life will change. If you don't you alone are at fault" (p. 349). Both these ethnographic studies signal the difficulties that literacy and literacy education posed in the lived experiences of women. They highlight the complex nature of attaining literacy and a literacy education for women, as well as the importance of the broader sociocultural context.

Another related line of feminist research has focused not on access but on the actual curriculum that girls and young women have been offered. Initially much of the work focused on the limits of literary material offered students; that is, the limited number of female-authored or female-centered texts, the stereotyping of male and female characters, as well as the phallocentric reading protocols used to interpret text. In addition it has been argued that conventional school-writing practices, particularly at the high school level, emphasize formal, linear, and logical expression, epitomized by the formal essay, and constitute a male rhetoric tradition that excludes female expression (Barnes, 1990; Caywood & Overing, 1989). To achieve success in school, university, and beyond, it was argued, a female student had to learned to be male—that is, to read (and write) like a man (Fetterley, 1978). Fetterley, like other feminist scholars and educators at the time, asked women and girls "to adopt the stance of a 'resistant reader' who does not identify as a male, but instead situates what she reads within a political context involving gender inequality and the neglect of women's experiences in literature" (Cherland, 1994, p. 14). This has proven difficult for a number of reasons.

Recent research continues to document the limits of literacy/literary experience for girls and young women in school. In a textual analyses of popular teen and preteen novels aimed at girls, Harper (Harper, in press; Bean & Harper, 2004; Harper, 1998), found that although young adult novels are offering a wider range of life possibilities for female characters, inevitably rigid gender categories reasserted themselves in the narratives, rendering independent females and their situations aberrant.

Research has also documented the difficulties experienced by girls and young women in writing against these narratives and discourses. Pam Gilbert in a 1989 study exposed the difficulty 10-year-old girls experienced in writing adventure stories for female characters and in finding story lines that did not involve marriage and female dependency. Despite their best efforts, the female characters

> Ended up being tied to marriage, fidelity and female dependence on male protection. When they [the girls] tried to write about independence, they instead wrote about male erosion of their independence. When they tried to write about women on their own, they wrote about daughters and fiancées ... the girls resisted the inevitability of marriage, physical domination and restricted freedom, but they had no speaking positions of authority available to them, no alterative dis-

courses which offered them other ways of construction the feminine. (Gilbert, 1989, pp. 264–263)

However, what has also become apparent though the 1990s was that efforts to provide a wider range of narratives and alternative discourses with feminist perspectives were not always well received by students, let alone others. Student response has proven to be less than predictable. Bronwyn Davies, in a series of landmark studies drawing on poststructural theory, found that at least some preschool children read against feminist narratives and continued to position female and male characters along very conventional gender lines (Davies, 1991; Davies & Banks, 1992). More recent research continues to support Davies' findings (Rice, 2000, 2002; Wason-Ellam, 1997). Some children continued to fit the feminist stories into conventional frames, believing that boys should do boys' activities and girls should do girls' activities. All the children focused on the importance of female beauty and in at least two studies (Rice, 2000, 2002) children were found to be less excepting of nontraditional male characters than nontraditional female characters. Fortunately, pedagogical intervention through drama and critical discussion was found to improve children's acceptance of nontraditional gender roles according recent research (Davies, 2003; Rice, 2000). Evidently simple exposure to feminist books, although important, isn't sufficient to create change. Adopting postmodern theory, it was evident that individuals actively struggled with and against the gendered subject positions available to them in text and in educational practice as the normal or natural "way to be" in the world (Jones, 1993). This struggle is well documented in many studies including the three example studies that follow.

## Three Example Studies

Meredith Cherland's text *Private Practices: Girls Reading Fiction and Constructing Identity* (1994) details her ethnographic study of seven 11- and 12-year-old affluent girls living in a small North American city, "Oak Town." The study focused the books the girls read in and out of school, *how* they read them, and what the reading of fiction meant to the girls. The study noted that reading fiction in the sociocultural context of the times was culturally sanctioned for girls but not for boys. Moreover, unlike the boys, the girls had "permission" to feel freely and deeply in their response to text and to secure friendships in the sharing of fiction. However, the instructional practices in the school where the girls attended did not acknowledge or value female experience of the world and highlighted "cultural imperatives that promoted ideas about expecting a hierarchy of power, looking to others for authority and devaluing any knowledge based upon their own (i.e., female) experiences of the world" (1994, p. 153). In addition, Cherland found that the Oak Town girls were subject not only to a cultural emphasis on female invisibility but also on female passivity. The girls resisted these discourses, using fiction to explore agency and, in this regard, to experience vicariously what was beyond what was culturally approved for them. At the same time, their extensive reading of horror and mystery stories reinscribed them within the discourses of female passivity: "to the grade six girls of Oak Town, it [horror] seemed to convey the message of female helplessness in the face of a pervasive and gender-specific threat of violence" (p. 189). Cherland's study demonstrated the precariousness and contradictory nature of subjectivity, as well as its connection to reading practices. It showed the active struggle of girls with text and discourse and suggested that this struggle was a potent place or site for advocacy work.

Margaret Finders (1997) conducted a year-long ethnographic study of young adolescent girls' literacy practices in and out of school contexts, which she published under the title *Just Girls: Hidden literacies and life in junior high*. In this study Finders followed two groups of Grade-7 girls in a junior high school considered one of the finest in the state and located in a small American town. Although the school population was almost exclusively Euro-American, there was a strong division between students from affluent homes and those working-class students from the "trailer parks." Finders followed girls in two social cliques, which she called "the tough cookies" and the "social queens." The tough cookies were a loosely connected group of girls from the trailer parks who were named as such by the heavy responsibilities they carried at home; the social queens were a tightly organized group of affluent and popular girls. Finders collected and analyzed the girls in and out of school literacy experiences. Evident in her findings were the ways in which literacy organized the lives and alliances of these girls with each other, the school, and their parents. What was particularly disturbing were the ways in which the progressive literacy program offered at their renowned junior high school failed to provide a transformative or liberatory education for any of these girls.

Their literacy program, under the guise of whole language, was less authoritarian than a traditional program, allowing for greater student choice, more personal response, and greater and more intense collaborate reading and writing experiences. However progressive this might appear, it was apparent from the study that the trailer park girls were alienated by this program, and more specifically by the middle-class assumptions that underpinned many of its initiatives. Rather than freeing students, the literacy program and junior high life in general constricted the girls' time, movement, and talk so that "only through literate underlife were these girls provided any opportunity for more freedom, independence, or responsibility" (Finders, 1997, p. 129). Moreover, without what we would call a critical literacy both sets of girls were not able to effectively challenge traditional gendered and classed discourses that were organizing their lives in and out of school, and most importantly the very literacy program in which they and their teachers were engaged. Both groups of girls were left vulnerable, trained either to be consumers and competitors for men's desires or simply silent and alienated, without political clout or economic resources: "While the social queens rehearsed their roles to secure their place in society through romance and commodities, the cookies reminded again and again that there was no place for them" (Finders, 1997, p. 128).

Finders repeats the call made by other feminists engaged in literacy education for a more critical school literacy program: "I advocate a pedagogy that situates reading not simply as an aesthetic experience but as a political act as well. ... Such a pedagogy would acknowledge the ways in which texts serve to enable and constrain social roles, the ways in which texts tend to normalize particular" (Finders, 1997, pp. 127–128). She places considerable responsibility on teachers: "If we deny our power as educators, we deny our students the opportunity to rewrite cultural and social scripts" (Finders, 1997, p. 128).

Helen Harper (2000) chronicled the responses of six 17-year-old young women to feminist avant-garde poetry. These young women, from various racial and socioeconomic backgrounds, were enrolled in a high school creative writing class. All struggled with the non-conventional and explicitly political nature of the feminist writing offered to them. Both in content and in form feminist literary writing engendered various degrees and forms of resistance, as evident in journal entries, interview data, and creative writing submitted by the young women. In analyzing the data, it was evident that there was a powerful and dangerous connection established between and among conventional literary and linguistic practices, femininity, and traditional heterosexuality (read as female passivity). Though not particularly surprising now, students' resistance to the disruptive but potentially liberating power of innovative feminist writing and feminist pedagogy more generally was unsettling to many feminist researchers. This research study, along with others, suggests that educators needed to consider the affective (i.e., desire and pleasure) in the production and consumption of politically explicit text and in the construction of self. As Valerie Walkerdine (1987) suggested, "If new content in whatever form does not map onto the crucial issues of desire, then we should be surprised if it fails as an intervention." (p. 62) More generally, Harper's study, like Cherland's and Finders', speaks to the need for close and careful examination of social, psychological, and historical context in developing feminist interventions (or any form of advocacy work) in literacy education. This context speaks not only to what happens in schools but also to what happens out of schools in the wider society.

These studies—in showing the gendered nature of literacy practices, the struggle with progressive language and literacy school programs, and even the struggle with explicit feminist texts and pedagogical intervention—exemplify the field. However, an exciting and relatively new line of feminist research that offers a broader perspective but relates nonetheless to advocacy work in literacy education is found in the field of feminist cultural studies.

## Feminist Cultural Studies
## and Advocacy Research in Literature

There are of course alternative spaces outside of the purview of adults and official school doctrine where individuals construct the world and themselves. One of these spaces is popular culture. A growing number of studies have offered textual analyses of pop culture products and events, as well as ethnographic studies of child and youth engagement with these products–events. A subset of these studies is focused on girls and women (e.g., Best, 2000; Inness, 1998a, 1998b; Mazzarella & Pecora, 2001) and at times with their engagement with popular literature and text-based media. Angela McRobbie's (1991, 1997, 2000) study of girls reading of teen magazines—"zines"—offered the first foray into this field, as did Linda Christian-Smith's study of teens' popular romance reading (1993). The Christian-Smith study drew on an early classic study by Janice Radway (1984). In her study, Radway offered an in-depth analysis of how women read romance fiction, from the perspective of women who were avid readers of the genre. Despite the tirades against romance novels as antifeminist and disempowering, Radway discovered that the women who read the novels found them to be sources of strength and pleasure. McRobbie and Christian-Smith found that, despite the popularity of nonsanctioned school materials, considerable ambivalence and contradiction existed in pop literature aimed at young women.

This line of research can be said to follow under the rubric of cultural studies and more specifically feminist cultural studies. Although broader in scope, the project of cultural studies is similar to the radical research cited throughout this chapter in that it focuses on power, knowledge, culture, and identity formation and looks to social transformation. It has a strong, though far from exclusive, emphasis on popular culture (pop art, music, literature, theater, etc.). Although culture is considered an object of study, it is simultaneously the site of political intervention; thus there is an ongoing preoccupation in cultural studies with radical social and cultural transformation (Grossberg, Nelson, & Treichler, 1992, p. 5). Scholars and educators in this field are focused on examining and challenging relationships among power, culture, and knowledge (Giroux, 1997) and, as in other fields discussed in this chapter, see themselves as politically engaged participants.

Feminist cultural theory developed out of a critique of the emerging field of cultural studies in the 1970s and 1980s. It draws on poststructural thought in examining the materiality of everyday life and on the discursive categories that organize and produce that experience. As

evident in Radway, Christian-Smith, McRobbie, and evident in the sophisticated work of Valerie Walkerdine (1990), it focuses on "everyday"
lives of women and young girls. It is concerned with the affective, that
is, with pleasure and desire, often understood through psychoanalytic
theory. What is apparent in these studies and others is that popular culture sites are ambivalent spaces, at times constraining and traditional,
and at other times liberating. They are, however, everyday spaces where
our taken-for-granted interpretations of the world and its possibilities
are made. And, as Nadine Dolby (2004) wrote, the study of popular culture can be used to "illuminate the connections between everyday acts
and the public sphere, and to map the new terrain of politics that opens
from this exploration" (pp. 275–276).

The inclusion of feminist cultural studies in advocacy research in literacy education is important because of its attention to

- The construction of subjectivity in discursive practices.
- The "everyday" of lived culture with an emphasis on popular culture.
- The affective domain of pleasure and desire in the production and
  consumption of text.
- The connection made between private and personal practices to
  political and public practices and structures.
- The broad definition of text and acknowledgment of pedagogi-
  cally space outside of the schoolyard. In doing so Cultural Studies, draws attention to the relationship, often the disjuncture,
  between school and nonschool sites of learning.

## Contributions and Critical Response

Studies in the area of feminist cultural studies and indeed much of the
feminist research in literacy education has involved textual analysis
and ethnographic methods: studies of how schooling, texts, and female
lives come together in particular ways that support and/or challenge
gendered and other power relations. Such research is designed to serve
women's interests, is designed to answer women's questions, and often places the researcher within the interpretative framework. Scholarship in feminist literary theory and feminist empirical linguistic
research has done much to expose and challenge the gendered assump-

tions and practices that underlie linguistic and discursive patterns. It offers alternative language and literacy practices that in some cases have been incorporated into everyday language and into textual practices in school classrooms. Feminist literacy theory has provided educators with new interpretations of canonical texts, alternative texts to consider and new protocols for the study of literary and non-literacy texts alike. Feminist research has also focused on agency, more particularly, resistance and engagement with school text and pedagogical strategies regarding gender. Recent work has forced on the role of fantasy and desire in textual practice in and out of school.

Rather than on "gender" per se, much of the focus has been on girls and women and the construction of femininity exclusively; but the focus of late has broadened to include boys, men, and the construction of masculinity, including female masculinity, in literacy education (Harper, in press; Bean & Harper, in press; Kehler & Martino, in press), although not all the research now being conducted on masculinity in relation to literacy is directly informed by feminism theory. This new broader gender perspective—which includes masculinity, as well as the continuing efforts to embrace women's differences across race, class, ethnicity, sexuality, and other forms of social difference, along with attention to the issues and research on the body, fantasy, pleasure, and desire—ensures feminist research will have even more powerful social and political impact. Whatever directions advocacy research takes, explicit, gendered forms of analysis will continue to offer a potent counternarrative that expands and complicates easy assumptions about the "oppressed" and the "oppressors," as well as the nature and workings of text and contexts, and of the mind and body in literacy education.

## QUEER THEORY AND ADVOCACY RESEARCH IN LITERACY EDUCATION

*Acts and gestures, articulated and enacted desires create the illusion of an interior and organizing gender core, an illusion discursively maintained for the purposes of the regulation of sexuality within the obligatory frame of reproductive heterosexuality.*

Judith Butler, 1990, p. 136

*Despite the explosion in scholarship and an apparent and slight clearing
in the public space, we remain in a defensive position: trying to teach tolerance, trying to teach the truth, trying to find ways to decenter and
destabilize the heterosexual normalization that so constructs the students we teach, indeed the public world that we inhabit.*

William Pinar, 1998, p. 6

Another counternarrative in literacy research and scholarship has been
inspired by "queer theory." Queer theory brings together two important theoretical discussions of the late 20th century: social construc-
tivist insights into sexuality and poststructuralist critiques of the
unified, autonomous self (Gamson, 2000). Queer theory calls for reading practices that are text centered and deconstructive. Like feminist
theory and postcolonial theory, it makes everyday experiences of marginality a ground for theory building (Gamson, 2000), offering new
ways of reading the world.

Meanings for queer theory keep changing because of its focus on
shifting identities and its deconstruction of the processes of sexual categorization. But it can be said that the word *queer* marks the *instability of
identity* and that queer theory works to question and destabilize *the
homo/hetero binary* in social life (Gamson, 2000). Queer theory is
grounded in poststructuralist theories of language that posit that the
meaning of the signified is never fixed, but is constantly deferred and
shifting. Meaning is generated through difference. Language works because there is difference, between signs and between a sign and that
which it signifies. Deconstruction, a critical practice that dismantles
language and rhetorical structures to reassemble them in a different way,
is queer theory's most useful tool.

Queer theory inspires research that considers and includes people
who are gay, lesbian, bisexual, transgendered, and/or questioning
(GLBTQ), but it is skeptical about these categories, seeing them as discursively constructed and unstable. Queer theorizing involves the ongoing deconstruction of sexual categories and identities. It reveals the
discursive practices, both textual and linguistic, that construct and
produce sexual subjectivities. Research inspired by queer theory sees
sexual meanings, identities, and categories as social and historical
products (Gamson, 2000).

Queer theory also deconstructs the homo–hetero binary in social life. It recognizes *heterosexuality* as a social and political organizing principle and it contributes to theorizing a politics of knowledge and difference. Reminding us that any identity is founded relationally, queer theory reveals an inside–outside dichotomy (Fuss, 1991) that constructs *heterosexuality* in language and images, a dichotomy that designates what heterosexuality is *not* and in this way reveals what heterosexuality *is*. The inside–outside binary (also important in feminist theory and in postcolonial theory) uses sexual identity to construct borders that exclude, repudiate, and oppress.

All research conducted by or about GLBTQ people is not inspired by queer theory and does not necessarily make use of it.[1] In listing the characteristics of queer theory then, it may be helpful to make the contrast, and to summarize what queer theory is *not*:

- Queer theory is not about gay and lesbian identity politics and struggles for equity. Rather, it is about deconstructing linguistic and textual structures that produce sexual identities.
- Queer theory does not focus on explaining homosexuality. Instead, it reveals heterosexuality as a political and organizing system, produced in the culture through language (discourse) that cites a homo/hetero binary.
- Where other research in literacy education conducted by and for GLTBQ people works at including gay and lesbian writers in the curriculum, and at describing inclusive pedagogies for reading and writing, research informed by queer theory does "identity work" (Blackburn, 2002) and is more likely to engage in projects of interpretation and theory development (Pinar, 1998).

## A Brief History

Where did queer theory come from? Others provide a more complete history than we can offer here (see Gamson, 2000; Pinar, 1998). But we can point out that the Kinsey reports[2] (Kinsey, Pomeroy, & Martin, 1948; Kinsey, Pomeroy, Martin, & Gebhard, 1953) worked to unsettle common sense ideas about "normal" sexual behavior, at least in North

America, where they were widely read and reported. Kinsey made it public and common cultural knowledge that homosexual feelings and behaviors were very widespread. They were normal in that they were nearly universal. Kinsey's surveys did *not*, however, find evidence of a coherent sexual core identity provided by nature, one that corresponded neatly to the gender category of male or female.

The idea that sexuality is not natural or biological, but rather socially constructed, began to take hold. Social constructivists in the 1970s and 1980s (working at the margins of the discipline of psychology) began to do minority group research, asking how sexual categories were created and experienced. Social constructionists (working at the margins of sociology and anthropology) began to research sexuality as a set of meanings attached to bodies and desires, meanings that were negotiated between and among people. Meanings can be challenged, and at a time in history when other scholarship was addressing political questions about social categories like race, class, and gender (asking why they existed and what their material effects on human lives might be), research and scholarship that worked at explaining heterosexuality and homosexuality as similar categories began to emerge. (See, for example, the essays collected by Ortner & Whitehead, 1981.)

Foucault's (1978/1990) explanations of the homosexual as a contemporary historical and cultural invention, constructed through discourse, worked as part of the postmodern crisis of representation that characterized the intellectual milieu of the 1980s. The arguments of Foucault (1978/1990), Lyotard (1984), Lacan (1977), Derrida (1987), and others inspired important theoretical arguments that contributed to the development of queer theory. Suspicious of grand narratives, rejecting the humanist belief that a unified and rational self existed, scholars working in the emerging field of cultural studies began to deconstruct the homosexual–heterosexual distinction and to argue that identities were fluid and shifting. Queer theory emerged in the 1990s, making use of poststructural theories of language as unstable and of meaning as always shifting. It deconstructed discourses of "heteronormativity" to critique the concept of "identity." By demonstrating in this way that all knowledge creation is political, queer theory contributed to challenging oppressive regimes of truth.

Eve Sedgewick's (1990) important work extended Foucault's idea that the reduction of sexuality to two neat categories (hetero and homo) was a historical invention, one that served the culture as a means of domination and oppression. Where earlier work in gay and lesbian studies had read same-sex desire as transgressive or deviant, Sedgewick inspired an important shift in thinking by arguing that the hetero/homo binary did not account for a range of sexual desires and practices that existed outside specific gender categories. Sedgewick's thinking helped to mobilize new theorizing concerned with sexuality as a normalizing regime, much like race, class, and gender (Spurlin, 2002).

Judith Butler's (1990) *Gender Trouble: Feminism and the Subversion of Identity* made another significant contribution to the development of queer theory. Butler made use of Foucault's idea that power is an effect of discourse, and that sex, gender, and desire are effects of a specific formation of power. She too rejected the usual binary frames for thinking about gender (male–female, homosexual–heterosexual) and the conceptions of power implicit in those binary frames. Seeking to "trouble" the gender categories that support gender hierarchy and compulsory heterosexuality, she proposed a "heterosexual matrix" for conceptualizing gender and desire, a matrix that would "unmask presumptive heterosexuality" to show that all sexual identity categories are the *effects* of institutions, practices, and discourses. Butler's (1990) image of a matrix conveys the complexity, the range of possibilities, and the interlocking dimensions of gender and desire.

Butler also pointed out that much of feminist theory had been assuming an existing identity for the category "woman" and the category "man," an identity that existed cross-culturally and was somehow essential in human beings. Butler argued that there was no natural sex prior to culture. Sex and gender are always open to multiple readings. She offered a *performative* theory of gender acts that dramatize cultural beliefs about gender and that produce and sustain cultural fictions of two genders as polar opposites. Gender, argued Butler, is an identity tenuously constituted in time, instituted through a stylized repetition of acts. Gender identity is performative, and gender reality is created and sustained through social performances. Because of this, there are performative possibilities for gender configurations outside the restricting frames of masculinist domination and compulsory heterosexuality.

Butler's (1990) ideas have proved very useful to scholars who work with queer theory to do advocacy research in literacy education. They allow literacy educators to go beyond labels like "gay" and "lesbian" to more complex understandings of gender and identity, to examine the ways in which the construction of difference is related to the construction of dominance (Pennycook, 2001). Butler has helped to make queer theory useful as a flexible, open-ended frame for research in psychoanalysis, semiotics, literary theory, film theory, and linguistics (Fuss, 1991), as well as in education.

Pinar's (1998) important collection of educational research and scholarship using queer theory presents a variety of applications from the 1990s. It includes essays that reinterpret the homophobic history of education (Sears, 1998; Tierney & Dilley, 1998) and that critique identity politics but also critique queer theory's unsettling of the collective identity that is essential to the political agendas of marginalized groups (Carlson, 1998; Meiners, 1998). Pinar's (1998) collection also offers essays that imagine and reimagine a queer pedagogy (Haver, 1998; Luhmann, 1998); that reflect on youth, popular culture and the construction of identity (Rodriguez, 1998; Steinberg, 1998; Walcott, 1998); that envision new forms of queer curriculum (Miller, 1998; Morris, 1998; Sumara & Davis, 1999); that envision new forms of research (de Castell & Bryson, 1998; Honeychurch, 1998); and that present challenges for AIDS education (Britzman, 1998a).

Pinar (1998) acknowledges both the significant contributions of James Sears to promoting understanding of the educational issues associated with homosexuality[3] and the contributions of Deborah Britzman (1995a, 19995b, 1996) to the history of queer theory in education. During the 1990s Britzman drew on Foucault (1978/1990, 1988), Sigmund Freud (1968), and Anna Freud (1979) to explore the discursive construction of sexual identities, to reflect on pedagogies that could call into question the "conceptual geography of normalization" (1995a, p. 152), and to work through the implications of the historicity of sex for creating curriculum that might incite identifications and critiques, and not close them down.

Britzman (1995a) has contributed to queer theory in literacy education by describing three reading practices that are useful for rethinking knowledge and for engaging in dialogue with the self and with difference: analyzing where meaning breaks down for the reader, provoking a dialogue between the self and the text, and theorizing about how one reads. Britzman (1998b) has continued her work of using psychoanalytic theory in queer theorizing, to help the field of education think what cannot be thought, and "stage the return of the repressed" (1996, p. 6).

In the past 5 years, queer theory has been used increasingly to mediate between intellectual inquiry into normative ideologies and social activism (Spurlin, 2002). In English studies queer theory provides both a mode of analysis and a strategy of opposition for challenging notions of fixed identity. It has worked both as a critical lens for reading (and rereading) the complexity of cultural signs and as a site for exposing and critiquing heteronormativity (Spurlin, 2002). Queer theory's current applications in literacy education most often concern either queer pedagogies for teaching reading, and writing or composition (Kopelson, 2002), or the uses of queer reading practices in the study of literature. But there is also Mollie Blackburn's work (2002, 2003a, 2003b, 2004), which uses queer theory to analyze identity work in the literacy performances of queer youth, to explore their ways of challenging power dynamics in working for social change. All three applications are invested in political struggle, although the investment works in different ways.

*Queer pedagogies* are in many ways related to Freirean critical pedagogies in that they critique the reproduction of knowledge and the cultural narratives that serve the interests of dominant social groups. Queer pedagogies challenge the assumption of real and stable gay and lesbian identities and they critique all identity-based approaches to teaching. They work to disrupt normative identities and to offer frameworks for interrogating and composing multiple aspects of the self (Kopelson, 2002). Performativity enters the composition classroom as strategic or tactical performativity, as theory in action (Butler, 1999), and a political project takes shape. Composition classrooms become sites for teaching students to write to shape and transform themselves and their societies. Queer pedagogies of performativity involve writing to escape confines, to exceed boundaries, and to transform thinking, to work toward and enact more democratic futures (Kopleson, 2002).

Other applications of queer theory in English Studies demonstrate *queer reading practices* that trouble social and sexual identities, interrogate social norms, and unsettle traditional interpretations of the world (see, for example, Jarraway, 2002; Schneider, 2002; Zeikowitz, 2002). They too work to denaturalize heteronormativity and to engage difference, but in the teaching of literature and culture. Queer reading practices do more than perform gay or lesbian readings of literary works or of authors from the literary canon. Instead, they analyze normative identities within particular historical, cultural, and political contexts for interpretation (Spurlin, 2002). Queer theory allows for readings that discern multiple and fluid sexualities among characters, that analyze the ways sexual norms have shifted throughout history, and that allow students to interrogate their own established cultural codes for reading. Through queer reading practices, literature classrooms can become sites for engaging with the instability of identity formations, and spaces for democratic deliberation and resistance, which may lead toward social change.

Blackburn's (2002, 2003a, 2003b, 2004) work does not focus on queer pedagogies or on queer reading practices per se, but still uses queer theory to inform advocacy research in literacy education. We will begin with one of her studies.

### Example Study: Literacy Performances

Blackburn (2003a) named the theoretical frames that inform her research as queer theory, critical feminism, critical race theory, and new literacy studies. Much of her research explores data she collected during her 3 years as an observer, researcher, and worker at The Loft, a youth-run center for GLBTQ youth in a large eastern American city. Youth at The Loft used literacy in many ways to author themselves into the world. Some were members of the Speakers' Bureau, a group within the group, educated as activists and hired to do outreach education on issues surrounding GLBTQ youth. They read to find, gather, and understand resources that would help them in their work. They wrote outlines for outreach sessions, and they wrote to communicate information on GLBTQ issues to others. Youth at The Loft, both inside and outside the Speakers' Bureau, read, wrote, and discussed poetry as ways to explore (and unsettle and rework) sexual identities. Citing Butler's (1999) concept of performativity, Blackburn calls these "literacy performances." She analyzes some of these literacy performances to show the efforts of queer youth to interrogate and disrupt inequitable power relations, in society and in their own lives and relationships, especially at The Loft, but also at home and at school. (For further discussion of Blackburn's research, see chapter 6.)

Blackburn (2003a) used queer theory to examine and explain the ways in which queer youth at The Loft both challenged and replicated inequitable power dynamics in the society at large. She sees the ways in which their literacy performances demonstrated their power to work for social change. She presents examples of queer youth reading and writing the world to disrupt existing power dynamics, by educating youth workers and teachers about economic issues facing queer youth who had often left home and were living on their own. She also shows queer youth challenging existing power relations by including transgendered youth (and not only gay and lesbian and bisexual youth) in their reading and writing and by providing compassionate portraits that made visible the sufferings of queer youth in school at the hands of teachers and other students.

But Blackburn (2003a) also saw that, within The Loft, the inequitable power dynamics of the society were sometimes replicated. Speakers' Bureau members had more social power than youth at The Loft who were not members, and they sometimes failed to recognize their own privilege when others challenged it. More powerful youth sometimes protected themselves from the accusations of others less powerful than they were. Blackburn worked to persuade more powerful youth at The Loft to look critically at their own power and privilege so that they could choose to share their power and choose to listen more closely, especially to their transgendered peers.

Blackburn's (2003a) research looks back and forth between literacy performances that challenge and disrupt existing power dynamics, and literacy performances that enact and maintain them. She implicates herself by describing her participation in those challenges and in those acts of maintenance. She makes her point clearly: If the goal is to work for social change, then the work is never done. Literacy educators and their students must continue to interrogate relationships between literacy performances and power dynamics, without hoping or expecting to achieve a perfectly just society. Justice lies in the learning through "perpetual interrogation" (p. 488).

**Example Studies: Queer Pedagogies and Curricular Practices**

*The intersections of queer theory and critical pedagogy are filled with numerous and exciting possibilities for productive classroom inquiry, cultural analysis, public deliberation and social (ex)change.*

William Spurlin, 2002, p. 10

Here we present three examples of queer pedagogies and curricular practices in use. In the first, Sumara and Davis (1999) began with Foucault's (1978/1990) idea that Western culture has entangled knowledge and sex, and with Britzman's (1995b) comment that every sexual identity is a shifting social relation. Sumara and Davis (1999) place their work within queer theory, interpreting normative pedagogy and curriculum as heterosexualized. They work to interrupt narratives of the heterosexual, in much the same way that feminist theorists work to interrupt narratives of patriarchy in the classroom.

This example of their research (Sumara & Davis, 1999) reports on two projects, one involving a group of gay, lesbian, and transgendered (GLT) teachers, and one involving children in Grades 5 and 6, their teacher, and some parents. In both projects, Sumara and Davis used the shared reading of literary texts as sites for critical inquiry. They designed reading activities that required readers to form literary identifications with characters and situations that both challenged and connected with their own lived experiences.

In the first project, the GLT teachers' reading and responding to Audre Lorde's *Zami: A New Spelling of My Name* produced a wide variety of responses and literary identifications that did not necessarily correspond to their sexual identities as gay, lesbian, or transgendered. Several gay males, for example, were unable to acknowledge the anger and frustration of the women depicted in the book, and the ways in which their own literary interpretations were shaped by misogyny. (The female teachers in the group had no difficulty in seeing this.) After 2 years of shared work, Sumara and Davis (1999) concluded that the literary identifications made could not be confined to notions of what might constitute a quintessential queer identity. They quote Sedgewick (1990): "even people who share all or most of our positionings ... may still be different enough from us, and from each other, to seem like all but different species" (p. 22).

In the second project Sumara and Davis (1999) report on, they worked with one teacher and her Grade 5 and 6 class, reading and responding to Lois Lowry's novel *The Giver*. This novel presents a future society where all historical memory has been lost, except to one person, the "receiver of memories" who keeps knowledge of the past, to advise the country's political leaders when necessary. Children in this society are raised in small families, each with one male and one female parent, but everyone except the Receiver of Memory is drugged to suppress their sexual feelings, and reproduction is managed through birth mothers. The main character, 12-year-old Jonas, is not drugged because he has been chosen as the next Receiver of Memory. He alone is then able to perceive colors, feel anger and grief, and experience the "stirrings" of sexuality. His identity changes as his knowledge increases, and he is no longer able to accept the way in which old people and babies are euthanized in his society, nor can he accept his father's role in that practice.

In focus group discussions that involved several of the children, their teacher, and Sumara, heterosexist assumptions and discourses emerged, as everyone worked to make sense of the story and understand its meanings. During the discussions, individual children assumed that only intercourse counted as sex, that the only sexual partners possible were members of the opposite sex, and that sexual desire would awaken in them when they reached a certain stage of development. The plot of *The Giver* also assumed that sexual feelings do not appear until adolescence, and that sexual feelings can and will still emerge in a society where history and memory do not exist.

Sumara and Davis (1999) analyzed these discourses and assumptions to reflect on ways of teaching to "amplify the imagination of learners" (p. 202) and to interrupt the heteronormative relations of curriculum. In asking questions and participating in these discussions, teachers have an opportunity to work with children to clarify these assumptions, to challenge their limitations, and to suggest that other ways of seeing the world are possible. Sumara and Davis (1999) suggested that all curriculum should recognize that sexuality is a necessary companion to all knowing; that heterosexual identity should be rendered problematic and destabilized, by making visible the unruly desires and pleasures that circulate through it; that curriculum ought to be more interested in understanding and interpreting differences among people, rather than noting differences among categories of people; that curriculum ought to focus on the ways in which identities shift; and that curriculum ought to be curious about experiences of desire, pleasure, and sexuality. In these ways, they argued, curriculum and heteronormativity can be *interrupted*, to expand learning and contribute to eliminating homophobia and heterosexism.

In another study of queer pedagogies and curricular practices in classroom use, Wayne Martino (1999) focused on the use of literary texts to interrupt straight thinking in an elementary English classroom in Australia.[4] He asked what approaches to teaching English could help students interrogate the effects of compulsory heterosexuality, and what ways of teaching might interrupt the familiar patterns of thinking that define sexuality in oppositional terms, and as a set of stable categories. Martino (1999) interviewed six teachers at a Catholic school (all White, two male) and their students (aged 12 and 13) about their study of the novel *Two Weeks with the Queen*, by Morris Gleitzman (1996), to explore the role that texts inclusive of queer characters might play in helping young people challenge stereotypes and question the limits of normality.

The novel all the teachers and students read, *Two Weeks with the Queen,* is about a young boy named Colin who is sent to London to live with relatives because his younger brother Luke is dying of a rare form of cancer and can receive treatment there. In a desperate search for a "top doctor," Colin visits a hospital where he meets a gay man, Ted, whose partner is dying of AIDS. Colin becomes Ted's friend, visiting him at his apartment when Ted becomes a victim of gay bashing. There Colin sees graffiti spray painted in red on the outside wall: the word *QUEENS*. Their friendship grows and deepens as Colin and Ted each endure the terminal illness of a loved one.

Martino (1999) found that in working with this novel the teachers were informed by liberal humanist ideologies of acceptance for individual differences. In discussions with students they challenged stereotypes and discrimination against gay people, and they encouraged tolerance. Students responded strongly to the novel. More than half of the boys (but only a few of the girls) rejected the novel, enacting "appro-

priate" masculine behavior by invoking misogyny and rejecting homosexuality as something sick and feminine, something they must be
opposed to. But many boys and girls produced overwhelmingly positive
and gay-affirming responses to the novel. These students (like their
teachers) used liberal humanist discourses of difference to argue for
tolerance, respect and acceptance for gay people.

Martino (1999) argued that this engagement with the novel can become a starting point for more critical work that could problematize
ideas about what is normal or natural. He suggested asking students,
"Who decides if someone is normal or not?" (p. 145). He suggested using texts from popular culture (television shows, music videos, magazines) to reflect with students about how gay characters are
constructed across a range of texts. He pointed out that it is already a
requirement in English classes to reflect critically on the world and to
relate the lessons of literature to one's own life. These ways of reading
can also be put to use in interrogating normality and in interrupting the
limits imposed by the hetero/homo binary. Martino (1999) implied
that it should not be too difficult for teachers to move beyond liberal
pedagogies to draw attention to the naturalization and normalization
of sexual identity. He sees great possibilities for reconstructing the social world in this work.

Zeikowitz (2002), who teaches courses in Medieval Literature at a
university in the American South, offers another example of advocacy
research in literacy education informed by queer theory. Zeikowitz's
college students are young adults, mostly White, middle class and
straight people who do not consider themselves oppressed and who do
not realize the part they play in maintaining an unjust society. Zeikowitz
attempts to use a "queer, critical pedagogy" in teaching literary texts
from the Middle Ages to examine the position of the Other, both in the
texts themselves and in contemporary society. His goal is to transform
students' thinking about categories of Otherness by teaching them to
"read queer," through engaging in a critical reading process that
denaturalizes the normativity that is tied to power structures. Zeikowitz
(2002) drew on conceptions of "a border pedagogy of postmodern resistance" (Aronowitz & Giroux, 1991) that involves students in critiquing
the cultural codes that shape their own identities, and in rethinking
received categories of Otherness.

The normative/queer (hetero/homo) binary has not remained stable across cultures and time periods. Zeikowitz (2002) helped students see the socially acceptable male bonding and erotically charged male intimacy that characterizes gatherings in Hrothgar's great mead-hall in *Beowulf*. He helped them discern Sir Gawain's homoeroticized gaze on the Green Knight's body, and the threat this poses to the homosocial character of King Arthur's court. He worked with them to examine the character of the Pardoner in Chaucer's *Canterbury Tales,* who may be a eunuch, and the contrast Chaucer constructs between the Pardoner and Harry Bailey, a model of medieval manliness and authority. In class discussions Zeikowitz taught students to examine the conceptions of "queer" prevalent in medieval times, and to compare and contrast those with contemporary conceptions of "queer." He asked, how would contemporary mainstream society view the Pardoner, or Sir Gawain's behavior, or the gatherings in Hrothgar's great hall? He encouraged students to identify the beliefs about masculinity and queerness operating in medieval times, and to attempt to empathize with queers from the earlier historical period.

Zeikowtiz (2002) then designed homework and classroom assignments that enable students to interact positively with both medieval and contemporary queers. In one assignment he asked students to compare and contrast their own reactions to the Pardoner with Harry Bailey's, and to justify both Bailey's responses and their own. He asks them also to speculate about how the Pardoner might describe Bailey, so that they can come to a deeper understanding of how "normality" is an arbitrary designation (see p. 77). In another assignment Zeikowitz asked students to first describe a monstrous figure, someone hideous or unattractive to them. Next they describe their reactions as heterosexuals to meeting someone who is openly gay or lesbian (all students adopt this viewpoint, even if they do not identify as heterosexual). Students then draw a boundary between acceptable and unacceptable appearances and behaviors in mainstream contemporary society, listing characteristics for each. They write about Grendel and the Green Knight as monstrous Others who pose a normative threat to the societies in which they exist. In these activities students cross cultural–historical borders and learn to interrogate how heteronormative American society views monstrous

Others (queers) as threats. They come to see how those boundaries have been constructed and invented.

Zeikowitz (2002) lists other assignments that, like these, encourage students to denaturalize their own social identities and to see the socially constructed norms that serve heteronormative society. Zeikowitz sees queer pedagogies as ways of influencing the world outside the classroom by redefining social and cultural norms to construct new communities. He believes that, by teaching students to engage in "queering the present," teachers can influence the world of concrete social relations to make it more just.

## CONTRIBUTIONS AND CRITICAL RESPONSE

Queer theory's limitations emerge from its strengths. Because queer theory problematizes representation, because it interrupts normativity and destabilizes identity categories, it calls into question the solidarity *within* identity categories that sustains political movements. Queer theory troubles the kind of identity politics that struggles to affirm sexual difference and win civil rights for gay and lesbian people (and for women). Instead, it analyses discursive and cultural practices that problematize all sexual identities, and in doing so it undermines many of the assumptions about gender that make GLBTQ and feminist advocacy work possible.

But queer theory is useful to advocacy research in literacy education in many ways. Its complex understandings of gender and sexual identity can help educators think about how schooling and literacy education work to heterosexualize and gender people and texts, and it can help us see the material effects of these processes. It can move advocacy beyond strategies of inclusive pedagogy and inclusive curriculum, to deeper understandings of oppression through education, and to new visions for antioppressive work in education.

Queer theory can help keep advocacy research attuned to the dynamics of discourse, and in this way help make advocacy research another site for calling identity into question. Importantly, queer theory reminds us to attend to the body as text. In literacy education, queer theory can serve as a critical lens for reading and rereading the complexity of cultural signs, and in this way inspire us to see education as a site for social transformation.

## Other Studies of Note

**Doll, M. A. (1998).** Queering the gaze. In W. F. Pinar (Ed.), *Queer theory in education* (pp. 287–298). Mahwah, NJ: Lawrence Erlbaum Associates, Inc.

Mary Aswell Doll is an English teacher who believes that English Studies ought to undermine common sense notions of the natural and the normal, by teaching the complexity of literature and by teaching the clarity of writing. Aware that our culture gains social control through fixing and unifying identity, Doll explains her desire to teach English in ways that undermine gender dogma in particular. She offers English teachers (and others who teach the arts) four strategies that can be highlighted in literature:

- *Shock*, as a way of queering the gaze of straight perception.
- *Jokes*, as another way of questioning the norm.
- *Myth*, as a way to work against "naturalness" to see with imagination's eye; and to disrupt the identity "human being" through transformations into animal, plant, minerals, the divine.
- *The perverse* (wilful countering), as a way to trouble the natural and normal, wrenching us away from ourselves.

Doll argued that these strategies can help the English teacher to confront the gaze of the homophobe, and disrupt notions of one, fixed gender identity.

**Kopelson, K. (2002).** Dis/integrating the gay/queer binary: "Reconstructed identity politics" for a performative pedagogy. *College English, 65*, 17–35.

In addition to making the theoretical contributions mentioned earlier, Karen Kopelson urges a performative pedagogy that calls for engagement and struggle with hard questions about identity and difference.

**Goldstein, T., Robinson, K. H., & Ferfulja, T. (Eds.). (2004).** Anti-homophobia teacher education [Special issue]. *Teaching Education, 15*(1).

Although the articles in this issue are more inclined to make use of critical theory than they are of queer theory, and although most of them are only peripherally related to literacy education, we do want to bring this good work to the attention of our readers. The article by Heather Sykes and Tara Goldstein (pp. 41–62) on performance ethnography as a curriculum activity offers many suggestions that could be applied in literacy classrooms, especially in Grades 6 through 12, and the resource reviews (pp. 117–125) are excellent.

The next chapter focuses on radical counternarratives that, though they may include a focus on gender and sexuality, address literacy education in relation to race and the postcolonial condition more specifically.

# 3

# Radical Counternarratives in Literacy Research II: Post Colonial Theory and Critical Race Theory

*[There are] two indivisible foundations of imperial authority—knowledge and power. The most formidable ally of economic and political control ha[s] long been the business of "knowing" other peoples because this "knowing" underpinned imperial dominance and became the mode by which they were increasingly persuaded to know themselves: as subordinate to Europe.*

Bill Ashcroft, Gareth Griffiths, and Helen Tiffin, 1995

*I remember asking myself in the first few months of my graduate school career, "Why is it these theories never seem to be talking about me?" But by graduation time many of my fellow minority students and I had become well trained: we had learned alternate ways of viewing the world, coaxed memories of life in our communities into forms which fit into the categories created by academic researchers and theoreticians, and internalized belief systems that often belied our own experiences.*

Lisa Delpit, 1995

*What comes, we now have to ask, of having one's comprehension of the world so directly tied to one's conquest of it?*

John Willinsky, 1998

## POSTCOLONIAL THEORY AND ADVOCACY
## RESEARCH IN LITERACY EDUCATION

Another kind of radical counternarrative apparent in literacy research and scholarship has been inspired by "postcolonial theory." Postcolonialism is a political and cultural movement that challenges the received histories and ideologies of former colonial nations and opens a space for insurgent knowledges to emerge (Pennycook, 2001). Postcolonial theory is a collection of theoretical and critical strategies used to examine the culture (the literature, politics, and history) of the former colonies of the European empires (Hart & Goldie, 1993). Research informed by postcolonial theory systematically reflects on the domination and subordination produced in encounters between the colonizer and the colonized (McCarthy et al., 2003). Postcolonial research draws attention to encounters between people who have been separated from each other, geographically and historically, and who come into contact in ways that involve conditions of coercion, radical inequality, and conflict (Pratt, 1992). Power relations and subjectivity (the discursive formation of the Self and the Other) are central concerns in postcolonial theory and research.

We place the advocacy research in literacy education informed by postcolonial theory in the category of "Radical Counternarratives in Literacy Research and Scholarship" because of the ways in which it makes use of poststructuralist theories of subjectivity, and the ways in which it disrupts the dominant culture's constructions of the Other. Postcolonialism in the academic world studies the experiences of the colonized at both local and global levels. It concerns itself with matters of slavery, migration, suppression, and resistance. It responds to traditional and established European colonialist discourses in the disciplines of philosophy, history, anthropology, literature, and linguistics. In the field of education, postcolonial theory has been useful for analyzing the ways in which western education and pedagogy operate in nonwestern contexts, placing some of the subjects of education at the center of discourse and relegating others to the margins. Postcolonial research demonstrates that education has been a tool for social and political control. Curriculum has been (and remains) a discourse through which the colonizer's knowledge has been distributed and validated (Viswanathan,

1989, 1998). As education has proceeded, the colonized subject of education has been required to identify with the values of the colonizer, and required to assimilate to the dominant culture. Assimilation, however, is an impossible project because it is simultaneously required and forbidden (Said, 1978).

These are some of the other premises and characteristics of the postcolonial theory and scholarship that inform literacy education's advocacy research:

- Like queer theory and feminism, postcolonialism is a problematizing practice. It questions social categories and challenges systems of privilege, and is therefore important to critical theory. It deconstructs discourses and destabilizes identities, and is therefore important to poststructural theories.
- Postcolonial research recognizes that "othering" occurs through language and discourse. The Self and the Other are constructed when those with social power (like the representatives of the conquering European empires) construct themselves as worthy and superior, by constructing those whom they dominate (the people of subjugated nation states and subjugated Indigenous peoples) as different and inferior (Said, 1978). Postcolonial theory connects language and power.
- In considering the construction of Self and Other, postcolonial theory remains aware of the construction of race, gender, ethnicity, and class. The construction of the Other is tied to a history of patriarchal, racist, colonial relations.
- In postcolonial theory, however, the Self–Other binary is not neat and immutable. It is always in flux.[1] Postcolonial research therefore makes use of concepts like "cultural hybridity" and "contact zones" (the contested social spaces between the "first" and the "third" worlds) as aids to understanding.
- Postcolonial theory has also been used to study the teaching and learning of the English language around the world, and the cultural politics of resistance and appropriation (Pennycook, 2001). *Resistance* occurs when the powerless find ways to alter, oppose, or negotiate the structures that oppress them, and reconstruct their languages, cultures, and their identities to their own

advantage (Canagarajah, 1999). *Appropriation* occurs when colonized people take over and reuse the language, culture and knowledge of the colonizer for their own purposes. (This relates to the term *cultural hybridity*.)

• Postcolonial literary theory has been used to challenge the dominance of British literature in English studies curriculum. Postcolonial theory rejects the grand narrative of universal human experience, and the universal value of excellent literature, and asks the questions: Whose literature? Whose excellence? Whose values?

## A Brief History

Postcolonial theory originated in the academy in the years after the Second World War, as "third world" colonies were gaining their independence from European imperial powers. In the wake of the Holocaust, scholars in the disciplines of philosophy, history, literary theory, anthropology, and linguistics began to question the salutary effects of empire (Hart & Goldie, 1993) and to study the discourses of imperialism that had made possible a world of slavery and genocide, racism, economic exploitation, and the devastation of indigenous populations. They concerned themselves with the position of the colonial subject and offered counter narratives to the long tradition of European imperialist narratives of history and progress. Among the foundational texts for postcolonial research were Frantz Fanon's psychoanalytic works, specifically *Black Skin/White Mask* (1952) and *Wretched of the Earth* (1963). Fanon (1963), a psychiatrist working in Algiers, studied the psychology of the colonized, and the effects of the violence of colonization (and also of the violence of decolonization) on the oppressed. He demonstrated ways in which colonialism had been legitimized and justified through ideologies of racism and progress, offering moving examples of the psychic suffering colonialism had produced. Another early and foundational text for postcolonial theory is George Lamming's (1960) *The Pleasures of Exile*, which explained the ways in which Britain, even after the loss of its Empire, has maintained cultural authority through the Eurocentric assumptions about race, nationality, and the Other, which return again and again to haunt cultural discourses, social life, and the production of writing (Ashcroft et al., 1995).

Over the past 50 years, scholars producing postcolonial theory have drawn on a variety of philosophical and political theories to challenge some of the central categories of Western humanism, especially notions of universalism. They have pointed to the ways in which knowledge and power and subjectivity are situated, produced in history, and constructed in local contexts. Throughout the 1960s, 1970s, and 1980s they have demonstrated that representations of the colonized have been produced in ways that justified colonial domination.

The history of postcolonial theory in the 1970s and 1980s can be traced in the development of concepts and terms contributed by people who worked in many disciplines, including literary theory, cultural studies, and film theory. We can mention only a few of the scholars who made foundational contributions to postcolonial thinking. Edward Said (1978), for example, drew on Foucault to argue that discourses of Orientalism *produced* the Orient as a figment of the Western imagination for consumption by the West, as a means of imperial domination. Homi Bhabha (1985) deconstructed colonialist epistemology, exploring the literary means by which the coloniser controls the imagination of the colonized, as "the book" and its "knowledge" assume a greater authority than the experience of the colonised people themselves. Yet, as colonial literature displaces the images of identity already held by the colonial society, contestation and opposition occur, and it is in these that "hybridity" and subversion occur, and domination can be displaced (Ashcroft et al., 1995). And Gayatrai Spivak (1988) questioned the possibilities for the recovery of a "subaltern voice." Could the subaltern speak, after being written out of the historical record? Could the perspective of the Other be taken into account, after being erased? Is it not an act of essentialism to attempt to construct a speaking position for the subaltern subject? Spivak opened possibilities in theory for difference to speak *itself*, in local contexts, in many places, and at specific moments, in various ways. Today there are postcolonial critical traditions in every nation and region.

The publication of *The Empire Writes Back* (Ashcroft, Grifiths, & Tiffin, 1989) was also important in the history of postcolonial theory. It made use of the postcolonial theorizing that had preceded it, but went beyond critiquing colonialism to emphasizing "hybridity." It collected and celebrated the writing of authors who combined indigenous traditions with the remnants of imperialism to write (in English) something newly postcolonial and oppositional.

During the 1990s the question of subject positions came to the fore in postcolonial theory (Hart & Goldie, 1993). Who was and is the postcolonial subject? The people of India, of African nations, indigenous peoples in settler nations like the United States and Canada, and women in all of these societies have been subjugated and colonized in a variety of ways. Postcolonalism resists becoming a totalizing method by engaging with difference in ways that have led to rapid growth in the field and have inspired new forms of postcolonial theory. Here we will mention two: Neocolonial theory and the intersections of feminist theory with postcolonial theory.

**Neocolonialism**

Neocolonialism is sensitive to the fact that times change and that colonial subjugation differs according to its historical moment. The structures that supported *colonialism* (the dominance by European nations in past centuries over the economic, political, and social systems of other countries) persist in many ways even after empires collapse and slaves are freed. Colonial discourses live on within a society, maintaining power imbalances in gender, race, and class by inflicting symbolic and material violence on indigenous and non-White peoples and women. The contemporary United States, for example, is "characterized by an internal *neocolonialism* that has its origins in the mutually reinforcing systems of colonialism and capitalist domination and exploitation that enslaved Africans and dispossessed indigenous populations throughout the 17th, 18th, and 19th centuries" (Tejeda, Espinoza, & Gutierrez, 2003).

The concept of neocolonialism has allowed scholars to make use of the concepts and tenets of postcolonial theory to examine complex contemporary social problems within nations and within social systems like education. Tejeda, Espinoza, and Gutierrez (2003), for example, have analyzed recent developments in California using neocolonial theory. They have pointed to the recent voter propositions (all passed by the California electorate) that eliminate health and educational services to those who cannot prove their citizenship, and that prohibit the use of the home language in teaching and leaning. They explain these as neocolonial tactics that position non-Europeans as Other and as inferior, and deny them access to full participation in democratic life. The nature of the domination, oppression, and exploitation of subordinated groups is different in neocolonialism, but these evils still exist.

Colonial constructs and imagery persist. One need only look at events in the United States after September 11, 2001, to see the West's sense of global mastery, the West's conceptions of the Orient and the Other, and the West's claims on civilization (wealth, knowledge, power) at work in the discourses of United States foreign policy. These ways of thinking have become common sense, and through them some people in some places are made to suffer and to serve. Neocolonial theory helps us see these discourses at work.

But neocolonialism also allows scholars to advocate for new groups of people in new ways. The argument is that, because social reality is malleable and can be transformed through human action, we are obligated to act to end the influences of the past on the present. Tejeda et al. (2003), and others, call for decolonizing pedagogies in public schools that will teach the colonial past and unmask the logic of colonial domination, that will challenge western regimes of knowledge and representations of the Other as inferior, that will highlight the ways in which these representations still exist in the discourses of contemporary life, and the harm that they do. Like postcolonial theory, neocolonial theory concerns itself with subject positions, but it critiques unjust social arrangements *within* societies, rather than between them.

## Intersections of Feminist Theory and Postcolonial Theory

Feminist theory, also concerned with subject positions, has intersected with postcolonial theory over the past 10 years in productive ways. There are striking theoretical similarities in feminist theory and postcolonial theory. Women, like all colonized subjects, have been relegated (by patriarchal domination) to the position of Other in the societies within which they live. They have experienced oppression and repression, like colonized races and cultures. Feminist theory, like postcolonial theory, seeks to reinstate the marginalized. Feminist theory too questions the forms and modes and discourses of dominance and subordination.

But feminism and postcolonialism have sometimes come into productive theoretical conflict. Feminism has undermined certain unwarranted assumptions in postcolonial theory. When women writers of colonized nations have represented the patriarchal oppression within their own societies (Petersen, 1995), they have sometimes been called to account for writing in ways that conflict with postcolonial agendas of decolonization and cultural restitution, and for representing their society's cultural values in less than positive ways. Feminist theory has supported the legitimacy of their demands for justice (Ashcroft et al., 1995).[2]

Postcolonial theory has in turn questioned some of the assumptions of western feminist scholarship, assumptions that have naturalized women's oppression under widely differing forms of patriarchal domination and ignored cultural differences (Mohanty, 1995). Feminist writing and political action that liberate in one context can colonize in another (Ashcroft et al., 1995; Spivak, 1995), and feminism must be sensitive to difference.

### Early Uses of Postcolonial Theory
### in *Literacy* Research and Scholarship

Postcolonial theory's influence on research in literacy education took shape as one strand in its history. John Ogbu, for example, has been studying the low school achievement of African American youth in Stockton, California, for more than 30 years, as it is measured by tests of literacy ability. He has used concepts from postcolonial theory to describe the direct colonial strategies that disadvantage Black children by denying their families access to housing in certain neighborhoods (and access to the excellent schools in those neighborhoods) and that disadvantage Black children by denying their parents access to income-generating work opportunities (Ogbu, 1990, 1991). He also engages with questions around the subjectivities and subject positions of African American children in California schools, explaining that these children respond to schooling in ways informed by their relationships with the White people who control the schools, their perceptions of their own status mobility, and their sense of their own cultural identity. He describes African Americans as an example of an "involuntary minority," a low status group born into American society as a result of slavery and

colonialism. He distinguishes this status from that of "voluntary minorities," immigrant groups who have "chosen" to escape oppression and
danger in the old country, and to seek opportunities in American society.
He points to case after case where the literacy achievement of involuntary minority students is much lower than that of voluntary minority students. He explains this as both an unconscious and a conscious choice by
African American children to reject the teachings and the values of the
school to resist the discourses that devalue them, and maintain their own
cultural identities. Ogbu is a cultural anthropologist, and he does not
cite postcolonial literary theorists in his work. But it can be argued that
he is himself a postcolonial theorist from a different discipline. Obgu
shares with Said, Bhaba, and Spivak an understanding of the damage colonialism does to the psyches of the colonized, and an appreciation of
the ways in which the colonized subject may struggle to resist.

So does Lisa Delpit (Delpit, 1988, 1995; Delpit & Dowdy, 2002),
whose work has also been important to advocacy research in literacy
education. (See chapter 4 for a description of how her work helped to
inspire a new direction in Whole Language literacy teaching, through
the Critical Whole Language movement.) Delpit (1988) made use of
the sociolinguistic research, which described the unacknowledged differences in the language practices of minority language groups (see
chapter 4), and of postcolonial theories of the construction of the
Other, to argue that indirect progressive literacy pedagogies were not
appropriate for, or effective with, minority children (specifically, African American children). Delpit does not directly credit postcolonial
theorists, but her work does make use of concepts from postcolonial
theory (Eurocentrism, and the power relations established and maintained in culture, discourse, and language, through the constructed
subjugation of the Other).

Willinsky (1998) has also contributed to advocacy work in literacy
education by outlining the colonial development of English as a subject
in Canada, and the lingering legacy of colonialism in the teaching of literature in North America. He begins by demonstrating that imperialism
has educated the world with peculiar and powerful ideas about race, culture, and nation, and that the educational legacy of imperialism results
in ethnic nationalism and genocide, as well as staggering divides between wealth and poverty. He argues, among other things, that educa-

tional research and scholarship have a contribution to make in revealing colonial legacies so that they can be countered and resisted.

### Reflecting on History: The Legacies of Colonialism

The past is not forgotten. It invests the present with meaning. The legacy of imperialism lives on in literacy curriculum and instruction, and in literacy education policy. It lives on in the portrayal of non-White and indigenous peoples as Other; in the way these people are seen as existing outside history; in the suggestion that there are evolutionary differences in the morality, cultural identities, and psychologies of these people that make them inferior; and in the ways culture and nationality are equated with race in schools. Willinsky (1998) declared that schools will have to help undo their own handiwork. Postcolonial theory will continue to be useful to those who teach about the colonizing and "othering" that occurs through language and discourse, who engage with issues in the teaching of indigenous languages and literature, and who examine representation and difference in literary theory.

### Postcolonial Theory in Literacy Education

Postcolonial theory from a variety of disciplines (history, linguistics, geography, anthropology, literary theory, and film criticism) has proved useful to advocacy research in at least four areas of literacy education. First, postcolonial theory has influenced *research on English language teaching*. Alastair Pennycook's (1998, 2001) explanations of the history of colonialism as the context for the teaching of English around the world describe the global politics of ELT (English Language Teaching) and support the analysis of research on language and literacy teaching for immigrant youth in North American schools. Lee Gunderson's research (2000, 2004) on immigrant and refugee ESL students in Canada, described in some detail later, considers colonialism and its effects on children's literacy learning in schools. Helen Harper's studies of White women teachers working with First Nations students in the Canadian North (2000, in press) also make use of postcolonial explanations of the construction of the Self and the Other to argue for teaching English in "the least harmful ways."

Second, scholars have used postcolonial theory to inform their *studies of the colonial legacies of literacy education* in general (Willinsky, 1998) and *government policies for literacy education* in particular (Luke, 1997; Luke, Nakata, Singh, & Smith, 1993; Singh, 1995, 1996). Third, scholars have addressed *colonialism in literacy teaching*. bell hooks (1994) has described the applications of postcolonial theory in her teaching of White university students in the American midwest, and Lisa Delpit has critiqued the cultural blindness of the assumptions White teachers make about African American children and how they ought to be taught to read and write (1998, 1995). Fourth, postcolonial theory has informed *research on the teaching of literature*, examining the ways in which colonialism shapes literature curriculum, and suggesting more inclusive pedagogies that support its study. Greenlaw (1995) has demonstrated postcolonial literary readings available to teachers and young people. Singh and Greenlaw (1998) have worked with Said's (1993) ideas for contrapuntal readings in the high school literature curriculum, offering examples of how a colonial work of literature can be juxtaposed with a postcolonial literary text, to disrupt constructions of the subaltern subject. And Handel Wright (2004) has explored new varieties of anticolonial literature studies in Africa and described the nature of African and African American literacies in high school English classes.

## Four Example Studies

MacGillivray, Ardell, Curwen, and Palma (2004) have used neocolonial theory to analyze the ways in which the Los Angeles Unified School District in California has been monitoring literacy teachers' instructional decisions, practices, and classroom environments since 1999, and the ways in which the colonial tactics of the school district have affected the subjectivities of elementary school teachers who must endure close surveillance, a standard curriculum, and overt control. District reading policy, created in response to very low standardized test scores in the district, has specified the reading curriculum (LAUSD teachers must choose one of three commercially published basal programs for grade one, *Reading Mastery, Success for All,* or *Open Court*) and quantified the number of instructional hours teachers must devote to it. Adherence to one of the scripted programs has been ensured through district in-service sessions, monetary stipends, "instructional coaches" placed at the school, and a frequent student assessment schedule.

MacGillivray and her colleagues analyze the forms of dominance inherent in this situation and find them reminiscent of classic colonial tactics. They explain that, in the process of colonization one group dominates and controls another through processes of socialization and coercion, and they present evidence that LAUSD teachers (like colonized subjects) have come to see themselves as dependent and in need of support. Their status as "Other," created by the district's rejection of their professional knowledge and the district's demands for their compliance, has changed the ways in which they see themselves. This process helps to make colonization self-sustaining over time, as subordinated teachers come to have difficulty imagining an alternate situation, and the new order comes to seem natural. Surveillance (Foucault, 1980) has been used to ensure teachers' compliance (through "instructional coaches" placed in schools to monitor teachers' adherence to the basal programs), and any resistance is used to justify ongoing monitoring.

Teachers do, of course, operate across the colonizer–colonized boundary, and MacGillivray et al. (2004) acknowledged that LAUSD teachers have responded to district mandates in nuanced and varied ways. Many teachers respond positively to certain aspects of the basal programs, but conversational analysis of transcripts of teacher interviews and group meetings shows that most teachers are well aware of district surveillance and the necessity to speak the party line. Teachers critique the basal program's overemphasis on phonics and the ways in which it prevents them from individualizing instruction and meeting student needs. But as time goes by teachers' professional identities are undermined. They are redefined (and they come to define themselves) as unskilled workers, restricted in using their professional knowledge. Many internalize the directives of the school district and come to see themselves as incapable and dependent. Though some resist at their own peril, many come to accept the ideology of the colonizer that sees female elementary school teachers as incapable, inferior, and in need of being controlled. MacGillivray et al. demonstrate that neocolonial theory offers a new language and a set of concepts useful for explaining a situation in which the complex act of teaching reading has been reduced, scripted, and controlled. They conclude with their concern for the effects of the colonizer's script on the literacy education of minority students, ESL students, and children from a wide variety of class and cultural backgrounds.

Lee Gunderson (2000) used the postcolonial concepts of *diaspora* and *Eurocentrism* and a postcolonial focus on the effects of migration in an exploration of the subject positions of refugee and immigrant teens in British Columbia high schools. Drawing on interview data from two large-scale studies of roughly 35,000 immigrant students from 132 countries who spoke 148 first languages (see Gunderson, 2004), Gunderson (2000) argued that the English-only system, which provides very little ESL support for these students, is both oppressive and unjust. He describes many ways in which immigrant teens are marginalized, and many manifestations of the racism they encounter in Canadian life. He presents the irony in the fact that, though immigrant students understand very well that their learning of English would benefit greatly from interaction with native speakers of English, they do not seek it out, because of the unfriendliness they encounter, and because their own cultural values do not allow or encourage it. But chiefly Gunderson (2000) pleaded with teachers to understand what it means to be a young refugee or immigrant in school, desperate to learn English, but unable to do so. He asks teachers to work hard at teaching the literacy skills these ESL students need to succeed at academic tasks.

Dropout rates for immigrant students have increased, and their achievement has declined. Learning to read and write is basic to becoming a contributing, participating member of society. School language represents the power code and gives access to academic knowledge. Acquiring literacy in English is no guarantee of economic success in the wider society, but it can help with students' integration into the dominant society, support their participation in society, and lessen their isolation. Gunderson (2000) points out that the Eurocentric views and beliefs of school boards and teachers shape the curriculum and determine instructional practices, and that these exclude the history, literature, and the arts of students' home cultures, and alienate immigrant students and parents, whose beliefs about teaching and learning are often quite different from those of the teacher and the school. He believes that teachers as a group tend to view immigrant students as inferior because their English is not standard, and that they take this to signify a lack of intelligence or ability to learn.

Gunderson (2000) presented the voices of the diaspora by describing the complexities of immigrant teens' experiences in British Columbia's high schools: their troubled interactions with Canadian teens, and with teens from other immigrant groups; their economic problems, exacerbated by racism; the setbacks some have suffered in war zones and refugee camps; the advantages and disadvantages of ESL classrooms, when there is access to these; the conflict between their parents' and their teachers' views of education; the home traumas caused by first language loss; and immigrant teens' struggles to construct their identities in ways that provide a sense of self worth. Gunderson (2000) concluded with another plea to school boards and teachers to be aware of their own power and their cultural biases, and the ways these are communicated in class; to make every effort to allow ESL students access to academic knowledge by allowing them to use dictionaries and to translate for each other in class; to develop programs of instruction that require interaction with native speakers of English; and to work at knowing *all* their students and valuing their cultural backgrounds. He has used postcolonial theory to illuminate for teachers their own roles in constructing and oppressing the contemporary subaltern.

Helen Harper (2000) reflected on language as a tool of the colonizer in her studies of women teachers of English Studies (both White and Aboriginal) in the Canadian North. Understanding that it is in Aboriginal languages that Aboriginal cultures and world views reside, Harper (2000) is concerned with how English language and literacy can be taught, if at all, "in the least harmful ways." Colonial conquest provides the historical context in which the women Harper interviewed teach English. In Harper (2000), a White teacher is disturbed that she is seen as the "oppressor" by virtue of her Whiteness. An Aboriginal woman is disturbed that she is aligned with the oppressor by virtue of being a teacher. Both women speak English as their first language and teach students with an Aboriginal first language. Both (without intending it) bring English Studies to their students in the Canadian North as one of the key instruments of colonization. To their credit, both are unsure about the value and the purposes of English literacy education for the students they teach. Are they working to provide students with tools they need to leave their home communities and compete in the outside world? (The Aboriginal parents and Elders of these communities hope not.) Are they preparing them for life on the reserve? (Do they need English for that?) Or are they teaching English so that students can use it to protect themselves from government policies? (This seems to them a more reasonable purpose.)

Harper (2000) pointed out that the Canadian government's *Report of the Royal Commission on Aboriginal Peoples* (1996) made a key commitment to salvaging Aboriginal languages and cultures and world views and makes Aboriginal language instruction in schools a central recommendation. White people teaching English language and literacy in the Canadian North must find ways to teach the colonizer's language (which embodies the values and the world views of the colonizer) in ways that are not harmful to Aboriginal language and culture. She pointed out that the language of the community ought to be the language of instruction in the school, at least in the primary grades, and that the school program and the curriculum must be embedded in the Aboriginal beliefs and perspectives of the home community. English Studies would be a curricular supplement in these contexts. Teachers would need to become knowledgeable about their students' home culture and language. Although it is not likely teachers would be able to learn to speak the local Aboriginal language fluently, they could learn quite a lot *about* it, and support students in using their first language knowledge in their English lessons. Code switching could be encouraged. Stories could be written in the home language, with translations into English, and the politics of translation could be discussed. English could be taught as a social and political tool, something to be used to promote First Nations interests wherever English is used. Harper (2000) reflected on ways in which teachers of English can refuse to participate in the legacies of colonialism and the continuing destruction of the languages and cultures of the indigenous peoples who have been colonized.

Singh and Greenlaw (1998) present a postcolonial approach to teaching high school literature, and the reading and writing that literature study requires. They contrast an *orientalist* pedagogy in use in many high school literature classrooms in the English-speaking countries that are former British colonies (Australia, Canada, New Zealand, and the

United States) with a *contrapuntal* pedagogy that could be used to counter its limitations. They make use of Said's (1978) concept of *orientalism*, his term for the ways in which the British colonizer constructed the Other in discourse as different and inferior. Singh and Greenlaw describe an orientalist pedagogy for teaching literature as one in which ideologically driven images and fantasies about Asia[3] and its peoples are reproduced, and the legacy of imperialism lives on. They point out that orientalist pedagogy continues to serve western political and economic interests that no longer involve conquering and subjugating the Other, but instead involve trading with and competing with the Other. Anglo-Pacific nations still desire to define and know Asia for political and economic gain, and orientalist pedagogy still works to position Asian people as absolutely different in these five ways:

- Orientalist pedagogy constructs Asian people as different and inferior, and therefore deserving of economic, cultural, and sexual subjugation. It exoticizes.
- It represents Asia as erotic and strange. It feminizes Asia, taking a masculinist (and therefore more powerful) stance toward the Other.
- It marginalizes and ignores the voices of Asian peoples.
- It characterizes Asia as stationary and unchanging.
- Finally, orientalist pedagogy continually reconstitutes itself. Its covert antipathy and its cultural hostility do not always look the same, but can take a variety of forms.

Orientalist pedagogies teach that there are hierarchies of race and nation that are natural and innate. But a contrapuntal pedagogy can undermine the legacies of imperialism and produce representations of Asian people that are more open and just. Singh and Greenlaw (1998) used Said's (1993) postcolonial literary theory as the basis for a new pedagogy that is "contrapuntal" in juxtaposing colonial texts (and their orientalist portrayals of Asians) with postcolonial texts, written from the point of view of the same Asian peoples and cultures. Teaching strategies involve establishing a dialogue between two or more works, through reading, discussing, and writing about the assumptions they make about Asian people. A contrapuntal pedagogy deconstructs the orientalist discourses of colonial texts to show how they maintain the power of colonial (or neocolonial) interests through stereotypes of Asian people, with postcolonial texts providing contrasting discourses and views. Contrapuntal pedagogy allows students to better understand their own views of themselves and others, and to understand how these views have been produced.

Singh and Greenlaw (1998) also provide a contrapuntal reading of three texts: a neocolonial novel, a postcolonial novel, and a postcolonial film. They demonstrate ways of helping students to avoid essentializing the Other, while engaging students in the complexity of the postcolonial predicament of interacting cultures. They demonstrate ways of avoiding the racism, sexism, and economic reductionism of orientalist pedagogy while encouraging students to question, to analyze, and to see themselves through the eyes of the Other.

## Challenges and Critical Responses

There have, of course, been criticisms of postcolonial theory and its uses in research. Postcolonial research has sometimes failed to take account of gender differences in the experiences of people within contact zones, and failed to take account of the differences in experiences of oppression for women and for men. Postcolonial research has sometimes failed to take account of positive cross-cultural interactions in the contact zone and the power and possibilities that exist in constructions of cultural hybridity.

It is certainly problematic when Western scholars theorize the experience of marginalized colonized people (Appiah, 1991). This can be a form of academic imperialism. Postcolonial theory should not be something that westerners engage in to gain credibility and tenure in the academy. When they do, their behavior is unethical. It becomes another form of colonialization. Postcolonial scholars must always take into account their own power, position, and privilege, and the fact that being in the institution makes their opposition to it weak and paradoxical. When postcolonial theorists and researchers do not take account of their own positions of privilege, they limit the effectiveness of their work.

Some might consider the fact that there are differences between postcolonialism and postmodernism to be a limitation of postcolonial theory. Certainly the major project of postmodernism (deconstructing the master narratives of European culture) is very similar to the postcolonial project of dismantling the binaries of imperial discourses (Ashcroft et al., 1995). Like postmodernism, postcolonialism makes use of poststructural theories of language and discourse, of subjectivity and subject positions, to challenge notions of universalism and to insist on difference. But unlike postmodernism, postcolonialism is grounded in the conviction that social reality can be changed, that the marginalized can be reinstated, and that greater justice is both possible and necessary.

Chief among the contributions of postcolonialism to research in literacy education is the challenge it poses to researchers to *attend to the history of imperialism* that continues to haunt education and literacy teaching. Postcolonialism has destabilized a number of disciplines and a number of historically specific approaches in the humanities to analyzing issues of racism, economic disparity, and linguistic and cultural difference. This has been helpful to researchers working to disrupt traditional European approaches to the teaching of language and literature. Postcolonialism has demanded that educators pay attention to indigenous languages and literary practices, and the ways in which these may be undermined and destroyed through the teaching of English language and literature (Semali & Kinchloe, 1999).

Postcolonialism has also helped literacy educators to historicize literacy instruction, the literary canon, and literature curriculum. It has helped literacy educators learn to read literary texts and literature curriculum documents in ways that help them avoid complicity in the subjugation of the Other. Educators have come to realize, for example, how problematic it can be in reading literature to be asked to identify with a character. They have some to realize that we cannot assume neutral, universal experiences across culture. Postcolonial theories support researchers and teachers as they engage in resistance to the legacies of imperialism, and attempt to work in ways that give voice to the marginalized.

But postcolonialism has also contributed by demanding that educators *consider how difference is inscribed in their advocacy practices,* as well as in their literacy teaching. It demands that they look critically at themselves. It has helped scholars examine their work and see their own complicity in oppression. It has, for example, challenged the discursive production of Third World Woman by Western feminists. It has helped White, middle-class feminists take account of women of color, arguing that the collective oppression of indigenous women results primarily from colonialism. It has shown researchers how to make use of poststructural theories of power, knowledge, and subjectivity to explain colonial relations, how to deconstruct the existing orthodoxies, and how to examine themselves and their own advocacy work for its colonialist tendencies. In doing so it has raised researchers' awareness of themselves as cultural carriers and social reformers.

Researchers who wish to contribute to social reform need to recognize and be aware of the material effects of a colonial history. In using postcolonial theory, postcolonial researchers and teachers can contribute to a politics of resistance, cultural regeneration, and emancipation to reconstitute the social order and transform the world.

## Other Studies of Note

Here are a few other studies informed by postcolonial theory. These too reflect on the domination and subordination produced in encounters between the colonizer and the colonized. There are no doubt many others.

**Hooks, b. (1994).** *Teaching to transgress: Education as the practice of freedom.* New York: Routledge.

Using concepts from critical theory and postcolonial theory, hooks reflects on her own teaching of English to White American university students. She argues that a teacher's most important goal is to teach her students to transgress against racial, sexual, and class boundaries to achieve freedom.

**Luke, A. (1997).** Literacy and the other: A sociological approach to literacy research and policy in multilingual societies. *Reading Research Quarterly, 35*(1), 132–141.

Using concepts from postcolonial theory, Luke considers the future of literacy research in multilingual societies. Pointing to the ways in which literacy and language education categorize the multilingual subject as "Other," both different and deficient, and to the ways in which policy interventions are embedded in complex sociopolitical and economic contexts, Luke calls for a sociological analysis of literacy as capital, and a new agenda for literacy research. Literacy practice is "situated, constructed, and intrapsychologically negotiated," and literacy skills are reconstituted and remediated in relation to variable fields of power and practice in the larger community. Government policy that decontextualizes literacy does not serve the interests of the Other. Instead it interferes with redistributive social justice and limits the educational achievement of the Other.

**Wright, H. K.** (2004). *A prescience of African cultural studies: The future of literature in Africa is not what it was.* New York: Peter Lang.

Wright argues for a paradigm shift, one that would turn educators away from literary and aesthetic approaches to the study of literature, and toward cultural studies approaches to the study of literature. This change would require a shift from the idea that literature is apolitical to recognition of the overtly political character of literary education. Wright makes use of postcolonial, Marxist, feminist, and poststructural theory to illuminate the need for such a change and to undermine the legacies of colonialism in literacy education.

## CRITICAL RACE THEORY AND ADVOCACY RESEARCH IN LITERACY EDUCATION

*Critical race theory is an intellectual movement that is both particular to our postmodern (and conservative) times and part of a long tradition of human resistance and liberation.*

Cornel West, 1995

*Specifically, critical race theory offers an alternative definition for the type of conversation about racism we believe is necessary and productive in literacy research. Critical race theory defines racism as a present and unavoidable force in the construction of our social reality. Racism is a system of privileged discourses and discriminatory institutionalized practices, which act upon our individual perceptions of reality. Our understanding of what is real is intrinsically racist because we have grown up in and live in a society with racist institutions and discursive practices.*

Stuart Greene and Dawn Abt-Perkins, 2003

*Literacy requirements have often been used in the service of racist big-otry ... I argue that one of the key components of the ideology of liter-acy became the notion that literacy belongs to Whites.*

Catherine Prendergast, 2003

Our fourth and final counternarrative in literacy research and scholarship is critical race theory (CRT), another example of what Edward Said has called "antithetical knowledge," another counter-account of social reality by sub-versive and subaltern elements of the reigning order (West, 1995).[1] Critical race theory begins with the premise that race is a social construction, not a biological characteristic. Race is an idea, a discourse, a system, a way of thinking that advantages some people and disadvantages others, a con-struction that serves certain powerful political and economic interests. Race is socially constructed, but critical race theory points out that race has profound consequences for material well being in daily life. In a racist soci-ety it is difficult to speak openly about race, because social norms are con-structed to serve the interests of the status quo, and taboos that silence explicit talk about race serve to maintain the naturalness of White suprem-acy, and to support the notion that poor people suffer because of their own deficiencies. Critical race theory makes race visible and demonstrates the ways in which the law and educational research (and all other social institu-tions in a racist society) have been influenced by a paradigmatic view that characterizes people of color as inferior (Tate, 1997).

CRT emerged in the United States within the field of critical legal studies in the years following the civil rights movement of the 1960s and early 1970s (Tate, 1997). Although critical race theory began in the United States, draws extensively on the civil rights history of the United States, and has often been applied in educational research in the United States, it is now being used to inform educational research in other coun-tries (see Monture-Angus, 2002; Razack, 2002; Schick, 2000). Its ten-ets, concepts, and arguments are proving useful in a number of disciplines and across educational contexts.

Tate (1997) identified these characteristics of CRT:

1. The goal of critical race theory is the elimination of racial oppression.

2. CRT begins with the recognition that racism is endemic in society.
3. CRT crosses epistemological borders, borrowing from the traditions of liberalism, law, feminism, Marxism, poststructuralism, critical legal studies, cultural nationalism, and pragmatism.
4. CRT interprets discourses of equity and equality of opportunity in light of their limitations.
5. CRT critiques the concepts of neutrality, objectivity, color blindness, and meritocracy as camouflages for the self-interest of Whites.
6. CRT challenges ahistoricism. It insists on a contextual, historical treatment of race, education, and equity. (To this end, CRT values, and theorizes from, the stories of people of color whose experiences have been formed by racism.)
7. CRT sees itself as part of an iterative project of scholarship for social justice.

One important way in which CRT makes race visible is to recount the history of racism, and to explain the ways in which the systemic forces of racism have been made *in*visible. Critical race theorists challenge the idea that racism exists outside history, as an aberrant attitude that exists in only some people. They point out that the U.S. Constitution was written to preserve property rights, not human rights. They point to the history of slavery in the United States, and to discriminatory laws that made segregation legal. They also tell the story of resegregation, through outlining the history of the civil rights discourses that informed legislation and litigation after 1954 (*Brown v. Board of Education*), discourses that the U.S. Supreme Court later appropriated to *subvert* legal moves toward racial equality. (Among these were discourses of color blindness, of equality of opportunity, and of meritocracy.) Today minority students living in poverty in the United States are more segregated than at any time since 1954 (Greene & Abt-Perkins, 2003). CRT reveals that this situation has a history.

### A Brief History of Critical Race Theory

It is generally agreed that the history of CRT begins in 1954 with *Brown v. Board of Education*, the landmark legal case in which the United States Supreme Court ruled that "separate but equal" schools for Black and White children were inherently unequal and unconstitutional, and ordered U.S. schools to "desegregate with all deliberate speed." In the years that followed *Brown*, the civil rights movement succeeded in changing a number of racist laws and institutions. But racial injustice in the United States did not disappear. It took new forms. Racism still shaped U.S. social structures, including education and the law. A few legal scholars began to examine the impact of social forces on legal change and legal discourse, and a new field emerged during the 1970s called *critical legal studies* (CLS).

Scholars within critical legal studies analyzed legal ideology and discourses to reveal the ways in which they were serving as mechanisms to legitimate the racist social structures of the United States. Where civil rights doctrine had called for "color blindness" so that all citizens stood equal before the law, CLS critiqued color blindness and called for "race consciousness" that did not ignore the importance of race in shaping the experience of the individual person. Where liberal discourses had called for "equality of opportunity," assuming a level playing field of social life for all people, CLS scholars critiqued the assumption that a level playing field existed and called for affirmative action programs. CLS critiqued Supreme Court decisions involving formalistic interpretations of "civil rights" that ignored the contextual realities of racialized peoples' lives.

Critical legal scholars drew on critical theories of systemic injustice *and* on poststructural theories of discourse and power to argue that the law is more than a vehicle that frees people or supports oppression. The law is a perspective on society, full of internal inconsistencies, and subject to varying interpretations over time. Scholars in CLS demonstrated that distributions of power in society are neither natural, rational, nor are they necessary (Tate, 1997).

Many CLS scholars have pointed to the limitations on achieving justice using dominant conceptions of race, racism, and social equality. But three scholars have made special contributions to a new body of theory (and a new intellectual agenda) that crosses disciplinary boundaries and finds applications outside the law: CRT (Tate, 1997). Civil rights lawyer and legal scholar Derrick Bell (1979, 1987, 1989) has used allegory and narrative to examine legal discourse in situated ways, and to inspire political activism to achieve racial justice. Richard Delgado (1990) began with the assertion that racism is normal, not aberrant, in American society. He went on to justify the use of stories or "voice scholarship" in critical race theory, arguing that people of color (unlike White people) live in a world dominated by race. He justified theorizing from chronicles of the experiences of people of color, arguing that reality is a social construction, and that stories are useful for destroying and changing mindsets, for building community, and for easing the minds of those who suffer. Third, Kimberley Crenshaw (1988, 1993) pointed to the ways in which legal interpretations proceed largely from the worldview of the interpreter. She called for new forms of social and legal theory that grounded analysis in the realities of the lives of the racially oppressed, that analyzed the hegemonic role of racism, and that attended to the interaction of gender, race, and class. (See Tate, 1997, for a fuller explanation of these ideas.)

CRT, incorporating these ideas, came to be applied in scholarship outside the legal arena. CRT found applications in history (see Omni & Wynant, 1994, for example), in literary theory (see Morrison, 1992), and in many sociological studies of Whiteness, White supremacy, and White privilege (see Bergerson, 2003; Fine et al., 2004; Kinchloe, Steinberg, Rodriguez, & Chennault, 2000; Valdes et al., 2002). In the field of education Tate, Ladson-Billings and Grant (1993) applied the ideas of Derrick, Delgado, Crenshaw, and others to analyzing school choice and voucher plans, standards-based reform efforts, and school desegregation efforts. Tate and Ladson-Billings (1995) and Ladson-Billings (1999) used critical race theory to counter the myths of cultural depravity and disadvantage that plagued teacher education. Ladson-Billings (1999) also traced the history of racist ideas that "culturally disadvantaged" children were defective and lacking, that "difference" was an educational problem, and that any child who was not White and middle class was abnormal. She advocated for teacher education that used the tenets of critical race theory to disrupt the discourse of what she refers to as PSWBW (Public School Way Back When), which valorized and idealized schooling before desegregation. Recently other educational researchers have expanded the applications of CRT beyond the Black–White binary to include the racialized experiences of Latinas/os, Native Americans, and Asian Americans (Solórzano & Delgado Bernal, 2001; Solórzano & Yosso,

2001, 2002; Yosso, 2002). These authors emphasized the intersections of race and racism with other forms of oppression and they argued for the extension of CRT arguments to include all colonized and marginalized people of color (Yosso, 2002).

Among the educational researchers seeking to build on poststructural and critical theories to better understand the role of race in U.S. schools and society, there have been literacy researchers making use of critical race theory in their work. Catherine Prendergast (2003) pointed out that in the United States literacy and racial justice became conceptually enmeshed and inseparable in debates over school choice, standardized testing, affirmative action, and reparations after 1954. Promoted as the means to racial justice, these initiatives did not produce it. Backlash against school desegregation efforts made it clear that White people too have an investment in literacy achievement, as a means for marking and preserving White privilege.

Educational research has a long history of relying on racial stereotypes about people of color to help support racist ideologies and specific political actions (Tate, 1997). Premised on the belief that people of color are biologically and genetically inferior to Whites, IQ studies have purported to "measure" differences among racial groups, to argue that low intelligence is at the root of social inequity, and that educational and legal policies must take this into consideration (Herrnstein & Murray, 1994; Hilliard, 1979; Jensen, 1969; Kamin, 1974; Madaus, 1994; and others). Literacy scholars have used arguments and concepts from critical legal studies and CRT to question and discredit studies from this "inferiority paradigm" (Tate, 1997).[2] Other scholars have used CRT to refute "the literacy myth" (Graff, 1979), which suggests that literacy will guarantee moral growth and financial security, regardless of other social factors. Since the turn of the 21st century, many more literacy researchers have been using CRT to make race visible and central in their work.[3]

### Two Example Studies

Catherine Prendergast's (2003) book-length study of "the tangled history of literacy and racial justice" in the United States uses critical race theory to make an outstanding contribution to advocacy research. Prendergast's five chapters present different aspects of that tangled history. In her first chapter she traces the discourses of civil rights legislation and rulings by the U.S. Supreme Court in the decades after *Brown versus the Board of Education,* to uncover the assumptions that shaped the legal decisions that subverted progress toward racial justice. Among these were the assumption that White identity has property value; the assumption that literacy is White property, and a characteristic of White identity; and the assumption that literacy is a neutral skill that is uniform and the same for all people, regardless of their culture or history (see also Prendergast, 2002). Prendergast (2003) argued that an "economy of literacy" exists, in that when desegregation occurs and racialized people are admitted to White educational institutions to acquire literacy, literacy is then devalued and perceived to be in crisis. The rhetoric of literacy crisis allows literacy standards to change and become more difficult to attain, so that literacy remains associated with Whiteness, through the White people who have the resources to attain the higher standards.

Prendergast deconstructed the rhetoric of the anti-affirmative action movement in similar fashion, pointing to a reconsideration of the concept of "rights" after *Brown versus the Board of Education.* She also analyzed the place of literacy in the American dream, by examining the presidential speeches of Ronald Reagan to reveal his distaste for the civil rights movement and his "melting pot" theory of the goals of immigration. Equating race with ethnicity, and portraying the failure to become assimilated as due to a conflict of cultural norms, Reagan rendered race (and the United States' history of racial discrimination) invisible. Throughout, Prendergast used critical race theory to reveal discourses and to construct arguments of use to literacy researchers working for racial justice.

Importantly, Prendergast (2003) looked back at Shirley Brice Heath's (1983) landmark study *Ways With Words: Language, Life and Work in Communities and Classrooms* to trouble and "locate" Heath's influential text in history. (See our chapter 3 section on situated literacies for a discussion of Heath, 1983.) Arguing that Heath was in effect a literacy researcher attempting to document the effects of desegregation between 1968 and the late 1970s (when the data for *Ways With Words* was collected), Prendergast (2003) pointed to a silence around race in the text, and the ways in which *Ways With Words* downplays racial differences between the communities of Trackton and Roadville, focusing instead on class differences. The historical context in which these communities existed, and in which their literacy practices were situated, is almost never invoked in the text.

Prendergast reexamined Heath's archived data to trace the ways in which Heath had to negotiate stereotypes, tensions, and taboos in her writing of the text. She used CRT to revisit anecdotes Heath's participants related, and to reveal the constraints on what Heath could say in her correspondence with other scholars. She does not blame Heath for being subject to those historical constraints. But she does use CRT to make race visible in Heath's story of life and education in the Carolina Piedmont, and to reveal how literacy became a means of asserting a separate White identity in the years after 1954.

Lastly, Prendergast (2003) reported on life and literacy education at High School X, a public alternative secondary school established in 1971 to offer an education in which racial difference could be spoken of openly, and the need for racial justice acknowledged. Every student at High School X was required to take a course in racial justice and the history of racial oppression. Actively involved as a participant-observer at the school in 1996, Prendergast attempted to study racism's impact on students' literacy practices. She found highly skilled and subtle uses of literacy in school. Students did use literacy, and used it well, to contest racist policy decisions by the school board, to name their social realities, and to resist the effects of racism in their lives. But their literacy achievements did not often lead to further education or to well-compensated employment in the years after school. Prendergast (2003) advocated for African American young people and forms of literacy education that engage them and allow them to be heard, offered within an educational context that does not promote their failure.

Arlette Ingram Willis (2003) provided a second example of critical race theory's uses in advocacy research in literacy education. Willis used CRT to reflect on her own troubled teaching of a literacy methods class for preservice teacher education students, both White and "minority." Willis told the story of the course, illustrating the students' responses to readings about social inequities, power, and privilege by quoting excerpts from two of her students' journals. One European American female student wrote of her fear of learning about racism and her own White privilege, and joined the other White students in remaining silent in class. One

Puerto Rican American male student wrote of his anger and resentment at being pitied by White students in the class, and became determined to challenge his White classmates and help Willis to teach them about racism. Tension mounted, as White students' silence announced their collective unity and underscored their Whiteness and privilege in a racialized society. Willis was forced to reflect on her own teaching about race as a woman of color, and to conclude that her own dedication to teaching about past and current racial inequities had led her to recenter Whiteness in her classroom. She came to understand that she was teaching her White students about race and privilege at the psychological and emotional expense of her students of color. Willis concluded by calling for teaching methods that draw students' attention to the intersections of race, class, gender, and power in literacy pedagogy and literacy content, and for classroom discussions of the intersections of race and literacy.

Willis drew on two important aspects of CRT in her analysis: first, the importance of acknowledging racism as always present and normal in American society; second, the use of narratives to contextualize lives and experiences. By centralizing issues of race and privilege within discussions of literacy research, and by calling for the teaching of multicultural literature written by scholars of color from a variety of cultures, Willis believes that literacy educators and teacher educators can redirect their efforts, to make race visible.

Willis (2000) has written elsewhere about using critical race theory to help White preservice literacy teachers overcome their resistance to learning about the United States' history of racism, and to help them overcome their beliefs in a meritocracy of American life that allows all people to achieve. She explained to them the ways in which their thinking and their actions may support "dysconscious racism" (King, 1991), an "uncritical habit of mind that justifies inequity and exploitation by accepting the existing order of things as given" (p. 135). Willis worked to teach future teachers to do critical readings of every curricular text. She breaks the silence about race in teacher education, even as she recognizes how emotionally challenging this may be for her students, regardless of their race and ethnicity.

## Contributions and Critical Responses

Critical race theory acknowledges racism and makes it visible in education and in all aspects of daily life. It theorizes racial epistemology and puts it to work in literacy research by refuting beliefs that low intelligence is at the root of societal inequities; that people of color are simple and lazy; that Whites are more intelligent, diligent, and deserving; that racial divisions in society are natural and inevitable (Tate, 1997).

Greene and Abt-Perkins (2003) suggested that critical race theory contributes to educational research by developing local knowledge, by theorizing White racial positions too, and by attending to ethics and consequences in literacy research. In these ways it inspires efforts at change. But they also argued that literacy researchers need to engage even more fully in the process of making race visible. Like many White educators, literacy researchers have avoided engaging with critical race theory because it is disturbing to acknowledge their own privilege and their own racism. They do not wish to attend to the ways in which the institutions of schooling and society have placed minority students living in poverty at a disadvantage in achieving access to quality education, housing, health care, and employment (Greene & Abt-Perkins, 2003).

Racism is not an aberration. It is built into the fabric of life in the United States (Nieto, 2003) and other racist societies. Racism in not an individual, ethical act. It is a social phenomenon open to critique, and CRT provides a guide to that critique. But even more than analysis and critique, literacy education needs useful and strategic ways to combat racism in its various educational forms, like high-stakes testing and such punitive policies as "No Child Left Behind." There is racism in many researchers' beliefs about the capabilities of children of color, and even in the ways they understand the nature of literacy (Nieto, 2003). White literacy educators especially need to make the problem of racism theirs to solve. CRT can help them advocate and work toward that end.[4]

## Other Studies of Note

**Lali, R., & Hinchman, K. A. (2001).** Critical issues: Examining constructions of race in literacy research. *Journal of Literacy Research, 33,* 529–561.

This study reviews scholarship on race, racism, and White liberalism, and offers a critique of the authors' own complicity as White liberal researchers in the social and political dynamics that support continuing inequity. It also offers suggestions for literacy researchers who hope their work will contribute to projects for social justice.

**Lamos, S. (2000).** Basic writing, CUNY, and "mainstreaming": (De)racialization reconsidered. *Journal of Basic Writing, 19*(2), 22–43.

This study uses CRT to point to the property value of White identity, and also to the complicity of the justice system in the U.S. in maintaining education (and literacy) as White property.

There are also studies that meet our criteria for advocacy research in literacy education, and that list critical race theory as *one* of their theoretical frames. For examples, see these:

**Mollie Blackburn (2002, 2003a, 2003b, 2004)** lists critical race theory as one of the theoretical frames that inform her work. See our chapter 2 on Queer Theory in literacy research for a discussion of Blackburn's work, and chapter 6 for an analysis of her views of social justice.

Kris Gutierrez, Jolynn Asato, Maria Santos, and Neil Gotanda (2002) also draw on critical race theory as one of several theoretical lenses in their analysis of the impact of California's Proposition 227 (which prohibits the use of the primary language in instruction) on pedagogy in bilingual and English-only education.

We leave the radical counternarratives that we have named in these last two chapters as feminist, queer, postcolonial, and critical race theories to address other kinds of scholarship that, though they may be influenced by these counternarratives, may be better named "Literacy as Social Practice" and "Linguistic Studies." We begin in the next chapter with the contributions made to advocacy research by studies that consider literacy as social practice.

# 4

# Literacy as Social Practice

In the past three chapters we have laid out two broad categories of advocacy research in literacy education. The first we have called *Critical Literacies*. The second we have called *Radical Counternarratives in Literacy Research*. Now we turn our attention to a third category that we are calling *Advocacy Research on Literacy as Social Practice*. Studies we have placed in this category focus on literacy as a complex social practice with consequences for individual lives. Like the critical literacy advocacy research we have discussed, they are political in that they are concerned with the distribution of power. These studies too aim to be transformative in that their intention is to bring the world closer to social justice by revealing the ways in which local literacies both reflect and help to construct larger social structures of inequity. These studies do not necessarily ground themselves in poststructural theories of the human subject, and in theories of language and shifting meaning, although they may.

This chapter is organized around four subcategories of advocacy research on literacy as social practice. They are as follows:

*Situated literacies*, which study tacit local norms for doing literacy.

*Multiliteracies*, which are concerned with redesigning futures for and with those "at risk."

Some studies of *adolescent literacies,* which focus on the complex, multifaceted, and multimodal literacy practices of adolescent learners.

A few of the studies grounded in *activity theory,* which show us in great detail how inequality and power differentials are enacted in literacy activity.[1]

## SITUATED LITERACIES

Advocacy research in the category of "situated literacies" is inspired by the discipline of anthropology and its approaches to the study of culture. It does not assume that literacy is some unitary thing that people *have,* but rather that literacies are things that people *do.* People grow up learning and living the meanings their culture has for things like literacy, and their culture's norms for doing literacy, and they enact those beliefs.

Studies of "situated literacies" can be distinguished from multiliteracies, adolescent literacies, and studies grounded in activity theory in these ways:

- Studies of situated literacies rely on the research methods of ethnography for studying cultural norms.
- They focus on tacit cultural norms for doing literacy and the shared local knowledge of families, communities, and individuals.
- They describe literacy *practices,* the behaviors, values, attitudes, feelings, and social relations (Barton & Hamilton, 1998), which are patterns belonging to a cultural group, situated in a particular time and place.
- They see literacy as something to be studied in a variety of domains (the home, the workplace, the school, the church) that are part of a culture.
- Situated literacies research focuses to a great extent on literacies *outside* of school, examining the literacy practices associated with one particular group of people to understand what literacy is *for them.*

Not all studies of situated literacies are *advocacy* research, but some do attempt to show how literacies are ideologically constructed and how they are embedded in power relations. Some focus on the local literacies of oppressed peoples and see literate activity as a collective resource for those people, essential to the kinds of local democratic participation required for a better world. We will review a few of those studies here, studies that describe the ways of acting and behaving through literacy that reflect, enact, and create the structures of society.

## A Brief History

Like Shirley Brice Heath (1983, p. ix) we credit Dell Hymes with encouraging researchers in the 1960s and 1970s, both those who were anthropologists and those who were linguists, to do research that would be relevant to practice in literacy education.[2] Heath's (1983) ethnography of "ways with words" in Trackton and Roadville inspired many later studies of situated literacies. Heath spent more than 10 years working in the Piedmont Carolinas area south of the Appalachian Mountains in the southeastern United States, conducting research on the language and social patterns of three communities there: Roadville, a White working-class community of families who had worked for four generations in the textile mills; Trackton, a Black working-class community of families who worked in the textile mills, but whose older members remembered life as small farmers; and White middle-class townspeople who did not identify with their neighbors, but whose sense of community centered on networks of voluntary associations across the region (like churches, the Elks Club, and the Junior League). Heath demonstrated, in vivid ethnographic detail, the contrasting ways in which these three communities told stories, used reading, used writing, and provided their children with orientations to language and literacy that the children then brought to school. Heath went on to detail the ways in which these "ways with words" conflicted with (or were consistent with) the expectations for language and for literacy they encountered in their teachers at school. She made the point powerfully that the schools that served the communities of Roadville, Trackton, and the townspeople were not neutral arenas for literacy education and social growth. They represented the interests of one social group, the townspeople, whose children came to school with the tacit linguistic knowledge, the skills and the values that would allow them to make sense of school and succeed there. The children of Roadville and Trackton came to school with different knowledge, skills, and values that conflicted with those of the school, leading to academic failure and diminished social futures. Heath called for new kinds of teacher training to familiarize teachers with the literacy norms and values of the children they would teach, so that race and class would not be so directly and easily reproduced at school, and so that society could change.[3] (But see also the Critical Race Theory of chapter 3, for commentary on the constraints Heath faced in speaking about race.)

Meanwhile, Denny Taylor and Catherine Dosey-Gaines (1988) were conducting the research for another enlightening and disturbing landmark American study, one that challenged traditional views of literacy as a single uniform skill that operated in the same way across races and classes. Ethnographers who, like Heath, used the research methods of ethnography (participant observation, open interviews, and document analysis) to study the literacy practices of one social group, Taylor and Dorsey-Gaines told the story of several families struggling with poverty in the South Bronx, all of whom had children doing well in school. Describing in vivid detail the daily misery of these African American women who were raising young children on very little money, they also described the ways in which these women used literacy to fill out welfare application forms, negotiate with government agencies over housing, plan their daily activities, and otherwise manage their lives. They presented what the children of these women wrote at home and at school, and described these children reading at home and engaging in disconnected and destructive literacy lessons at school.

In doing so, they presented a dramatic challenge to researchers who used sex, race, economic status, and setting as "variables" in studies of literacy achievement, assuming that there would be correlation. The people they studied were highly literate and made brilliant uses of literacy in their particular circumstances, as they struggled through their lives, but literacy did not save them from their poverty in a society that did not value them and that offered them no support. Taylor and Dorsey-Gaines closed their study with a call for educational policy that takes account of the social, political, and economic forces that impact on people's lives, and with a call for coherent and connected social programs that help poor people. They called for societal change.

Also in the 1980s, in the United Kingdom, David Barton and others were conducting ethnographic studies of reading and writing in local communities, documenting the ways in which literacy practices are social, located in the interactions between people. Seeking to explain what it is that people *do* with literacy, Barton and Hamilton (1998), to offer one example, studied the literacy practices of the community of Lancaster in northwest England in the 1990s. Starting from the premise that literacy is best understood as a set of social practices, and that these can be inferred from events mediated by written texts, Barton and Hamilton offered a description of Rita, a local woman reading a recipe to bake a pie. Locating their description in the domain of the home, the researchers analyzed their observations of and their conversations with Rita to show how she used literacy to create something for her own pleasure, to connect with her daughter Hayley, to share her resources with her friends, and to make gifts. The Lancaster study included many other examples from the domains of Lancaster workplaces, churches, and schools, and many new examples of the *functions* of literacy (both private functions like *threatening* and *dreaming*, and public functions, like *providing evidence* and *creating ritual*). Details of the literacy differences in each domain and function help us to see the pressure of social conventions and attitudes as they support dominant literacy practices, which in turn are part of broader cultural practices. Also situating literacy in social history, Barton and his colleagues help us understand the ideologies and the traditions on which these literacy practices are based.

Andrea Fishman (1988), for another example, researched literacy practices in the home and school lives of an Amish family in Pennsylvania. Within the context of a close friendship that Fishman developed with an Amish woman and her family during the 1970s, she conducted an ethnographic study of their literacy practices and framed an account of their cultural beliefs about literacy. In uncovering the "Old Order" principles on which Amish life is structured, and the ways in which Amish students viewed mainstream school literacy practices (like writing in dialogue journals) as intrusive and inappropriate, Fishman shed light on the subtleties of the home culture's impact on literacy achievement in school.

In recent years Barton and his colleagues[4] have framed their research as *critical* ethnography, showing how literacy is ideologically constructed and embedded in power relationships, and they have connected their research to issues of global justice. One contribution that the study of situated literacies can make to the struggle for justice is this: It can help people grasp the *particulars* of inequalities of power, inequalities in the distribution of wealth, and in access to information and to education. It can bring into graphic relief the differences in literacies enacted where people have *more* material resources, and where people have less. By helping us understand how every situation is different, and that literacy needs, purposes, and practices grow out of particular lives being lived in a particular social context, situated literacies research can help us grasp the need for a more equitable distribution of material resources within developed countries and around the world. Barton (1994) called for the provision of adult education to provide opportunities for those who have received the least educationally, and demanded political commitment to the eradication of poverty as necessary to the provision of literacy.

Brian Street has also made a significant contribution to advocacy research in situated literacies over the past 20 years. Referring to studies of the social nature of literacy coming from a number of disciplines as "the New Literacy Studies," Street has distinguished his own studies of literacy as "ideological" and social from studies of literacy as psychological and a set of neutral skills (Street, 1995). Where Barton and his colleagues have often focused in depth on one local context at a time, Street's contribution has been to look at literacies as they are situated across cultures. Reacting against psycholinguistic research that has located literacy in the mind of the individual person, Street (1984) called for research that would study literacy practices as they arose in local contexts. Street (1993) then collected ethnographic accounts and case studies of situated literacy practices in a variety of locations and across cultures. In focusing on literacy as something that happens between and among people, Street helped to make the cross-cultural comparison of literacy practices possible. Juxtaposing studies of literacy practices in several African villages and nations (Bledsoe & Robey, 1993; Bloch, 1993; Lewis, 1993), with poor Hispanic communities in the United States (Rockhill, 1993), with Hmong immigrants in Philadelphia (Weinstein-Shr, 1993), and with urban African American adolescents (Camitta, 1993), Street demonstrated the power of contrast in the study of situated literacies across cultures. Data Street gathered has pointed to the social (rather than to the psychological or cognitive) consequences of literacy, showing how literacy is *ideological* in its connections to social institutions and to power relations. Street (1995) made connections to discourses of literacy in international development, and in this way too helps to open the way for research that connects literacy with social justice.

In one such study, also mentioned in chapter 2, Kathleen Rockhill (1993) showed how literacy was important in the power dynamic between Hispanic immigrant men and women in Los Angeles. Interviewing these people, Rockhill documented the longing for literacy among Hispanic women who wanted to attend adult education classes to have a life outside their homes and find possibilities for a hopeful future. She also documented the anger, fear, and violence of their husbands when literacy education challenged traditional patriarchal male–female arrangements in marriage. Rockhill offered her ethnographic stories of women's longing and desire as a corrective to the professional discourse of adult education, which has used a lack of motivation to explain these women's lack of participation.

**Three Example Studies**

Here we will mention three recent examples of advocacy research in this tradition of situated literacies. First Deborah Hicks (2002), in a study that will be examined again in chapter 5, has researched literacy learning in the lives of two young working-class children (Laurie and Jake) in a small town in the mid-Atlantic region of the United States. Following the children through the first 3 years of their schooling, Hicks conducted an ethnographic study of their literacy learning at home and at school. Although Hicks (2002) concerned herself mainly with understanding the ways in which the children's working-class norms for literacy and its uses were not affirmed or appreciated at school, and the ways in which school literacy norms and practices proved alienating and difficult for them, she does align herself with situated literacies research by inquiring into the nature of literacy enacted in particular domains (at home and at school), and in specific local contexts at a particular historical moment.

Hicks (2002) met all the criteria for situated literacies research outlined earlier. She conducted an ethnography to uncover tacit cultural norms for doing literacy; she presented the shared local literacy knowledge of families, communities, and individuals; she described literacy practices (behaviors, values, attitudes, feelings, and social relations) in a particular time and place. She studied literacy in domains outside of school, as well as in school.

But Hicks (2002) also positioned herself as an advocate by declaring her intention to use the results of her research to benefit the children and the teachers she studied. She took a critical view of social class as a system of privilege and dominance that works to distinguish sets of literacy norms. Yet she also took a poststructural view of the discursive construction of gendered and classed subjectivities in literacy learning, and called for greater cultural sensitivity in literacy teachers and in school instructional practices. Although she is part of the tradition of situated literacies research, Hicks (2002) went beyond it and does more.[5]

Another recent example of advocacy research in the tradition of situated literacies is Cynthia Lewis's (2001) study of the social nature of literary interpretation and response in an elementary school classroom. (This study is described in more detail in chapter 4, as an example of recent sociolinguistic advocacy research.) Careful to attend to cultural norms and practices, Lewis's research goes beyond explanations of how literacy practices are shaped by particular contexts. She uses poststructuralist theory to explain how human subjects are produced through discourses in specific sites, and foregrounds the inequities of social power and status that literacy practices work to produce. Lewis also tells an older story of how children whose home norms and values are different from those of the school may exercise their agency to reject the school's literacy practices, and refuse to participate in the school and cultural norms those practices assume and require. Those who cannot and will not affiliate with the school's literacy practices (and the society's) pay the cost in their material lives.

Our third example of recent situated literacies research comes from the United Kingdom. Eve Gregory and Ann Williams have studied literacy in the lives of people living in the East End of London in the late 20th century. Gregory and Williams (2000) used ethnographic methods to study the literacy practices of the Bangladeshi-British people of Spitalfields, a neighborhood in London's East End, and the monolingual English speakers of the neighborhood, both in school and in the public domains of clubs, places of worship, and recreation. Gregory and Williams (2000) made it clear that their intention is to dispel certain deep-seated myths concerning the teaching and learning of reading in urban, multicultural, multilingual neighborhoods. They target four such myths: the myth that equates poverty with poor literacy skills; the myth that equates early reading success with a particular type of parenting; the myth that the mismatch between the language and learning styles used in the home and those demanded by school leads to early reading failure; and the myth that there is one correct method of teaching initial literacy. In studying the details of literacy practices in social and historical context, they reveal the wealth and importance of literacy activities in the lives of poor children; they find many ways in which parents and other adults introduce children to literacy before school and during the early school years; they highlight the ways in which children blend (or "syncretise") home, community, and school languages and learning styles to enhance their achievements; and they present a number of successful teaching methods that have supported the children of this neighborhood in learning to read. From the first page to the last, this book allows the poor people of Spitalfields in London's East End to speak up for their children, most of whom are learning to read in an economically disadvantaged neighborhood, in spite of the discursive structures that work against them.

Gregory and Williams (2000) also situated the peoples and the places of this neighborhood historically. They reported on the childhood memories of the oldest people in Spitalfields who recall their own learning of literacy. They traced patterns of migration to Spitalfields over several centuries and examined the neighborhood's place in the social and economic history of Britain. Within this broad history they embedded the history of schooling (and literacy provision) for the poor in the City of London over the past 500 years, emphasizing the situated literacy practices of Jewish immigrants who sent their children to Hebrew school, of poor English Londoners who learned to recite the poetry of Empire in school, and of Bengladeshi immigrants who now send their children to Bengali community schools to learn the tenets of Islam. Literacy had a role to place in the survival of the poor people of the East End, and still does. But literacy education also enriched their cultural traditions and sustained first languages. Literacy can be used as a powerful means of defiance in the lives of the oppressed. But Spitalfields children can and do find opportunity and joy in literacy in school today.

Through all of this, Gregory and Williams (2000) were respectful of families and the ways in which education at home complements literacy education at school. They emphasized the literacy successes of poor children living in London's East End and they call for literacy education that respects their breadth and depth of knowledge, their wealth of experiences, and the joy they find in reading.

**Contributions and Critical Response**

Studies of situated literacies have the potential to relate the private and the public, and to frame local literacy practices with the larger sociological and cultural structures of inequity. First, situated literacies research keeps us aware of the importance of specific social and cultural contexts for literacy. These studies show that literacy practices, including literacy lessons, are never the same. The social class and ethnic norms of the participants, and the power relations in local contexts, shape literacy practices in specific social locations at specific moments in time. Literacy practices, in turn, contribute to producing social structures of inequity and privilege.

Second, this kind of advocacy research, by making it very clear that literacy is not one thing for everybody, by deepening our understanding of other people's literacy practices, makes us stop and think and reflect on the ways we do things. In this way it can help mainstream educators see their own privileges, to see how literacy instruction serves *their* interests, and not the interests of the marginalized.

Situated literacies research teaches us to expect endless variety in literacy practices. It counters our tendencies to overgeneralize our research findings and it helps to remove the constraints on what we are able to see. By making us understand the *need* for change and helping us to *desire* change, this kind of advocacy research can, perhaps, help us believe in the possibility of change.

The assumption most researchers of situated literacies make is that, once we *see* differently, we will act differently. But that is a problematic assumption. We often see and understand, but then do not know *how* to act. If we are to change the world through literacy education, we will need to find new ways to work in classrooms and new forms of research to inform our best efforts. We will also need the courage to face new knowledge squarely and to act on it.

## OTHER STUDIES OF NOTE

**Barton, D., & Tusting, K. (2005).** *Beyond communities of practice.* Cambridge, UK: Cambridge University Press; and Barton, D., Hamilton, M., & Ivanic, R. (2000). *Situated literacies: Reading and writing in context.* London: Routledge.

These two books contain a range of research studies of situated literacies. Some of these studies can be considered advocacy research.

**Cherland, M. (1994).** *Private practices: Girls reading fiction and constructing identity.* London: Taylor & Francis; and Finders, M. (1997). *Just girls: Hidden literacies and life in junior high.* New York: Teachers College Press.

Although descriptions of the Cherland study will appear in chapters 2 and 5, and a description of the Finders study appears in chapter 2, it is worth noting that Cherland's (1994) and Finders' (1997) studies of sixth-grade girls' literacies follow in the tradition of situated literacies research that we have been discussing here. Both accounts are full ethnographies of literacy in a community and focus on making clear the tacit local gendered norms for reading (Cherland, 1994) and for writing (Finders, 1996). Both report on life at home, as well as at school. And both call for rethinking the practices of school curriculum and instruction that position girls as disadvantaged subjects.

**Gunderson, L., & Anderson, J. (2003).** Multicultural views of literacy learning and teaching. In A. I. Willis, G. E. Garcia, R. B. Barrere, & V. J. Harris (Eds.), *Multicultural issues in literacy research and practice* (pp. 123–142). Mahwah, NJ: Lawrence Erlbaum Associates, Inc.

These authors report on immigrant parents' reactions to the whole-language literacy curriculum their children have encountered in Canadian schools. Here the values of the larger community were in conflict with the values of a smaller community situated within it. The authors highlight the situated character of literacy instruction, and argue that when teachers are aware of local norms for literacy, they stand a better chance of clearing the way for all children to learn.

**Majors, Y. (2003).** Shoptalk: Teaching and learning in an African American hair salon. *Mind, Culture and Activity, 10,* 289–310.

Yolanda Majors (2003) studied the language and literacies of African American women working in and using a beauty parlor in a midwestern

American city, to make visible the culturally relevant ways of teaching and learning in that community, which could support learning in school.

**Moje, E. B. (2000a).** "To be part of the story": The literacy practices of gangsta adolescents. *Teachers College Record, 102,* 651–690.

Moje (2000a) studied the literacy norms and practices of young multiethnic teens in an urban classroom in Salt Lake City, Utah. This study is considered in detail in the *Adolescent Literacies* section of this chapter. Here we acknowledge that it is also an example of situated literacies research.

**Nieto, S. (2000).** Language, literacy and culture: Intersections and implications. In T. Shanahan & F. V. Rodriguez-Brown (Eds.), *49th Yearbook of the National Reading Conference* (pp. 41–60). Chicago: NRC, Inc.

In this article, presented as a conference plenary address, Nieto situated her own and her family's literacy in social and political context. She outlined the tenets of sociocultural theory and pointed to the fresh perspectives on difficulties in literacy education that sociocultural theories can offer. She concluded by pointing out that race is not a personality trait or a psychological problem, but rather an institutional system and a manifestation of economic and political power. (Nieto's work also appears in chapter 3 in the section on Critical Race Theory.)

**Willis, A. I. (2002).** Literacy at Calhoun Colored School, 1892–1945. *Reading Research Quarterly, 37,* 8–38.

Although this study is not grounded in anthropology and does not use ethnographic research methods, in one sense it *is* a study of situated literacy. It certainly ought to be mentioned in this chapter on Literacy as Social Practice. The literacy Willis lays before her readers is historically situated in time and place (Alabama, in the southern United States). Willis constructs a genealogy of literacy and the power–knowledge relations involved in one local struggle for literacy. Her focus is on tracing the discursive formations that limit meanings for literacy and access to literacy in a school intended to help African Americans become literate, and to reveal the workings of political violence in ways that might allow for them to be "unmade" today. (See more descriptions of Arlette Willis's research in chapter 3 in the subsection on Critical Race Theory.)

## MULTILITERACIES

Multiliteracies research shares with situated literacies research its view of literacy as social practice. It is clearly advocacy oriented. Its goal is to ensure that all students come to full and equitable social participation in public, community, and economic life (Cope & Kazalantis, 2000). Although it has only a 10-year history, multiliteracies research has stimulated much discussion about changes in literacy pedagogy, calling for literacy instruction that takes account of the multiple linguistic and cultural differences that characterize society in "New Times" (Hall, 1996). New Times are times of fast capitalism and changing economic realities, times of computer-based hi-tech industries, times characterized by the ascendance and democratization of popular culture. Multiliteracies theory calls for a pedagogy that will provide access to newly necessary languages of work, power, and community, and that fosters the critical engagement necessary for economic participation and success. To make the point briefly:

- Multiliteracies calls for the teaching of a variety of text forms associated with a range of technologies, so that all students gain competent control of many representational forms.
- Multiliteracies theory calls for advocacy research and scholarship based on the premise that basic *skills* are necessary, but that higher order thinking, depth of intellectual engagement, *critical* literacy, and connectedness to the world are also necessary for the literate citizen of today's world.
- The term "multiliteracies" names research and pedagogy that is concerned with redesigning the future for and with those "at risk" (New London Group, 1996).

### A Brief History

Twelve years ago, in the fall of 1994, a group of 10 academic theorists from a variety of disciplines met in New London, New Hampshire, to consider the future of literacy teaching and what would need to be taught in the rapidly changing future. They were Courtney Cazden, Bill Cope, Norman Fairclough, James Gee, Mary Kalantis, Gunther Kress, Allan Luke, Carmen Luke, Sara Michaels, and Martin Nakata. Grounding their discussions in their awareness of the critical factors of local diversity and global connectedness, they articulated two important arguments:

- First, literacy pedagogy cannot remain centered on language alone. Other modes of meaning are also dynamic representational resources (visual, audio, spatial, and behavioral). Technologies of meaning are changing rapidly. Literacy is now multimodal, and one set of skills and one set of standards can no longer constitute the ends of literacy learning.
- Second, we live increasingly globally interconnected working and community lives. Literacy pedagogy must deal with linguistic differences and cultural differences. Literacy workers must see themselves as active participants in social change (New London Group, 1996).

There are several important theoretical contributions to the articulation of these arguments. One is Gee's (1992) assertion that discourses (which he defines as ways of using language, of thinking, and of acting that can be used to live as a member of, or identify someone as a member of, a socially meaningful group) are inherently ideological. Discourses are "identity kits," which allow one to act in certain social roles, and which are intimately related to the distribution of social power. Discourses (with a capital *D*) are also communities of practice. Children arrive at school as members of one community of practice, of one social group, or perhaps more than one, and as competent in a primary discourse. Control over certain discourses can lead to the acquisition of money, power, and status in a society (although it will not necessarily do so). Any given discourse puts forth certain concepts, viewpoints, and values at the expense of others, and marginalizes the viewpoints and values of other discourses. But the discourses of power that can lead to the acquisition of social goods will most easily empower those whose discourses of identity are least in conflict with them. The individual person is the point where many conflicting, socially and historically defined discourses meet.

Multiliteracies theorists made use of these conceptions of discourse and difference in framing their visions of literacy instruction for a better world. The New London Group (1996) concluded that "learning to read" ought to involve the acquisition of a variety of discourses. Schooling and literacy instruction ought to enable students to go beyond the primary discourse of the home, to the acquisition of secondary discourses to be used in workplaces, stores, government agencies, businesses, and churches. "Literacy" should be seen as the acquisition of the languages of these secondary discourses. Recognizing that the nonmainstream child will have more conflicts in acquiring dominant secondary discourses (like writing and speaking Standard English) because they conflict with his or her primary discourses of home and the secondary discourses of his or her community, and recognizing that this is a factor in social gatekeeping, the New London Group called for literacy instruction that stresses the acquisition of many "literacies," the secondary discourses of many representational forms.

The acquisition of these many discourses and representational forms is essential for full participation in civic life in New Times (Hall, 1996; Luke & Elkins, 1998). As rapid changes in world economic systems and in communications technologies transform local communities and the world of work, literacy pedagogy must take account of the ways in which people constitute complex meanings in and through relations with these many technologies and their resultant texts (a concept called *intertextuality*) and literacy pedagogy must also take account of the ways in which people combine different modes of meaning to create and innovate (a concept called *hybridity*). Control over these discourses is important, not only because it provides access to new worlds of work, but also because it is necessary for the critical framing that will enable human subjects to understand the workings of power and ideology in society, and so provide them with a basis for designing their own social futures.

The concept of "design" is an important one in multiliteracies theory and research. Although it is not possible to do justice to the complexities of the designs framework here, we can say that it is based on a particular theory of discourse (Fairclough, 1992) that involves three elements (available designs, designing, and redesigning), all of which are aspects of meaning making seen as an active and dynamic process. *Available designs* are resources for meaning making that take the form of languages from many semiotic systems (film, photography, popular music, and other "languages" that are both visual and aural). *Designing* is the process of shaping emergent meaning, not by repeating available designs, but by transforming those available resources of meaning. The *redesigned* is the outcome of designing, a new meaning, something through which meaning makers remake themselves. They reconstruct their identities and are themselves transformed (New London Group, 1996). The emphasis here is on the increasing complexity of modes of meaning, and on their complex interrelationships.

Multiliteracies theory then proposes four components of literacy pedagogy that ought to occur in schools. The first is situated practice, which requires a community of learners to engage in meaningful uses for literacy that draw on their own backgrounds and life experiences, and that meet their social and material needs. The second component is overt instruction, which refers to active intervention on the part of the teacher to scaffold literacy learning by making information explicit, and by calling to consciousness what the learner already knows. The third component of literacy pedagogy is critical framing, which involves learners in placing what they are learning in a wider context as they work to account for its cultural and historic location, to more deeply understand and creatively extend what they are learning. The fourth component is transformed practice, which juxtaposes and integrates different discourses (and social identities) to put new meanings to work in new contexts and cultural sites (New London Group, 1996).

### Example Studies

Multiliteracies theory has inspired a number of examples of advocacy research. One such example is the New London Group's book on the design of social futures, edited by Cope and Kazalantis (2000), which builds on the multiliteracies theory of 1996 and calls for literacy pedagogy to change. It offers more detailed explanations of why multiliteracies theory is necessary for New Times (notable here is Carmen Luke's chapter on technological change and the cognitive orientations and skills that new technological forms require). The volume also describes design elements in greater detail (see especially Kress, 2000) and outlines literacy pedagogy for students who will be members of multiple lifeworlds. This is pedagogy that accepts cultural and linguistic difference in classrooms as the norm in an increasing globalized society, and takes account of the many different text forms associated with a variety of technologies. It is pedagogy that seeks to help students gain control of many representational forms, and works toward access for all, without erasing different subjectivities (see Courtney Cazden's interesting discussion of the tensions involved). This volume also includes examples of multiliteracies projects in practice in South Africa and Australia. It calls for schools to become arbiters of difference, places where differences will function as productive resources, and a sense of common purpose may be created. The multiliteracies vision of the future would first be lived in schools and would include work relations of collaboration and commitment, active citizenship for diverse communities, mass media access, and the creation of communities of learners that are diverse and respectful of individuals (Cope & Kazalantis, 2000). Through this vision, equitable access for all would be assured.

Michael Newman (2002) has provided a recent example of literacy research that uses the multiliteracies theory elaborated earlier as an analytic framework, in this case to examine the concept of academic achievement. While teaching remedial and ESL students at the City University of New York, Newman came to wonder what it was that other students could do that his had so much trouble with. Turning first to information theory and cognitive science, Newman interviewed four proficient undergraduates and their professors, and examined the literacy artifacts they produced, to investigate the nature of academic literacy. He then described academic literacy as a game of normatively Designed rules for communication and interpretation. He followed the New London Group in extending conceptions of literacy to include print, linguistic, spatial, visual, auditory, gestural, and multimodal forms; in using the concept of design to analyze the complex systems of communication and interpretation that constitute academic literacy; in proposing a curriculum for college-level remedial literacy teaching as explicated design; and in proposing a multiliteracies pedagogy of four components (situated practice, overt instruction, critical framing, and transformed practice).

In a very different study Chandler-Olcott and Mahar (2003) investigated girls' "fanfiction" writing in a seventh-grade classroom in upper state New York, and used multiliteracies theory to understand the ways in which two girls, marginalized from the upper middle-class peer culture of their school, used their interest in *anime* (Japanese animation) to design personal texts written for their own social purposes. The girls collected anime-related videos, comics, and other memorabilia to support their recreational writing of fanfictions, stories they produced for themselves and other "insiders" familiar with the anime-inspired source material. Chandler-Olcott and Mahar observed that teachers were never made part of the audience for the girls' fanfictions, and that the writing of fanfictions was not acknowledged or sanctioned by school literacy instruction in any way. Using the multiliteracies theoretical framework to explain to themselves the details of what they were witnessing, Chandler-Olcott and Mahar came to see the girls' writing of fanfictions as the construction of meaning, as a process of designing through which the meaning makers remade themselves. They explained the girls' use of popular culture as a source of available designs, and the girls' complicated composing processes as designing. Composing was a multimodal process involving the integration of various visual, linguistic, and audio designs in one text. The girls' fanfictions were illustrated stories that borrowed from anime cartoons certain visual and spatial elements, elements that the girls chose to incorporate in the Web pages where their fanfictions were posted. The girls practiced intertextuality, linking a variety of cultural texts to produce their work, and relying on readers' knowledge of previous texts. They combined characters from more than one television show, for example, drawing on a variety of discourses about heterosexual relationships that play out in many of the media and print texts of our time. The girls' complicated and sophisticated fanfictions were examples of the redesigned, constructed through a process that involved the creation of *hybrid* texts woven together from a variety of discourses and genres.

All this allowed the girls to do identity work around female heterosexuality and issues of power. And all this was invisible at school. The authors advocate that teachers acknowledge these invisible forms of students' literacy to understand and know their students (and their lifeworlds) better, so that they can do a better job of overt instruction and critical framing in literacy instruction. Here is the link to advocacy research: Teachers must be aware of these hidden processes and multimodal designs to provide classroom teaching that will engage *all* students in literacy learning, so that students can come to control many forms of literacy, and use them to achieve full and equitable social participation in public, community and economic life.

We also note that some researchers are attracted by the call for multi-literacies, but still want to rely on critical pedagogies in literacy education. One of these is Eric Weiner (2002), who uses the work of Gee (1999) and other multiliteracies theorists to transform university remedial programs for migrant workers. (Weiner's study is also described in chapter 1 as an example of critical literacy research.) Demanding that remedial adult literacy programs move beyond basic skills to include concern with critical inquiry and the responsibilities of citizenship in a public democracy, Weiner encouraged his students to engage with structures of power by analyzing the discourses of racism used in articles taken from *Newsweek* and the *New York Times*. His concern was to help his students understand how power produces knowledge, and how to read to act on the world. He cites Freire (1998) and Giroux (1999) rather than the New London Group, but he does speak of "multiple literacies" and adds to basic skills a curricular focus on higher order thinking, depth of intellectual engagement, critical literacy, and connectedness to the world, arguing (like the multiliteracies theorists) that these are also necessary for the literate citizen of today's rapidly changing world.

### Contributions and Critical Response

When we assess the contributions of multiliteracies theory and research to advocacy work for social justice, we can reach these conclusions:

- Multiliteracies work points to the value of difference in literacy classrooms, and names difference as the normal state of affairs in literacy classrooms at this historic moment.
- The multiliteracies work keeps us focused on the future *consequences* of literacy pedagogy and research as we live them now.
- It pushes us to look closely at the many kinds of literacies the world requires, now and in the future.
- It provides us with a discourse of obligation to "at risk" students, who are not getting from literacy education what they need to succeed in changing workplaces and in changing public spaces.

In our estimation, there are also two critiques of the contributions made by the multiliteracies advocacy research and scholarship. First, although multiliteracies theory is intended to be practical, and to inform teachers' daily work, its technical language and theoretical complexity may be obstacles to the understanding of teachers (Chandler-Olcott & Mahar, 2003). Second, advocacy research informed by multiliteracies theory does not so much *challenge* the status quo or seek to change it, as it does struggle to deal with its consequences. The multiliteracies emphasis on understanding the forces at work in the present and on coping with those forces in the future may (although this is certainly not its intention) have the effect of drawing attention away from the need to transform the world.

**Other Studies of Note**

**Alvermann, D. E., & Hagood, M. C. (2000).** Critical media literacy: Research, theory, and practice in "New Times." *Journal of Educational Research, 93*(3), 193–205.

Alvermann and Hagood recognize the demand to reinvent literacy curriculum in ways that acknowledge and teach new forms of textual representation and new technologies for "New Times" (Hall & Jacques, 1990; Luke & Elkins, 1998; New London Group, 1996). This article reviews research and argues for teaching students to make political connections through the study of *critical media literacy* (the critical study of all texts, print and nonprint, including the texts of popular culture) in school.

**Grabill, J. T., & Hicks, T. (2005).** Multiliteracies meet methods: The case for digital writing in English Education. *English Education, 37,* 301–311.

Grabill and Hicks use multiliteracies theory to argue for the use of Information Communication Technologies (ICTs) in the teaching of writing, and for the recognition of new literacies and multiliteracies in English education courses. They outline the changes in writing that have resulted from computer technologies; ask teachers to reimagine the technology-writing relationship; and encourage teachers to teach for critical understandings of technology and writing to engage the (social and cultural) revolution.

**Lalik, R., Dellinger, L., & Druggish, R. (2003).** Fostering collaboration between home and school through curriculum development: Perspectives of three Appalachian children. In A. I. Willis, G. E. Garcia, R. B. Barrere, & V. J. Harris (Eds.), *Multicultural issues in literacy research and practice* (pp. 69–99). Mahwah, NJ: Lawrence Erlbaum Associates, Inc.

Working to establish a pedagogy of multiliteracies, these authors designed literacy curriculum for their students that not only valued and celebrated Appalachian cultural forms, but also encouraged engagement in new literacies and modes of representation. They describe this work as helping children to develop new literacies as part of the process of studying existing literacies.

## ADOLESCENT LITERACIES[6]

Adolescent literacies research, generally speaking, includes a broad array of studies that make use of a number of different research methods. Some studies focus on content area literacy instruction, some on high school literature study, and some on how adolescents are positioned in school classrooms and in literary texts. Most of the research on adolescent literacies attempts to advocate *for the age group*, on the assumption that age is one of the categories that produces power inequities, and in light of the fact that in North America publicly funded education is providing little financial and moral support for continuing attention to the development of literacy skills in adolescence (Moore, Bean, Bradyshaw, & Rycik, 1999; Moje, 2000b; Moore, Alvermann, & Hinchman, 2000; Rycik & Irvin, 2001).

In our view, most of the research in the category of adolescent literacies is not advocacy research. But there *are* studies of adolescent literacies that do stand in solidarity with teens and their communities, and that contribute to improving their material, economic, and political circumstances. There are some studies of adolescent literacies that attempt to open spaces for social and personal possibility (Simon, 1992), that are intended to help create a global community, that envision a more just world, and that point the way to social action (e.g., Sturtevant et al., 2006).

Those studies of adolescent literacies that *are*, in our view, advocacy research belong in this chapter because they contribute to our understandings of literacy as social practice. Some focus on tacit cultural norms for doing literacy, or on the shared knowledge of adolescent communities. Some describe the literacy practices of adolescents situated in a particular time and place. Some study adolescent literacies in school, and some study them in domains outside of school. But the studies we have chosen to review here have this in common: They represent research that relies heavily on highly contextualized descriptions of the lives of teenagers, and their experiences with and against school literacy materials; and they are studies that advocate for the marginalized. Their goal is to undermine and alter the systems of privilege that have produced historically the patterns of literacy achievement in adolescence that have led to unjust social consequences.

## A Brief History

Several scholars have considered which kinds of research may have led to the emergence of adolescent literacies as a field of study in the 1990s. A. Luke (2000) suggested that studies of adolescent literacies can be situated within the postwar studies of social class and school achievement that produced these well-established research findings: Unequal school achievement by social class and culture tends to establish itself strongly in the upper primary and middle school years. Moore and Readence (2001) mentioned Katz (1971), who made connections between privilege and power and literacy as he looked back at the school policies of compulsory attendance and curricular tracking, first imposed on poor people and ethnic minorities in the 1880s, and which were intended to produce workers for industry. Moje, Young, Readence, and Moore (2000) pointed out that the studies of adolescent literacies developing in the 1990s departed sharply from studies of content area reading and from studies of secondary reading remediation, both of which grew out of cognitive psychology. Reacting against psychology, adolescent literacies research during the 1990s seemed to take inspiration from the sociological and historical scholarship of Stuart Hall (1996), who began to deconstruct accepted understandings of youth and teenagers, and to call for greater complexity in characterizations of adolescence. Anyon, Apple, Fairclough, Gee, McLaren, and others studied school literacy, unmasking the power relations in education that have constructed different outcomes for different students, and other researchers interested in adolescence made use of their ideas and approaches.

As the International Reading Association has continued to call for research and well-informed instruction that focuses on this age group (Moore, Bean, Birdyshaw, & Rycik, 1999), literacy researchers have begun to study differences in the literacy norms and styles of different subgroups of teenagers, and some have examined the ways in which the concept of "literacy development" is raced and classed. Nancy Lesko's (2001) recent genealogy of adolescence as a cultural construction has provided applications of poststructural theory useful for the field.

At the 1999 convention of the International Reading Association, four prominent researchers in the field of adolescent literacies (Elizabeth Moje, Josephine Peyton Young, John Readence, and David Moore) called for a focus on the needs of marginalized adolescent readers in these "New Times," and for the inclusion of critical literacy in high school literacy programs. Making a strong argument for a Freirean approach to literacy instruction, they called for teaching adolescents that there is a world of unequal power and resource distribution; that there is systemic privilege based on ethnicity, race, gender, and class; that texts and responses to them are ideologically charged; that it is possible to interrogate texts to uncover the ideologies embedded in them and operating in them; that texts can be deconstructed to show how reality is presented and what world views are excluded and made invisible (Moje, Young, Readence, & Moore, 2000). They cautioned literacy teachers not to force a critical analysis on adolescent learners, but rather to create space where students can resist, pointing out that "This is hard work, but it is work that could lead to a more fair and just world" (p. 408). They concluded with a call for action on the part of literacy teachers and researchers, asking them to become politically oriented, vocal, active participants in the world.

More specifically, Harper and Bean (2006) have argued that schooling needs to more closely align radical democratic citizenship with adolescents and their 21st-century literacies. They suggested that the field of adolescent literacies with its important findings and insights into teens' multiple and new literacies, multiple texts and modalities, youth culture, and the material and discursive construction of social difference and identity can support such efforts. In a related line of research, Bean and Harper (in press) also encouraged the use of contemporary young adult literature in exploring notions of individual freedom and collective responsibility in our global community.

The example studies we describe next show other researchers making visible the unequal power relations in literacy practices and events, and attempting to create space for students to make a difference.

**Example Studies**

Bob Fecho's (1998) report on a critical literacy inquiry in his urban high school English classroom began with "a collision" between Standard English and Black English vernacular. Fecho's students reacted with anger to Nikki Giovanni's (1971) poem "Beautiful Black Men," assuming that the poem parodied Black English. Fecho used the incident to make language the object of study, and to engage students in critical research projects that focused on connecting language to race, connecting language to power relations, and analyzing under four language themes: Standard English, Black English, slang and profanity, and code switching. Literacy became a tool for bringing codes of power under scrutiny, through the acquisition of those codes (Delpit, 1988; Freire, 1970). Students became aware of the role language played in the construction of their personal identities and they began to see themselves as members of racial, ethnic, and class-based communities with less social power.

Fecho named the first implication for practice raised by this study: the need for teachers to acknowledge the political nature of language and literacy study. He argued that for students to learn and accept standard English, they need to become critically aware of the role language plays in everyone's life. He called for valuing the linguistic competency and diversity in urban classrooms, so that students are less resistant to learning the codes of convention valued by the mainstream culture, less reluctant to acquire the language of the oppressor, and more inclined to actively critique the language and literacies that affect their lives.

Elizabeth Moje (2000a) provided us with another example of advocacy research. In a study of the literacy practices of "gangsta" adolescents in Salt Lake City, Utah, Moje analyzed their literacies as tools, rather than as forms of deviance or resistance to school norms. She took pains to present the seventh-grade boys and girls she studied, adolescents representing a number of different ethnic groups and races, as meaning makers, as people who used their unsanctioned literacies to claim social space, construct their identities, and participate in the world ("to be part of the story"). Moje analyzed graffiti writing, the practice of "tagging," journal and note and letter writing, prayer parodies, and other literacy practices these adolescents engaged in, to show what these unsanctioned practices accomplished for them. Moje found that their literacy practices aligned these adolescents with gangs, and moved them to new levels of membership in gangs. They used literacy practices to demonstrate commitment to the gang, to disparage other rival gangs, to make sacred vows, to express their fears and concerns, to engage in acts of aggression. Their alternative literacy practices were tools of power for gangsta adolescents.

Moje (2000a) reported that, in the course of the study, she came to see herself "as an advocate for these youth, and I committed myself to providing a space in which their voices could be heard and their practices understood" (p. 659). Assuming that identity practices are articulated at the intersection of class, race, gender, culture, and age, Moje devoted herself to presenting the complexity of these adolescents' literacy practices and the multiple purposes they served, working to present her analyses as a way of speaking *with* the young people she studied, rather than for them (p. 660).

Important to her advocacy work is Moje's recognition that the literacy practices of gangsta adolescents, which function as identity markers and accomplish many things for them, also have negative effects on their life chances. Their literacy practices are clearly also acts of resistance against teachers and the school literacy practices that silence and marginalize them, positioning them as people who do not belong and cannot succeed. Gangtsa literacy practices contribute to reproducing the marginalization of these young people, to their vilification in school, and to their identification as "at risk" and as "problems." Moje also documented culturally biased, racist, classist, and sexist ideologies among teachers, family members, and community members that also limit the school success of these youth. On behalf of gangsta adolescents, Moje demanded literacy instruction that accepts and values a broad variety of literacy practices in the classroom and that teaches the literacy practices of mainstream social power. She called for working with youth to engage them in action-oriented reading and writing projects that will teach them to use their metadiscursive knowledge to understand how the past informs the present, to question their own life experiences, to question larger social values and norms, and to reposition themselves as thinkers and agents of change.

Gee and Crawford's (1998) critical discourse analysis of after-school interviews with two teenage girls provides us with a third example of advocacy research. Although both girls were White, one (Sandra) was 14 years old and working class, whereas the other (Emily) was 15 years old and upper middle class. Gee and Crawford use the tools of discourse analysis and narrative analysis to show the ways in which "social class flows out of the material circumstances of one's life: where, how, and with whom we live, act, and move with quite different access to different sorts of activities, experiences and forms of knowledge" (p. 226). They offer their work to teachers as a way to gain insight into the identities of their adolescent students, and the "ways with words" (Heath, 1983) they bring to the literacy classroom.

Gee and Crawford first analyze the interview transcripts for what the girls are saying when they speak as an "I." They show that when Emily (the upper middle-class girl) speaks as an "I," she speaks as a knower and claimer, assessing and evaluating things, events, and people. Sandra (the working-class girl) uses "I" statements to talk about how she feels, as she describes social interactions and paints a social world that is "negatively tinged." Where Sandra is a responder and her interview structure is picaresque, Emily's interview is biographical and about the trajectory of self through time and space. Gee and Crawford next analyze the interview transcripts for key motifs (repeated images and themes). Sandra's interview is patterned with motifs of disconnection, not caring, and laughter as a way to disconnect from authority. Emily's interview is patterned with motifs of activity, achievement, and assessment.

Lastly, Gee and Crawford (1998) analyze the narrative structure of each girl's interview, showing that Sandra's (working class) narrative is classically "oral" in structure, containing multiple substories within a tightly organized and unified frame. Sandra's narratives are characterized by text echo and by large amounts of parallelism, by reversals and inversions. Emily's (upper middle class) narrative approach is quite different. She presents a theory of the world in narrative form, a world where people like herself pursue a life trajectory through achievement space as it is defined by school and other public institutions, and where there is risk and stress. Gee and Crawford point out that school language is not liable to appeal to either girl. Sandra is cut off from the achievement trajectory Emily expects to follow. Sandra lives in a world of accidents, of play, a world in which what counts is the laughter you effect in others. Emily, on the other hand, struggles to find the connections between words and the "nature" of the people who speak them. She tells stories of misinterpretation, in which someone she thought was the "right" kind of person is revealed to be a "poser" who does not see the world as Emily sees it, as a meritocracy where privilege and success are earned through individual achievement.

Gee and Crawford (1998) undermine the idea that classrooms and literacies serve upper middle-class students, and do not serve working-class students. They demonstrate the consequences of social class, and show that the adolescents of neither social class are well served. They conclude by calling for reimagined teaching and classrooms where working-class and upper middle-class adolescents are served in ways that bring together and enlarge both social worlds.

Gee (2000) has continued to work elsewhere with the implications of this and other similar studies, making the link to literacy instruction more directly. His work belongs in this chapter on literacy as social practice because he argued against seeing literacy as a "stand-alone mental ability," and for seeing literacy as socially situated and inextricably connected to "identity work." Studying the discourse practices of teenagers, Gee argued, will reveal their lifeworlds, and the distinctive social languages and identities that characterize those lifeworlds. What we learn can guide us (teachers) in working with students to create social literacies that will equip working-class teens to face the future, while they interrupt the distancing strategies of upper middle-class teens who hold to a belief in their own essential merit and worth. What is at stake, says Gee (2000), is the creation of "literacies through which we can all read and write more equitable selves and worlds" (p. 22).

We will offer one final example of advocacy research into adolescent literacies. Alvermann, Moon, and Hagood (1999) in a book intended for teachers called *Popular Culture in the Classroom,* described their work with middle school students that focused on analyzing the politics of pleasure in films and in popular music. Teaching critical media literacy units, which were informed by theory from cultural studies, feminist studies, and critical theory, they sought to help adolescents use resources from popular culture to challenge and change authoritative cultural norms. Their goal was to help adolescents see the gender, race, and class biases in the popular media, to help them understand that relations of power are at stake in people's daily interactions around popular culture forms.

Alvermann et al. (1999) reported on what could be called collaborative action research with adolescents in school. It is research that seeks to identify pedagogies that can help young people understand how print and nonprint texts of everyday life construct their knowledge of the world and the various social, economic, and political positions they occupy in the world. They call for teachers to work at creating communities of active young readers and writers who expect to exercise agency, who expect to decide themselves which textual positions they will assume or resist in complex social and cultural contexts. They advised teachers to respect the expertise and the pleasure in popular culture found by the young people they teach, but also to teach critical analysis. They called for teaching adolescents to unpack the assumptions in popular images; for teaching that engages youth in discussions where they need to discriminate, choose, manage, and assess; for teaching that demonstrates to young people that meaning is a terrain of struggle.

### Challenges and Critical Response

Adolescent literacies research does not always make strong connections between the lives of young people and the workings of power. It may be that adolescent literacies research has not yet realized its potential to engage in or contribute to advocacy work for teens. Most of it does not yet adequately address complex issues around adolescents' access to and alienation from social institutions; it does not yet focus extensively on their positions and identities within cultural fields of community life and work, education, and consumption; it does not yet engage young people with texts and discourses of power (A. Luke, 2000). The four studies we describe earlier are exceptions to the rule. They study adolescent literacies, they engage with relations of power, and they advocate for young people and for critical ways of teaching.

There are some studies of adolescent literacies that do demonstrate that adolescent identity is complex, shifting, and multiple and that, for many contemporary teens, literacy practices are equally complex, multifaceted, and multimodal. Much recent adolescent literacies research defines literacy broadly to include many ways of engaging with popular culture, in and outside of school contexts. It demonstrates the narrowness of school literacy practices and school identities, shows the harm that they do, and occasionally critiques progressive pedagogies (see Moje, Willes, & Fassio, 2001, for example, to see how Writing Workshop can be made more responsive to the needs of marginalized students). In these ways, adolescent literacies research promotes change within schools for better, more relevant pedagogical content and method. But most adolescent literacies research goes no further than that.

The studies we have described earlier (Alvermann et al., 1999; Fecho, 1998; Gee & Crawford, 1998; Moje, 2000) do more. They are examples of advocacy research because they call for staging the conditions for students to rethink and reenact their social and semiotic relations of power in the world (A. Luke, 2000). Fecho (1998) and Alvermann et al. (1999) could have been included with other critical literacies research. Gee and Crawford (1998) could have been included in our next chapter with linguistic studies. Moje (2000a) could have been placed at the beginning of this chapter with other studies of situated literacies. We have drawn them together here because of their common focus on adolescents, and because they all encourage educators to work to "change the subject" of adolescent literacies, first by turning diversity and complexity into productive resources valued in school (A. Luke, 2000), and second by teaching the literacy codes and conventions of the dominant society. They assume the intelligence of teens and advocate for teaching that will ensure their access to and participation in the future.

**Other Studies of Note**

**Alvermann, D. E., & Hagood, M. C. (2000).** Fandom and critical media literacy. *Journal of Adolescent and Adult Literacy, 43,* 436–446.

Alvermann and Hagood offered research into what it means to be an adolescent "fan" of alternative popular culture texts. In our view, their most important point comes at the end of this article: Citing Bourdieu

(1979/1984), they pointed out that cultural tastes are used to place people in different social groups and to legitimate social class distinctions. They asked teachers to consider the relationship between cultural tastes and social inequity as a topic for investigation in their critical media literacy units.

We would like to point out that there are several studies mentioned in the first two sections of chapter 4 that focus on adolescents. (See Cherland, 1994; Finders, 1997; Fishman, 1988; Moll & Diaz, 1987; Weiner, 2002.)

There are also studies included elsewhere in this book that focus on adolescents. See Blackburn (2002, 2003a, 2003b, 2004) and Martino (1999) in chapter 2 (Queer Theory), for example.

As we go to press, the second edition of Donna Alvermann, Hinchman, D. Moore, S. Phelps, and D. Wolf's edited text *Reconceptualizing the literacies in adolscents' lives* is forthcoming. This text may offer more advocacy work in this field of adolescent literacies.

### Activity Theory[7]

There is a wealth of research and scholarship growing out of the tradition of activity theory, especially cultural–historical activity theory, but there are few examples of *advocacy* research on literacy education that have been inspired by it. We have chosen two example studies whose authors emphasize their affiliation with activity theory. The transformative potential of this work is obvious, as is the debt to the discipline of cultural psychology and to Vygotsky; but there are difficulties in positioning their work. Please consider this last section of this chapter as a short speculation, if you will, one that suggests a slightly different source and direction for advocacy research in literacy education and highlights the work of a group of brilliant researchers.

The example studies we will present share these characteristics:

- Like all research grounded in activity theory, they focus on culture's role in the human mind at work in society (Cole, 1996; Vygotsky, 1978).
- As examples of advocacy research, they show in vivid detail how inequality and power differentials are enacted in literacy instruction and in literacy activity.

- As examples of advocacy research inspired by activity theory, they connect the microanalyses of language and literacy use with the macroanalyses of discourse and power. They connect psychology, sociology, and culture through specific examples of literacy in use.

## A Brief History

Activity theory appears to have grown out of the need to reimagine the discipline of psychology (Hull & Schultz, 2001). Michael Cole (1996) has recounted the history of psychology to show its development as the ahistorical, scientific, positivist study of the universal mechanisms of the human mind and human behavior. He also recounts the history of the "new" discipline he calls *cultural psychology*, which sees the human mind as inextricably bound up in the historically variable and culturally diverse intentional worlds that it is constituted by, and that it also helps to constitute. Cole recognizes Bruner's (1990) contributions to a cognitive psychology that turns away from behaviorism and toward a focus on the process of making meaning. But he also credits the Russian psychologists Leontiev, Luria, and Vygotsky with creating a cultural–historical approach to psychology that emphasizes the development of human psychological processes through culturally mediated, practical activity. A basic premise of this approach to psychology and to research is that the analysis of human psychological functions must be grounded in humans' everyday activities, and that these activities should be the focus of research.

Making good use of the work of Vygotsky (1978) and Luria (1979), some researchers using activity theory have focused on the mind in society, on revealing culture at work in the human mind, and on literacy. Scribner and Cole's (1981) monumental study of literacy among the Vai people of Liberia showed us how culture and activity work in and through literacy, and gave us the term *literacy practice* (a conception of literacy as multiple, not unitary, that is crucial to all the studies mentioned in this chapter). In the 1990s literacy researchers began to use activity theory to ground studies of literacy as an integral part of human life, enacted in everyday activities, studies that put learning and the workings of the human *mind* front and center.

Both Scribner and Cole, for example, have been concerned with applying their research findings to education. Scribner has used her activity theory perspective to study literacy in the workplace, and Cole (1996) has worked to establish after-school activity systems for children that juxtapose work and play, and engage children in activity that requires thinking through literacy (Hull & Schultz, 2001). Cole has also used activity theory applications to design reading instruction.

Luis Moll is another who has contributed significantly to the history of advocacy research in literacy education through activity theory. He credits Au (1980) and Heath (1983) for demonstrating that knowledge of literacy practices in one context (the home community) can be used in another context (the school) to make literacy instruction more effective for children who are linguistically and culturally different from the mainstream. But because he is inspired by cultural–historical psychology (Vygotsky, 1978; Wertsch, 1985), Moll's research has worked with the idea that reading and writing are psychological tools that mediate human interaction with the physical and social environment. (A zone of proximal development exists [Vygotsky, 1978], which is simply the distance between what children can accomplish independently and what they can accomplish with the help of adult or more capable peers.) Literacy instruction in this view ought to focus on designing activities and providing social supports that allow individual competence to develop. Writing is one child–adult classroom interactional system of activity, and knowledge of community social and psychological literacy practices can help teachers design activities that provide effective zones of proximal development.

In seeking that knowledge, Moll and Diaz (1987), for example, studied writing in the homes of a bilingual community in California to collect information useful for the teaching of writing in schools to limited-English-speaking students. Their ethnographic findings were that parents and other adult community members were very concerned with social problems like youth gangs, unemployment, and the need to learn English, and that they saw the development of writing as an essential element of the good education they desired for their children. In collaboration with junior high school teachers, Moll and Diaz used these findings to support the design of writing activities to be done as homework. One such activity involved writing an essay on the value of bilingualism, based on information the students collected through surveys and interviews with family members. As the work progressed and small groups were employed, students needed less direction from the teacher, and began to produce expository writing that was stronger in expression and structure. Moll and Diaz (1987) concluded that it is profitable to focus on social content in designing writing activities, because community social life is relevant for learning, and because writing is critical for the analysis of social life. Writing activity that calls for students to communicate about something locally relevant and important to them holds great promise for helping poor and marginalized students develop the writing competence that will allow them to act on the world.

The studies described in the section that follows provide recent examples of the uses of cultural–historical activity theory in advocacy research into literacy as social practice. They demonstrate the continuing usefulness of activity as a unit of study, *and* show that the study of activity can be connected with larger political purposes and aims (Hull & Schultz, 2001).

**Example Studies**

In one study drawing on the tradition of activity theory, Kris Gutiérrez and her colleagues (Gutiérrez, Baquedano-López, Alvarez, & Chiu, 1999) have studied what Cole (1996) called "productive joint activity" in an after-school computer program called Las Redes (Networks), located at a port-of-entry urban elementary school near the Los Angeles International Airport. (See chapter 6 for another description of this study, offered for a different purpose.) The program makes a conscious effort to promote the cognitive and social development of the children who attend (mostly Latino/a, African American, and Tongan students). It also fosters collaboration among UCLA undergraduates, university faculty, other community adults, and the children involved. The program is designed with concepts from activity theory in mind (encouraging people to use social processes and a variety of cultural resources to construct potential zones of proximal development in child–adult collaborations [Vygotsky, 1978]; considering language as the central mediating tool in fostering productive joint activity; and viewing collaboration as a process of coproducing knowledge through sharing material, sociocultural, linguistic, and cognitive resources; Gutiérrez et al., 1999). The authors describe the program as a flexible adaptation of the general principles around which Michael Cole conceptualized the Fifth-Dimension after-school projects (see Cole, 1996).

Gutiérrez and her colleagues focused their research on the e-mail exchanges between the children who attended Las Redes and "El Maga," an entity they describe as residing in cyberspace, ambiguous in gender, and accessible only through email. The mysterious El Maga made use of personal knowledge of the children's everyday practices in the after-school computer club, and of the children's linguistic and cultural repertoires, to coparticipate with the children to create learning in a routine literacy activity (e-mail). The children were asked to recount to El Maga the ways in which they accomplished their computer learning tasks, and solved the problems they encountered in playing computer games. The children engaged in elaborated writing and problem solving, often with the assistance of an undergraduate volunteer, in their attempts to find out more about the identity and the personal characteristics of El Maga. These e-mail messages helped to create dynamic spaces for learning, as bilingual and hybrid linguistic practices were treated as resources, and as the children collaborated with El Maga in cyberspace.

The research findings for this study make it clear that encouraging hybrid language practices (encouraging responses in more than one language, encouraging code switching, and refraining from privileging one language over another) stimulates literacy learning and development. The report cites other research that shows that there are dramatic gains in the learning of bilingual students who make use of their home languages in literacy-learning practices. The report also points explicitly to the urgent need for meaningful collaboration and rich contexts for literacy learning of the type created at Las Redes, "particularly in a time when English-only, anti-immigrant, and anti-affirmative action sentiments influence, if not dominate, educational policy and practice" (Gutiérrez et al., 1999, p. 92).

In another study Gutiérrez, Baquedano-López, and Tejeda (1999) have argued for the use of multiple, diverse, and sometimes conflicting mediational tools to promote the emergence of "third spaces" (zones of proximal development) for expanding learning. They use findings from their ethnographic study of the literacy practices of one dual immersion elementary school classroom to show how "hybrid" activities, roles, and practices can lead to productive contexts for literacy development. "Hybridity" is a term the researchers use to make sense of diversity in learning contexts. In classrooms that incorporate a number of cultural contexts, many voices, and a variety of scripts for learning, conflict and tension are intrinsic. When the resulting tensions in activity rupture normative practice, new hybrid activities and improvisations emerge and transformation can result. Hybridity can therefore be very positive, as hybrid language and schooling practices bridge the gap between home and the school. In practical terms, the authors advocate the use of the use of diverse, alternative texts and language codes and registers, ways of participating, and ways of sharing expertise (even through unauthorized side talk). They place a high value on respecting the languages, social practices, and beliefs of all the members of the classroom community, and see these as positive resources for literacy learning. Conflict then is not something to be avoided, but something that acts as a catalyst for learning. Hybrid strategies allow marginalized children to move to the center of classroom life, and their literacy abilities to develop. The contribution of activity theory to this research is the understanding that hybrid strategies have not only social, but also cognitive consequences. They mediate children's intellectual development, as they support teachers who must "negotiate or traverse the diverse and often conflictual urban classroom landscape (301)."

**Contributions and Critical Response**

Guttierrez advocates. She and her colleagues choose to study marginalized children. Her work reveals brilliant young minds coping with a world of difficulty, and extremely capable with language and literacy. She calls for the kind of literacy education that would acknowledge and support cognitive and social struggles for self-expression and better futures. Importantly, she and her colleagues also connect their research findings to the broader political context that limits opportunities for bilingual and marginalized children. They contest the view that literacy is one thing for all children, and demand literacy curriculum and instruction that intentionally violates federal guidelines and programs.

We are also aware of a tradition of research on writing in higher education and in workplaces that draws on cultural–historical activity theory (Russell, 1997), but does not advocate. We know of other studies of writing in elementary schools that make use of cultural–historical activity theory (Cazden, 1992; Sperling, 1996), but again, do not advocate. Studies grounded in activity theory *can* arm us in the struggle for social justice by providing specific examples of young minds at work in literacy activities, making use of all the resources, and especially all the linguistic resources available to them. The work of Guttierez et al. (1999) could perhaps have been included in our next chapter on advocacy research from sociolinguistics. But Guttierez makes use of the theoretical constructs of activity theory (the zone of proximal development, and the mind internalizing what was first external to it). She and her colleagues do take inspiration from Vygotsky; they do sociologically informed cultural psychology; they attend to literacy; and they advocate for the worth of the children they study. For these reasons, we recognize their work as advocacy research.

**Another Study of Note**

**Green, B., & Kostogriz, A. (2002).** Learning difficulties and the New Literacy studies. In J. Soler, J. Wearmouth, & G. Reid (Eds.), *Contextualizing difficulties in literacy development: Exploring politics, culture, ethnicity, and ethics.* New York: Routledge/Falmer.

This book chapter links critical literacy, cultural–historical psychology, and the New Literacy Studies to examine the relationship between the label "learning disabled" and the social, political, and pedagogical context in which that label has meaning. The theoretical frames, which include activity theory, make notions like "disability" problematic. The authors explain the logic of school classifications as a generalized technological apparatus (Foucault) that normalizes those labeled "abled," to argue that the culture *produces* disability.

**Concluding This Chapter:**
**Why Advocacy Research on Literacy as Social Practice?**

Research on literacy as social practice arms us in the literacy wars that continue to be waged in the early 21st century. As we write this, the United States Department of Education, supported by the American president, continues to promote laws and policies that assume literacy to be a purely psychological skill, or set of skills, the same for every individual of every race, gender, ethnicity, and class. American school children are being subjected to high-stakes standardized tests, as if it were possible and appropriate to categorize and compare their literacy achievements without regard for their social situations and circumstances, and as if the playing field on which literacy education operates were a level one. Research on literacy as social practice (on situated literacies, multiliteracies, and adolescent literacies) presents the particularities of literacy learning in many contexts, and compels those who are willing to read it to understand social inequity and to face its consequences.

# 5

# Linguistic Studies

*I believe, if linguistics is to realize its potential for the well being of mankind, it must go even further, and consider speech communities as comprising not only rules, but also sometimes oppression, sometimes freedom, in the relation between personal abilities and their occasions of use.*

Dell Hymes, 1973

Many of the "disciplines of knowledge" around which universities organize themselves contribute to advocacy research in literacy education. Where chapter 4 focused on research inspired by sociology and anthropology, this chapter will focus on advocacy research grounded in linguistics. Again, the categories overlap. People like Dell Hymes and Shirley Brice Heath (1983) have shown the relevance of *both* anthropology and linguistics for educational practice, and many valuable advocacy studies are grounded in both. For the purposes of this book, we are outlining in separate chapters the advocacy research that does more to emphasize *culture* and the research methods of anthropology, and the advocacy research that does more to emphasize *language* and the research methods of linguistics.

The number of studies making use of linguistic knowledge and investigating the nature of language and linguistic functioning in literacy lessons and events is very large. We have therefore chosen to organize this chapter in three subsections, each one devoted to a different stream of advocacy research inspired by linguistics. The first subsection provides an overview of *sociolinguistic* advocacy research in literacy education. The second subsection overviews *psycholinguistic* research and scholarship. The third section concerns *critical discourse analysis*. The three subsections can be thought of as intertwining threads that together form a strong cord. We could perhaps have subdivided this chapter in another way. But in what follows we will explain our thinking about these three "threads," to distinguish among them.[1]

- The sociolinguistic advocacy research included here focuses on speech, on the rules for speaking used by particular communities of speakers, on variations in those rules, and on how social competence is produced *in joint interactions*. Sociolinguistic advocacy research explains the conditions and meanings of language use. In literacy education, it often describes the organization and use of linguistic features in the teaching or learning of literacy, to direct attention to the ways in which language both reflects and helps to constitute access to knowledge and social power.[2]

- The psycholinguistic advocacy research included here begins with a focus on the human mind, and on the cognitive microprocesses that are part of reading activity. But it frames its emphasis on language and cognitive processes with awareness of the social arrangements that influence the development and use of those processes. It uses both (knowledge of cognitive processes and knowledge of social arrangements) to critique instructional methods that limit the learning of some children, and to offer instructional alternatives that will support the learning of all children. But it also ties language use to people's positions within society, to structured privileges, to politics, and to greater or lesser social power.

- The research involving critical discourse analysis included here provides detailed analysis of language in use that highlights the relationship between language and power, and the constructing character of discourse. This research analyzes both the larger structures of discourse that are important in sustaining and producing unequal power relations, and also the micropractices of language and conversational style that are closely tied to social identities. Some of it advocates for greater acceptance of minority languages and nonstandard varieties of English in schools.

## PART I: SOCIOLINGUISTIC ADVOCACY RESEARCH

*Sociolinguistics is nourished in important part by the obvious relevance of its subject matter, joining other academic fields in which concern for education, children, ethnic relations, and governmental policies, find expression ... perhaps what is needed is not research, but substantial doses of money, love, and democratic participation ...*

Dell Hymes, 1973

Sociolinguistic research is characterized by its concern for the social, as well as for the linguistic. Sociolinguists study what competent language users know and do in joint interactions with others. They analyze instances of language in use, as people perform their social competence and work to achieve their social purposes. They explain the ways in which variations in social functions give form to language, and they lay out the tacit rules for using language that communities share, rules that work to produce social contexts.

Sociolinguistic research is about communicative competence, and about social action. It advocates when it demonstrates the ways in which the systematic failure of working-class and minority children is accomplished in schools, in and through language interactions. Sociolinguistic advocacy research in literacy education analyzes the language of literacy lessons in school, and/or the language of literacy in use outside of school, in an effort to demonstrate the ways in which differential literacy achievement is accomplished; the ways in which social inequities are reproduced; and the ways in which differential access to knowledge is granted (Collins, 1987).

### A Brief History

Hymes (1973) pointed out that the term *sociolinguistics* gained currency around 1963, when certain linguists began to do more than describe the structure of language, and also concerned themselves with the integration of language and sociocultural context, and the analysis of function (p. 326). Hymes (1962) had argued that the ethnographic methods of anthropology and sociology ought to be used in linguistics, to create a new field of study he called "the ethnography of speaking."

Hymes (1973) later described the linguistics that emerged as grounded in the assumption that language is socially *constituted*. Language does not exist apart from the social. The goals people have for language are part of what language is. Language and social setting interact to jointly construct the culture.

During the 1960s and 1970s sociolinguistic research took off in a number of directions. Labov (1966) studied dialects, Gumperz (1968) studied speech communities, Bernstein (1972) studied codes, Fishman (1978) studied language domains, and Halliday (1973) described functional diversity. Brilliant sociologists like Schegloff (1972) and Goffman (1961) provided fascinating linguistic analyses of everyday social interactions. It is beyond the scope of this brief review to recount the history of each of these streams in detail. This chapter will trace only two lines of sociolinguistic research that have had consequences for advocacy research in literacy education.

One of these begins with the work of William Labov (1966), who studied dialects in use, demonstrating their variation and their validity. Labov conducted studies of the dialects of English found in New York City, giving special attention to Black English dialects. He analyzed language recorded in use, in naturally occurring social contexts (at a neighborhood dance, for example, rather than in a laboratory setting). Labov demonstrated through linguistic analysis that these dialects were regular, rule-governed, systematic, and expressive, not inferior in any way to Standard English, the prestige dialect. Labov's work immediately undermined the idea that African American children were linguistically and cognitively deficient, by demonstrating the logic of their language and the competence of their linguistic performances. If these children were failing in school, it was not because they were linguistically deficient.

The other line of research that grew out of sociolinguistics and inspired later advocacy research is the work of the ethnomethodologists, some of whom studied literacy lessons. Garfinkle (1967), Mehan (1979), and Heap (1977, 1982) provided microanalyses of language in use that demonstrated that social life was a joint accomplishment. Mehan (1979) and Heap (1981) both examined the procedures, interactions, and negotiations that took place in classrooms during literacy lessons, and found the pattern (initiation, reply, evaluation) and the power and knowledge asymmetries that characterized teacher–student interactions during reading lessons. Mehan (1979) analyzed reading lessons in one classroom to demonstrate the tacit psychological knowledge of the social structure that was an inseparable part of reading and learning to read. Heap (1981) demonstrated that every instance of classroom reading was different, constituted by its context, according to the social organization of the reading activity. Ethnomethodologists conducted microanalyses of language in the classroom to show teachers and students creating, constructing, negotiating, and maintaining both broad and situation-specific social forces and structures.

A number of sociolinguistic researchers in literacy education moved toward advocacy during the early 1980s. We can mention a few startling and highly influential studies from this period. Sara Michaels (1981) analyzed the intonation contours and the narrative structure of the sharing time stories of Black children, and the contrasting intonation contours and structure of the stories of White children in the same class, to show that the Black children used a topic-associating narrative structure, whereas the White children used the topic-centered narrative structure of their teacher. Because sharing time stories were collaboratively produced in interaction with the teacher, the White children who used the teacher's topic-centered discourse style were more successful in telling their stories, and the Black children were systematically less successful. They experienced the teacher's questions as interruptions, rather than as helpful scaffolds for their story telling, and the result was fragmentation of their topics and misinterpretation of their intent. When the teacher became aware of the logic and regularity of the Black children's discourse structure, she took the first step toward improving her communication and collaboration with these children during sharing time.

Around the same time, Kathryn Au (1980) was studying the language of classrooms where Hawaiian children were failing to learn to read, and finding that the participation structures of traditional school reading lessons were quite different from the participation structures of speech events in Hawaiian culture. Native Hawaiian children were competent in *talk story*, which involved lots of mutual participation and conarration, and which contrasted sharply with the usual pattern (teacher initiation/student reply/teacher evaluation) of reading lessons. Hawaiian children were being characterized by their reading

teachers as "unmotivated." When Au and her colleagues devised reading lessons that resembled Hawaiian *talk story*, Hawaiian children
were able to bring all their cultural and linguistic resources to bear on
learning to read, and their reading comprehension increased dramatically (Au & Jordan, 1981).

James Collins (1986), another sociolinguist concerned with the fact
that so many minority children were not learning to read in school, studied language use in reading group instruction in a first-grade classroom,
with four different reading ability groups. He explained differences in
the intonation patterns that characterized the reading aloud styles used
by the children in each group as they interacted with their teacher's correction strategies. He found that children in high-ability groups tended
to place tonal nuclei at the ends of clauses, where low-ranked readers
tended to place tonal nuclei in the middle of clauses. The teacher responded to these different ways of "chunking" texts by handling equiva-
lent errors in different ways. Identical miscues prompted low-level
linguistic instruction focused on decoding for the lower groups, and
more broadly ranging instruction about clauses, expressive intonation
and textual inferences, more focused on comprehension, for the higher
groups. Children in the lower groups did not receive much practice in
applying their knowledge of spoken language to the task of reading,
whereas children in the higher groups did. The teacher appeared to have
an implicit model for what literate behavior should sound like, and to
have differing expectations for students' readiness and ability to read
when their spoken language patterns differed from her own. Collins and
Michaels (1986) later worked together to isolate systematic differences
in discourse style in the classroom interaction of literacy lessons, and to
point out that disharmonious interactions with the teacher during reading instruction diminished the student's access to the kind of instruction
and practice necessary for the acquisition of literacy.

Taking another approach, McDermott and Gospodinoff (1981) set
out to italicize the claim that minority children were failing in school because of a mismatch between their own linguistic interactional rules and
those of the teacher, who usually came from a more powerful social
group. Sociolinguistic researchers were emphasizing the fact that minority group children and majority group teachers have different
interactional systems that result in miscommunication, and that

miscommunication leads to alienation and failure. McDermott and Gospodinoff (1981) analyzed classroom interaction to show that the miscommunication between the teacher and her students during reading lessons is not an accident, but that it represents a sensible interactional accomplishment on the part of everyone involved. They pointed out that, when linguistic and social miscommunication occur, people usually repair the miscommunication. They are fully capable of doing so. But there are cases where establishing communicative code differences marks people off as coherent and often antagonistic groups, and establishes politicized ethnic borders. When children and teachers do not repair minor communicative code differences in interactions during reading lessons in school, it is likely that relations between the teacher and the children are being used to maintain ethnic borders (p. 219). McDermott and Gospodinoff (1981) analyzed a disruptive incident during reading time in a first-grade multiethnic classroom near New York, in which a minority group boy interrupted the teacher while she was working with the lowest reading group, from which he had previously been excluded for disruptive behavior. They argued that, in the short run, everyone involved benefited from the miscommunication: the disruptive boy received attention, and the teacher and the lowest reading group received a break from the discomfort of their intense organizational negotiations during the reading lesson. In the process, ethnic borders and identities were maintained. But in the long run, the bottom reading group got only one third of the time the top group got with the teacher and the text, and they did not learn to read. As time went by, the race and ethnicity of the children in the bottom group became more salient in negative ways. Failure became a systematic part of the social contexts in which the children and the teacher were immersed, and of the social conditions under which they came together to teach and learn to read and write.

Other sociolinguistic research studies from the 1980s that were important to the history of advocacy research in literacy education include the following:

• Perry Gilmore's (1985) study of literacy achievement in Grades 4 through 6 at a school in a low-income urban Black community. The major literacy problem parents and teachers identified was "attitude," and "attitude" was the most important factor in assigning children to low ability groups in reading. "Attitude" was displayed through gendered forms of "stylized sulking," and through the girls' sexualized performances of dance "steps." Cultural in origin, the sulking displays functioned for Black children as face-saving devices when they were disciplined in the classroom, and "doin' steps" served the girls as a form of artistic expression. But middle-class teachers interpreted these ritualized displays, which worked to align students with Black vernacular culture, as "bad attitude." Social resistance was understood as literacy skill deficiency, and this led to academic failure for many of the children.

• Robert Aronowitz's (1984) study of reading comprehension tests and the ways in which some children failed to understand the special demands of those tests. He interviewed young test takers about the strategies they used for choosing an answer from a number of possible choices, and explained how they failed to understand the coherence of the written discourse of the test. Pointing to his analysis of the complex and interesting strategies they used in selecting "incorrect" answers, Aronowitz argued that assigning children to ability groups on the basis of their reading comprehension test scores was misguided, and damaging to their chances for academic success.

• Jenny Cook-Gumperz's (1986) explanations of the differing ideologies of literacy education throughout history, and the ways in which these served the political purposes of the times.

• David Bloome's (1987) studies of reading as a social process in urban, predominantly Black, working-class middle school classrooms. Intending to produce research that would inform political debate and educational policymaking, Bloome used sociolinguistic and ethnographic methods (including close analyses of videotapes of classroom interactions during reading lessons) to demonstrate the ways in which social and cultural factors mediated students' interactions with printed text. He found that students assumed a passive, "alienated" stance toward extended text during reading lessons. The stance (recurrent across classrooms) functioned as a frame for reading lessons. It was accomplished in interaction with the teacher, constructed through the tasks she assigned, and it worked to allow teacher and students to operate appropriately within institutional constraints. The prescribed curriculum was covered, but without students' genuine engagement with the text.

- Luis Moll and Rosa Diaz's (1987) study of literacy in a working-class bilingual community in San Diego. (See also chapter 3, Activity Theory, for a description of this study's place in another category's history.) The project sought to understand the writing that occurred in homes and other community settings, to explore ways of using that information for the teaching of writing in schools, for the benefit of limited-English-speaking students. Working toward instructional change, the researchers engaged teachers in implementing a series of "writing modules" that involved the students in writing activities related to the community's concerns (youth gangs, unemployment, immigration, and the need to learn English). Through structured homework assignments, parents and other community members were involved in the classroom writing activities, and genuine student engagement with the process of writing occurred. Students wrote more, and improved their English verbal expression, reading, and vocabulary.
- Henry Trueba's (1987) ethnographies of bilingual–bicultural education for Mexican American children in the United States, which demonstrated the ways in which opportunities to learn in U.S. schools were not equal for language minority children who were acquiring English through another culture in their homes. Explaining that children's ability to participate meaningfully in school learning activities depended on specific and substantial cultural and linguistic knowledge, he argued that language minority children therefore found it more difficult to learn to learn. Trueba (1989) also explained ways in which culture and literacy were linked to the phenomenon of minority students dropping out of school.

Sociolinguistic advocacy researchers in the 1980s attempted to contribute to concrete change in literacy classrooms that would benefit poor, racialized, and language minority children. In the 1990s, sociolinguistic research continued to focus on access to literacy as institutional gatekeeping, as it catalogued and described the ways children used language in competent and exciting ways that teachers had not traditionally seen and understood (see Collins, 1991; Fordham, 1991; Gutiérrez, 1992; Larson, 1995; Michaels, 1991; Solsken, 1993); and it continued to describe the ways in which ideology was being constructed and enacted in school literacy activities, so that power was distributed in certain ways, and society and culture were reproduced (see Auerbach, 1991; Freebody, Luke, & Gilbert, 1991; Fecho, 1998; Gee, 1996; Gutiérrez & Larson, 1994).

We conclude this history of sociolinguistic advocacy research with a description of Betsy Rymes' (2001) study of language and teenage identity at an urban charter school in Los Angeles, as an example of one direction in which sociolinguistic research has gone. Like much recent sociolinguistic research, it does not focus on literacy education alone. But Rymes does advocate. She uses traditional sociolinguistic methods of close analysis of language, and a sociolinguistic focus on teachers and students in interaction, to link issues of school reform with issues of language and identity. Her microethnography of life at City High, a charter school designed to cater to students who had already left high school, presents the characteristic linguistic features and the textual structure of the stories students told about "dropping out," as they presented themselves as people who had behaved reasonably and honorably in the actions that led to their expulsion and times in jail. Rymes also analyzes the structure and the language of other, more successful students' stories of "dropping in," as they used language to narrate themselves as not responsible for previously leaving school, and to align themselves with the values of their teachers and the school (work hard, leave the past behind, believe that it isn't too late). City High closed after only 15 months in existence, but Rymes came away with recommendations for teachers who work with adolescents. She recommends that teachers listen to students' stories, and listen "dangerously," opening themselves to the kind of fear that many adolescents live with and the violence they engage in to truly empathize and feel their vulnerabilities. She asks teachers and school administrators to attain all the local knowledge they can, and to understand that they are the co-authors of their students' lives. Nearly every chapter ends with the implications of Rymes' analysis for school reform: Understanding the ways in which social phenomena like "dropping out" are reproduced on a microlevel in conversations may show us how they can be reversed. Understanding our own contributions to the ways in which lives are lived and narrated makes us (teachers, administrators and researchers) responsible for changing interactions and outcomes, and for helping our students survive.

## Example Studies

Here we will present two recent examples of sociolinguistic advocacy research in literacy education. One advocates for young people who are recent immigrants to the United States, whose first language is not English, and one advocates for working-class children in classrooms where progressive pedagogies are in use. Both analyze instances of language in use, and both also make use of interviews, participant observation, and other ethnographic methods, adding these to the interactional analysis that sociolinguistic research has traditionally done.

The first is Ellen Skilton-Sylvester's (2002) case study of Nan, a Cambodian teenager living and going to school in Philadelphia. This work was part of a larger study involving 3 years of participant observation in the homes and at the school of seven young Cambodian girls, all the children of refugee families (Skilton-Sylvester, 1997). The larger study found that there were important differences in what these girls wrote at home and what they wrote at school: differences in genres, in the social and academic prestige of writing, in the functions of writing, and in the volume and quality of written texts. At the school the girls attended, being good at literacy had negative peer-group consequences. As the children of Khmer refugees who had escaped from the genocide of the Pol Pot regime that had murdered people for being literate, the girls were culturally Cambodian. They were growing up within a culture in which women had traditionally been given little formal schooling. But in spite of many social, historic, and cultural reasons why Cambodian girls might turn their backs on literacy, these girls enjoyed an active writing life at home that was nearly invisible at school (p. 62). Nan was a prolific writer at home, producing plays, fictional and nonfictional stories, captioned pictures, and letters. But at school Nan struggled with academic literacy, and her teachers despaired of her ability to read and write in English.

Skilton-Sylvester described the ways in which Nan's home literacy practices were oral, visual, and creative. At home, her strengths as a speaker, artist, and storyteller were assets, but they did not help her at school, where the written word was more valued, and accuracy mattered more than meaning. A prolific writer at home, Nan's right to express herself through writing was constrained in school. Skilton-Sylvester concludes that, if Nan had learned to write in her native Khmer, she might not have fallen so far behind her Native-English-speaking peers in school in her ability to understand and create texts in English. She advocated for children like Nan by pointing out that Nan was not unintelligent or uncooperative. She was complex, diligent, and committed to learning. Nan had strengths and cultural preferences, and she used all the resources she had at hand in attempting to learn academic literacies at school. But she failed, and possibilities for her future were curtailed. Skilton-Sylvester argued that teachers at school must allow their students who are learning English as a second language to use all their multimodal resources to perform literate acts in the classroom, so that they can use literacy to convey meaning, build relationships, "do social work," and succeed. She concludes that their out-of-school literacy resources "can be a foundation for school literacy, if we are able to read the words and the worlds that children bring with them to school, and help them to engage in new and related words and worlds as they use writing to do the social work of school" (p. 88).

Cynthia Lewis (2001) provided a second recent example of sociolinguistic advocacy research (this study is also described briefly in chapter 4, Situated Literacies). Lewis (2001) is an ethnography of classroom life, involving interviews and long-term participant observation, as well as analyses of language in use. Lewis spent a school year in a fifth- and sixth-grade classroom in a small, predominantly White midwestern city, following five students as they read and responded to literature with their teacher and classmates. This was a classroom where literature was valued, in an elementary school with a diverse population, located in a community with a wide range of income levels. The focal students can be described in several ways: three were boys and two were girls; three were fifth graders and two were sixth graders; two were working class and three were middle class; two were of low or middle ability and three were of high ability. Lewis's book also focuses on four classroom practices involving literature: read-alouds, peer-led discussions, teacher-led discussions, and independent reading times, explaining how these practices were shaped by discourses and rituals within the classroom, and by social codes and dominant cultural norms beyond the classroom. Looking closely at moment-to-moment interactions, Lewis documented the shifts in power and status that shaped and changed the classroom culture, and the experiences of the five focal students. In the process she explained issues of social class, gender, and race in the school and in the surrounding community.

Lewis (2001) framed her study with theories of classroom literary practices as enactments of power relationships and cultural norms (Cherland, 1994; Simpson, 1996), and with theories of identity performances (Butler, 1990, 1993). She analyzes the "ritual power" of read-aloud practices, in which most of the boys remained on the margins, while the teacher worked to create an ethos of classroom community and common bonds. She analyzed the language of peer-led literature discussions, in which textual interpretation was shaped by interaction embedded in sociocultural conditions. She underscores the ways in which status and power were negotiated in these groups, as peer leaders controlled talk to achieve social and interpretive power. Next Lewis analyzed the language of teacher-led literature discussions, through which the teacher attempted to foster resistant readings and critical stances. In these groups the negotiation of social roles went underground, and teacher and students focused on textual interpretation. Finally Lewis analyzed discussion of "free choice" texts during independent reading time, when students displayed their knowledge of popular narratives as a form of subcultural capital, and social codes and discourses that opposed those of the classroom were played out. The focal students for this study positioned themselves and were positioned differently in each of these literary activities.

Lewis (2001) advocated through her insistence that the close analysis of classroom interaction can help teachers to a better understanding of the social and power relations (especially those of social class and gender) that influence the ways in which students speak and act in these literary activities. She encourages teachers to capitalize on that better understanding, to create spaces within which students can negotiate more equitable roles, and openly comment on them. She also encour-

ages teachers to help students examine and question a literary text's social and cultural construction, so that they become able to recognize and
address inequitable power arrangements at work in the world. Lewis argued that teachers must take the responsibility for understanding how
the literary practices they use *do* and *do not* recruit children's affiliation
(Gee, 2001), and for understanding how gender and social class work in
that affiliation. Arguing for the inclusion of teacher-led literature discussions, which require a critical stance, Lewis advocated for the creation of literacy classrooms able to produce people who can both use
and critique literature, to change themselves and their society.

**Contributions and Critical Response**

Sociolinguistic research has made three important contributions to advocacy work in literacy education:

1. First, it has provided evidence of the sophisticated linguistic competence of children who speak nonstandard dialects of English.
2. Second, it has described and demonstrated discontinuities in the
   interactional norms of the home language and the school language
   of children who are failing to become literate.
3. Third, it has drawn attention to the difficulties of minority children
   in school and raised questions about what could be done to help.
4. Most importantly, it has thoroughly undermined theories of linguistic and cognitive deficit in children who fail to become literate.

These are fine contributions, but sociolinguistic research has also
been criticized for its static, liberal view of society that makes it difficult
to deal with questions of social justice (Williams, 1992). It often has an
air of inevitability about it that may discourage literacy teachers. In focusing on linguistic competence, and in focusing on mismatches in
interactional norms, it can appear to locate the construction of disadvantage in the language of literacy classrooms, and not in the world outside
the school. And in analyzing (almost entirely) instances in which communication goes wrong and children are disadvantaged, it fails to provide instances of positive and productive interactions around literacy in
which things go well and literacy is learned.

## Other Studies of Note

David Bloome, mentioned earlier in our history of sociolinguistic advocacy research in literacy education, has continued over the past 20 years to do brilliant advocacy research through the sociolinguistic analyses of language interactions in literacy classrooms. (See Bloome, 2001; Bloom & Katz, 1997; Bloome, Katz, & Champion, 2003; Christian & Bloome, 2004.)

In chapter 4 we have described several studies that make use of sociolinguistic research methods, as well as other methods (Fecho, 1998; Gutiérrez, Baquedano-López, Alvarez, & Chiu, 1999; Gutiérrez, Baquedano-López, & Tejeda, 1999; Hicks, 2002; Moje, 2000; Moje, Willes, & Fassio, 2001).

See also **Joel Dworin (2003),** Examining children's biliteracy in the classroom. In A. I. Willis, G. E. Garcia, R. B. Barrere, & V. J. Harris (Eds.), *Multicultural issues in literacy research and practice* (pp. 29–48). Mahwah, NJ: Lawrence Erlbaum Associates, Inc. This case study uses sociolinguistic theory, activity theory, and critical theory to illuminate one child's acquisition of literacy in two languages, and the potential value of that achievement for his access to the world around him.

### PART II: PSYCHOLINGUISTIC ADVOCACY RESEARCH

*There are many possible reasons for reading difficulty apart from hypothetical brain disorders. Personal, social, or cultural conflicts can interfere critically with a child's motivation or ability to learn to read, and it is also possible for something to go wrong during instruction.*

Frank Smith, 1986, p. 2

Psycholinguistic advocacy research in literacy education is characterized by concern with linguistic theory, by intense interest in the functioning of the mind in language and literacy acquisition and production, *and* by concern for the ways in which inappropriate literacy curriculum and instruction contribute to stratifying society and creating oppression.

Psycholinguistic advocacy research attacks practices like standardized testing, scripted reading curricula, and ability grouping, all of which are among the means by which schooling in general and literacy instruction in particular work to stratify society. It undermines them with linguistic knowledge of how people acquire language and learn to read, and with theory from cognitive psychology about why these practices are inappropriate and counterproductive for the learning of the individual child. It also offers alternative assessment techniques, curricula, and instructional frames. In doing so it takes a political stance, showing that literacy education is not politically neutral. As Altwerger and Saavedra (1999) pointed out, literacy education can be a tool of critical inquiry, as well as a tool of passive transmission. It can work to transform an oppressive society, as well as to sustain and reproduce that society. Psycholinguistic advocacy research makes these points.

The field of psycholinguistics has made well-informed and rational challenges to existing educational practices by offering a coherent theory of how reading and writing work, and by asking pertinent questions: Do standardized tests really test *reading*? What happens in the mind when a person reads? Does ability grouping work to the advantage of all those children who wind up in the lower groups? Are prepackaged curricula and basal readers consistent with what we know about cognitive functioning? Psycholinguistic theories of reading and writing have long been and are still being used to challenge educational practices that have no basis in how the human mind works, revealing them to be tools of power and dominance that have helped to maintain race and class inequities.[3]

## A Brief History

Until the late 1960s most research on reading took a narrow, experimental approach to answering the question, "What happens when people read?" Experimental research conceptualized reading as consisting of sets of behaviors. But by the late 1960s the fields of psychology and linguistics had begun to free themselves from the theoretical constraints of behaviorism, and public concern about literacy was growing (Bloome, 1987). There were many more research studies in psychology, linguistics, and education that investigated issues of meaning and comprehension in mental activities such as reading. By the late 1960s new forms of research that blended fields (sociology and linguistics; anthropology and education; psychology and linguistics) were emerging.

One such blend was the new interdisciplinary field of psycholinguistics. Building on earlier research, Kenneth Goodman published *The Psycholinguistic Nature of the Reading Process* (1968). Frank Smith published *Understanding Reading* (1971). Reading research began to study reading in use in "naturally" occurring social contexts, as researchers chose to begin with the premise that readers and writers constructed meaning by using cognitive and linguistic processes to serve their communicative purposes. Making use of insights from the research of cognitive psychologists like Cole, Scribner, Griffin, and Ferreiro, psycholinguistic researchers like Frank Smith (1971) and Kenneth Goodman (1973) did research they intended to be applicable to classrooms.

The development of sociolinguistic ethnography (Gumperz, 1968; Hymes, 1962) did affect this psycholinguistic research. Sociolinguists emphasized the complex variations in language that were linked to its social uses and functions, in the everyday events that were part of broad social and cultural structures. Psycholinguists recognized this work as valuable (they did not disagree), but they chose to emphasize the central role that people's minds play in face-to-face interaction, as they construct an interpretation of what they are doing and what they are trying to communicate. What is happening in the minds of readers and writers? What does it have to do with language? What does it imply for classroom instruction? These were the questions that inspired psycholinguistic research, which sought better theory and knowledge about reading to reform and strengthen practice.

Psycholinguistic researchers, working with the classroom in mind, collectively articulated the premises that together formed a psycholinguistic theory of reading. That theory is explained in the writings of Frank Smith and Kenneth Goodman, and very clearly presented to teachers in Edelsky, Altwerger, and Flores (1991). It can be summarized in this way:

- Language is composed of four interrelated, interdependent and inseparable subsystems of tacit rules for producing language (both oral and written).
- The phonological subsystem specifies which sounds and combinations of sounds are possible under particular conditions in a

given language. (Graphic and graphophonic rule systems tie spelling to the sound and meaning systems of language.)

- The syntactic subsystem is composed of rules that structure sentences in terms of acceptable word order and grammatical relationships.
- The semantic subsystem determines the ways in which words and sentences can convey meaning.
- The pragmatic subsystem concerns the connections between all aspects of the social context (the general situation in which an instance of oral or written language occurs) and all other aspects of language.

Psycholinguistic theory emphasizes the ways in which these systems operate together, and the ways in which language is acquired. Children learn language and use language through constructing hypotheses (that is to say, by making predictions) about how the subsystems of language work and interact to produce meaning. In social interaction, their hypotheses are confirmed or disconfirmed, and they revise their tacit knowledge of the rules for language production and use (Ferreiro, 2003; Ferreiro & Teberosky, 1982).

These psycholinguistic premises for language learning and use have implications for literacy instruction. Because the language subsystems operate together, instruction that separates them is counterproductive. Language develops through meaningful use and in interaction with other people. It is not a matter of sequential skill mastery. Children need to use language orally for a variety of authentic purposes (like peer projects in school) for language to develop well. The need for meaning and purpose in language use extends to written language too. People who are learning to read do not need to practice the separate subsystems of language. They do need to make use of information from all the subsystems of language as they make predictions about the meaning of print.

Many literacy researchers (Ken and Yetta Goodman, for example) and teachers used psycholinguistic reading theory in the 1970s to engage in advocacy for children who were not learning to read. Concerned that inappropriate methods for teaching reading were disadvantaging some children, they attempted to reach teachers, to make theory accessible to them, and to thereby change classroom literacy instruction. They were in some ways quite successful. Psycholinguistic theory made great sense to classroom teachers, and in the late 1970s and early 1980s the grassroots Whole Language movement was born. (See Edelsky et al., 1991, for a description of the Whole Language movement in the United States. See Comber, 1994, for comments on the history of the Whole Language movement in Australia.)

There were other forms of linguistic research flourishing during the 1970s and 1980s that no doubt contributed to the thinking of psycholinguistic researchers. There were the sociolinguistic studies described earlier. There was also the remarkable work of Sylvia Ashton-Warner (1963), a teacher of Maori children in New Zealand. Ashton-Warner (like Freire) emphasized the use in literacy instruction of key words that were especially meaningful for the learner. She saw writing as a psychological tool for communication and thought, as she insisted on the intelligence of the children she taught.

Psycholinguistic research differed from the work of ethnomethodologists and sociolinguists who studied the workings of language in the traditional, skills-based teaching of reading, and who often did not question the efficacy of skills-based instruction. Psycholinguistic researchers objected to the ways in which traditional literacy instruction conflicted with what was now known about the human mind and the linguistic and cognitive processing involved in the act of reading. They saw themselves as in conflict with those who did *not* object to skills-based instruction.

These strands and influences within psycholinguistic research were unified in an emphasis on *meaning and thinking* that was psychological. It was the emphasis on *language and meaning* that was psycholinguistic. (It was an emphasis on the socially situatedness of the language and meaning that was sociolinguistic.) Psycholinguistic researchers recognized that writing and reading are complex, recursive, social, and cognitive processes. Both writing and reading involve orchestrating multiple cueing systems to produce a text that functions pragmatically in a situational context. Reading, like writing, is an act of composing. (See the work of Jerome Harste, Carolyn Burke, Kenneth and Yetta Goodman, and Frank Smith for further explanations of psycholinguistic reading theory; and Edelsky et al., 1991, for classroom examples of readers and writers constructing and exploring possible worlds).

One important advocacy movement that psycholinguistic reading theory inspired was the campaign against basal readers in the United

States in the late 1980s. Several psycholinguistic researchers joined forces to articulate the ways in which the publishing industry, for the sake of profit, ignored new knowledge about how children learn to read. They argued that literacy education was failing children, especially poor and minority children, by using basal readers that made use of a different (and incorrect) theory of reading. Behind the assertion that basal readers were at fault was the implication that society was at fault. In 1988 a *Report Card on Basal Readers* (K. Goodman, P. Shannon, Y. Freeman, and S. Murphy) implied that inadequate literacy instruction served to help maintain the unjust social status quo.

We can see the connections between psycholinguistic theory and research and advocacy work for social justice in the history of the Whole Language movement in the United States. The idea that psycholinguistic theory ought to inform classroom practice and literacy instruction had a powerful effect on teachers and literacy consultants. The theory called for knowledgeable teachers who understood the linguistic and cognitive theory that implied a certain kind of classroom practice. Many public school teachers, hungry for intellectual community and the opportunity to apply professional knowledge to the benefit of the children they taught, responded strongly. University researchers and teacher educators supported them, and a grassroots Whole Language teachers' movement took shape.

The idea that language (including written language) is learned through use had great liberatory potential, as did the idea that learning to read and write is like learning to speak (Edelsky et al., 1991). Both ideas meant that teachers did not need to rely on published materials. They only needed to set up their classrooms so that children would be required to authentically use written language for real social purposes. Psycholinguistic reading theory and its instructional applications supported the idea that one could use language for any purpose, even for transforming sociopolitical reality. This is a powerful idea that Paulo Freire and his followers had already acted on in Brazil and Cuba and elsewhere. But teachers in the United States, Australia, and Canada in the 1980s and 1990s (as today) were working within an individualistic capitalist society that discouraged looking to sociopolitical reasons for children's problems, or for solutions to them. Looking for psychological solutions to educational problems (especially through teachers' acquisition of "scientific," rational knowledge of linguistics, cognition, and appropriate teaching methods) was more consistent with the philosophy of individualism that pervaded society as a whole, and with the history of educational psychology. Literacy problems were believed to reside in the individual child, and solutions were the responsibility of the individual teacher. To a largely female, White, middle-class teaching force, psycholinguistic solutions to educational problems seemed reasonable and appropriate, and social revolution did not. For these and for other reasons, the Whole Language teachers' movement did not align itself with progressive political forces and the ongoing struggle for social justice.

In the United States, the Whole Language movement's emphasis on linguistic knowledge for well-educated teachers did lead to a shift in the kinds of materials adopted in districts whose instructional leaders saw the benefits in encouraging teacher professionalism. But those materials continued to be commercial packages. Publishing companies accommodated by producing "Whole Language" instructional materials to preserve their commercial markets and profits. These materials were often not consistent with psycholinguistic theory, and their use subverted teachers' reliance on theory, and teacher autonomy and professionalism. Still, the Whole Language movement spread and to some extent succeeded, for a time.

Then scholars of color began to argue that the Whole Language movement was White and mainstream, that it served White middle-class children better than it did children of color who did not posses the tacit knowledge of standard English dialect and the middle-class "ways with words" that the movement assumed (Delpit, 1988). During the same years, the Whole Language movement suffered from a conservative backlash. Recognizing and fearing the liberatory potential of project-oriented instruction that freed teachers and allowed for literacy to be learned through the kind of meaningful, purposeful use that could subvert the sociopolitical status quo, conservative forces offered standardized test scores as a (mis)measure of what Whole Language had failed to accomplish. The media were enlisted to push the perception that Whole Language was a failure (lead articles were published in *Time* magazine and in *Newsweek* on "The Reading Wars," for example). Public opinion turned against Whole Language, and the movement faded.

(See Altwerger & Saavedra, 1999; Edelsky et al., 1991, for fuller accounts of this history.)

Public opinion also turned against the Whole Language movement in Australia (Comber, 1994). The Australian movement had fulfilled some of Whole Language's liberatory potential by emphasizing children's personal strengths, and by allowing for children's self-regulation and self-direction. It had also contributed to the development of teacher research, and had encouraged teachers in reflective practice, positioning them differently in the production of knowledge (Comber, 1994). But because it emphasized individualistic pedagogies like process writing, and individualistic concepts like "personal voice" and "authorship," and because it ignored power relations and gendered and other ideological aspects of classroom writing (Gilbert, 1992), it became the object of critique by those concerned with the potential for literacy in transformative education for social justice. Genre theorists (Martin, 1984, 1991) criticized psycholinguistic theories and Whole Language pedagogies for not making explicit to disadvantaged children the "genres of power" and the kinds of language that would gain them greater access to social power and to life chances. Baker and Freebody (1986, 1989) analyzed the ideological messages in school textbooks, and the ways in which reading teachers privileged some cultural discourses over others (Luke, 1993); and critical literacy pedagogies began to be developed as alternatives to Whole Language (Comber, 1994).

And yet, even though the United States and Australian Whole Language teachers' movements of the 1980s and early 1990s did not become movements for social justice, psycholinguistic reading theory continued to develop, and new thinking about the liberatory potential of instruction based on psycholinguistic theory was produced. One key idea was that language did not simply exist *within* a social context. Language was socially constituted (Hymes, 1973). The interrelated subsystems of tacit rules for producing language were not only phonological, syntactic, and semantic. They were also pragmatic, or social in nature. As Dell Hymes and others continued to explain, the social context cannot be separated from what language is. Language must have a meaningful purpose, or it isn't language. Reading and writing require hypothesis generating as part of meaning-making transactions, and these occur within a sociohistorical context.

Early psycholinguistic theory acknowledged the existence of a pragmatic subsystem of language rules, but did not fully acknowledge the importance of this pragmatic subsystem in learning to read and write. Pragmatics existed in the background of psycholinguistic reading theory, as "context." Sociolinguistic research perhaps encouraged that view, presenting contextual factors as if they influenced the production of language but were separate from it. Then Edelsky's (1984) *Writing in a Bilingual Program: Habia Una Vez* demonstrated the ways in which the pragmatic subsystem interrelated with all the other subsystems of language, and the ways in which writing occurred through social contexts. Edelsky's analysis of children's writing demonstrated once again and in a bilingual instructional context that it is not helpful to separate language into bits for the purpose of instruction. It makes much better cognitive sense to keep language whole, and wholeness means encouraging children to use not only the phonological, syntactic, and semantic knowledge available to them, but also any social and pragmatic resources available to them. Edelsky found that historically low-achieving "Hispanic American" children were becoming literate in a bilingual (Spanish and English) whole language program where they were both allowed and encouraged to use all their linguistic resources freely, from both languages, and where they were allowed to write for real audiences and purposes. She analyzed their writing for instances of code switching, spelling, punctuation and segmentation, structural features, stylistic devices, and content to show important relations between first and second language acquisition and use. She offered evidence that teaching skills and correcting errors is not as helpful to bilingual children's literacy learning as supporting them while they write their intentions, and she connected harmful instructional policies to a social context that disadvantaged bilingual children and their families.

The Edelsky (1984) study was an important contribution to advocacy work using psycholinguistic theory and research, because it demonstrated the benefits of instruction that is consistent with linguistic and cognitive knowledge of how literacy is learned. It argued against instruction which conflicts with this knowledge and disadvantages those children who are not allowed to use all their linguistic knowledge in literacy learning in school. Later advocacy research has made use of this sociopsycholinguistic model. Consider for example the work of

Gutiérrez, Baquedano-López, Alvarez, and Chiu (1999), who make much the same argument: Children ought to be allowed to bring *all* their linguistic and cultural resources to the project of literacy learning. (See chapter 4, "Activity Theory," and also chapter 6 for a full description of Gutiérrez et al., 1999.)

Psycholinguistic theory is useful to advocacy work in literacy education because it can be used to support changes in oppressive forms of instruction. We live in a society in which the doctrine of individualism that sustains capitalism (Apple, 1993) shapes schooling and literacy instruction. But the individual language learner is a social being. Intelligence and reading ability are social activities that people accomplish together. They are not skills or traits given to individuals. The wrong kind of individualistic instruction teaches a hidden curriculum, ensures unequal access to literacy learning, and plays an important role in maintaining and reproducing a stratified society. Psycholinguistic theory can be used to demonstrate this process at work, and to subvert it. It can be used to advocate for social transformation. And in more recent theorizing and research, it has.

### The Critical Whole Language Movement

As more educators in Australia, in the United Kingdom, and around the world began to write during the late 1980s and early 1990s about "critical literacy" (the project of teaching reading and writing for social change and for political enfranchisement), psycholinguistic advocacy researchers took note. In the United States, Carole Edelsky (1994) called for a retheorizing of Whole Language, and the Critical Whole Language movement took shape (see also chapter 1 for a discussion of this shift). In the later 1990s teachers began to *acknowledge the political role* literacy (and literacy instruction) plays in maintaining systems of power and domination in a classed society (Altwerger & Saavedra, 1999, p. xi). The Critical Whole Language movement subscribes to sociopsycholinguistic theories of reading and whole language instruction, and endorses the kind of progressive pedagogies consistent with those theories: reader response pedagogies, transactional reading pedagogies, writing process pedagogies, and curriculum-as-inquiry pedagogies. These ways of teaching and learning are acknowledged as cognitively and linguistically appropriate, and psychologically "correct," but, like traditional whole language instruction, they do not go far enough. They do not, as a first priority, tie language to power, tie text interpretation to societal structures, or tie reading and writing to perpetuating or resisting (Edelsky, 1994). Progressive pedagogies and whole language instruction ought to take the role of language in perpetuating or constituting systems of domination and make that the central topic for classroom instruction. The Critical Whole Language movement does make highlighting the relationship of language and power a primary enterprise for the literacy classroom.

For the past 40 years teachers and researchers have used psycholinguistic reading theory to justify a set of commitments in practice (see K. Goodman, 1968, 1982, 1996; Y. Goodman, 1985; Y. Goodman, D. Watson, & C. L. Burke, 1987, 1996). Those commitments have centered on applying cognitive and language theories in reading instruction that will support *all* children in learning to read. The Critical Whole Language movement still calls for that commitment in practice, but demands more explicit connections between instruction and systems of authority. It argues that classroom instruction based on skills theory can reinforce hierarchical systems of authority, and that classroom instruction based on psycholinguistic theories can demonstrate the democratic principles of critical democracy and justice (Edelsky, 1999).

Psycholinguistic theories focus on the individual, but the goal for literacy education is societal. Literacy education, indeed *all* education, ought to be for the purpose of creating a participatory democracy (Edelsky, 1994). The Critical Whole Language movement has inspired advocacy in the form of collaborative action research conducted in classrooms by teachers, sometimes structured through cycles of planning, action, and reflection. (Examples of this kind of research can be found in Edelsky, 1999, and Allen, 1999.)[4]

One key premise of this research is that language in use sheds light not just on individual experience, but also on people's societal positions, structured privileges, and on the creation of greater or lesser social power. Readers make meanings from texts, but they make them from existing possibilities for meaning that have been culturally and historically produced (Mellor, Patterson, & O'Neill, 2000). The classroom study of language in use should therefore foreground the political, sociological, and historical character of reading practices. Critical Whole

Language teaching and research still assume that there *are* universal psychological processes in oral and written language that all human beings share, but they also assume that language and language practices are fundamentally social and ideological in character. The human mind is, according to this view, where the social and the ideological are located, and where we see them at work.

And yet, teachers and researchers should be careful not to think about empowerment as merely a psychological process. Critical Whole Language calls for an emphasis on *praxis*, for recursive reflexivity in the service of political consciousness. It calls for instruction that engages students in critique, but which also offers them hope, and opportunities to take action (Edelsky, 1994, 1999). Critical Whole Language research, then, is advocacy research that seeks to end systemic classism, sexism, racism, and all systems of domination and privilege. It works through critical literacy pedagogy that supports children in their development as readers and writers, as it supports children in learning about society. It teaches the word, and the world.

Edelsky (1999), adapting a list created by Bob Peterson (1994), identifies the general characteristics of Critical Whole Language pedagogy through which advocacy research emerges. The first three on her list are characteristic of the instruction inspired by psycholinguistic reading theory over the past 40 years. The last three go beyond that theory. Critical Whole Language instruction:

- Involves no (or very few) exercises.
- Is grounded in students' lives.
- Offers a safe place to learn.
- Takes a critical stance.
- Is pro-justice.
- Is activist.

The collaborative action advocacy research Critical Whole Language has inspired centers on doing instruction better, on following the curricular interests of the children as well as on guiding them, and on sharing stories of classroom learning with others who wish to teach for democracy. It is research into instruction that takes a sustained look at social issues to bring about democracy, to bring about an end to systemic privilege and domination, and to create a new political climate where people can have a significant say in what affects their lives (Edelsky, 1994).

**Example Studies**

Here we offer two examples of recent advocacy research that have followed from the psycholinguistic tradition in literacy education. The first, a collaborative study, was conducted in an inner-city school in Arizona where most students were Spanish speakers from low-income families. The second, an action research study (see again End Note 4), was conducted in an affluent suburban middle school where most students were monolingual English speakers. Both studies were conducted by teachers in their own classrooms.

The first study, by Cecilia Espinoza and Karen Moore (1999), traces the evolution of a "curriculum-as-inquiry" (Harste, Short with Burke, 1988) unit the two teachers taught in a multiage (Kindergarten through second grade) class. They began with a desert study. As the desert study was concluding, the bilingual children of the school were taking an interest in and learning to sing the songs of Tish Hinojosa, a Mexican American folk singer and activist, songs that dealt with injustice and social change. One of Hinojosa's songs, called "Something in the Rain," dealt with the struggles of farm workers over the use of pesticides in the grape fields of California. The children in Espinoza and Moore's class connected the song with the respect for the land they had developed during their desert study, and with the illnesses of their own relatives who were working in the grape fields. They were moved by the song's descriptions of other children who were suffering from being poisoned by pesticides while their parents watched in helplessness. Espinoza and Moore supported their students as they "embarked on a journey of inquiry" that followed the children's questions and interests. They helped the children gather information about farm workers and desert agribusiness. They learned about La Causa, a workers' movement initiated by César Chávez. Taking every opportunity to explain to others how boycotting would help farm workers struggling with poor working conditions, low wages, and pesticide use, the children began to boycott grapes and demanded that parents in their community and others at their school do the same.

Espinoza and Moore say that this experience helped them see that with the right kind of experiences at school, children will learn to care about the world, and will see the possibilities for taking action and working for justice. They continued to allow the curriculum to follow their students' interests by studying the life and work of César Chávez. They then provided biographies of other people who had fought for human rights and for the environment, people who had a vision to follow. The children talked and wrote about how the people whose stories they were reading could help them make decisions about their own lives. The children began addressing problems in their own community around the school and, with their parents' help, found some solutions.

This work in the community happened at a time when the children were also studying the news and the media, and the unfair and inaccurate ways in which the media portrayed Hispanic peoples. The children moved from studying migrant labor to a study of poems written in both Spanish and English, poems that advocated for the rights of others and concerned themselves with the lives of the poor and the needy. The children came to realize why poetry has so often been considered dangerous by totalitarian regimes. Over the course of 2 years in this multiage classroom, the children learned to read and to write through their pursuit of the knowledge that would allow them to work for human rights and so influence the world.

What was psycholinguistic about this pedagogy and this instance of teacher research? Like other Whole Language teacher research before it, this study focused on theoretically sound classroom practice. The children were not required to do exercises. Instead they read and wrote for real purposes, to engage in and influence the world. This study made use of project learning, and inquiry-based learning, on the psycholinguistic assumption that language and literacy will develop best in meaningful use, and it followed the children's interests, to maximize that meaningfulness. The curriculum was active, and grounded in the children's lives.

But unlike much of the psycholinguistic research before it, this study is also an instance of advocacy research, intended to move the world toward social justice. In this study the stakes are high. Children must learn to read and write well so that they can participate in the kind of democracy where people decide together what their society will be like. Literacy is a tool in the struggle for human rights, for the environment, and for justice. The most effective literacy instruction possible is shown to be a necessary part of education for democracy.

The second study, by Abigail Foss (2002), reports on action research conducted in Foss's 4-hr-long eighth-grade English classes, located within a middle school of 600 students in an affluent and insulated neighborhood in Tucson, Arizona. Most of the 13- and 14-year-old students Foss taught were monolingual English speakers, Christian, and from middle to upper class homes. Believing that it is important for *all* children to identify and problematize the systems within which we live every day, Foss sought the best ways of practicing critical literacy with students who had inherited social positions of privilege. Believing that her students would be miseducated, and receive only a partial education, if they were not exposed to critical views of power and systems of dominance, Foss worked at teaching literature in ways that highlighted historical and lingering social inequalities, and required critical conversations. She organized her teaching around three themes:

- First, the institution of the school and how it functions in our lives.
- Second, the identification of individuals' multiple subject positions and the development of an understanding that experiences, such as reading, are socially constructed.
- Third, the recognition and problematizing of the privilege that permeated the lives of her students.

Required to teach *To Kill a Mocking Bird,* Harper Lee's novel of segregation and racial injustice in 1930s Alabama, Foss engaged her students in activities that illuminated the three themes. She asked them to write about how school functions in the novel, and to connect the main character's experience of school with their own. She asked her students to form small groups to discuss the common themes in their writings. She gave them photocopies of critical articles to read about schooling and curriculum and asked them to "conduct a conversation with the author" by underlining key phrases and responding in the margins. She posed critical questions and discussed possible answers with individual students and with the class. As the unit progressed, Foss engaged students in diagramming the intersections of their own identity categories. Finally, she asked students to write their reflections on privilege in *To Kill a Mocking Bird,* and to consider MacIntosh's (1998) article, "White Privilege: Unpacking the Invisible Knapsack."

Over the course of the unit, Foss dealt with the student resistance she encountered with patience, and with information. She reflected on her teaching and on her students' reactions and responses to it, and then devised new ways to reach her goals. It is this engagement in repeated cycles of planning, action, and reflection that makes her work action research.

What is psycholinguistic about the Foss (2002) study? Like other psycholinguistic research before it, this work highlights the link between theory and appropriate methods and classroom practice. It uses progressive pedagogies based on reader response theory and transactional reading theory. It focuses on what is happening in individual students' minds. It involves few exercises, it is grounded in students' lives, and it offers a safe place.

But the Foss (2002) study is also an instance of advocacy research because it takes a critical stance, and because it is pro-justice. It engages privileged students in analyzing systems of privilege and dominance and teaches them to look at the world from the viewpoint of the disadvantaged (Connell, 1993). It interrupts the taken-for-granted, and engages students in considerations of unequal power relations. It meets all of the criteria for critical whole language research and practice, except the last. It does not yet require activism. Foss (2002) closes her report by worrying that sometimes her students felt that the world was overwhelmingly bleak. Her report does not cite Edelsky (1994), nor make use of Edelsky's argument that research and practice must engage in critique but also go beyond it, to engender hope, and engage students in action. Perhaps in the next cycle Foss's planning will include opportunities for her students to engage in activism, as they respond to new awareness of their own privilege.

**Critical Responses And Contributions**

There are two obvious criticisms that could be made of psycholinguistic advocacy research. The first, which could be made from the perspective of critical theory, is that its premises are too individualistic. The second criticism, which could be made from the perspective of poststructural theory, is that its premises are too universalist.

First, the psycholinguistic theory that informs the advocacy research discussed earlier focuses on the individual mind and what happens in it, and so it can fail to take up the question of *why* it happens. When it fails to address race, gender, and social class, it fails to consider the social structures and the practices of injustice that affect the human mind. The reading theorists whose work inspired the Whole Language movement, too narrowly concerned with reading theory and cognition, did not look beyond the individual person who was reading or learning to read. Critical Whole Language teaching and reflective scholarship does look beyond the individual to the society, but it sometimes runs into trouble when it stops short of a full and critical consideration of social systems of privilege and power, and when it does not call for justice. Where this kind of advocacy research does succeed, where it uses psycholinguistic theory and practice in working for justice through engaging learners in activist projects, it can be truly transformative. Where it falls short, it is merely individualistic and humanistic, and it contributes little to social change.

Second, psycholinguistic advocacy research can be accused of grounding itself in universalist theories of cognition that do not take account of the cultural and social processes at work in the production of "mind." It does not make use of poststructuralist theories of subjectivity as constructed by individuals in interaction with many cultural discourses. It does not locate the individual's identity in an historical moment, nor does it envision identity as something different for each person, and constantly in flux. Instead, it sometimes appears to ground itself in dualistic thinking that splits the Mind from the Body, and which envisions "mind" as something existing apart from the body, as a separate entity where the psyche resides. Psycholinguistic theory fails to explicitly acknowledge the ways in which social identities like gender, race, and social class are multidimensional, complex, and interlocking; and this keeps it from fully appreciating the complexity of what surrounds the ability to read, and of what counts as reading.

Finally, it should be noted that, because psycholinguistic advocacy research takes place in schools and is so completely concerned with classroom practice, it cannot escape the restrictions of the institutional context in which it occurs. One of these is the amount of time available to teachers for planning, reflecting, and writing about their accomplishments.

On the other hand, psycholinguistic theory adds a missing piece to advocacy research. Clearly racism, poverty, and cultural differences do influence the development and the operation of the human mind. Sociolinguistic research has shown us the social processes by which more poor and minority children fail to learn to read. Psycholinguistic research's focus on the capable mind and what it *can* do helps us advocate against the social conditions that interfere with literacy acquisition and limit the ability to read. It undermines the language deficit theories that blame the victim, offering instead a view of the language learner who is always hypothesizing about meaning, and actively working to make sense.

Psycholinguistic research continues to provide ammunition in "the Readings Wars" (Goodman, Goodman, Rapoport, & Shannon, 2003) in the United States. When conservative political forces have attempted to use a "scientific" discourse of literacy for controlling literacy curriculum and literacy teachers, to structure a society that blames poor people for their own suffering, psycholinguistic advocacy research has been used to discredit the "science" that claims to ground reductive pedagogies and scripted reading curricula (Strauss, 2003).

Psycholinguistic advocacy research also has immediate educational benefits for children. In drawing together university-based researchers and classroom teachers, it provides shining examples of methods all teachers can use in working for justice. At its best, it demonstrates Freirean principles at work as individual and collective consciousness is raised, and it inspires educators to action.

**Other Studies of Note**

**Edelsky, C. (2005).** *With literacy and justice for all: Rethinking the social in language and in education* (4th ed.). Mahwah, NJ: Lawrence Erlbaum Associates.

Carole Edelsky has published several editions of this book updating her collected essays, each of which advocates by applying sociopsycholinguistic thinking to some aspect of language and literacy education.

**Altwerger, B. (2005).** The push of the pendulum. In L. Poynor & P. M. Wolfe (Eds.), *Marketing fear in America's public schools: The real war on literacy.* Mahwah, NJ: Lawrence Erlbaum Associates.

Like several other educators in this volume, Altwerger applies psycholinguistic and other kinds of theory to challenge the Bush government's legislated and policy approaches to centralized and destructive literacy education.

**Altwerger, B., & Strauss, S.L. (2002).** The business behind testing. *Language Arts, 79,* 256–262.

Bess Altwerger continues to advocate by using psycholinguistic and critical theory to undermine the legitimacy of the conservative Right's agenda for literacy education.

### PART III: CRITICAL DISCOURSE ANALYSIS

*I have written [this book] for two main purposes. The first is more theoretical: to help correct a widespread underestimation of the significance of language in the production, maintenance, and change of social relations of power. The second is more practical: to help increase consciousness of how language contributes to the domination of some people by others, because consciousness is the first step towards emancipation.*

Norman Fairclough, 1989, p. 1

*It would not seem too far-fetched to suggest that critical applied linguistics may at least give us ways of dealing with some of the most crucial educational, cultural, and political issues of our time.*

Alastair Pennycook, 2001, p. 23

Critical discourse analysis (CDA) clearly belongs in this chapter on research inspired by linguistics. Like sociolinguistic and psycholinguistic research, critical discourse analysis demonstrates the creativity inherent in language use, and highlights the social purposes language accomplishes. But where *sociolinguistic* advocacy research focuses on the ways in which texts are socially produced and performed, and on interactional norms that can disadvantage some students and privilege others; and where *psycholinguistic* advocacy research focuses on the cognitive capacities that produce language, and on instruction that will benefit the individual and serve the society; *critical discourse analysis* demonstrates the ways in which discourse defines and positions human subjects, constructing "truths" about the world. Where sociolinguistics says that language is socially produced, and psycholinguistics says that language is cognitively produced, critical discourse analysis says that it is in language that we can see the construction of social identities and individual minds. The contrasts are not entirely due to theoretical differences, although there are some. The contrasts are a matter of emphasis. To oversimplify, sociolinguistics begins with people interacting in the construction of texts; psycholinguistics begins with people cognitively constructing texts; and critical discourse analysis begins with texts constructing people.

James Gee (1992, 1999) has described "discourses" as "identity kits," sets of ways of using language and of thinking and acting that identify a person as a member of a socially meaningful group. Discourses, says Gee, are inherently ideological, and intimately related to the distribution of social power and to hierarchical structure in society. Each person acquires a "primary" discourse at home as an oral mode, and other "secondary" discourses (like literacy) in other social contexts (like the school). Secondary discourses are easier to acquire if they do not differ much from one's primary discourse. Discourses are produced and shaped by cultures, and so "discourse" can also be defined as a set of culturally specific values that are constituted through language, and demonstrated in its use (Gutiérrez, Rymes, & Larson, 1995).

CDA is about examining discourses and the construction of knowledge, power, and identity through the close analysis of language texts. CDA analyzes language in use, to demonstrate how discourse systematically constructs versions of the social world and positions subjects in relations of power, with political consequences. It analyses specific instances of language in use to highlight the ways in which discourse is shaped by society, and the ways in which society is shaped by discourse.

CDA often involves a three-part analysis of that language in use (Fairclough, 1992):

- First it provides description, an analysis of the linguistic features at work in the oral or written text under examination, the lexical items, and the textual devices used (devices like pronominalization, modes, imperatives, and interrogatives).
- Next it provides interpretation, which shows how the linguistic features of the text work to position subjects and create social relations and a view of the social world.

- Finally it provides explanation, which may tie all this to large-scale ideological formations (like racism and patriarchy) and to relations of power; or which may concern the construction of knowledge, power, and the human subject.

CDA, then, makes connections between power and linguistic interactions (looking at who has control over topics, who interrupts, who takes more turns, and more), and makes connections between power and meaning (explaining ideology as subtext; Pennycook, 2001, p. 83). CDA makes use of poststructuralist, neo-Marxist, and feminist theories in its analyses of language, to ask and answer questions about who succeeds and who fails in schools, and how, and why. It offers evidence that reality (what we experience and know) is constructed in and through language. Difference and school failure are not individual developmental problems, nor are they community deficits. CDA shows that they are constructed in talk and in written texts. Literacy research has made good use of CDA to critique and challenge dominant institutional practices (Luke, 1995) that disadvantage minority children and youth, and deny access and equity.

### A Brief History

During the 1980s the social sciences took a "linguistic turn," and began to focus more on the study of language. This was in response to postmodern theories of language that unsettled and deconstructed the old humanistic view that language is transparent, that it corresponds to an external and preexisting "reality" and simply names and reflects what is real. Foucault's work (1972, 1979, 1980) had traced the history of the ways language had been used to construct binaries and hierarchies, which were thought to reflect the innate, intrinsic order of the world (St. Pierre, 2000). Foucault described the constructing character of discourse (Luke, 1995, p. 8), explaining how discourse actually defines, constructs, and positions human subjects, in broader social formations *and* in local sites. Discourses systematically *form* the objects about which they speak. They achieve knowledge–power relations by constructing "truths" about the social and natural world, truths that become the common sense beliefs by which governments rule and monitor their

populations, and by which members of communities define themselves
and others. But Foucault saw discourse as more than simple top-down
manipulation. He also saw that communities participate in discourse in
local ways, both resisting and becoming complicit in their own regulation. Discourses are internalized, and people also discipline themselves
(Foucault, 1980). Foucault's work began to inspire linguists to shift
from thinking about text and discourse as constructed artifacts to the
study of how texts construct social formations, and individuals' social
identities (Fairclough, 1989, 1992; Kress, 1989, 2003; Lemke, 1995),
and it began to inspire researchers to analyze pedagogic discourse to
show how it is implicated in systems of "governmentality" (Baker &
Luke, 1991; Freebody, 1991; Luke, 1991).

In response to all of this, educational researchers making use of linguistics produced some brilliant work. The development of research
methods in the fields of interactional sociolinguistics, the ethnography
of communication, and ethnomethodology (all of which used discourse
analysis) contributed to the development of *critical* discourse analysis
by demonstrating ways of analyzing discourse to highlight the consequences of language and discourse for minority students. Baker and
Luke (1991) collected the work of scholars concerned with applications
of these ideas about discourse for literacy education (specifically, reading pedagogy). Both psychology and sociolinguistics had "stopped
short of theorising or analysing adequately the social and discursive histories and forces which influence what reading is made to be, how reading is done, for students in schools" (Baker & Luke, 1991, xiv). Baker
and Luke argued that framing sociolinguistic analysis with critical theories of knowledge and cultural transmission, of discourse, and of cultural and economic reproduction would illuminate how school reading
constitutes readers, and also works to constitute society.

Fairclough (1992) also credited important developments in "critical
linguistics" research at the University of East Anglia during the 1980s,
specifically the work of Fowler, Kress and Hodge, which centered on
the ideological analysis of the grammatical and vocabulary features of
written texts. This work involved a critical orientation to language
study that refused to take language conventions and practices at face
value, and refused to ignore their political investments. Bourdieu
(1991), Habermas (1979), and Foucault (1980) were all important in-

fluences on this work, and critical discourse analysis continued to develop. Unlike sociolinguistic research, CDA did not stop with detailed linguistic analysis of language in use in local sites. It began there, but then went on to follow Foucault by linking the local to a broader analysis of discourse and power.

**Example Studies**

Allan Luke's (1992) study of literacy events in an Australian Grade One classroom provides an early example of critical discourse analysis that makes careful and productive use of both poststructural theory (specifically, Foucault's discourse theory) and neomarxist theory (specifically, the critical sociology of Pierre Bourdieu) to demonstrate the ways in which literacy events construct and position the literate child through the discourses of pedagogy. Luke's study demonstrates some of the ways in which literacy instruction is a material social practice, and a form of inscription (of body writing and mapping), through which a certain kind of literate child is produced, and through which class and gender are represented and reproduced (p. 109).

Luke's first transcript centers on a teacher seated on a chair beside an enlarged print book mounted on an easel, with 5- and 6-year-old children seated on a rug around her. The illustrated book tells the tale of "The Three Billy Goats Gruff" with pictures and with written text. In Luke's first transcript, the teacher directs the children as they comment on an illustration, telling them to "sit up straight," "face the front," and "sit down." Her grammatical constructions invite the children to rearrange their bodies into a "correct" formation, to willingly participate in constructing a collective to perform what counts as reading in this situation. The teacher invites the children to engage in a "technology of the self" (Foucault, 1988) as they interactively construct subjectivity during the lesson. But there are some who do not participate willingly, and for these the teacher invokes a "technology of power" (she threatens them with staying in at recess).

In Luke's second transcript, the teacher and the children "read" the text of the folk tale together. The teacher leads. Her voice volume, pitch, and stress are followed by the children, although differently by the boys and by the girls. Again, subjectivity is established in terms of a collective identity, as particular postures, silences, and gestures are put on display. The teacher's authoritative reading of the text is marked on the student body, which contributes to the building of a literate "habitus." Luke explained Bourdieu's (1977) concept of the habitus as a "structuring structure" of properties, schemas, habits, and tastes that come into play in the shaping of subjectivity and that figure in the acquisition of social-class based patterns of language and literacy. Although Luke used Foucault (1988) to comment on the moral regulation of bodies in the first transcript, he used Bourdieu's (1977) ideas in the second transcript to explain pedagogy as a structure that contributes to the reproduction of social class. Luke explained that Foucault does not preclude the possibility of ideology at work in literacy events, and Bourdieu does not ignore the construction of the human subject in linguistic interactions. It works well to bring the ideas of both to bear on literacy events. Foucault's poststructuralist ideas support the view that the discourses of literacy lessons are built around claims about truth and reality, which are articulated in material practices in classrooms, and which inscribe the subjectivity of the student. Bourdieu's ideas explain that the inscription of subjectivity contributes to the construction of a bodily habitus, which marks the student's cultural capital in classed and gendered ways. Both sets of ideas are extremely useful to a critical discourse analysis that seeks to demonstrate the language of literacy events in service to the disciplinary regime of the school.

Gutierréz, Rhymes, and Larson (1995) have provided an American example of critical discourse analysis that demonstrates the construction of power in the interaction between the teacher and the students in a ninth-grade classroom, where the students were predominantly African American and Latino, but some were also European Americans. This study analyzed classroom discourse during a current events lesson and discussion that required a certain kind of reading, and was intended to teach that kind of reading. The authors use discourse analysis of face-to-face interaction in the classroom as a way to show that who gets to learn and what is learned are connected to larger societal structures and social relationships.

Their discourse analysis first presents the teacher's monologic script, which limits dialogue and reflects dominant cultural values. In the transcript analysis, the teacher gives a current events quiz on the "world of news," which has been constructed in that day's *Los Angeles Times*. The teacher's questions, vocabulary choices, and grammatical constructions make it clear that what counts as curriculum is reflective of middle-class values and routines (like reading the morning newspaper). The teacher responds in ways that discount and turn away from what the students do know about current events, as the teacher's intonation patterns work to construct knowledge as something the teacher alone possesses. In these ways the teacher's power over the students is maintained through language forms that stifle dialogue and interaction and critique, and the teacher's knowledge displaces the local and culturally varied knowledge of the students.

Gutierrez, Ryme, and Larson (1995) also analyzed another section of video data to demonstrate that the students contribute counterscripts that do not comply with the teacher's view of appropriate participation. Having shown that the teacher's script positions students as ignorant and wrong, the authors explained how students contest the teacher's constructions by countering with changes in volume, voice quality, intonation contours, and dialect. Students do not entirely disrupt the teacher's script, but they change "the key," using jokes and discordant contributions to display their own forms of knowledge and competence. They build a counterscript. When the teacher begins asking questions about the U.S. Supreme Court case *Brown v. Board of Education,* one student "rekeys" the line of questioning by associating the court case with the popular musician James Brown. Some students do continue to try to guess the teacher's intended meanings, but others help to build a new script that reinterprets the teacher's current events lesson as a music trivia game show, and contributes to classroom "underlife" (a range of activities people develop to distance themselves from the surrounding institution; see Goffman, 1961).

The study then examines a "third space," a place where the teacher's script and the students' counterscript intersect in the same key, where information can be shared without anyone's knowledge being discounted, and where artifacts like newspaper texts become available for critique. The authors present a section of transcript in which a student departs from the counterscript about a popular musician to ask an authentic and personally relevant question about race in the American South, and in which the teacher departs from her current events script to give an important and direct answer to the student's question. The authors call this nonscripted intersection a "third space," where authentic interaction can potentially occur. However, discourse analysis also shows that, when this potential for authentic and critical interaction arises, the teacher and the students quickly retreat to the scripts they are more comfortable with, and possibilities for merging students' interests with instructional goals, and for sharing relevant knowledge, are undermined and terminated.

The authors closed by encouraging teachers to work at creating more meaningful contexts for learning in this third space. They called for teaching that works in the third space to transform oppressive curriculum, to value local knowledge as the vehicle for the development of multiple kinds of literacy, and to undermine traditional power arrangements and replace them with new scripts invoked at local sites. Gutiérrez, Rymes, and Larson (1995), taking a positive and hopeful turn, call for the construction of a "new sociocultural terrain" that will allow for the joint reconstruction of what counts as knowledge, and the joint reconstruction of forms of knowledge representation. They call for classrooms to become sites where no one's cultural discourses are secondary, where it is acknowledged that all discourses have cognitive and sociocultural benefits.

This example of critical discourse analysis offers a situated and dynamic portrait of knowledge, power, and identity being created in classroom interaction, and connects this with systems of oppression that are maintained when learning is limited. This is advocacy work, informed by poststructuralist theories of the construction of the human subject, which states clearly that it intends to do more than simply underscore (yet again) the ways in which minorities are oppressed and marginalized. It intends to do more than blame the teacher. The authors make their transformative political intentions clear, by suggesting ways in which teachers can relinquish traditional notions of power and students can participate in redefining curriculum as social practice, and in creating new contexts for literacy learning.

Rebecca Rogers (2002) provided a third example study of advocacy research using critical discourse analysis. Rogers used CDA as part of a 2-year ethnographic study of the literate lives of two African Americans living in urban poverty, June Treader (a woman who attended the Adult

Literacy Center where Rogers worked) and her oldest daughter Vicki (age 10 to 12 at the time of the study). Rogers was interested in why children who come from nonmainstream homes often fail to do well in school. She spent time tutoring both June (at the Adult Literacy Center) and Vicki (at home); she interviewed June, Vicky, and Vicky's teachers; and she spent time with both June and Vicky in their community activities and at the school. Using CDA, Rogers (2002) analyzed June's language in use in three different domains: the home, the local social services office, and the school. She identified and illustrated three different discourses at work in these domains: a discourse of schooling, a discourse of mothering, and a discourse of the CSE (Committee on Special Education) meeting.

Rogers (2002) found that the June's language was characterized by *the discourse of schooling* when she discussed reading, a discourse that assumes that reading is a skill that can be reliably and objectively tested by an external authority. June took up a subject position of literacy failure within this discourse, in spite of the fact that she was able to handle all the literacy demands of her household and negotiate written texts for the school, for health care, and for social services. But Rogers also found that June's language was characterized by a *discourse of mothering* in her home and community work, a discourse of advocacy and strength and experiential knowledge, both of and for her children. Through the discourse of mothering June Treader resisted her daughter Vicky's placement in a special education classroom. But, when Rogers analyzed the *discourse of a CSE meeting* held at the school, she found that June was almost entirely silent. The language used by the four professionals present was characterized by discourses of schooling (which involved statements of deficit and references to testing), discourses within which June saw herself as a literacy failure; and also by forms of turn taking and metadiscursive framing that controlled June's contributions and often silenced her. After 50 min at this meeting June agreed to the placement of her daughter in a special education classroom.

Rogers (2002) went beyond critical theory to use CDA to present the multifaceted nature of literate subjectivities, and the complexities of the ideologies that operate through them. There is more to June Treader's story than conflict between opposing discourses. June herself values the discourses of schooling that diminish her own literate abilities, and even uses these discourses in her interactions with her children at home. The ideologies of her home and her children's schools are compatible, not in conflict. She does not believe that the literacies she uses every day have value, because they are invisible to the school. Rogers pointed out that in the process of acquiring the discourses of schooling, June Treader also acquired the ideological relationships and concepts that discourse promotes, and this rendered her unable to resist the institution of the school.

Rogers (2002) called for critical literacy instruction in the classroom that will show students how to look for gaps and how to challenge the assumptions embedded in texts. She also pointed to the possible uses of CDA for uncovering the cultural models that are attached to family literacies, and the ways that these both help and hinder people's efforts to help their children become literate and attain school success. "Literacy in June Treader's life is paradoxical" (p. 265), says Rogers, because literacy embodies enormous complexities. Ideology operates from within. Through CDA we can see which subjectivities are evoked in which discursive contexts. Negative consequences for people's lives can come about when discourses align, as well as when they conflict.

### Contributions and Critical Response

CDA has contributed to advocacy research by demonstrating the centrality of language, text, and discourse in the constitution of human subjectivity and social relations, and also in the constitution of social control and surveillance. As a research technique, CDA has been used to study matters of identity, control, and power not only in education, but also in the fields of feminist studies, critical legal studies, communications and media studies, multiculturalism, and critical race studies. In education, CDA has been used to undermine the ideologies of educational common sense, and to demonstrate the political consequences of language and discourse in classroom lessons and literacy texts (Luke, 2002). These are important contributions.

Pennycook (2001) pointed out, however, that much important work in CDA (the work of Fairclough and Kress, for example) has been located within a modernist emancipatory Marxist model of knowledge and the world. It continues to use positivist, rational, and enlightenment modes of meaning. It claims to be a *scientific* discourse, and it assumes the possibility of an ideal order outside of ideology (p. 84). This work, says Pennycook, lacks self-reflexivity and fails to problematize the status of scientific knowledge. It does not show awareness of Foucault's (1980) notion of *truth claims*, which are produced within discourses that are neither true nor false. Much of CDA appears to have a traditional view of ideology, in which power is manifested in language and discourse. Pennycook (2001) called for a CDA that remains aware of (and is explicit about) its own politics of knowledge, a CDA that acknowledges that there is no right position and no truth outside of ideology.

But of course, critical discourse analysis is dynamic. It continues to change. Recent uses of CDA *have* moved away from neo-Marxist assumptions that ideology is unified and coherent, and that there are systematic consequences to the texts and discourses of mass capitalism. Recent examples of critical discourse analysis have taken a more Foucauldian view of the unpredictable complexity of discourse in local sites. CDA no longer always assumes that there is systematicity and intention in discourse. It does more to recognize that discourse can be random, idiosyncratic, and unpredictable. It also seems to takes more account of Derrida (1980), recognizing that absences and silences in discourse can also have powerful political effects (Luke, 2002).

The recent work of Gunther Kress (2003) has moved in these directions. Kress analyzed discourses at work in this "new media age," in which literacy is no longer just a matter of language, but is now also a matter of multimedia design. Image is in many ways displacing print, and moving to the center as the dominant medium of communication. This will, Kress argued, produce large scale social and cultural effects, including shifts in relations of power. Kress analyzed discourse to demonstrate the ways in which language creates and positions human subjects, but also to demonstrate the democratic potential of new information and communication technologies, and their cognitive and epistemological consequences.

And James Gee's (2003) *What Video Games Have to Teach Us About Learning and Literacy* points to the kind of contribution critical discourse analysis may make to advocacy research in the future. Gee provided a positive analysis of the language and structure of video games, to summarize the "central truths about the human mind and human learning" (p. 9) that are revealed in the ways in which video games are learned and played. He shows that in the playing of video games learning and identity are melded, and human agency is exercised. He suggests that we can study the discourses of video games, to understand the "play" of social identities and political perspectives as they work for and against each other, and to practice "a form of self-defense" (p. 200). He advocates for literacy instruction in schools that is designed with the learning principles used in video games in mind.

Critical discourse analysis in the past has had certain limitations. Luke (2002) pointed out that CDA has most often been characterized by a negative focus on ideology critique. It has tended to focus on demonstrating the suppression of diasporic identities by the dominant classes. This has been useful in advocacy research that seeks to demonstrate the consequences of ideology and social structures in literacy education. But Luke believes that CDA could do more to document the forms of text and discourse that mark the *productive* use of power in the face of economic and cultural globalization (Luke, 2002). CDA, he argued, ought to augment its strong focus on ideology critique with the study of texts that model the productive use of power and discourse in new conditions and in New Times.

Freire and Macedo (1987) argued almost twenty years ago that there *can* be dialogic, democratic exchanges in literacy education that do *not* oppress. CDA ought to show literacy educators what those exchanges would look like, and what they can accomplish. CDA might be used to demonstrate what *could* be, and what *ought* to be. As Luke (2002) suggests, critical discourse analysis could move toward providing examples of the use of language in the production of positive social power, by making use of new and hybrid techniques for linguistic analysis, and of emerging social theories.

## Other Studies of Note

**Rogers, R. (Ed.). (2004).** *An introduction to critical discourse analysis in education.* Mahwah, NJ: Lawrence Erlbaum Associates, Inc.

This book contains 11 different essays that illustrate the uses of CDA in a variety of educational contexts today. Several deal specifically with literacy education.

**Wilkinson, L., & Janks, H. (1998).** Teaching direct and reported speech from a Critical Language Awareness perspective. *Educational Review, 50*(2), 181–190.

This study engaged Grade 11 students in eight classroom activities based on CLA, which led to marked improvement in their ability to critically read reported speech.

**Janks, H. (2001).** Identity and conflict in the critical literacy classroom. In B. Comber & A. Simpson (Eds.), *Negotiating critical literacies in classrooms* (pp. 137–150). Mahwah, NJ: Lawrence Erlbaum Associates, Inc.

As she has for the past 15 years, Janks continues to use critical language awareness and the techniques of CDA to make sense of classroom literacy learning. (See also chapter 1 for a description of Janks' contributions to Critical Literacy research.)

**Gee, J. P. (2000).** Teenagers in new times: A new literacy studies perspective. *JAAL, 43,* 412–420.

James Paul Gee, over the past 10 years especially, has made use of CDA to demonstrate the ways in which literacy is inextricably connected to identity work. In these studies he examined the ways in which American teenagers of different social classes fashion themselves in language as different kinds of people, and argued that school curricula and instruction should take full account of the social languages and literacies that constitute identity work, because it is through these that people "can read and write more equitable selves and worlds" (p. 419).

**Gee, J. P., & Crawford, V. (1998).** Two kinds of teenagers: Language, identity and social class. In D. Alvermann, K. Hinchman, D. Moore, S. Phelps, & D. Waff (Eds.), *Reconceptualizing the literacies in adolescents' lives* (pp. 225–245). Mahwah, NJ: Lawrence Erlbaum Associates, Inc.

Gee and Crawford offered a critical discourse analysis of the language of two teen girls, one working class and one upper class, and the ways in which social class gets constructed in discourse. They connected the features of discourse they identify with the larger social structures of class, and the ideologies that preserve social hierarchies. This is advocacy because the study shows the misery that results from the personal consequences of class for the girls' lives, and then calls for changes in the school English curriculum to serve both girls better. (This study is also mentioned in chapter 3 under Adolescent Literacies.)

**Gee, J. P., Hull, G., & Lankshear, C. (1996).** *The new work order: Behind the language of the new capitalism.* Boulder, CO: Westview.

Gee, Hull, and Lankshear used CDA and other techniques to analyze the language of the new global capitalism that characterizes "New Times" (Hall, 1996), and the new patterns of global economic exchange that have altered the ways in which work is now defined and organized (Rizvi & Lingard, 1996, Foreword). The authors used forms of CDA to analyze a vocabulary that accompanies organizational change and is suggestive of democracy (words like "collaboration," "participation," and "empowerment"), to show that this discourse is inherently contradictory. Although the language preaches democracy and empowerment, it does not permit workers to question the underlying assumptions of the new business capitalism. The language is an apparatus of control, masquerading as reform. The authors argued throughout the book that the words and deeds of the new capitalism ought to become the central focus of a critical literacy that enlists citizens around the world in analyzing what kinds of economic and social arrangements will work to the benefit of all people in the global community (p. 153).

# 6

# *Why* Social Justice?
# Ethics for Advocacy Research

*The voices of indignation and protest have resounded through the years in response to injustice and human suffering ... social justice is a concept contingent on particular historical circumstances. It does not exist in some supersensible realm, anymore than in the minds and souls of individual human beings.*

Maxine Greene, 1998, xiii

*I have never been afraid of believing in freedom, in seriousness, in genuine love, in solidarity, or in the struggle in which I learned the value and importance of indignation.*

Paulo Freire, 1998, p. 98

The first five chapters of this book have laid before us definitions, histories, and examples of advocacy research in literacy education. This chapter will reflect on *why* researchers advocate. It will consider the concept "social justice" as the end or purpose for advocacy research in literacy education. It will take up the challenge to articulate more clearly the connections between advocacy research in literacy education and the project of social justice. It will also reflect on the ethics that inform and color advocacy research. It will consider the need for a shared vision for the future of advocacy research and outline some challenges for the future of advocacy research in literacy education.

This chapter begins with a consideration of the conceptions of social justice embedded in four different studies, each one an example of advocacy research in literacy education, and each reviewed in an earlier chapter of this book.[1] In many ways, the studies are similar. They all assume that a better world is possible through literacy education. They all demonstrate commitment to the idea that human beings matter, and that education can contribute to the achievement of human potential. They all advocate for children. There is some overlap in the theoretical perspectives that frame these studies. But here I will emphasize the ways in which they are distinct, to *contrast* their approaches to doing research for social justice, and their beliefs about social justice and ethics. Our intention is to present the studies and then work backward from them, to reflect further on the differences in these researchers' views of justice. We will close this chapter with some reflections on ethics for advocacy research.

These are the example studies, listed in the order in which they will be reviewed:

- Gutiérrez, K. D., Baquedano-López, P., Alvarez, H. H., & Chiu, M. M. (1999). Building a culture of collaboration through hybrid language practices. *Theory Into Practice, 38,* 87–93.
- Hicks, D. (2002) *Reading lives: Working-class children and literacy learning.* New York: Teachers College Press.
- Cherland, M. (1994) *Private practices: Girls reading fiction and constructing identity.* London: Taylor & Francis.
- Blackburn, M. V. (2002) Disrupting the (hetero)normative: Exploring literacy performances and identity work with queer youth. *Journal of Adolescent and Adult Literacy, 46,* 312–324.

These studies have been chosen because each is grounded in a different discipline, and because the research each describes is colored by a different body of theory. Together, these studies present a range of meanings for social justice. This chart, although overly simplified for the sake of clarity, will serve as an advance organizer for the discussion that follows:

TABLE 6–2
Four Examples of Advocacy Research in Literacy Education

| The study | Gutierrez et al. (1999) | Hicks (2002) | Cherland (1994) | Blackburn (2002) |
|---|---|---|---|---|
| Discipline | Psychology | Philosophy | Sociology | Literary theory |
| Theoretical orientation | cultural-historical activity theory | narrative theory | feminist theory | queer theory |
| Research methods | ethnography and discourse analysis | ethnography and discourse analysis | critical ethnography | ethnography and document analysis |
| How to do research for social justice | "Unconceal" race and ethnicity. Serve the interests of the least advantaged. | Unconceal social class. Confront the myths of psychology. Use literary writing to convey lived experiences. | Unconceal gender. Change cultural beliefs and social structures. Redistribute power. | Unconceal sexual identities. Change the "subject." |
| Vision for achieving social justice | Be compassionate. Keep schools from damaging children. | Feel with children. See. Then engage in creative teaching actions. | Redistribute resources. Unsettle systems of power and privilege. | Destabilize identities to free and affirm people, and to enable agency. |

**Gutiérrez, K. D., Baquedano-López, P., Alvarez, H. H., & Chiu, M. M. (1999):** Kris Gutierrez and her colleagues (1999) conducted research on an after-school computer program called *Las Redes* ("Networks"), located at a port-of-entry urban elementary school near the Los Angeles International Airport. (See chapter 4, "Activity Theory," for another description of this study, offered for a different purpose.) The program made a conscious effort to promote the cognitive and social development of the children who attended (mostly Latino/a, African American, and Tongan students). The researchers studied e-mail exchanges between the children who attended Las Redes and "El Maga," a mysterious figure without a gender who lived in cyberspace and who could only be reached through e-mail. The children wrote to El Maga about their problem solving in their computer-learning tasks and in their playing of computer games, activities they engaged in often with the assistance of an adult volunteer. Because El Maga encouraged the children to use both their languages, the e-mail messages became spaces for the use of hybrid linguistic practices. The researchers then conducted microanalyses of the children's language and literacy use in this situation and attempted to show how inequality and power differentials were enacted in these literacy activities, and how they were resisted. Their findings were that encouraging hybrid language practices (encouraging responses in more than one language, encouraging code-switching, and refraining from privileging one language over another) stimulated literacy learning and development. The learning of these bilingual immigrant students who made use of their home languages in literacy activities was enhanced. Meaningful collaboration and rich contexts for literacy learning (like those created at Las Redes) provide best for the literacy learning of bilingual and immigrant children. The authors concluded by pointing out that these are not the ideas that dominate educational policy and practice in the United States today.

**Deborah Hicks (2002):** Deborah Hicks, having spent years studying how children engage with classroom discourses in urban multiethnic classroom settings in the United States, decided to focus this particular research project more narrowly on the literate engagements of children growing up in poor and working-class White families. (See chapter 4, "Situated Literacies," for another description of this study, written for a different purpose.) Class differences are often glossed over in the United States, and (Hicks argued) White poor and working-class children are often viewed negatively, and without cultural sensitivity. She argued that White working-class children experience painful cultural dissonance in middle-class classrooms, and that teachers and researchers need to strive for critical practices that address diversities of *class*, as well as those involving relations of ethnicity, race, and gender.

Hicks (2002) spent 3 years following two White working-class children (Laurie and Jake) through their first years of schooling in a small town in the Mid-Atlantic region of the United States. The teachers and the administrators of the school, located in a blue-collar working-class neighborhood, cooperated generously with Hicks, keeping the children in the same classroom for the 3 years of the study, and allowing Hicks to participate in instructional activities and to conduct classroom observations and collect data in a variety of ways. Hicks engaged with the teachers in oral inquiry processes (developed by Carini, 1982) to review the progress of the two children in reading and writing. She spent considerable time with the children at their homes, getting to know their families and discussing their progress and their needs with their parents. Hicks also tutored the two children at home, hoping to counter and overcome the difficulties they were experiencing at school. She said that her hope for the research project was to engender advocacy for the children, their families, and their teachers, but that larger educational and societal constraints muted the effects of her advocacy. She knew of pedagogies aimed at social justice and access to literacy, but was unable to make them happen in a school that embraced both traditional and progressive values and teaching practices. Teaching was constrained by the institution.

Hicks' (2002) research recounts the histories of working-class lives in part through stories of her own childhood, of the lives of her own parents and the parents of Jake and Laurie, as well as through stories of Laurie and Jake themselves. She strives for *historicized* research that follows the slow and evolving nature of lived time. The theoretical frames she uses to orient and analyze her research data include *sociocultural psychology* (specifically the work of Vygotsky, 1934/1986); *critical psychology* (including the work of Walkerdine, 1988, 1990); and *philosophy and its connections to literature,* and the emotions and attachments literature engenders (including the work of Martha Nussbaum, 1990; Raymond Williams, 1977; Iris Murdoch, 1991; and Mikhail Bahktin, 1993).

Hicks (2002) believed that writing social science research in literary ways serves as a form of action in the world. Seeking links to the political activism expressed in the work of feminist theorists Jane Miller (1990, 1996) and Valerie Walkerdine (1988, 1990), Hicks wrote some of the stories of Jake and Laurie in novelistic style, using a literary voice to relate the richness and the complexity of their lives. She reflected on the children's painful literacy engagements in school amidst well-intentioned progressive pedagogies that bump them up against middle-class practices and expectations they do not understand. She conveyed the values, attachments, and identities the children experience in their working-class homes, and then juxtaposed these with school conflicts.

Hicks' (2002) writing is not entirely novelistic and literary, however. Hicks' research also contains sections of critical academic writing in which she urges readers to consider the histories of class and gender locations as starting points for reflection and critical action. She argued that the philosophical discussions she intersperses with the children's stories are part of her agenda for social activism. She argued for critical literacy practice, which she defines as teaching actions that draw on listening, watching, feeling, and understanding. Through these actions, she believed, teachers can eliminate the negative effects of class conflict in school, and find ways to value and support working-class children and their ways of becoming literate. Change, she argued, has to entail a moral shift, a willingness to *see* those who differ from us. Crossing class boundaries to teach requires hard work and struggle. Hicks believed that this is the *praxis* of which Freire (1999) wrote. We can only change the world we *see*.

Hicks (2002) applauded multiple forms of social activism through research. She celebrated Heath (1983) for combining the study of language practices with advocacy alongside teachers and community members. She celebrated Walkerdine's feminist critiques of psychology and education, which deconstruct and unsettle systems of oppression and provide ammunition for the battle to change teaching practices. And she made her own contribution through this study, using her writing to counter the myths and metaphors of educational psychology, and to confront the hegemony of an education system that devastates children like Laurie and Jake.

**Meredith Cherland (1994):** Next we offer a critical and sociological study of the reading practices of seven 11-year-old middle-class White girls. This is an example of feminist research (Stanley & Wise, 1993), because it privileges the experiences of girl children; because it attempts to show how children use literacy (as they use everything that comes to hand) to *enact* or do gender (West & Zimmerman, 1987); and because it analyzes reading as a way to participate in a society that privileges male people over female people. It makes the feminist assumptions that knowledge is embodied, and produced through experience, and that the personal is political. (This study is also mentioned in chapter 2, "Feminist Theory," and briefly in chapter 4, "Situated Literacies.")

This study was a year-long ethnography of the home and school lives of seven girls. It was a *critical* ethnography that framed the views of the participants with a view of society, as structured through systems of privilege and power. It made use of data from participant observation and ethnographic interviews to tell stories of the girls' reading lives, and to analyze those stories for the ways in which the girls enacted the culture around them. The findings explain how the girls enacted the culture's beliefs about time, about gender, and about individualism through their reading at home and at school.

Gender has a role to play in structuring an unjust society, and literacy has a role to play in constructing gender. This research presented narrative vignettes, stories that showed girls reading more fiction and different fiction from the boys they sat beside in school. It showed girls reading fiction to enter into social relationships with their mothers, and with each other. It showed girls speaking a discourse of feeling and intuition in their discussions of literature, where the boys in their classes made use of a discourse of action and logic. As cultural beliefs about gender and reading directed and shaped their literacy practices, both girls and boys participated in cultural reproduction through reading, and an unjust society was reproduced from one generation to the next. This study called for new methods of literature instruction to highlight the structures and themes that reveal the ways literary texts serve the interests of the status quo. Understanding what is happening is perhaps the first step toward social change.

**Mollie Blackburn (2002):** In this study, Mollie Blackburn used queer theory (Butler, 1990; Gamson, 2000) to inform the ways in which she analyzed transcripts of the literary talk and the poetry writing of a group of young lesbian women at an after-school center for GLBT youth (ages 12–23) in Philadelphia. Blackburn led the group in reading poetry about GLBT experience, and supported the group's members in writing and presenting their own poetry about their lives. Her research analyzed certain of the poems the girls wrote to destabilize gender constructions in their readings of the world (Blackburn, 2002). One important piece of Blackburn's research analyzed the poetry written by Justine, a

14-year-old African American lesbian writer who engaged in "identity work" in Blackburn's after-school group by performing herself in the poetry she wrote and presented. Blackburn concluded that through her poetry Justine "authored herself into the world" as a beautiful and powerful dyke who would one day have power over those who victimized and marginalized her.

Blackburn's 2002 study (see also chapter 2, "Queer Theory," where Blackburn's other research is reviewed in detail, and for a different purpose) used ethnographic methods to explore literacy *performances*, and through them the construction of *identity*, as ways to empower teens and effect social change. She used the work of Butler (1990) on performance theory to shape the concept of *literacy* performances. Where linguists would speak of literacy events, and sociologists would speak of literacy practices, Blackburn focused on literacy performances that were also performances of identity. She used a poststructuralist view of identity as something people construct for themselves, in interaction with the cultural discourses that surround them. Blackburn suggests that, because literacy performances (like poetry writing) are similar in each enactment but also different in each enactment, they destabilize identity. It is in these literacy performances, and their contributions to destabilizing identity, that literacy holds the hope for social change.

## ORIENTATIONS TO SOCIAL JUSTICE IN ADVOCACY RESEARCH

Because moving the world closer to social justice is the purpose or goal for advocacy research, advocacy research exists as part of a long western tradition of concern for justice, and as part of the discourses of justice circulating today. But the authors of advocacy research studies operate in a postmodern intellectual milieu that no longer accepts without question normative theories about the transcultural nature of rationality and justice, or accepts the idea that justice exists outside history. And yet, they do not entirely abandon all of the principles of distributive justice and compassionate justice. Like other authors throughout history, they make use of whatever cultural discourses move and inspire them.

The authors under discussion are qualitative researchers, sensitive to social contexts, viewing the world as socially and discursively constructed, and they do not seek or apply the universal principles of justice outlined by Kant (1959), for example, which emphasize adherence to a rational and logical moral law. Nor do the authors of these studies sub-scribe without question to the rationalist views of John Rawls (1971), who argued that justice is not related to moral law or to any higher moral order, but rather that principles of justice will be arrived at when self-de-termining individuals exercise the equal rights of citizenship. Rawls paid little attention to economic circumstances or to the role compassion might play in justice. He did, however, suggest that the principles of jus-tice that individual members of a society come to agree on should be ac-ceptable to anyone in any position in that society. To achieve this acceptability to all, Rawls argued, the inequalities in society should be arranged to benefit the least advantaged, and justice can then be achieved. The authors of our exemplar studies do act on their desire to serve the interests of the least advantaged. Rawls' assertion that justice requires social institutions like education to intervene actively to miti-gate disadvantaging circumstances (and ensure equal benefit) remains an important (if rationalist) idea for advocacy research.

But, of course, there are other ideas about justice informing advocacy research. Maxine Greene (1998) contrasted the conceptions of justice in the writings of Kant and Rawls with those of Amelie Rorty (1988), pointing out that Rorty highlights the emotional and affective dimen-sions of ethics and justice by challenging the ideal of self-sufficiency and pointing to the importance of embodied relationships, mutuality, care, and concern. Greene also reflected on the approaches to justice de-scribed by Iris Marion Young (1993), who suggested that justice can be achieved when people engage in dialogue and listen to each other, so that they come to understand each other's experiences and claims, and grow in concern for each other's welfare. Some of these views are also implied in our exemplar studies. (A discussion will follow.)

But advocacy research today must exist without widely agreed-on principles of justice that it can work toward achieving. There are no more "grand narratives of legitimation" (Lyotard, 1984) to which advo-cacy researchers can subscribe, and justice is only one more discourse among others. Lyotard (1984) has told practitioners that normative theo-ries of justice are illegitimate, and that practitioners are responsible for legitimating their own practices of justice. Foucault (1979) has under-mined Marx's views of capitalist society as a totality traversed by one major social division (class) and has offered a view of society as constructed in the crisscrossing threads of interwoven discursive practices. The analytic categories of gender, race, and class have been destabilized (Butler, 1990), and Stuart Hall (1996) has warned researchers inclined toward critical theory that they can only make use of a "Marxism without guarantees."

There are no guarantees of justice, no clear agreements as to what it is, and researchers know that. The advocacy research of the past 15 years embodies a variety of critical traditions struggling with how to envision and articulate political projects for our social life. Marxist discourses still inform some advocacy research, whereas postmodern and feminist poststructuralist discussions of the relation of power–knowledge and the construction of identity inform other advocacy research. Critical literacy researchers inspired by Freire, and others who understand literacy as situated social and linguistic practice, have not entirely abandoned the belief that progress and justice may be possible, although they temper their views with postmodern awareness that changing social conditions require different ways of framing problems and different epistemologies (Popkewitz, 1995). Researchers inspired by poststructuralist thought problematize all foundational categories, but contribute greatly to our understanding of the politics of whose knowledge is most important in the world, and why. None of the current advocacy research studies we have reviewed rely only on Marxist discourse. None rely solely on postmodern deconstructions of Truth that may lead everywhere and nowhere. Advocacy researchers are working in an age of multiple orientations to the nature of justice and visions for how to achieve it. Next, by way of illustration, we attempt to trace some of these orientations as they play themselves out in our four example studies.

## Multiple Views of Social Justice
## Implied in the Four Example Studies

What beliefs about the nature of social justice are operating in the four examples of advocacy research in literacy education that are described earlier? First we can ask, what do Gutiérrez et al. (1999) believe about social justice? Gutiérrez and her colleagues do research which seems to assume some of Rawls' rationalist views of justice, but they have left

Kant behind. Nothing in their research argues that justice is related to universal moral law or to any higher moral order. Their research focuses on and advocates for the children of recent immigrants to the United States, and for other children whose first language is not English, and that focus declares their interest in benefiting the least advantaged members of society. It implies an interest in a society where self-determining individuals exercise equally the rights of citizenship. So too does the list at the end of their article of the reactionary discourses of injustice that color the social context for their work. They implied that these discourses must be countered and their effects ameliorated. They attempted to show *how* social institutions like education can intervene actively to mitigate disadvantaging circumstances, specifically for the bilingual poor children they study and work with.

Gutiérrez et al. assumed that access to an education that provides for one's cognitive and social development is a child's right, and that educational practices that deny this are wrong and unjust. When children are denied the right to use their home languages (and all the linguistic resources they have in their repertoires) for learning, this is a disadvantaging circumstance. It limits their access to the kind of education that other children, whose first language is the language of their teachers and the school, can much more easily access. Denied the right to use their home languages at school, the children's literacy learning is limited. Encouraged to use their home languages in literacy activities, the children's learning increases dramatically. Justice will be done when all children have access to rich learning environments, and are not hampered in their learning by linguistic attitudes and instructional policies that diminish and limit them.

Like Rawls (1971), Gutiérrez and her colleagues in this study do not explicitly attend to economic circumstances as disadvantaging, although they imply their interest by choosing to study poor children. They are out to keep the schools (not the economy) from damaging children. They demonstrate their care and concern by choosing to study children disadvantaged by poverty and disadvantaged by instruction that does not value the knowledge they bring to school, and by arguing for their better education with great enthusiasm and passion. The ideal of justice implied in their research comes close to the justice described by Rorty (1988), who pointed to the importance of embodied relationships, mutuality, care and concern. The caring relationships portrayed between and among the children and the adults at Las Redes are an important part of this research and the remedies it proposes. And, in addressing their research report to those who make educational policy (as well as to other literacy educators), Gutiérrez and her colleagues act on Young's (1993) idea that in working for justice we must come to understand each other's experiences and grow in concern for each other's welfare.

## WHAT DOES DEBORAH HICKS (2002) BELIEVE ABOUT SOCIAL JUSTICE?

Hicks (2002) shared some orientations to social justice with Gutiérrez et al. (1999). Like them, Hicks is working to benefit some of the least advantaged members of society (Connell, 1993; Rawls, 1971). Like them, she believes that access to an education that provides for one's cognitive and social development is a child's right, and that practices that deny this kind of education are wrong and unjust. Like them, she deplores language attitudes and instructional policies that limit and diminish.

But Hicks (2002) directed more of her energy to the concerns of *compassionate justice* (Rorty, 1988), encouraging teachers to establish embodied relations of care and concern for the children they teach, and to work at understanding the experiences of the Other (Young, 1993). Hicks (2002) is in part a call for *empathy,* intended to help and inspire classroom teachers to find the social imagination that will allow them to share the lived experience of the Other. She wants teachers to understand the particularities of working-class lives, to *feel* and to *see* them. She points to the ways in which the theory and practices of developmental psychology divert our gaze from the specificities of class, gender, and race. The discourses of cognitive learning hide students from their teachers, and in doing so they subvert empathy.

Hicks (2002) is *not* someone who believes that empathy for the other is the only requirement for the establishment of justice. She does follow Nussbaum (1990) in believing that it is through sympathy and acts of imagination that we can find a kind of "poetic justice," which can serve as a foundation for dignity, freedom, and democracy. She does believe that empathy will serve the cause of social justice. But Hicks (2002) implied that a passive empathy alone will not transform consciousness or move the world toward justice. She implied that empathy must lead to action, that it is a teacher's duty to engage in the practical struggle to find the situated histories of the students she teaches, even though those histories are hidden by the educational discourses that surround them. Choosing to search and find, choosing not to ignore, but to *see,* is a political act, a challenge to power.

Hicks' (2002) answer is to begin with empathy, but one that is informed by feminist poststructural theory, an empathy that calls for understanding the lived subjectivities of children, but that is socially and politically sensitive. Empathy should move teachers toward more responsive kinds of literacy practices with working-class children. Empathy should be the starting point for critical literacy practices in the classroom. Justice will be established when working-class children are no longer devalued in school, and when they benefit from teaching practices that allow them to learn. Hicks (2002) implied that these children whose lives teachers are to imagine do not need empathy as much as they need justice.

For Hicks (2002), social justice is something that might be approached through a critical literacy that is a form of social activism, because it involves readings of situated lives and commitment to creating teaching practices that extend from those reading of children's lives. Hicks pointed out that this is what Freire did. He began with his students' lives, and showed them how to read their lives differently.

Hicks (2002) believes that research writing is also a form of social activism and a way to work for justice. Her work unsettles the gendered and classed regimes of truth that disadvantage children in the classroom, and critiques the educational discourses that ignore them. Her stories are speech acts that are intended to evoke memory, history, and reflective awareness, and that work to shape literacy research and critical teaching practice. Hicks sees research as the struggle to confront the hegemony of an educational system deeply informed by devastating metaphors and myths of mainstream psychology, which construct a politics of learning and achievement that marginalizes Laurie and Jake and their cherished identities and attachments. She sees social justice as a call for a moral shift, a call for willingness to open ourselves up and do the hard work that lies at the heart of teaching and writing.

## What Does Cherland (1994) Believe About Social Justice?

Working from a different perspective, Cherland's (1994) study[3] focuses on cultural enactments of gender through reading. Focusing on middle-class White girls, Cherland concerns herself with describing the reproduction of the culture and of an unjust society, making use of concepts from critical theory like r*esistance*, *agency*, and *hegemony* to show injustice at work in the lives of girls. In her view justice will require the kind of social transformation that will overturn the categories and systems that distribute resources of wealth and power differentially, and that limit the lives of individuals in subordinated and marginalized groups. Justice will come when we change or do away with those systems, and when resources, power, wealth, and privilege are redistributed to serve the interests of all people.

Cherland's (1994) study, like those of Hicks (2002) and Guttiérrez et al. (1999), implies a belief that individuals matter greatly, and that justice is in part about individuals and their physical and psychic well being. But Cherland was more explicit about the systems of privilege and power that produce injustice. In Cherland's research, individual identities are key to the reproduction of the culture and its inequalities. Cherland's research portrays the individual distress caused by social systems of privilege like patriarchy, and highlights Bourdieu's (1991) ideas about the experiences of symbolic violence at work in the culture's subordination of girls and women. Girls resist, and they struggle to exercise agency, and in this lies the hope for social transformation. But when the structures of the larger social order and individual subjectivities come together at school, gender is created and recreated in social practices with political dimensions, practices that embody complex relations of power and inequality, and patriarchy is preserved.

For Cherland (1994), the situation is grim. Dismantling systems of privilege like patriarchy is terribly difficult, because patriarchy interlocks with other systems of privilege like race and class that serve the interests of the powerful. Like Hicks (2002), Cherland (1994) provided a rich portrait of life at school, and suggests practices that will empower children. Cherland (1994) too focused on the construction of subjectivity as the ground on which injustice is constructed and can be countered. But unlike Hicks (2002), Cherland (1994) did not end with a call for working with individual subjectivities. She emphasized the critical Freirean idea that people can challenge and change the oppressive characteristics of society at large, and that justice will require systemic *social* transformation.

### What Does Blackburn (2002) Imply About Social Justice?

Blackburn's (2002) research implies quite a different, more troubled, postmodern, and uncertain view of what justice might be. There *is* a Freirean element to Blackburn's (2002) work, in its call for reading the word and writing the world. She did say that the girls she worked with in this research study were "marginalized" and "oppressed." But this is not a critical study. Blackburn declared herself immediately as concerned with "identity work". This study is about changing the self to acquire and exercise greater agency. It is about effecting social change, but it is not about addressing the social structures of gender, race, and class.

The view of justice implied in Blackburn (2002) is that the systems that construct injustice are discursive systems, constructed on the ground of language, and that they must be contested there. Literacy is transformative first of the self, and then (through the self) of the social world. Blackburn's work is rooted in the poststructural idea that subjectivity is the arena in which we live and struggle (as is Hicks' work), and that we can't be too sure about what the outcomes of justice should look like. We will, it is implied, come closer to justice when lesbian teens suffer less and are less affected by the discourses that devalue and demean them. Justice, when it is achieved, will exist in the everyday social arrangements and discourses that value all people as worthy, and that allow them to exist in peace and with dignity.

Blackburn (2002) like Cherland (1994) believes that identity is something people perform. But where Cherland (1994) believes that identity performances enact and reproduce the social order, Blackburn (2002) believes that identity performances *are* the social order. Blackburn's study is about deconstructing and disrupting the regimes of truth that constitute injustice. Justice for all will perhaps never be achieved, but social change for individuals like Justine is possible.

### Researchers' Views of Truth, Self, Knowledge and Power

All four of the examples of advocacy research under discussion are to some extent about the construction of subjectivities. Gutiérrez et al. (1999) focused on the cognitive processes that the human mind employs in interaction with others in rich zones of proximal development (Vygotsky, 1978). Hicks (2002) and Cherland (1994) attended to the ways in which systems of class and gender shape what human beings can see and accomplish. Blackburn (2002) attended to "identity work" in the lives of lesbian teens. All four studies express belief in the possibility of transformation. None of the studies saw the establishment of justice as a matter of adhering to a priori moral principles. Caring is implied in all of the studies, but is made explicit as a value only in Hicks (2002).

The range of views of social justice implied in these four studies is produced by a range of views of the nature of truth, knowledge, and power. Consider *truth*, for example. At one end of a range of beliefs about the nature of truth are traditional critical views that reality is a social construction that can be changed, and that systems reproduce social realities over time. At the other end of that range are postmodern ideas about reality and truth as multiple, produced in and through language and discourse. Gutiérrez et al. (1999) and Cherland (1994) come closer to the critical view of truth in their focus on the construction of social realities that produce disadvantage, whereas Hicks (2002) and Blackburn (2002) come closer to the poststructural focus on searching for multiple truths produced in discourse.

The four example studies also offer a range of views about *the nature of the self*. At one end of a range of beliefs is a critical view of the self as historically and politically defined according to categories of race, class, gender, religion, and sexual orientation. Cherland (1994) perhaps came closest to this view, although Gutiérrez et al. (1999) were also fully aware of history and politics as factors in the formation of the individual. At the other end of that range of belief would be the idea that the self is constituted in language, and therefore is unstable, shifting, always in flux. In this view the self is performed, and through processes of crisis and resistance can be resignified. Hicks (2002) showed children performing their identities in discourses that conflict with those of the school. Blackburn (2002) also presented the self as performance, showing the ways in which the self can also perform resistance and resignify itself.

The four example studies also offer a range of views about *the nature of knowledge*. At the critical end of the range is the view that knowledge is a way of seeing reality, produced to serve certain vested interests, and that what counts as knowledge is valued because it supports systems of power and privilege. At the poststructuralist end of the range is the view that all knowledges are partial, historically, and socially contingent, that the world is unknowable, and that knowledge is an effect of power. Again, Cherland (1994) and Gutiérrez et al. (1999) operate toward the critical end of the range, although Cherland (1994) is more explicit about how gender interests are being served by arrangements at school. Hicks (2002) demonstrates the partial nature of knowledge, and ties this to class as a system. Blackburn's (2002) research demonstrates ways to look beyond the already known in the production of knowledge.

Advocacy research also varies in its views of *the nature of power*. The more critical view would be that power results from the unequal distribution of wealth and resources and social privilege, according to categories like race, gender, and class. Cherland (1994) is most inclined to see the world in this way. Gutierrez and her colleagues (1999) also see power at work in these categories, and they too are concerned with disadvantage for those who possess less social power. Hicks (2002) contrasts the differences in power and privilege within categories of social class. But Blackburn's (2002) view of power is quite different. She shows Justine *performing* power that is positive and productive. In this view, which is more poststructural and less critical, knowledge can be positive as well as negative. It *flows through* social networks, and does not *result* from systems.

These differences in beliefs about the nature of reality and truth, about the self, about knowledge and power, lead to *differences in researchers' goals for their advocacy research*. Those whose beliefs are more critical seek to reveal the workings of privilege and power; to empower people to act against privilege and to resist power. They seek to shatter systems of inequity and so change the world. Cherland (1994) and Gutiérrez et al. (1999) have these kinds of goals. Those who see the world in more poststructuralist terms seek to deconstruct regimes of truth (Lyotard, 1984), interrupt the way things are, and to disrupt identities. Hicks (2002) and Blackburn (2002) have these kinds of goals.

The point of this discussion is not to come to a deeper understanding of the four example studies. The point is that there have been and continue to be many beliefs about the nature of reality, truth, and power–knowledge at work in advocacy research in literacy education. All the studies reviewed in the first half of this book imply something about the nature of truth, and the nature of power–knowledge. All have goals, and together they imply a range of beliefs about the nature of social justice and how to pursue justice. Some see the task as working for distributive justice, for the more equitable distribution of resources, wealth, knowledge, and power. Almost all imply that seeking justice requires compassion, and working to end human suffering. Some do more than others to address the conditions that will allow people to reach their full potential. Some are more inclined to work at the level of subjectivity, and to concern themselves with the performance of identities. Some are more inclined than others to see justice as a complex and unstable concept whose meanings shift.

## WHY SEEK SOCIAL JUSTICE?
## AN ETHIC OF RESPONSIBILITY FOR THE OTHER

*One of the great advances of our time is the recognition that the Other shares in the human condition.*

Maxine Greene, 1995

*We have an ethical responsibility to retreat from stances of dispassion.*
Michelle Fine, Lois Weis, Susan Weseen, and Loonmun Wong, 2000

*We must meet the specters armed with nothing, no rules, no truths, no certainties ... The only responsibility worthy of the name comes with the removal of grounds, the withdrawal of the rules or the knowledge on which we might rely to make our decisions for us.*

Thomas Keenan, 1997, p. 1

The beliefs about justice that inform advocacy research in literacy education today do not concern themselves with *morality*, the rules and customs observed by any one social group. They do appear to be informed by *ethics*, ideals concerning what is good, what ought to be, and how people ought to conduct themselves. There is no clear agreement about appropriate ethics for advocacy research. There are many ethical points of view. Lyotard's (1984) conceptions of "regimes of truth," and Foucault's (1997) explanations of them have undermined and unsettled Truth, to the point where Truth can no longer be seen as universal or absolute. Truth has multiple forms, and varies by nation, by gender, by class, and by race.

Advocacy researchers today cannot and do not operate as if universal Truth forms a foundation for justice or for ethical conduct. They are more inclined to see discourses of truth as an integral feature of the power relations that marginalize and oppress, and that must constantly be assessed as strategies of control and domination. Discourses of truth demand deconstruction. Foucault (1997) suggested that *freedom* might provide an alternative to truth in outlining a basis for ethical conduct. Instead of doing advocacy research to establish truth, perhaps we ought to advocate to establish freedom.

Quinby (2002) suggested that advocating for equitable education as a practice of freedom will contribute to the development of individuals and the societies in which they live, so that individuals can then cultivate greater justice. She called for global awareness that recognizes as good certain freedom-based practices of social justice (like equitable education, full and equitable employment, an end to poverty, and an end to the oppression of women). When freedom is extended, and practiced, people will be able to construct justice. But Quinby is not conceptualizing freedom as personal liberty, as Rawls (1971) did. She sees freedom as the conditions that will allow people to act not in their own individual best interests, but rather to act on the *responsibility* they feel for each other, so that socioeconomic transformation will occur.

What advocacy researchers in literacy education seem to have in common is an ethic of responsibility for the other. We see this in all the variety of ways in which advocacy researchers assume the need for social change, and in the ways they intend their research to contribute to social change. We see it in the concern of Gutiérrez and her colleagues

(1999) for the cognitive development of the bilingual child, in Hicks' (2002) concern for the misery of two working-class children, in Cherland's (1994) concern for the oppression of young girls, and in Blackburn's (2002) concern for young lesbians. The status quo is not acceptable to those who advocate, because the status quo disadvantages the other, and causes the suffering of the other.

The idea that we are each responsible for the other echoes down through the history of the world's religions. Judaism, Islam, and Christianity all contribute theistic discourses of moral responsibility and accountability to the cultural context in which advocacy researchers operate today. Christian authors and televangelists speak of a restored relationship with God, of a redeemed future, and of hope for a new creation in which all can share. Christian philosopher James Olthuis (1997), fully aware of postmodern critiques of reason, and understanding that knowledges cannot be neutral, dispassionate, and disinterested, suggested that deconstruction can open a prephilosophical space of proximity to the other (p. 2), as a place of ethical and spiritual responsibility, as a space where God is Love. He writes of an "economy of love" in which love expands and increases through being given, seeing the Christian vision of love as one among many. Meanwhile organizations like Oxfam, World Vision, and Catholics for a Free Choice enact a variety of Christian versions of Love, advocating for others and working for justice in the name of Love in a variety of ways.

At the same historical moment, of course, the Judao-Christian Bible is quoted in discourses that marginalize gay and lesbian people, that suppress women, and that justify enduring poverty. Discourses that perceive oppression as natural and ordained by God negate an ideal of freedom. In countering these discourses, some intellectuals argue that God is another metanarrative (Lyotard, 1984). Some believe that human beings can live by the values of religious traditions, or even of the Enlightenment, without returning to the beliefs and "truths" which justify them (Rorty, 1988). Others reject this belief.

Humanism (which includes belief in a stable, coherent self for each human being; belief in reason, and in universal foundations for knowledge; belief that conflicts between truth, knowledge and power can be overcome) is like the air we breathe. We cannot entirely escape it (St. Pierre, 2000, p. 478). But advocacy researchers do work in a social context where poststructuralism undermines humanism at every turn. Foucault's work on discourse has changed the way we think about language and how it operates in the production of the world (St. Pierre, 2000, p. 485). Derrida's (1980) contention that meaning can never be found, but must always be deferred, has influenced many researchers who have given up on finding out exactly what is going on. As Denzin (1997, p. 263) pointed out, living and working outside postmodernism is not a choice researchers can make. Most researchers know they are seeking to discover multiple truths and tell symbolic and partial tales.

And yet there is an ethic to which many advocacy researchers cling. They persist in acting on a sense of responsibility for the other. Discourses of ethical caring have helped to sustain their efforts. These are ethical perspectives that differ from the traditional, in that they are not associated with rights or duties. Neither are they utilitarian (based on the notion that whatever produces the most good will be ethically correct). They are not sustained by universalist principles of fairness and justice. Instead, these perspectives are anchored by an understanding of relationships, and an ideal of responsibility that grows out of networks of relationship (Ryan, 1995). Noddings (1984) has suggested that caring is the fundamental basis for ethics, and that when we care we step into the other's frame of reference, seeing and feeling their situations as they see and feel them. This is a complex (perhaps impossible) task for researchers who are of a different class or race or gender from the other they study. Unequal power relations must be recognized in research that is informed by an ethic of care, and power must be shared. In research informed by an ethic of caring and a concern for social justice, no one should be hurt.

Megan Boler (1999), pointing out that an ethic of care is part of the production of empathy, argued that there are risks involved when people engage in empathy, and that empathy alone cannot sustain an ethic of responsibility to the other, or inspire transformative action in the world. Empathy is not necessarily the route to inspiring change. Empathy, which implies full identification with the other, is at the same time founded on a recognition that the self is not the other. Inspiration to act for change may require seeing oneself as implicated in the social forces that create the obstacles that others confront. More than empathy, it is the awareness of one's own privilege and one's own complicity in the systems that sustain it, that may produce an ethic of responsibility to the other.

Of course there are many cultural discourses and material factors that work to undermine an ethic of caring for advocacy research. Researchers who live in privilege must not speak "for" others who are poor and marginalized, without writing themselves (and the racial and economic structures that sustain their lives of privilege) into the text. Researchers who "care" must ask themselves how they came to have the power to "see" and to speak about what they see. Today's researchers must acknowledge the historical moment and the social context in which they write, which is a time of ideological assault on the poor. Fine, Weis, Weseen, and Wong (2000) acknowledged that a lot of qualitative research has reproduced a colonizing discourse of the "Other" that does nothing to disrupt common sense or transform public consciousness about poor people and the working class. They call researchers to use emergent postmodern texts to interrupt this othering (p. 108), and to place the voices of poor people at the center of national debates about social policy around the world.

Fine et al. (2000) also points out the problems with the reality of "community." Simplistic calls for an ethic of caring community in educational research will accomplish nothing transformative. Race, ethnicity, gender, class, generation, and sexual orientation all mark dramatic differences in human experiences, and coalitions are few. The people who live in the same geographic neighborhood are not likely to live in harmony, or to see the world in the same ways. Researchers will have to work at uncovering the common ground and the shared languages of the people they care for and do research with. Fine et al. (2000) called researchers to "move delicately between coherence and difference." They suggested that, although feminist ethnography and other forms of advocacy research depend on an ethic of caring human relationship, engagement, and attachment, researchers must always remain aware of the inequality in the research relationship, and of the ways in which their research methods can leave research subjects exposed to exploitation.

If an ideal *can* help and sustain advocacy research, perhaps the ethical ideal of a caring community is the ideal that can. This would be a *democratic* community that would exist as a practice of freedom. Later chapters in this book will amplify that thought. But an ethical ideal of caring democratic community must always be interrupted by a poststructuralist emphasis on contradiction, heterogeneity, and multiplicity that concerns itself with difference and is politically engaged (Fine et al., 2000). There is no universal ethic for advocacy research, and yet there is. In the words of Elizabeth St. Pierre (2001), "In the moment of decision, I am alone, except for the other, all the others, all the specters in time to whom I am responsible" (p. 1).

### Challenges for the Future of Advocacy Research

Several scholars have called literacy researchers and teachers to construct and then rally around a shared vision for the future (Artiles, 2003; Luke, 2002; Powell, 1999). If advocacy researchers are to continue in their work for a better world, if they are to avoid the passivity and paralysis that may threaten their work, then they *need* a strong, overarching normative vision for the future of educational research. If we are to engage with issues of social justice and human rights in the context of rapid economic and cultural change, and in a postmodern intellectual milieu, then there are ethical and political dilemmas facing us.

What is worth working for, what is worth living and dying for, beyond and without the nation state? The people who destroyed the World Trade Towers on September 11, 2001, certainly have a vision of what is worth dying for, of what is worth killing for. As Allan Luke (2002) has pointed out, their vision for the future includes religious belief, political ideology, ideals of nationhood, a view of human rights, and normative visions of "the good life." They know that people do not live and die for the expansion of capital, or for the production of capital. They stand against this morally barren view of neoliberal governance (Luke, 2002).

Advocacy researchers in literacy education need an ethical and political metanarrative of their own. What kind of theory might support such a vision of a just world? Luke (2002) has suggested that we need a kind of critical educational theory that will inform our research, but one that is hybrid and polyvocal, one that does several things at once.

- It would have to be critical theory that dreams, to articulate visions of social and cultural utopias.
- It would have to be critical theory that blends in continued skepticism toward totalisation and essentialism.

- It would have to foreground the dilemmas of learning to live together.
- It would have to be epistemologically sensitive to the local, the "cultural," and the diasporic.
- It would have to invent an explicitly normative and yet self-critical metanarrative.

Paulo Freire had that kind of powerful normative vision for education. But at this moment in history, many educational researchers do not. As we look back over the first half of this book, we can see in the dilemmas that confront advocacy researchers in literacy education *six challenges* that could lead us toward a shared vision for the future. The first three challenges have already been implied in this chapter. The last three challenges will be expanded on in the chapters that follow.

**The Challenges**

1. To continue *to highlight and theorize power relations* and their material and discursive effects in our work.
2. *To articulate more clearly the connections between advocacy work in literacy education and the project of social justice*, of creating a more equitable and compassionate society. We will need to envision both an ideal "literate citizen" and a strengthened "democratic community." In short, the challenge is to speak more of freedom, ethics, and of moral purpose. This will require articulating in theory and in practice a "pedagogy of commitment" against a "pedagogy of method."
3. *To promote the social and community nature of advocacy work*. This will require valuing the interests of the community over and above the interests of the individual. We will need to abandon the masculine hero image of the researcher-advocate as the rugged individualist warrior, to work with and in community. We will need to recognize many sites and communities, including the academic community, for advocacy work.
4. *To attend to the materiality of bodies in our work* and to our own subject positionings within advocacy work. In part this means acknowledging that advocacy isn't simply the work of the mind. It is

also the work of the body that reflects the history of the body, individually and socially. This will require attending to the place and power of desire and pleasure, fantasy, and the irrational in the re-inscription of dominant ways of being in the world.

5. *To anticipate the conservative backlash and prepare for it.* This means building allies across social movements locally and globally; it means continuing to name and promote advocacy research in literacy and its ethical and moral projects to the community at large; it means countering and resisting the domestication of radical work in institutions like schools, while remaining strategic in all our efforts.

6. *To stay critical and complex (and reflexive) in our theorizing, and humble in our efforts.* This means remaining open to critical and complex understandings of literacy, and the issues that surround literacy and advocacy work. It means staying fluid in our understandings of identity and community. In staying humble, we must articulate and acknowledge the limits of what we, individually and collectively, can do.

# 7

# The Literate Body

*"Bodies are essential to accounts of power
and critiques of knowledge."*

Elizabeth Grosz, 1995, p. 32

*The gradual and orderly surrender of one's body
is the project of elementary school*

Madeleine Grumet, 1988, p. 111

*Teaching and learning unfold
in the register of desire*

Jo Pagano (in Kelly, 1997, p. 22)

In this chapter we look at one of the key challenges identified in the previous chapter, acknowledging the discursive and material body in advocacy research and scholarship in literacy education. Of course, the body has always been of key importance for those whose teaching and research is explicitly embedded in advocacy agendas and in social justice issues more generally. At the heart of advocacy work has been questions and challenges concerning which bodies are and are not present in public schooling, how bodies are named and produced in schools, and how hierarchies of bodies are organized and subjugated by social class, race, ethnicity, gender, and other forms of social difference. For those who work in literacy education, the concern has been about which bodies become literate, about what literacy is offered to

**229**

which bodies, and about the representation and "reading" of bodies in school text and classroom practices. Although not considered as "bodies" per se, but as human beings, socially and discursively organized (e.g., boys–girls; Blacks–Whites–Asians; working–ruling classes, student–teacher), bodies are nonetheless inherent in advocacy efforts. However over the last decade, under the purview of postmodern and feminist theory and research, the body has become much more complex, and less determinate, while at the same time gaining in significance as a site of power. The implications of such have been felt in all areas of academic and social endeavors and perhaps most particularly in scholarly work explicitly concerned with challenging the status quo. As noted by Wanda Pillow (2000) "the body has gained both attention and importance, not only in feminist and postmodern theories but also more broadly in social theory as a place from which to theorize, analyze, practice, and critical reconsider the construction and reproduction of knowledge, power, class, and culture" (p. 199).

Viewing the body as a site for the inscription of power and culture is a relatively recent phenomenon. For much of the last two centuries social institutions have relied largely on medical models of the body as a fixed system of muscle, bone, and organs, that transcends history and culture. However for more than a decade now, as Erica McWilliam (1996) noted, "a project of re/covering the importance of the body as a field of political and cultural activity has been underway … bodies are now fashionable topics in a range of disciplines from media and cultural studies to sociology and philosophy" (p. 17). In his own inimitable style, Terry Eagleton (2003) noted, "There will soon be more bodies in contemporary criticism than on the fields of Waterloo" (p. 129).

This more recent scholarship has tended to theorize the body in one of two ways as either "inscriptive," referring to a "Nietzschian Foucauldian notion of the social body upon which social law, morality and values are inscribed" or as a "lived body" referring to the "lived experience of the body, the body's internal or psychic inscription" (Grosz, 1995, p. 33). The inscriptive or governed body is pliable or "docile" as both the object and instrument of power. According to Foucault, the production of the docile body became particularly intense in the 18th century with methods of control that focused on the operations of the body, its movements, gestures, dress, and attitudes at the level of the individual. Religious sects, the prison system, the school system, and the military came to bear striking similarities to each other in the control and management of the body. Rather than brute force, new microlevel methods of regulating and monitoring, and eventually self-monitoring of the body, "assured the constant subjection of its [the body's] forces and imposed upon them a relation of docility-utility, [what] might be called 'disciplines'" (Foucault, 1979, pp. 137–138). These disciplinary regimes ensure that the body becomes "more obedient as it becomes more useful and conversely more useful as it becomes more obedient" to particular interests (Foucault, 1979, p. 138).

However the body can resist, as Elizabeth Grosz (1994) noted, the body is "the field on which the play of powers, knowledges, and resistances is worked out … it is acted upon, inscribed, peered into; information is extracted from it, and disciplinary regimes are imposed on it; yet its materiality also entails a resilience and thus also (potentially) modes of resistance to power" (p. 149). She comments further:

> It is not simply that the body is represented in a variety of ways according to historical, social, and cultural exigencies while it remains basically the same; these factors actively produce the body as a body of a determinate type … [But] bodies are not inert; they function interactively and productively. They act and react. They generate what is new, surprising, unpredictable. It is the ability of bodies to always extend the frameworks which attempt to contain them, to seep beyond their domains of control, which fascinates me. (Grosz, 1994, pp. x–xi)

It may be that the ways in which the body resists have to do with the numerous disciplinary regimes and discourses to which it is potentially subjected. Any discourse in asserting itself, binds off, but at the same time, implicitly suggests an alternative: an outside. Foucault (1981) wrote, "Discourse transmits and produces power, it reinforces it but it also undermines and exposes it, renders it fragile and makes it possible to thwart it" (p. 10). Alternative discourses explicitly or implicitly offer means of resistance. Such resistance found in the interplay of alternative and dominant discourses is key to advocacy efforts. However, it may also be, as Grosz suggested, that resistance also has something to do with the body's experience "as lived," that is, by its psychically and internal inscription. Desire, emotion, and more generally the phenomenology of the body-as-lived or the body-as-flesh may resist or seep out from social inscription. But what seeps out is, of course, not the "real" body but a body constructed by its history of social inscription and "lived" experience.

Much of the contemporary scholarship on the inscribed and lived body challenges the Cartesian separation of mind and body: a separation that has been at the center of school life. Sheila Landers Macrine (2002) commented, "The human body has historically been written out of knowing, learning, thinking, and teaching and therefore only the mind remains, which is thought to be distinct and superior to the body" (p. 135). But as many scholars are beginning to argue, such thinking does not reflect the actualities of teaching and learning, where in fact the body and pedagogy "are inextricably entwined," where all teaching and all learning are embodied (O'Farrell, Meadmore, McWilliam, & Symes, 2000, p. 1).

Newly emerging research and scholarship by Brent Davis and Dennis Sumara (in press) deploys complexity theory to argue that what has been absent from educational research including advocacy research is an acknowledgment of the tight connection between biology, neurology, culture, and educational contexts. In part, they suggested that "one's internal, biology-based dynamics must be understood to affect and to be affected by one's physical experiences, which in turn unfold in social and cultural circumstances, which in turn shape and are shaped by intercultural and biospheric circumstances" (in press). This research holds promise for redirecting attention to the connection between and among individual and collective bodies, their biology, culture, and learning, connections that defy simple cause and effect. We hope to explore this further in relation to advocacy research as this scholarship becomes available.

Not only are the body and pedagogy entwined but in these "New Times" (Luke & Elkin, 1998) the body is increasingly connected to if not characterized by technology. The concept of the "cyborg," for example, encapsulates not only a connection but a melding of body and technology. Of interest to literacy educators, text is involved in this melding. The recent influx of communication technologies is profoundly affecting the relationship between text and the body. The private, docile, and self-confessing body, described by Foucault, has become the cyborg body of Internet e-mail, chat rooms, and blogs. It is at the same time organic, mechanical, and technological. In a historical note, Lankshear, Peters, and Knobel (1996) commented,

> With the impact of the Restoration, the human body ceased to be perceived as public spectacle and become privatized and self-constituted in such (types of) texts as in the diary, the lady's journal and the confessional genre more broadly ... [more recently] Donna Haraway's accounts of the collapse of subject categories and of boundaries of the body through the intervention of twentieth century technology ... suggests ... the boundaries between technology and nature are themselves in the midst of a deep restructuring. (p. 162)

At the same time recent scholarship suggests that the body, cyborg or otherwise, has become more integral to identity formation and re-formation, that is, to self-styling, so becoming infinitely more fluid than ever before. Shapiro and Shapiro (2002) wrote:

> In this postmodern world essentiality and permanence in identity and lifestyle strategies give way to fluidity and contingency as our life-world is interrogated for its capacity to provide meaning, recognition, pleasure and opportunity ... Individuals can no longer rest content with an identity that is simply handed down, inherited, or built on tradition. A person's identity has, in large part, to be discovered, constructed, and actively sustained ... [the body] has become central to the process by which a person's identity is to be managed and constructed. It is the visible carrier of self-identity and is increasingly integrated into our life-world decisions and choices. It is thus an increasing focus for liberation politics. (p. 6)

The inscribed body, lived body, biological body, cyborg body, and, as Svi Shapiro suggested, postmodern body, speaks directly to issues of power and desire, resistance, and regulation, and thus to liberation politics. Although advocacy workers must continue to pay attention to the question of which bodies (and voices) are materially present and absent in school classrooms and school texts, the focus in this new scholarship suggests that more complex questions and issues also need to be addressed. This chapter draws on some of this new scholarship to consider how particular attention to the body as a site of power and desire might better inform and potentially disrupt advocacy research in literacy education in important ways. In this examination, we weave the concepts of the governed body, transgressive or erotic body, cyborg body, and the fluid postmodern body of self-identity and self-management, while knowing that bodies can and do seep in and out of any effort to categorize them.

## SCHOOLING THE BODY

As mentioned previously, scholars have argued that schools like other social institutions are organized in accordance with Western philosophy and the Cartesian mind–body separation. In this split the mind epitomizes the best in mankind, the body, the most base. The body is, in effect, viewed as "Other" to the mind (Vick, 1996). According to McWilliam, the mind does more than reflect the best in human beings; it has been seen as constituting one's very humanity. She (1996) wrote, "the fact remains that, in the history of Western thought, a mind/body dichotomy has privileged the mind as that which defines human 'being,' while the body has been interrogated as the excess baggage of human agency" (p. 16). Macrine (2002) notes, "The mind is seen as the highest and closest thing to God. The body, conversely, is seen as an albatross levying a heavy drag on self realization" (p. 135). Many educationalists have argued that the division between mind and body and privileging of the mind operates to the detriment of students and their learning. Svi Shapiro wrote, "Traditional learning asks students to become bodiless beings or no-bodies; we ask them to alienate themselves for their feelings—the aesthetic or bodily experiences from the emphasis on cerebral knowledge" (Shapiro & Shapiro, 2002, p. x). Others have argued that it is not that students become bodiless in schools, but that their bodies are attended to only to be controlled and managed:

> It is not that the human body as a physical essence has been ignored. Educators, for example, have certainly stressed the importance in relation to the training of young people. The idea of "a healthy mind in a healthy body," of a necessary relations between the "physical" and the "mental/cognitive," has been at the heart of childhood education, physical education programs and popular physical culture for over a century ... the body's importance perceived in the main in terms of its careful management to enhance or to avoid distracting from mental effort. (McWilliam, 1996, p. 16)

In schools, as in other social institutions, the bodies of individuals are subjected to the "panoptic" (all seeing) gaze of authorities. Foucault (1979) suggested that "a relation of surveillance, defined and regulated, is inscribed at the heart of the practice of teaching, not as an additional or an adjacent part of it, but as a mechanism that is inherent in it and which increases its efficiency" (p. 141). As noted by Sue Middleton (2002), this "relation of surveillance" constitutes much of teachers' everyday work. It includes "monitoring the spatial location of students (where they may be and with whom they may mix); the postures students may assume within their allocated spaces inside and outside the classroom (static or moving, sitting in rows or in groups, in desks or on the floor); and the surveillance and standardization off their dress and demeanor" (p. 211).

Moreover, many researchers have noted that particular pedagogies incite both students and teachers to constantly self-monitor the body and its deportment to consciously position themselves in relation to social norms. In addition attention to the body is often premised on a notion that the inner mind can be read from the body and its movement. Malcolm Vick in his analysis of three teaching methods texts noted that each offered teachers means of assessing the mind based on a particular reading of the body. Vick (1996) argued it is the body that has been the real focus pedagogy: "despite the apparent excision of the body from pedagogical space by the positing of the mind as the true subject of pedagogy, the fact that the mind is an imaginary object, inferable and accessible only 'through' the body, paradoxically made the body central to pedagogy" (p. 113).

The ways in which pedagogical method organizes and authorizes particular "readings of the body" forecloses other interpretations, for example of the feminine body or the masculine body. Vick called for a careful consideration of what has been excluded in authorized readings. Of course many discourses infuse pedagogical and popular contexts in these contemporary times, so that teachers may be exposed to various readings of the body, authorized or not. However Lucy De Fabrizio (2004) suggested that,

> while teachers have gained a multitude of ways to read and understand the body, they nonetheless remain threatened by it in the classroom … the threat teachers feel is the confrontation with particular

bodies and the particularities of those bodies exactly as they resist sub-
sumption by generalized knowledge, prescriptive practice, blanket
policies of equity, and a host of other platforms that are necessary for
the institutional structuring of teaching. (pp. 3–4)

As De Fabrizio indicates, the particularities of bodies confound uni-
versalized readings. All student bodies, but perhaps most particularly
those whose discursive and material histories and locations lie outside
of dominant culture, undo the pedagogical and social norms that constitute teachers' work. They mess up the tidy generalities used to organize,
produce, and normalize teaching and schooling practices.

Student bodies are not the only threat to pedagogical norms and universal readings. Teacher bodies too have been perceived as an impediment to
pedagogy. Teachers were and are to be in effect *bodiless* to ensure the rig-
ors of learning in the supposedly cognitive and rational environment of
the classroom. For female teachers this is enormously difficult because,
historically, women have been determined by their bodies: the female
body the marker of womanhood (Conboy, Medina, & Stanbury, 1997).
Moreover the "respectable" female body has largely been confined to the
domestic sphere rather than in the public and professional world. Thus the
female teacher body has been viewed as suspect even in what has been
seen as women's "true profession"—teaching—and subjected to intense
regulation. The marriage bar of the early and middle 20th century protected teaching jobs for men and ensured that sexually active and preg-
nant female bodies were absent from classrooms. Now familiar, historical
research has documented the degree to which women's dress, activities,
demeanor, deportment, and living arrangements were the subject of contractual arrangements (Apple, 1986). In a similar way professional teachers associations have historically named and regulated what constitute the
"professional" women teacher in part by means of dress and bodily deportment (Cavanagh, 2003).

Recent neoliberal conceptions of the professional teacher have
sought to standardize teaching practice and so standardize both male
and female teacher bodies and their actions. The fact that "bodies bear
the marks of our culture, practices, and policies" (Pillow, 2002, p. 214)
means that within a neoliberal discourse of "the professional teacher"
individual markings are erased or overwritten, metaphorically and actu-

ally, by larger state marking of the teacher body. Such efforts subordinate difference, producing one body, the same as the next, and one context, the same as the next. Teacher bodies, as well as student bodies, located in and at the geographical or social margins, bearing the markings therein, often cannot easily display such similarity or compatibility with state norms, even if they try. Their bodies, their histories and locations can be viewed, even to themselves, as failing to support authorized pedagogical practice and policy, and as transgressing teacher "professionalism" more generally (Dillabough, 1999; Harper, 2004).

It is important to mention those teachers' bodies that have been viewed as inherently threatening to students and communities: the homosexual body. These bodies have been target of intense efforts to marginalize and exclude them from the profession (Blount, 2005; Cavanagh, 2005; Harbeck, 1997; Khatt, 1992; Rofes, 1985). Various campaigns continue to portray gay, lesbian, and bisexual teachers as evil, diseased, and/or criminal and directly or indirectly recruiting schoolchildren into a homosexual lifestyle. Although gay, lesbian, and bisexual educators have gained greater visibility and have begun to organize to protect their livelihoods, the educational context if not society at large remains hostile to them and to any self-styling of the homosexual body (Blount, 2005, p. 2).

The desire to manage and control the threat posed by the bodies of teachers and students ignores what has become increasingly evident to at least some scholars, that teaching and learning are embodied, contextualized practices. Teaching, for example, can be seen as intensely physical: a bodily performance. Denise Kirkpatrick and Stephen Thorpe, in an examination of the construction of the "good teacher" evident in teaching awards given to university professors in Australia, found that good teaching was characterized as an individual act of display, transmission, and passion. They stated succinctly, "award-winning teaching is a spectacle" (2000, p. 175). Moreover it is a spectacle that must engage the emotions, including pleasure and desire.

Some scholars make the claim that teaching and learning are intimately bound together with pleasure and desire (e.g., Gallop, 1995; McWilliam, 2000, 1999; O'Brien, 2000). Erica McWilliam and Alison Jones (1996) suggest that, rather than "the excess baggage of pedagogy," the body is inherent in teaching in part because Eros is necessary

and indeed a structuring component of pedagogy (p. 133). Carmen Luke
(1996) claimed that, as an art and craft,

> pedagogy is seduction and performance: we cajole, humor, invite,
> persuade, and convince in efforts to "seduce" students into the
> knowledges we embody, over which we have authority, and over
> which we want our students to "see" and grasp in that pleasurable mo-
> ment of (en)-light-(enment). (p. 289)

More explicitly, Jane Gallop argued that teaching is best understood
as a libidinal experience rather than a cognitive endeavor. She wrote,

> At heart a Freudian, I believe that our professional impulses are subli-
> mated sex drives. The pleasure I get from working with graduate stu-
> dents, the intensity of my wish that certain promising graduate
> students will choose to work with me, and the satisfaction I get from
> seeing the imprint of my teaching in their work all strongly suggest a
> sexual analogy. (1997, p. 87)

More specifically she sees transference, the tendency to position people in the position of parents, as a powerful form of love and "an inevitable part of any relationship we have to a teacher who really makes a
difference" (1997, p. 56).

The notion that the body and in particular Eros might be involved in
pedagogy raises red flags for many. Fear and concern has instigated considerable efforts to regulate teacher–student relations, often in ways to ensure that the body remain absent from pedagogy. Universities, for
example, now have weighty policies and procedures pertaining to issues
of sexual harassment and abusive pedagogical relations. Such efforts are
important but may eclipse significant lines of thought and action. Elspeth
Probyn (2004) suggested that the hyperawareness of the sexualized or
erotic body in pedagogy produces a situation where "theory is safer than
grounded analysis and discussion" (p. 34). She argued the more abstract
the theory the better attention is deflected from students' and teachers'
material bodies and their history. We do know, for example, that

> much of the literature that focused on the relation of the body of the
> teacher to the learner as productive (and seductive) does not inform the
> modern educational disciplines. It is not more likely to be encountered

in literary criticism, and this has been a loss to educationalists to trying to engage the "mindful bodies" of students. (McWilliam, 1996, p. 133)

Even minimal acknowledgment of this literature ensures, as Susie O'Brien (2000) stated, that, "at the very least, the sexualized body in pedagogy must no longer be simply dismissed as deviant" (p. 51). The fear and threat posed by the erotic body and the specter of sexually abusive pedagogy may make distance education look infinitely less "dangerous." Certainly in the minds of many, one of the advantages of distance education is that physical bodies are not involved. However a certain threat remains even with virtual bodies, as McWilliam and Jones (1996) noted ironically,

the utopian vision, i.e., that future teachers have no body to teach (with), might well be achieved through technological moves towards the "virtual" university, including the replacement of academic teachers with instructional designers who never actually engage with student bodies, much less with the substantive issue of pedagogical desire—if only there were not already so many reports of harassment on the Net! (p. 136)

Rather than consciously ignoring or excessively regulating actual and/or virtual bodies, educationalists need to consider how passions, desire, and the body are organized and produced in powerful and productive teaching and learning. Otherwise fear itself will ensure the entrenchment of the mind–body separation, and the enduring "fixation of mainstream educational discourse on the rational and the cognitive" to the detriment of us all (Sherry Shapiro, 1994, p. 61, in McWilliam, 2000, p. 133; also Shapiro & Shapiro, 2002). Moreover in the very effort to regulate and police the body Eros away may in fact reappear. Sadean scholars claim that discipline or policing form a dominant mode of eroticism in our society (Gallop, 1988). If so, then, as McWilliam warned,

In working hard to shore up best pedagogical practice by hauling sandbags of regulating policy into place to guard against any unforeseen outpouring of Eros, policy makers engage policing and also eroticizing work. And whatever its good intentions and proven outcomes, making policy more explicit must always have the perverse effect of eroticizing certain students' bodies, rendering them more "harassable" than others.

Thus Eros gets expelled form pedagogy, only to reenter in its many guises via the back door. (2000, p. 35)

However we might wish it differently, the body, and the emotions—particularly fear, pleasure, and Eros—are all deeply involved in learning and teaching. One pedagogical site where there is a marked fixation with the cognitive, and yet at the same time an often-unacknowledged concern with the regulation of the body is in literacy education.

## PRODUCING THE LITERATE BODY

In many ways, the literacy teacher can be seen to school the mind and the body—or better put, the "mindful body" (Strathern, 1996)—as well as to teach directly and indirectly about the mind and body, in the course of his or her embodied pedagogy.

The fundamental task of literacy teachers, beyond keeping student bodies at school, is to produce bodies that read and write. On the surface, learning to read the word and the world would not seem to involve the body very much; however, as with all other aspects of teaching and learning, the body is integral. Ray Misson and Wendy Morgan, among others, have demonstrated that reading, which appears a purely cerebral activity, has considerable corporeal dimensions. They indicate that, although the literate body is more obviously still, it nonetheless responses to text. Tears, laughter, groans, changes of breathing, muscular shifts, changes in expression can and do occur. During reading, Misson and Morgan (2000) argued, the

> body and text are engaged in a complex interaction. Essential to the aesthetic/reading process is not just the writing of the text on the reading body, but the body reacting to the textual material. The body does not simply receive but asserts itself in response to the text. That is, it is involved both in perception and reaction. (p. 96)

Moreover, such bodily responses to textual stimuli, its form in time and space, and demand for empathy are culturally determined, and, as such, are taught and managed. In this the social and the biological are intimately connected, each continually charging each other. To acknowledge this is to alter conventional notions of the body. Rather than romantic, spontaneous, and untrainable, Peter Cyles (2000), among others, asserted that the body and its "pleasure and desire can be helpfully thought of as discursively organized, and ought to be understood as teachable and learnable, indeed regularly taught and learned" (p. 23).

Not only pleasure and desire but the whole range of the affect is involved in teaching, and in particular the teaching of powerful texts that can produce what Elspeth Probyn (2004) called the "goosebump effect," "that moment when a text sets off a fission of feelings, remembrances, thoughts, and bodily actions" (p. 29). Such moments can be profound and Probyn in addressing Women's Studies teachers warns us all about the need for an "ethics of the affective in the classroom" to both acknowledge the work with affective reaction and to consider the limits of what is appropriate in classrooms particularly with what may prove high disturbing to students and/or teachers.

On a very mundane level, literacy teachers implicitly or explicitly teach students how and where the body reads, how one opens and handles a new book and other behavioral aspects. Perhaps more significantly, they teach the skills and techniques of handwriting, and in doing so discipline and monitor the mind and body. Alison Jones (2000) has noted that teachers' surveillance, "first of the techniques of handwriting, and progressively of the expression of the students' thoughts, remains focused on writing, which students are required to submit to their teachers' changing and always intense, scrutiny" (p. 151). In examining handwriting primers, Jones found a strict notion of the ideal body regarding pen holding. In such texts, the "dynamic tripod grasp" together with other instruction and monitoring, "the body becomes a machine whose movements can be calculated, controlled, and made efficient" (p. 152). Similar to Malcolm Vick, Jones argued that, through the writing body, the mind of student is delivered to the teacher for judgment and correction. But more than just the mind, one's character, one's gentility, and, for young women, their femininity has been assessed by way of their handwriting. As Jones noted, "To my teachers, it was clear from the telltale signs of my 'lovely' writing that not only was a I good pupil, but more fundamentally a child—a girl—of good character" (p. 154).

Pleasure is organized in relation to the pedagogical discipline of the literate body as either the illicit pleasure of transgression or the pleasure in submission and in the pleasing of others. Jones (2000) commented on her own desire, "Via perfect writing, I desired to deliver the perfect mind to my teachers. The predictable and painstakingly even shape of my words signaled my willingness to conform, to be controlled, which pleasured my teachers" (p. 153). Less obvious, the act of handwriting itself can be seen to offer a kind of sensual pleasure:

> The feel of the clean white sheet of paper, beneath one's flattened fingers, the faint chemical smell which it emits, the thrill of being the first to mark its virgin expanse, the flow of ink which follows the movement of the pen's tip. Traces of one's own body on the page. (Jones, 2000, p. 152)

Surely this is the pleasure young children and teens experience with their new and colorful pencils, pens, markers, and scribblers at the onset of the school year.

Even in these days of the printed rather than handwritten text, the clean and distant perfection of the typed page offers a kind of pleasure in the precise, hygienic look of the page. Certainly, the student body almost seems to disappear with word processing although its traces to the discerning teacher may be read it in the choices in formatting and the quality of the printing. Similarly in distance education student and teachers' bodies may also appear to disappear but oddly enough Eros and pleasure with virtual bodies continue as bodies are read and written online. Bodies are created and recreated online without any necessary reference to the physical body. The pleasure in reinventing the self outside of the limits of the signification placed on the actual body can be freeing, although how one chooses to reproduce and re-represent the body online still relies on discursive formations at hand.

Pleasure and Eros can be seen to organize and school the literate virtual and material body; pleasure, Eros, and other emotional responses are themselves schooled. As suggested previously, the body taught to read, write, and respond in particular ways to textual content and form. The mindful bodies of students are schooled to produce the authorized readings of texts, or at least a range of authorized meanings. In this Roger Simon (1992) reminded us that "schools are tantamount to 'dream machines,' sets of social, textual, and visual practices intended to provoke the production of meanings and desires that can affect people's sense of their future identities and possibilities" (p. 40). Such dream machines provide what can be imagined as possible. The social, textual, and visual practices of school literacy that discipline bodies and minds, dreams and realities can, as feminist and postcolonial literary scholarship has noted, serve to delimit the horizon of possibilities for minorities and female students and more generally all students as they learn to read and write and respond to bodies in hegemonic ways.

How we learn to mark or not the bodies represented in text and the body of reader has enormous implications on individuals and on the collective psyche. Toni Morrison, for example, commented on how the 400-year-old presence of African and African American bodies in America and more particularly in American literature has been actively ignored. She marvels at how readers nonacademic and academic alike have rendered insignificant African American literature: "What is fascinating, however, is to observe how their lavish exploration of literature manages not to see meaning in the thunderous, theatrical presence of black surrogacy—an informing, stabilizing and disturbing element—in the literature they do study" (1992, p. 13). Having learning to read and respond in particular ways, to mark and unmark bodies, readers become rooted intellectually and emotionally to interpretations of the bodies in text and in life, including one's own.

Not only is one's relation to his or her body lived out through the mediation of discourse, but that body is itself coerced and molded by both representation and signification. Discursive bodies learn on and mold real bodies in complex and manifold ways. But as mentioned earlier, the body can resist, and thus so can literate body, however regulated and schooled it might be. Whatever the dialectic between the body-as-flesh and the body-as-text, it requires the deep and abiding attention of advocacy researchers.

### The Body in Advocacy Research in Literacy Education

Attending to the scholarship concerning the body-in-text and the body-in-flesh, the inscribed body and lived body, and the material and the cyborg body would seem to offer some potent insights for those who work in literacy education committed to a social justice agenda. First it would seem that such scholarship demands that advocacy work refuse the split between mind and body and instead attend to the "mindful bodies" in our classrooms and in our research. Advocacy work in literacy education is always then a cognitive–emotional, mind–body experience. At the very least it is crucial to remember that the affective makes us care about things (Probyn, 2004). Thus teacher's and learners, and researcher's, pleasure and Eros and other bodily responses are embedded in advocacy work in literacy and need to be considered even as such feelings defy control. Such a focus leads to questions about the ways in which and how bodies are being read in text, how bodies defy their inscription in text, how bodily cognitive pleasure and desire is schooled and regulated even in our most liberatory pedagogical efforts.

Attending to the particularities of "mindful bodies" of students and teachers may prevent the assumption of universal and predictable effects and also the reification of teaching and learning strategies. Indeed this is what Freire warned us about in his refusal to name and specify his own pedagogical methods for others to follow. Attending to "mindful" bodies focuses pedagogical concern on teachers, learners and communities, and on their local particularities and situated histories that, marked on the body, prevent routinized practice. In addition to methodological concerns, such attention may allow greater sophistication in analyzing the myriad of ways in which mindful bodies live in the present moment, as well as understanding the monotonous regularity in which oppression resinscribes itself in bodies over time and space.

But even attending to such particularities, research and pedagogy liberatory or otherwise cannot be entirely predictable in its effects because notions of pleasure, Eros, and other emotions and affects are embedded in how we read the word and world, and troubles even our most innocent efforts. Thus, to espouse a liberatory agenda is to embark on a pedagogy journey that is, in Deborah Britzman's words, "scary." "More often than not, things do not go according to plan: objectives reappear as too simple, too complicated, or get lost; concepts become glossed over, require long detours, or go awry. ... In short, pedagogy is filled with surprises, involuntary returns, and unanticipated twists" (1991, p. 60). Moreover, to acknowledge the body and the affective is to be reminded that, in any pedagogy journey, there is "dynamite aboard."[1] Such acknowledgment is important, as Peter McLaren (1990) reminded us that

> Yet it is necessary to acknowledge the capacity of individuals to at least partially recognize the constitution of the self, is what makes lib-

eration possible. ... It is also a precondition for refleshment, or forming a space of desire where we can assume self-consciously and critically new modes of subjectivity hospitable to a praxis of self and social empowerment. We must never forget that we can act in ways other than we do. (p. 163)

We believe it is crucial to consider the body as lived in advocacy research and to analyze how body and its pleasures are shaped in text, in practice, and in and by literacy research: more succinctly, how advocacy in literacy education—reading the word and world—affects the lived–textual body. This refers to learners and teachers and of course to those who conduct advocacy research and scholarship.

## The Bodies of Advocacy Researchers and Educators

The theorizing of Giles Deleuze (1992) suggests that the body is not a monolithic entity, but composed of an infinite number of particles, continually arranged and rearranged, and affecting and affected by the particles of other bodies. It is thus important for advocacy researchers to consider not only the material and affective history of learners and teachers, but their own bodies, and in doing so to consider their bodies in relation to other bodies. It is to consider the bits and pieces of particular bodies—that is, the movements, gestures, behaviors, emotional expressions, locations, and reactions that connect or don't connect with learners and others. In the case of advocacy work it may be to undo any totality of the advocacy researcher and educator to allow for reconnection with others in text or in person in the name of forwarding social justice, equity, and compassionate in democratic life. It is to fragment and pluralize the body–self, and so it is to "risk the self" as Deborah Britzman (1995) reminded us. But this is not to give *up* the body—to be bodiless—nor is it to give *over* the body—to surrender it—but instead to acknowledge it, insist on it, and engage its complexities and particularities and the "circuits of affect" that open connections (and not) with other bodies in literacy education without hiding behind abstraction (Probyn, 2004). We would add that this applies not only to the bodies of individual advocacy researchers and educators, but to the field generally, that is to the "body" of advocacy research and researchers that currently exists.

This is something we have only begun to think about in relation to this text and the body of research we describe.

### Advocacy, Desire, and The Body of Citizenship

Ursula Kelly (1997) concluded her text, *Schooling Desire*, stating that "The precise location of hope within the erotic character of pedagogy is in the use of that energy to promote collective good" (p. 137). Early in her book, oddly enough, she attached this idea to citizenship:

> If it is the (often unstated) purpose of schooling to mold and meld citizen desire, I would argue that it is the project of a radical pedagogy not only to identify this process, but to provide the opportunity to address the collective and often contradictory investments that are identity and the particular embodiment of identity-as-desire as constitutive engagements with/in the social. (Kelly, 1997, pp. 39–40)

The molding and melding of citizen desire and identity in the process of literacy education in context of American democracy is considered in the final chapter of this text. Over the course of completing this book, it has become our belief that advocacy research and scholarship ultimately finds higher ground in these troubled days when firmly embedded in the discourse of democracy, democratic schooling and its production of the literate body, so it's there we go.

# 8

## Literacy, Democracy, and Freedom

*A democracy is more than a form of government;*
*it is primarily a mode of associated living,*
*of conjoint and communicated experience*

John Dewey (1916)

*The progressive educator must always be moving*
*out on his or her own,*
*continually reinventing me and reinventing*
*what it means to be democratic*
*in his or her own specific cultural and historical context*

Paulo Freire (1997)

*Literacy must be part of a discourse*
*that seeks to realize the democratic tenets*
*of freedom and justice for all.*

Rebecca Powell (1999)

The relationship of democracy and freedom to literacy has been long accepted but, with odd exception, rarely explored. It has been easy to agree with the Jeffersonian notion that a citizen who can engage in the literacy practices of the nation secures a stronger democracy and greater freedom. But such easy agreement belies the contractions, limitations, and ambiguity that underlie the terms *democracy*, *freedom*, and *literacy* and their connection. Patrick Shannon (2001) noted that, although most educators have agreed the terms are linked, "many define democracy, the state and freedom differently and theorize language and its roles accordingly" (p. 10). Moreover he stated that, "language educators often confront these links [between democracy, freedom and literacy] as hostile contradictions rather than working dialectics" (p. 10). For literacy educators deeply committed to issues of social justice and equity, this is all the more true. In part this is because freedom, democracy, and literacy have a commonsensical, taken-for-granted, apple-pie-like quality to them that camouflages the philosophical or ideological contradictions, tensions, and practical difficulties of realizing democracy and freedom in literacy education and in society in general.

Freedom is particularly difficult in this regard. Isaiah Berlin (1958/1970) wrote that, "Like happiness and goodness, like nature and reality, the meaning of this term is so porous that there is little interpretation that it seems able to resist" (p. 6). Colin Lankshear (1997) claimed that "[E]veryday usage of freedom is prone to ... sometimes being unduly vague and ambiguous, and at other times connoting too much ... freedom has been used to name diverse and often incompatible educational and sociopolitical ideals and practices" (p. 64). Similarly, Maxine Greene (1988) suggested that there is both absolute emptiness and yet absolute power attached to the term:

> The United States presents itself as the apostle of freedom. It resides in our tradition, the world is told. It lies at the core of the American dream ... [yet, it] is a taken-for-granted possession. Born into it, the young are expected to defend it, whether or not it means anything in their personal lives. Their government, in the meantime, making its own selective determinations, describes itself as the guarantor of freedom everywhere. (p. 26)

The idea of democracy is also difficult. Although often touted as a single and unified concept, it carries considerably ambiguity and plurality. Frank Cunningham, in his text *Theories of Democracy* (2002), cited five forms of democracy: liberal democracy, radical democracy, participatory democracy, deliberative democracy, and democratic pragmatism; and he provided the example of a Chinese student who, having risked his life in the Tiananmen Square, where some of his friends had lost theirs in the cause of democracy, notes, "neither he nor they could claim to know just what democracy is" (p. 2). J. Baecler (1995), among many scholars, commented,

> [I]t is difficult to reach a common understanding of what the word means. Democracy is a free regime? Undoubtedly. But what is freedom? A regime of equality? Perhaps. But how many crimes have been committed in the name of equality? A regime of majority rule? And suppose the majority favours absurdities and outrageous acts? And, to begin with, is democracy a political regime, a form of social organisation, a state of mind or a set of behaviour patterns? Or is it all of them and still more? (in Davies, 2000, p. 279)

In her text *Pedagogy, Democracy and Feminism: Rethinking the Public sphere*, Adriana Hernandez (1997) maintained that

> Democracy through the times, has been and still is the discourse that sets the terms for critique of current affairs and institutional orders and creates the basis for change. Although, we should agree, that language of democracy is anything but uniform. Democracy carriers the most diverse and conflicting meanings and concepts which are not always liberating enough, and sometimes not liberating at all. (p. 31)

Carole Edelsky (2004) reminded us that democracy during the Mc-Carthy era looked considerably "different and meant something different from how it looked and what it meant in the Sixties" (p. 8). Moreover, we would add that democracy has come to mean something quite different again in these "New Times" (Luke & Elkins, 1998).

In the 21st century, radical and progressive educators, among many others, have become increasingly alarmed by the ways in which democracy has been defined and aligned with corporate culture and commercial values. Henry Giroux (2003) argued that although the important legacy of public education has been

> to provide students with the critical capacities, the knowledge, and the values to become active citizens striving to realize a vibrant democratic society ... this role is facing an unprecedented attack from the proponents of market ideology who strongly advocate the unparalleled expansion of the corporate culture. (p. 119)

He is particularly appalled by the link between consumer and citizen:

[a]lthough many observers recognize that market culture exercises a powerful role in shaping identities, it still comes as a shock when an increasing number of young people, when asked to provide a definition of democracy, answer by referring to "the freedom to buy and consume whatever they wish, without government restriction." (Giroux, 2003, p. 120)

Michael Apple (2000) noted that the American citizen is often equated with the American consumer, and freedom is redefined as a set of consumption practices but that this couplet has a long history. In the Canadian context, Ken Osborne wrote that "there is a tension between the demands of democracy and the imperatives of capitalism, that the present and future of democracy are at risk, and that education has some part to play in ensuring its survival" (2001, p. 29). However, Nadine Dolby (2003) reminded us that "consumption is not necessarily and inherently a private practice with no radical democratic possibilities. Individuals and communities have been mobilized as citizens within the framework of consumption, and consumption practices have changed the spaces of democracy" (p. 271). She offered examples of consumer boycotts that have affected corporate behavior and corporate responsibility in a democratic life.

Despite its complexity and importance, the concept and practice of democracy has suffered from a certain level of neglect in the field of education. In his text, *Living Dangerously: Multiculturalism and the Politics of Difference*, Giroux (1993) claimed there has been little discussion about educating for democratic life:

The retreat from democracy is also evident in the absence of serous talk about how as a nation we might educate future generations in the language and practice of moral compassion, critical agency, and the utopian horizons of social imagination. The discourse of leadership appears trapped in a vocabulary in which the estimate of a good society is expressed in indices that measure markets, defence systems, and the Gross National Product. Missing in this discourse is a vocabulary for talking about and creating democratic public cultures and communities that are attentive to the problems of homelessness, hunger, censorship, media manipulation, and the rampant individualism and greed that ... has become the hallmark of the last decade. (p. 11)

Both then and now Giroux calls for a renewed focus on democracy and democratic schooling.

Educators, families and community members need to reinvigorate the language, social relations, and politics of schooling. We must analyze how power shapes knowledge, how teaching broader social values provides safeguards against turning citizenship skills into workplace-training skills, and how schooling can help students reconcile the seemingly opposing needs of freedom and solidarity. (2003, pp. 122–123)

Similarly, Greg Dimitriadis and Dennis Carlson in their text, *Promises to Keep: Cultural Studies, Democratic Education and Public Life* (2003), suggested it is time to "give new meaning to the promise of democratic education and public life" which they believe lies in a "new progressivism" (p. 3). In these times when we are in the sway of what Carol Edelsky (2004) among others have called an "anti-democratic dynamic" with voting participation rates falling, increasing inequality of wealth, and increasing punishment for dissent, she argued there is a need to explicitly teach democracy: "to develop a genuine democracy rather than what now masquerades as such, it is urgent to very deliberately teach it."

Public education has always been at the center of the democratic project and in particular with liberal-democratic theory since the time of Jean-Jacques Rousseau, John Locke, and John Stuart Mill, and certainly with Thomas Jefferson (Miron & Dhillon, 2004). Educating the citizen to participate fully in the public space of democracy, knowing their rights and obligations, ensures the survival of the democratic state and its freedoms. Then and now the call for a stronger democracy has meant reform of democratic education and inevitably this has entailed literacy education. As noted by Harvey Graff (1987), literacy and democracy has tightly aligned since the development of Athenian democracy. Graff noted that, in ancient Greece, "the Western tradition of an educated electorate, schooling in literacy as preparation for citizenship, and the equation of literacy and democracy were born" (p. 23). Centuries later, literacy, as will be discussed, lay at the center of the emerging democracies in America and elsewhere, and has continued to do so, but the nature of that connection and the politics of literacy education more generally shifts and changes according to the times and circumstances.

As cited throughout this text, those radical and progressive educators whose work in literacy education explicitly involves advocacy research have been particularly critical of contemporary literacy education and its role in democratic life. Rebecca Powell (1999) suggested "that literacy and language instruction in schools has often failed to provide students with the communicative competence required for true democratic participation" (p. 64). To create a more powerful democracy, she like others argued for a more critical and moral literacy. Powell stated, the "discourse promoted through literacy instruction ought to be a moral discourse—one that strives to overcome prejudice, to defy elitism and to develop a more equitable and compassionate society" (p. 59).

The remainder of this chapter offers a more detailed discussion of the historical and contemporary discourses that have named and linked the concepts of democracy, freedom, and literacy education. In addition, the chapter traces the contemporary ways in which this connection has been articulated in the praxis of social advocacy work in literacy education; it speculates on the strategic possibilities of how this work may yet be strengthened in efforts to contribute to the revisioning and strengthening of democratic education in literacy research and practice committed to social justice. This chapter serves as a conclusion to this text for it leads us to what we believe is higher ground on which advocacy research and practice in literacy education can be supported and expanded in light of the enormous challenges of the 21st century.

### FREEDOM IN DEMOCRACY: DEMOCRACY IN FREEDOM

Democracy is, as Greg Dimitriadis and Dennis Carlson described, "a moving target, an unfinished project, open to re-visioning, with no original, authentic fixed or final or unified meaning" (2003, p. 7) and therefore any effort to find some pure and original meaning or some natural connection between democracy, freedom, and literacy, is misguided. And we make no such effort. But at any historical moment, *democracy, freedom*, or any other term has a kind of horizon of meaning or meanings, contingent as that might be, that is deployed in ways that may or may not expand human potential and social possibility. Making visible this horizon of meaning and its legacy would seem an important step in understanding and strengthening the role advocacy research might play in creating stronger literacy education and ultimately a more democratic society.

Historically it is evident that in much of the western world democracy as a political system takes its legacy from ancient Greek philosophy, infused with the political assumptions and beliefs of the Enlightenment, and, at the time of the American independence, a growing belief in the power of science and capitalism as a means to understand and organize social life. At the time of the American Revolution after centuries of bloody European civil and religious wars, governing institutions were seen as absolutely necessary to master the passions and control the propensity of mankind toward mutual animosities and the forming of factions around social difference (i.e., religion, race, class, gender, region, nation, language). Government, by regulating behavior, adjudicating conflicts and securing a notion of the "common good," would ensure social order, security, and prosperity. In exchange for the consent of citizens to state power and authority, the government was to defend and protect citizens' individual rights and freedoms. In effect the government "would guard the passions of individual for the sake of order and guard [or protect] the guardians for the sake of freedom" (Shannon, 2001, p. 11).

Such agreement was seen as contractual in nature, as Dimitriadis and Carlson (2003) commented,

> Aside from the Greek tradition of democracy as primarily a way of life organized around habits of civility, practices of freedom, and public dialogue, the promise of democracy has been linked in American culture to a liberal Enlightenment discourse of contractual rights. This discourse of democracy constructs democratic citizens as contractual subjects, whose consent to be governed is made contingent upon the state, in effect promising to protect their personal rights and freedoms through a system of laws and courts. (p. 6)

The rights and freedoms promised have included, among other things, the freedom of thought, speech, movement, and association, and the right of national citizens to be self-governing. Liberal and liberating at the time of the American Revolution, such a "contract" named citizens as subjects of their own duly elected government as opposed to a monarchy, dictatorship, or aristocracy. Free to choose those who would govern them, and assured of protection and fairness under the law, citizens, in exchange, had to acquiesce to the needs of society as a whole, that is to "the common good." Maximizing individual freedom and at the same time delimiting the freedom of the citizen to establish fairness, equality, and consent to the common good makes liberal democracy a difficult project. Ensuring individual freedom, but also collective unity and "common good," remains an underlying tension. And yet it was believed that, "[w]ithout freedom, the natural taming of the physical and social worlds through science and capitalism would be impossible, and without government [limiting freedom] science and capitalism would lead men to seek undue advantage over one another" (Shannon, 2001, p. 11).

One of the means of organizing such contradictory goals was to name and limit the areas in which the state held power in the lives and freedoms of its citizens. Liberal democracy delineates public and private spheres. In doing so it organizes citizenship and governmental authority in very particular ways by confining state authority to the public sphere. But even there, authority was to be minimal. It was assumed that "while there may be a need for laws this should remain limited, that there ought to exist a certain minimum area of personal freedom, which must on no account to be violated ... It follows that a frontier must be drawn between the area of private life and that of public authority" (Berlin, 1958/1970, p. 9).

The line between state authority and individual freedom, between private and public sphere, has been made and remade over time. As will be discussed, much of the late 19th and early 20th century saw increasing state involvement in what might be named the private sphere. But wherever the line was drawn, most conceptions of freedom or liberty concern the ability of the individual to make choices and act on them without coercion. Nell Noddings (1999), in describing liberal democratic societies, stated,

> it is not simply that citizens of such democracies are expected to make intelligent choices in voting, more important, they are left to their own guidance on a wide range of life choices ... What rightly concerns us is the maintenance of a form of government under which our right to

make choices is held sacred. The choice of where to live, with whom to associate, what sort of work to do, which professionals to consult, which merchants to patronize, how to spend our leisure time, how to worship, what to read … these choices we cherish. Voting is often little more than a powerful sign that we do cherish these choices. (p. 579)

Barriers to choice are therefore of crucial concern of any democratic government or citizen. These barriers can take several forms. Most formulations of freedom and its barriers have come to be understood along the lines offered by Isaiah Berlin in his famous 1958 essay "Two Concepts of Liberty." In his essay Berlin named and defined negative and positive liberty and, in the context of the Cold War, promoted negative freedom as the better of the two. Negative liberty consists of the absence of material obstacles to the exercise of individual choice: barriers that are external to the self. Such barriers might include physical force, laws, policies, and practices exerted by human beings that are overtly coercive and prevent or limit choice of others. Government needs to concern itself with eliminating such barriers, clearing the path for whatever choice may or may not be made by the individual. Positive freedom concerns the conditions necessary to take advantage of opportunities that negative freedom makes possible. It includes not only external barriers but also internal barriers such as one's fears, compulsions, will, and desire that frustrate choice. Negative freedom does not attend to the choices actually made by an individual, only that choices be available, whereas positive freedom attends to what is and is not chosen within a particular context.

Positive freedom demands the provision of conditions that individuals may not be able to create on their own. For example, "freedom of education" may be possible if legal restrictions that might prevent one from attending are removed (negative freedom), but this freedom rings hollow if a student cannot afford tuition, if a student is handicapped and there is no wheelchair accessibility to the school, or if a fear of failing prevents them from acting on this freedom (positive freedom). As outlined by Nancy Hirschmann (2003) negative freedom assumes an autonomous, self-reliant individual, positive freedom, posits a more communal and contextual sense of self.

Whether freedom is negative or positive, a democratically elected government is not absolutely necessary to establish and secure such freedoms. A benevolent dictator may work to ensure freedom for citizens. What distinguishes choice in a democracy surely must be the freedom to choose the government of the day. In colonial America there was a degree of scepticism about ability of "the people" (i.e., White, male, propertied landed yeoman) to do so, that is, to act on their freedom to choose their government, intelligently and rationally. Indeed popular democracy created a great unease in colonial America: an unease that some say continues to this day. Some would argue that giving power to the masses was pure folly; as Noam Chomsky (2000) writes, "Fear of democracy is deeply entrenched. Alexander Hamilton put it clearly when he described the people as a 'great beast' from which governing elites have to be protected" (p. 44). Most at the time of colonial America accepted the argument that, if the people were to participate in self-rule, they had to be qualified to do so, that is, to use their freedom to make well-informed, rational choices. The ability to read and write and to think rationally was considered crucial to making such choices.

### Literacy Education and Democracy

Public education would provide such literacy; however, this did not mean the elimination of social strata. Thomas Jefferson ensured that the fundamentals of language education, arithmetic, and history would be offered for 3 years of publicly supported primary schooling to improve the minds of citizens "in order to enable them to follow the arguments presented by those in authority" (Shannon, 2001, p. 11). A minority of students would be selected to continue their education at their families' expense to become low-level administrators and civil servants, teachers, and (a smaller number yet) lawmakers. Jefferson's notion was "to supply the new country 'with a natural aristocracy,' who were selected for their powers of rationality and a literate citizenry whose White male members of some means were able to vote" (p. 12). Women, slaves, and indigenous people were not included in the category of citizen and, although some might receive private education or training, public education was denied to them and to all relegated to the private sphere. The role of the citizen was defined exclusively in relation to the public sphere and to rationality: a category that discursively and materially excluded all but the White, propertied, male populace (Dillabough & Arnot, 2000).

Although formal public schooling figured strongly in the democratic formations of colonial America, it was not a strong feature of Athenian democracy. There democracy was understood as more than "a process of decision making and self-governance"; it was seen as "a way of living together in which people are always engaged in a form of self-education through public dialogue, debate, questioning their beliefs and stay open to new ways of thinking about what is good and just" (Carlson & Dimitriadis, 2003, p. 5). Harvey Graff in his classic text *The Legacies of Literacy* (1987) chronicled a form of primary schooling in the rudiments of reading, writing, and arithmetic in Athens, but similarly indicated that more faith was placed in the family and the metropolis—the public sphere of debate and discussion as an ongoing means of molding and educating the democratic citizen. Nonetheless, the alignment between formal literacy education and democracy would begin to take root.

Literacy education in Athens and later in colonial American depended heavily on transmission methods. It emphasized rote learning, repetition, and recitation, as students were "slowing taught their letters first, then the syllables and words, before they confronted texts" (Graff, 1987, p. 25). Literacy involved only the abilities to decode and encode text such that one could be informed in making political choices. In this, literacy was viewed as a neutral skill that would allow for access to information and political argument thus ensuring freedom of choice and an effective and strong democracy. Freedom was aligned with rationality and literacy and linked with particular bodies such that White masculinity subsumed rationality, autonomy and knowledge, and in public sphere, citizenship.

Throughout but certainly by the turn of the 18th century, the aims of public schooling also included the development of moral and democratic character:

A law-abiding, virtuous and national citizenry who could read the augments put forth by the natural aristocracy of the republic would free themselves to vote and to participate in the economy as they found possible. Schools provided the methods and contents to develop these patriotic, moral, and economic habits of rational action and mind. (Shannon, 2001, p. 14)

In developing the values, desires, and preferences for a democratic citizen, schools were shaping citizens for democratic society. Public schooling and in particular literacy education would ensure the preservation of freedom and the democratic state by developing moral and rational citizens. This particular rendering of literacy, democracy, and freedom and their connection has not disappeared but has and continues to be deployed in arguing for reforms to schooling and specifically literacy education. However, alternative and more expanded notions of democracy, liberty, and literacy education began to gain prominence in America and elsewhere in the 19th and early 20th century.

## Democracy, Progressivism, and Literacy

Through the 19th and 20th centuries, democracy, freedom, and public schooling took on wider meanings and purposes with the demands for greater participation of women and others in social and political life, by the increasing numbers of immigrants, in particular non-Anglo Saxon immigrants coming to North America, and by an economy shifting rapidly from agrarian to industrial. Government institutions took on greater responsibility to address the challenges these demands and shifts presented. However, democracy itself may have also contributed to change. Ken Osborne noted that the increased governmental involvement in citizens' private and public lives may have happened regardless of the social and economic challenges of the time. He (2001) wrote,

> democratic government was no longer confined if it ever really was to matters of high policy, international trade and relations, law and order, and the like. It now includes and indeed is dominated by far more immediate and personal concerns: sewage and sanitation, clean water, public health, pensions, housing, child-rearing, roads and land use, and the other aspects of people's daily lives, as a direct result "of the democratization of politics, whereby so-called ordinary people, once they had the right to vote, pressed for action to deal with their needs and priorities" (p. 220).

In addition it was argued convincingly by many, including British scholar T. H. Marshall, "that in order to exercise political and civil rights, citizens had to be accorded basic social rights. Without a safety net that provided food, shelter, clothing, medical care, and education for everyone, citizenship was not equally available" (Dolby, 2003, p. 268). For people to participate in democratic life, basic resources, or at least equal opportunity to secure such resources had to be assured.

The scope of government involvement in the private and public sphere expanded, and rather than protecting citizens *from* governmental interference to protect individual freedom, freedom was viewed by some as secured *by* governmental involvement. With the enfranchisement of women and the increasing number of minorities and immigrants, and an ongoing concern with social class, this meant in part that the state was seen as responsible for ensuring minority rights and greater egalitarianism. Thus, rather than merely a set of political arrangements, comprising whatever institutions were thought necessary to turn the idea of self-rule into a reality, democracy and liberty were expanded to include equity and social justice, so that, "democracy was seen, at least on the left, as including a concern for social justice—hence, of course, the term 'social democracy' which a hundred years ago enjoyed a far more radical connotation than it has today" (Osborne, 2001, p. 33).

Providing quality education to all became central to educational reform in the face of the often elite and undemocratic nature of 18th and 19th century schooling. In 1884, Francis Wayland Parker, among others, complained that American public schools served the aristocracy rather than the masses, and asserted that indeed "the myths of education as the means to social, economic, and political advancement were the primary means by which the gaps between the society's have and have nots were maintained" (quoted in Shannon, 2001, p. 15). The expanded expectations of education in a democracy are evident in Parker's comments. Not only was democratic education to provide an electorate that could understand and vote in an informed and rational manner, but to offer to all in a democracy a fair and equal opportunity to develop their potential.

Increasing democracy was understood as more than a political structure that assured each citizen the vote—liberal democracy—it was also understood as "a way of life" (Dewey, 1916), as "post-liberal democracy" (Bowles & Ginitis, 1986), and as "popular democracy" (Engel, 2000), among other terms. Carol Edelsky (2004) referred to what she names as a "living democracy," and suggests these newer conceptions hold in common three basic premises: the equal opportunity to develop potential, having a voice in decisions that have society-wide consequences, and greater equity in resource distribution. As mentioned earlier, schools including literacy programs were viewed as crucial to providing greater equity in resource distribution by providing the means for all individuals to improve themselves and partake in democratic life and prosperity.

In addition, many progressives including Dewey suggested that schools themselves needed to operate as a living example of democracy. Although students would not have the complete freedom to, for example, choose their teachers, as much as possible school life should reflect democratic values and structures. Lynn Davies (2000) spoke to this, suggesting that,

> The key components of democracy—and thus a democratic school— would be participation, legitimacy, accountability and respect for human rights ... A parallel set of tenets for democracy would be transparency, participation and challenge, that is, a system where: the ways of operating are open and clear to everyone, and those in power are accountable; there are mechanisms for people to participate in decisions on matters that affect them; and, the organisation is continuously open to criticism and change through legitimised formal and informal processes of challenge, such as opposition parties or a free press. (p. 289)

School structures that ensure transparency, participation, and critique are important but so is the specific content and methods of everyday lessons. Basic literacy offered in traditional schools was necessary but insufficient to meet the needs of democratic life, but so too were progressive efforts, and Dewey "worried that expanding literary skills without also expanding critical skills might actually undermine democracy. He recognized that the new mass media were creating an era of 'information-overload.' In such and environment democratic decision-making faces a new threat, tyranny through propaganda" (Riley & Welchman, 2003, p. 106). To be free from undue influence, to frame purposes and directions, and to participate in public projects citizens needed to be independent, self-motivated, critical thinkers who actively and collectively pursued knowledge, working for the improvement of democratic life.

In this "Dewey envisioned the individual as a potential creator or new knowledge in an educational contexts as the means by which a nation advances itself. In fact he viewed the creation of new knowledge to be a responsibility of the individual to the Nation by participating in its progress" (Hasbrook, 2002, p. 61). Citizens in Dewey's democracy required an education that would promote the cooperative development, testing, and refinement of new ideas and institutions for the good of society. His model of schooling is that of the open, collaborative scientific community. Therefore, citizens required the "intellectual, social and communicative virtues essential to collective, cooperative inquiry" (Riley & Welchman, 2003, p. 96). In part this meant school lessons that enhanced interaction across social and class divisions, and developed a more critical, active, and interactive literacy for the masses than had ever been envisioned by colonial America.

Louise Rosenblatt, Dewey's contemporary and collaborator, has done much to expand on the connection between the democratic nature of schooling and literacy, more specifically literary study. Rosenblatt named the political nature of literacy/literature study early in here career. In 1938 she stated that "[t]he study of literature can have a very real, and even central, relation to the points of growth in the social and cultural life of a democracy" (p. v). She and others who have followed her footsteps have insisted on the centrality of the personal responses of individual readers to text. In doing so, she offered students less authoritarian literary lessons that allowed readers to find their own way into texts. As noted by John Willinsky (1991), for Rosenblatt, "This was literature for a liberal democracy with her increasing stress on an economy of freely engaged transaction with the text" (p. 116). In her early scholarship individual responses were understood and organized within a larger social context of reading and readers—a transaction between the reader, text, and the larger social world. Although beginning with the individual response, Rosenblatt's approach connected readers and citizens in sharing individual literary responses. Rosenblatt argued that such an approach broadened one's life experience and foster the understanding of and empathy for others that democratic life demanded. Rosenblatt also claimed in sharing and discussing literary responses, readers could develop a more critical attitude toward accepted opinion and undue influence, which was also necessary for democratic life. In 1990, Rosenblatt, speaking of literary study in relation to contemporary problems with democracy, reiterated the value of her approach. In words reminiscent of Dewey nearly 60 years earlier, she wrote, "The political indifference of many of our citizens, their acceptance of appeals to narrow personal interests, and their vulnerability to the influence of the media are important symptoms [of problems with democracy]," and she stated,

> I can reaffirm the belief uttered so many years ago. We teachers of language and literature have a crucial role to play as educators and citizens. We phrase our goals as fostering the growth of the capacity for personally meaningful, self-critical literary experience. The educational process that achieves this aim most effectively will serve a broader purpose, the nurturing of men and women capable of building a fully democratic society. (1990, p. 107)

The literacy promoted by Rosenblatt and Dewey attempted to enfranchise more students, and by creating the "mental habits" and dispositions for working critically and collectively, to create citizens who could and would participate in the improvement of democratic life—to participate in what today might be named as "deliberate democracy." Deliberate democracy "refers to a coming together to think through learn from, and become part of the political process" to create a better world (Willinsky, 2000, p. 205). The goal of creating a better world is key. In this, the aim of democracy and for democratic schooling is not deliberation for sake of deliberation, or for participation for the sake of participation. Pedagogy and for that matter democracy itself are to serve important ends, as Roger Simon (2001) in speaking about a critical "pedagogy of empowerment" reminds us:

> Without a vision for the future a pedagogy of empowerment is reduced to a method for participation which takes democracy as an end and not a means. There is no moral vision other than the instance on people having an equal claim to a place in the public arena. Of course this is extremely important, but without something more empowerment becomes an empty and abstract moral that is unable to call into question existing contradictions between human capacities and social forms. It provides us with no guidance as to what forms of knowing and learning might help enhance our chances of developing a just and

compassionate society when justice and compassion are so urgently required. (2001, p. 147)

Social improvement, and a moral vision, was for Dewey and the Progressives key to their understanding of the purposes of democracy, democratic schooling, and literacy lessons. Social equity and freedom were central themes. As noted by Noam Chomsky (2000), Dewey believed that reforming education could lead the way to a society in which "the ultimate aim of production is not production of goods but the production of free human beings associated with one another on terms of equality" (p. 37). Evidently even freedom was a means rather than a goal in Dewey's writing. In his 1938 text, *Experience and Education*, Dewey commented,

There can be no greater mistake, however, than to think of such freedom as an end in itself ... For freedom from restriction is to be prized only as a means to a freedom which is power: power to frame purposes, to judge wisely, to evaluate desires by the consequences which will result from acting upon them; power to select and order means to carry chosen ends into operation. (p. 41)

Freedom was key to the creation of knowledge and to the potential transformation and improvement of democratic life.

There is much that those committed to advocacy work in literacy education have and can take from Dewey, Rosenblatt, and other early progressives. Their notions of democracy, freedom, education, and literacy continue to inform advocacy efforts. However, continuing economic and social inequalities locally and globally, dramatic technological change, philosophical disenchantment, and political disenchantment have lead to a desire among at least some for a more radical democracy and a more radical literacy education that might better meet the demands of the 21st century. In addition there has been ongoing critique from the left (and the right) of the progressive movement. For those on the left, the liberalism of Dewey and Rosenblatt has been seen as failing to make class conflict, gender, and racial inequalities sufficiently problematic to creative viable social change (Freire & Macedo, 1987). Certainly Dewey emphasized the building of democratic community through critical inquiry, interaction, empathy, and a sense of the common good, and he would also stress unity and civility in social and political life. Writing during the Russian Revolution and First World War, he would write of the importance of an education that provides the "habits of mind which secure social changes without introducing disorder" (1916, p. 99).

Melissa Hasbrook (2002) suggested that Dewey was too unable to confront social difference:

> Dewey advocated harmony for the sake of unity. As he linked progress with the improvement of "group habits," his intent to overcome differences was not about confronting differences within educational sites. For example addressing what teacher about "other nations," Dewey promoted a focus upon "commonalities." (p. 62)

Although Hasbrook may be overstating Dewey's intent to "overcome difference," since Dewey did, after all, insist that critical inquiry and dissent were important to democracy, radical thought in the late 20th century has placed greater emphasis on radical and incommensurate difference in the democratic collective. In general there has been a more complicated, less individualistic understanding of freedom, and on a more politically explicit and potentially potent literacy education articulated in these times than that offered by the early progressives.

## DEMOCRACY AND FREEDOM
## AS RADICAL DIFFERENCE IN A RADICAL COMMUNITY

As discussed at the outset of this chapter, radical educators and activists have noted that talk of democracy and democratic life was strangely absent in the discussions of schooling through much of the last part of 20th century. Many have voiced concern about the ways in which corporate interests have, in the vacuum, been aligning notions of democracy and democratic schooling with consumerism and the ethos of late capitalism. Until very recently the question of what would constitute democratic education has evidently been important only for philosophers of education (Riley & Welchman, 2003). Particularly after the events of 9/11, many have called for public discussions: Roger Simon (2001) wrote,

> Surely it is time to re-open public discussion about the aims of education to ensure that our current policies and practices are consistent with the core qualities of democracy; democracy not narrowly de-

fined as a form of government, but as Dewey characterized it—as a way of life, as an ethical conception, and hence always about the democracy still to come. If this sounds utopian, so be it. (p. 32)

Some have begun to answer these calls, utopian or otherwise, but as Westheimer and Kahne (2003) have noted, "what has most strongly characterized recent discussions of democracy and education—in particular those that followed the attacks on the World Trade Centre and the Pentagon—has been a striking lack of consensus about what democracy requires of citizens and of schools" (pp. 9–10). Although acknowledging the need for at least a provisional path forward, the fact that there has been a lack of consensus is hardly unexpected. In part this may be a consequence of the shock, alarm and confusion brought on by 9/11, but it is perhaps also an inevitable result of democratic life itself in these postmodern times.

Radical social, and postmodern thought, with its emphasis on difference and on social power, rejects the notions of a single, universal truth and thus that a unified popular will or absolute consensus is possible or for that matter even desirable. Such thought helps support the notion that dissent and difference are not problematic in a democracy but constitute its very foundation. Chantel Mouffe, a leading intellectual on democratic life, pointed out,

We must accept the inevitability of conflict and antagonism as fundamental and constitutive elements of political life. Therefore, instead of perceiving those traits as problematic, as an obstacle to a movement of total stability and homogeneity, they should be perceived as the healthy traits that allow for constant transformation and prevent that movement of stability as a menace to the liberties of the members of society that do not coincide with what the "general will" at a certain historical moment might be ... In this way liberal democracy seems to me to be able to offer fundamental elements for a discourse of radical and pluralistic democracy that articles at the same time equality and difference, the individual and the social, the political and the ethical, all in an open process of negotiation. (1992, p. 31)

Even Dewey noted that, "rather than being impediments, disagreement and dissent are thus key aspects of participation, they are the engines of growth in a democracy" (Dewey, 1916, in Edelsky, 2004). A stronger emphasis on a pluralistic and radical democracy demands the fostering of and engagement with difference. It is a democracy that is, by its very nature, noisy. The many voices, many perspectives that can and should fuel democracy suggests a more active democratic citizen than the one limited to voting in electoral process as traditional constituted in liberal discourse. This radical, pluralistic version of democracy recognizes many sites of democratic activity. In comparing liberal with radical democracy, Nadine Dolby (2003) noted,

> Liberal democracy ... is a very slow process of change, and if citizens hope for their actions to have an effect, they must curtail those actions to a narrow band of electoral activities ... Radical democratic theories, in contrast to the liberal theories ... explore the idea that electoral politics is not the only site of agency and power within society ... Instead many sites become potential loci of change and transformation, including people's small, often discounted, everyday acts. (p. 268)

Dolby speaks to popular culture as one of many political and pedagogical sites where people come to know intellectually and affectively society, both the self and collective, and she believes that it is a site where social and political change and transformation can occur.

The insistence on the noisy nature of a pluralistic and radical democracy—one that insists on and fosters many sites, many voices, and many perspectives—requires a space or site for listening to the collective, the "metropolis" if you will, and, of course, requires its citizens have the ability to hear the "other" on the other's own terms. Regarding a collective site, Maxine Greene, among others, speaks to the importance and value of public space. She wrote (1988),

> My concern is to find out what we can do to open such spaces where people speaking together and being together can discover what it signifies to incarnate and act upon values far too often taken for granted ... [where] we must intensify attentiveness to the concrete world around in all its ambiguity, with its dead ends and its open possibilities. And attending, as Dewey and Freire have helped us to see, is not merely contemplating. It is coming to know in ways that might bring about change.

She and Henry Giroux speak to the value of schools as sites for "coming to know" and rewriting democratic life in one's own life. Giroux

(2003) stated, "Educators must defend schools as essential to the life of the nation because schools are one of the few public spaces left where students can learn about and engage in the experience of democracy" (p. 123). Linda Darling-Hammond (1998) concurred: "if equality, humanity, and freedom are the promise of democracy, then education is the promise-keeper" (p. 79; see also Westheimer & Kahne, 2003, 2004; Kahne & Westheimer, 2003).

According to Maxine Greene and others collective public space in schools or elsewhere is crucial in finding and actualizing freedom. In this, she offers a counter discourse to the notion of negative freedom cited earlier in this chapter. As discussed earlier, negative freedom emphasizes the ability of individuals to pursue their own self-interests unfettered by social constrains, obligations, or governmental "interference." Although, as Nel Noddings (1999) suggested, this view of freedom is inherently American, it ultimately erodes our sense of responsibility for one another. In addition Charles Taylor indicated a danger of nihilism is that "the self which arrived at freedom by setting aside all external obstacles and impingements is characterless, and hence without defined purpose" (1985, p. 157). Maxine Greene offers a more generative (and generous) model of freedom. In her model freedom comes from and indeed is dependent social involvement. She stated "Freedom is made possible only when people come together ... in a life consciously lived in common" (1984, p. 80). Like Dewey, Greene spoke of collective democratic projects and maintains that "freedom shows itself or comes into being when individuals come together in a particular way, when they are authentically present to one another ... when they have a project they can mutually pursue" (p. 16). Meagan Morris (2000) explained further that

> Freedom for Greene, is freedom-in-community. Freedom has to do with "connectedness" or being together in community. Freedom means dialogue, "reinterpreting situations," and opening perspectives. Greene emphasizes that freedom is a dialectical movement between the individual's freedom and the freedom of others, between what is possible and what is not. (p. 130)

It is in community—in the dialectic between self and other—that new and alternative possibilities of thought and action are brought into being, where people are freed "to surpass the given and look at things as if they could be otherwise" (Greene, 1988, p. 3). Greene stated categorically that it is

> unthinking any longer for Americans to assert themselves to be "free" because they belong to a "free" country. Not only do we need to be continually empowered to choose ourselves, to create identities within a plurality; we need continually to make new promises and to act in our freedom to fulfil them, something we can never do meaningfully alone. (1988; p. 51)

Freedom viewed in this way is not found in an external world on an open plain, empty of people, where possibilities are created or found in personal psychology of isolated individuals, but instead is forged in the dense interaction of the self in the social environment. Greene is not the first or the only to speak of freedom in this way; many others including Freire spoke of such freedom.

However, there has been most recently some who have questioned the possibility of dialogue and "mutual projects" required by radical and progressive versions of democracy and its freedom-in-community. In Megan Boler's (2004) edited text *Democratic Dialogue in Education: Troubling Speech, Disturbing Silence*, various theorists address the question of whether inclusive democratic dialogue is possible in a society divided by power and privilege, where all voices do not carry the same weight. The difficulties are daunting as advocacy researchers and educators well know. Drawing on her experience teaching Maori and white students in New Zealand, Alison Jones' response is to question the entire enterprise of democratic dialogue or what she calls the "talking cure" to social inequalities and injustice. Jones (2004) stated,

> Dialogue is based, however cautiously it might be considered in a dominant group fantasy or romance about access to and unity with the other. This is the fantasy of a democracy based in consensus reached as a result of rational debates across different views and groups. It is a truly magnificent, if flawed, romantic ideal. (p. 62)

However critical Jones is, in the end she remains surprisingly optimistic that practical democratic work can be done without direct collective dialogue:

With more critical understanding of the complexities and contradictions inherent in apparently benign and progressive desires for dialogue in education, we might reduce our romantic expectations of dialogue, and set about working alongside and with each other in different ways. Dialogue, if it occurs, will most likely be a serendipitous by-product of that more oblique engagement. (2004, p. 66).

For Jones and others, the emphasis on dialogue can negate difference in the desire to find and secure unity and sameness, rather than engaging incommensurate difference however obliquely as we work toward a more equitable and democratic society.

The warnings of Jones and others about the project of engaging democratic dialogue are well founded, but, as suspect as such dialogue might be, it is necessary, as Barbara Houston (2004) noted: It is "the fundamental activity of democracy" and "it is hard to imagine how one might sustain democracy in its absence" (p. 106). Houston spoke to the need for democratic dialogue particularly that devoted to issues of social justice: "I support attempting democratic dialogue about matters of social injustice in education, making sure that the challenges of it and the obstacles it become part of the discussion" (p. 107). The difficulties (perhaps the impossibilities) of dialogue become, in her estimation, part of democratic talk, not a reason to withdraw from it.

Nancy Hirschmann (2003), in her text *The Subject of Liberty*, suggested the kind of analysis needed to inform our thinking and our dialogue in democratic life. Hirschmann focuses particularly on freedom, which she understands as the articulation and enactment of choice. Drawing on social constructivism, Hirschmann suggested that our choices are determined by our desires, preferences, beliefs, and values, which are produced, organized, and shaped by our individual and collective social identities, which are in turn produced in the social realm. She called for a close and detailed examination of the social and discursive contexts in which people live out their lives to understand the viable choices and actual freedoms available. If democracy is fundamentally about choice and freedom it is imperative for us to consider the social construction of choice:

If choice is key to freedom, then what is necessary to understanding freedom is an examination not only of the conditions in which choices are made but also of the construction of choice itself; what choices are available and why, what counts as choice, who counts as a chooser, how the choosing subject is created and shaped by social relations and practices … the processes of [an individual's] choice making must be situated in a larger social and discursive context for choices to have meaning. Indeed, such contexts are needed to make choices possible; they are the logical precondition for choice. (p. 202)

Peter McLaren (2000), drawing on the work of Iris Marion Young, also suggested the open and careful analysis of options and preferences in context:

In the age of global capitalism, when so-called democratic schooling has become a laughable appellation, Iris Marion Young's concept of communicative democracy can prove instructive. Democracy in Young's view is not simply about registering one's preferences in a vote, but about becoming critically reflexive about one's preferences. It entails a move from motivated self-interest to collective interest, through examining the social knowledge available in a context free of coercion (pp. 176–77).

Although there may be no discursive context free of coercion, nonetheless a move to collective democratic interests would seem to demand a critical and self-critical analysis of the social conditions, social contexts, and social knowledge available that creates who we are and what choices and freedoms are possible in efforts to expand the democratic project. This suggests a particular kind of literacy education, one that many advocacy researchers and educators are now engaged.

## LITERACY FOR A RADICAL DEMOCRACY

*How in a society like ours, a society of contesting interests*
*and submerged voices, an individualistic society,*
*a society still lacking an "in-between,"*
*can we educate for freedom?*
*And, in educating for freedom,*
*how can we create and maintain a common world?*

Maxine Greene, 1988, p. 116

Much has been suggested about the schooling and the literacy education required by a democratic society. From our perspective, schools need to foster participation and encourage, engage, even embrace the possibilities and tensions of commonality and difference. Conceiving democracy as a radical plurality, as fueled by difference and dissent, means that schools as public space must become sites for both the performance and analysis of social, cultural, and other forms of difference within the framework of democratic life. This is exciting but certainly not easy work. Greg Dimitriadis and Dennis Carlson (2003), in discussing school choice, addressed some of the tensions of acknowledging and sustaining difference, identity, and choice, but also the possibilities such work suggests:

> If we think of education as occurring in learning communities, in which individuals are inducted into particular discourses of self-production and meaning making, then it is clear that these communities must now be understood as speaking in diverse voices, as organized around affinity as least as much as geography. Thus, progressives often support some version of choice in public education, such as charter and magnet schools, which potentially allow marginalized groups to constitute themselves around empowering narratives of self-production and community. Of course this could also lead to an isolation of various affinity and identity groups and a failure to come together around any shared visions of democratic public life. Perhaps a better response among progressives would be to support heterogeneity within schools, with space allowed for the constitution of groups around difference and identity, and also for the crossing of borders and the construction of hybrid, nonessentialist identities ... Democratic communities of learning in the twenty-first century must be communities of difference without normalizing centers; and public education, we believe, must play a role in building and sustaining such communities. (pp. 23–24)

As suggested, public education must support and sustain "communities of difference without normalizing centers." Literacy education then must work to engage diversity without domesticating it. To help us get a sense of this, Dimitriadis and Carlson provide the common example of reading noncanonical popular texts concurrently with more

traditional literature, or of reading Eurocentric histories of American
along side histories written by those subjugated or silenced in dominant narratives, together with other discourses, "that bring into view
'the subaltern gaze on the eye of power, while simultaneously
problematizing the very construct of centre and periphery'" (McCarthy, in Dimitriadis & Carlson, 2003, p. 24).

This suggests the critical literacy that many advocacy workers are already engaging. It is a literacy that names and analyzes dominant and
subordinate forms of knowledge and their construction as hierarchical.
It is the critical literacy of Freire, McLaren, Giroux, and others that considers that all material and discursive contexts are constituted by and in
power relations and that insists on a schooling that both performs and in-
terrogates the world as it exists to pursue greater social justice. As noted
by Joel Spring (1994/1998), within this philosophy,

> the primary task of education it to help students understand the so-
> cial construction of knowledge in the framework of power ... in the
> search for methods of eliminating social injustice and decreasing in-
> equalities in power ... [and] gives people the ability to participate in
> a democratic state and the tools to equalize the distribution of
> power. (p. 27)

Of particular importance to literacy educators, as discussed elsewhere in this book, these tools, under the guise of postmodern/
poststructural thought and linguistic study, have come to include a critical approach to the constituting effects of language and discourse. As
Dennis Carlson in his most recent text, *Leaving Safe Harbors: Toward
a new Progressivism in American education and public life* (2002),
suggested,

> Language, and the mythic core of language, are now understood to
> play a generative and formative role, to shape both our reading of texts
> and the texts themselves. Language thus becomes the central concern
> of a new progressivism in education, and the role of language in consti-
> tuting the world along particular lines ... until people are able to
> "re-think" self, world, and other, they have not really changed, no
> matter how much more information they have access to, no matter
> how many textbooks they read. (pp. 179–180)

Rebecca Powell (1999) proposes five criteria useful in formulating a pluralistic, radical literacy education with attention to the political workings of language and discourse:

1. Literacy instruction ought to promote freedom of thought through encouraging diverse perspectives and welcoming productive critique.
2. Literacy instruction ought to encourage student's communicative competence by considering the social, cultural, and hegemonic dimensions of language use.
3. Literacy instruction ought to be consciously political.
4. Literacy ought to be taught in ways that make students aware of the power of language for transformation.
5. Literacy ought to be taught in ways that nurture a community of compassion and care. (1999, pp. 64–65)

A radical, pluralistic democracy that insists on the apparent impossibility of dialogue and collective work in and among groups and individuals who are positioned differently by power and privilege demands a literacy that will support participation, interaction, and critical analysis in ongoing efforts to find and secure democracy and freedom-in-community in the times in which we find ourselves. This means seeking out the points of energy in and across difference. It also means connecting the multiple sites and texts of democratic activity so that literacy promoted in school communities engages literacies outside of schools in the many sites where democratic activity is or can be undertaken. From the previous chapter it also means connecting school literacy lessons to the material and discursive circumstances of the body, and asking, among other things, how democratic life is lived on and by the collective and individual body and how desire and pleasure is schooled in and for democratic life. Whatever else, a critical and compassionate literacy for the 21st century is ultimately articulated and can be firmly grounded in the collective writing and rewriting of democratic life. It is where advocacy researchers and educators seek and can find higher ground.

### A Post-9/11 World and Post-9/11 Literacy

This project began with feelings of guilt and despair over the events of 9/11, the Iraq war, and the more general sense that left-leaning progressive and radical voices were being lost in education and indeed in much of the world. Since we began writing, the world has not improved much. Men, women, and children continue to lose their hopes if not their lives in Iraq, Afghanistan, and the Middle East, among a host of other war or war-like zones; various forms of domestic and international terrorism continue; the gap between rich and poor expands; and a conservative agenda continues to dominate the political scene here and elsewhere. It is not an easy time to be a liberal let alone a radical. But in writing this book we have found great or at least sufficient hope and energy, despite these "No Child Left Behind" (or Standing) times. In part this is because there is an amazing record of brilliant and defiant research and teaching conducted in a literacy education committed to advocacy. Our book has only scratched the surface. Moreover it is a record that continues to expand, offering powerful energy and insight for the future possibilities, some of which we've highlighted in this text. There is much here to renew our intellectual commitment to our field and to advocacy work.

Oddly enough our hope also comes from tensions, that is, in dialectics found in the theoretical work being done in this field we constitute as advocacy research in literacy education. There is, in our estimation, a productive energy in the tensions between theory and practice, between the postmodern and the neo-Marxist perspectives and among the various radical social theories. And it may well be that resolution is unproductive. Like democracy, creative and productive research and scholarship may depend on and be sustained by difference and dissent from in and out of the field.

Although we acknowledge that there may be no revolution, we are convinced that change is always possible and that, even on "higher ground," movement rather than stability names our historical condition, though in the end there are no comforting absolutes, as Dennis Carlson (2002) cautioned,

> Progressives must resist the desire, born out of insecurity and fear, to "fix" the world under a clarifying gaze, to offer students and the "the public" ready answers to perceived problems, to stay with what is comfortable and safe. For one thing, there are no safe harbors, even if we may like to pretend there are. There is no one, unified, unchanging truth that we can rest our feet upon, no firm foundations that we can

use to define who we are. Beyond this, one could say that the current cultural terrain of late modern or "postmodern" culture is one in which truth and value are more un-fixed than ever before. (p. 180)

This is not an excuse to do nothing, but instead an assurance of possibility in the brave development of provisional rather definitive initiatives. In the end it is to be humble in our efforts, dynamic in our thinking, grounded in our present day material circumstances, attentive to discourse, and at home with uncertainty.

We do take great comfort in this final quote. "Democratic progressivism presumes that there is no end of history, that progress toward a better, more humane, equitable, and caring world is always being challenged, that we must continuously think anew as we move upon an historical stage that is open and unfinished" (Dimitriadis & Carlson, 2003, p. 8). Thus history, democracy, and literacy education, open and unfinished, invite us forward.

# Notes

## CHAPTER ONE: PAULO FREIRE AND CRITICAL LITERACIES

1. In outlining Freire's biography we draw on Peter McLaren's extended description in his 2000 text, *Che Guevara, Paulo Freire, and the Pedagogy of Revolution*, which appears slightly altered and abbreviated as "Paulo Freire's Pedagogy of Possibilities" in Stanley Steiner et al. (2000), *Freirean Pedagogy, Praxis, and Possibilities*, and as "A Legacy of Hope and Struggle" in Antonia Darder (2002) *Reinventing Paulo Freire: Pedagogy of Love*. Our sources also include Ana Maria Araujo Freire's introduction in her and Donaldo Macedo's 1998 edited text *The Paulo Freire Reader*. Ana Maria Araujo Freire was Freire's second wife and his widow.

2. Donaldo Macado (1998) reported in detail the lukewarm attitude evident at the Harvard Graduate School of Education. He noted, for example, that the school does not offer a single course specifically on Freire's theories and ideas, whereas the Harvard Divinity Schools offers a course entitled "education and liberation" where Freire's ideas are a central focus.

3. These four points are condensed and modified from those outlined in the work of McLaren (2000b).

## CHAPTER TWO:
## RADICAL COUNTERNARRATIVES IN LITERACY RESEARCH I

*Feminist Theory and Research in Literacy Education*

1. David Smith, now at the University of Alberta, in conversation during a graduate class at the Ontario Institute for Studies in Education in 1991.

*Queer Theory and Research in Literacy Education*

1. There are many examples of advocacy research in education *by and for GLBTQ people* that make little or no use of queer theory. For recent examples see Kumashiro's (2002, 2003) brilliant applications of poststructural, feminist, and psychoanalytic theory (as well as queer theory) in creating classroom practice for social change. See also the 2003 special issue of *Teaching Education,* which offers articles concerned with educating future teachers to understand homophobic oppression and its consequences, and to provide them with strategies for anti-oppressive classroom practice.

   In literacy education, GLTB advocacy research outside of queer theory often takes the form of teacher research that seeks to transform literature curriculum and pedagogy, to make them more inclusive of the experiences of gay and lesbian people. See, for example, Athanases, 1999; Gonzales, 1994; Hammett, 1992; King and Schneider, 1999; essays included in Garber, 1994; and some sections of the Teaching Tolerance web site at www.tolerance.org

2. The Kinsey reports (Kinsey et al., 1948; Kinsey et al., 1953) were controversial books about human sexual behavior, based on data from hundreds of interviews conducted by Alfred Kinsey, an American zoologist at the University of Indiana at Bloomington, and others. Kinsey's research findings challenged conventional beliefs about sexuality, and concluded (among other things) that more than 90% of people were to some extent bisexual, that 10% of people were homosexual, and that masturbation was almost universal in human males. Although Kinsey's methodology has

been critiqued and his data revisited and analyzed differently, his original estimates have held and are widely accepted to this day.

The Kinsey reports caused a sensation at the time of their release and were vigorously attacked by conservative groups. They no doubt contributed to (or expressed, or were produced by) changes in public perceptions of sexuality in the second half of the twentieth century.

3. James T. Sears has a long history of working in education to challenge heterosexism. Over the years he has made use of a variety of theories to help teachers and parents imagine the lived experiences of growing up gay in American society and schools (1988, 1990), to help educators envision a curriculum that is inclusive of gay and lesbian people (1992; Letts & Sears, 1999), and pedagogies that are open and inclusive of all identities (1997, 1999). He has also worked to unsettle the discourses of conservative religious groups that enter into contemporary curriculum debates to maintain oppressive normative structures (Sears with Carper, 1998). Although Sears has often used critical theory to frame his discussions of equity and justice and the politics of heterosexism, more recently he has also made use of queer theories to challenge teachers to reconceptualize their work (1999). Sears is not a literacy educator, per se, nor is he himself a queer theorist. But he has contributed a large body of distinguished advocacy work to the field of education, work that has been very useful to advocacy workers in literacy education, and we want to mention him here.

4. It is interesting to note that Sumara and Davis (1999) conducted their research in Canada, and that Martino (1999) worked in Australia, both outside the conservative educational climate of the United States.

## CHAPTER THREE:
## RADICAL COUNTERNARRATIVES IN LITERACY RESEARCH II

*Postcolonial Theory*

1. Postcolonial theory has been criticized when it seems too deterministic and essentialist, and does *not* allow for subjectivity in flux.

2. For an excellent example of this dynamic in action, see bell hooks' chapter on her interactions with Paulo Freire (hooks, 1994). 3. Singh and Greenlaw (1998) used Asia as their example, but their descriptions of orientalist and contrapuntal pedagogies would of course apply to the study of literature about other colonized peoples as well.

### Critical Race Theory

1. Where did these "counternarratives" (feminist, postcolonial, queer and critical race theory) come from? Chapters 2 and 3 have allowed us to address the many research studies in literacy education that are not applications of Freire's ideas, and not explorations of critical literacies, studies that do not begin with the researcher's ties to an established discipline like sociology or linguistics. Where could we place research that emerged from theory that broke new ground, and that sought to apply scholarship that had not traditionally inspired research in literacy education?

We thought about our own early work (Helen's research on teenage women and their readings of feminist avant-garde poetry, and Meredith's research on 11-year-old girls and their readings of fiction), and the fact that after many years we both still think of ourselves as feminist researchers. We looked and found that many of the studies we were attempting to classify made use of feminist theory to claim space for studying literacy in the lives of girls and women.

We then thought that perhaps a consideration of "standpoint" might allow us to generate some other categories. Working from the poststructural premise that what you know has everything to do with where you are in the world, we decided that postcolonial theory and queer theory could also be subcategories of the scholarly counternarratives that were inspiring some of the advocacy work in our field. That worked: Feminist, postcolonial, and queer theory would be the subcategories for chapters 2 and 3.

For a while, we thought that cultural studies might work as another subcategory. But most of the cultural studies research fit elsewhere in the book. We also wondered if we ought to have a subcategory that made *race* central in its analyses. We knew that we had research studies that made race central in all the other categories and subcategories of research in this book (see Ernest Morrell's work in critical English Studies in chapter 1, for example; many of the studies we had included in the postcolonial section of chapter 3; and several studies in the sociolinguistics subsection of chapter 5). But was there a body of advocacy research in literacy education that was unified by an emphasis on race, and that made use of counternarratives about race?

We decided to learn more about *critical race theory* and its applications in education. We read "Critical Race Theory and Education: History, Theory, and Implications" by William Tate, and found that CRT grew out of critical legal studies in the United States, which reconsidered the premises of the Civil Rights legislation of the 1960s and 1970s. Then, because an international conference called "Critical Race Theory in Education" caught our attention, we looked carefully at the literature. We found that there were some research studies in literacy education that made use of CRT, and which advocated. Clearly, we needed to include this section on something we had almost missed.

2. Catherine Prendergast (2003) has made the powerful argument that advocacy research in literacy (whether or not it uses CRT) is itself a byproduct of the American civil rights movement and its challenges to White supremacy. Out to defeat cognitive deficit explanations of variation in literacy achievement, out to show the unrecognized proficiencies of the people who were failing at official (culturally biased) measures of literacy, but who had multiple culturally situated literacies of their own, literacy researchers began to call for tolerance of cultural variation in literacy practices. But that was not enough to change the discourse of deficit that plagued literacy education, because it did not provide scholars with a way to discuss the impact of larger social forces and events on literacy achievement. Deconstructions of deficit thinking could not stand up to cultural taboos against speaking openly about race and racism (Prendergast, 2003). Critical race theory has provided what was missing.

3. As with all histories, different scholars construct the history of CRT in different ways. We have written only one possible overview of the development of CRT and its applications in education, relying heavily on Tate (1997) for a history that includes educational research. See Crenshaw, Gotanda, Peller, and Thomas (1995) for a collection of important writings in the history of the movement. See Ladson-Billing (1999) for a history that speaks to teacher education, and Prendergast (2002) for a history that traces the legal decisions that sustained the value of literacy as White property.

4. Because CRT's applications in literacy research are quite recent and fewer in number when compared with other counternarratives in literacy research (feminist, postcolonial, and queer theory), we would characterize this subcategory as "emerging."

### CHAPTER FOUR: LITERACY AS SOCIAL PRACTICE

1. Our subcategories for this chapter are our own (somewhat arbitrary) choices. They do overlap and bleed into each other. We could have organized this chapter differently, and we caution our readers to remain aware of that. In the end notes that follow, we will take up some of the issues we have had to deal with in assigning characteristics to subcategories, and in assigning specific studies to subcategories. For now, we remind our readers that these are not the only categories possible in a consideration of literacy as social practice. They are simply the ones we have constructed for this book.

2. Some might credit Scribner and Cole's (1981) landmark study of literacy among the Vai with pointing the way to situated literacies research, and to some extent we are sure that it did. However, Scribner and Cole were (and are) psychologists, and were focusing on the mind in society. We have chosen to cite their work later in this chapter, in connection with the history of advocacy research grounded in activity theory. Although their study of the Vai is the study of literacy in one community, although it is accessible and reads like ethnography, we categorize it here as a brilliant example of cultural psychology, rather than as an example of anthropology.

We place Hymes at the start of our overview of situated literacies because we want to highlight the fact that many advocacy researchers who have studied situated literacies are both anthropologists *and* linguists, like Heath. Our distinction between "situated literacies" and "linguistic studies" (see chapter 5) is sometimes a fine point. Anthropologists study language in pursuit of cultural knowledge, and linguists study culture in their pursuit of linguistic knowledge. We have categorized advocacy studies as "situated literacies" or as "linguistic studies" on the basis of which discipline they seem to us to favor, but we realize that this is a difficult distinction to make, and that others might see the matter differently. (Please note that we also credit Hymes at the beginning of chapter 5.)

3. Recently Catherine Prendergast (2003) has reexamined Heath's (1983) archived data, to bring the tenets of critical race theory to bear on it. She said,

Critical race theory's conception of racism as the rule and not the exception ... is valuable for understanding the communities of *Ways* [*With Words*]. Trackton children are not simply engaging in strategies to survive in the community of Trackton and are not ignorant of the linguistic practices outside their community. They are always/already socialized into discourses of racism and very aware that group identifications based on race significantly shape their everyday experience. Strategies for dealing with the basic inconsistencies and inherent contradictions of life in a racist society can be seen as part of the Trackton way of life. (p. 92) (See chapter 3 for a discussion of critical race theory.)

4. There are other distinguished researchers of situated literacies who have worked with Barton. See Barton, Hamilton, and Ivanic (2000), and Barton and Ivanic (1991), for examples.

5. Here we face another problem with our subcategories of advocacy research on literacy as social practice. What do we do with literacy researchers who choose *not* to attend to systems of privilege and power, but whose brilliant research on literacy as social practice contributes to the struggle for social justice by becoming ammunition in the hands of advocates? Anne Haas Dyson comes to mind. Dyson studies the language of marginalized young chil-

dren and the writing they produce, revealing the ways in which they draw on many dimensions of social context (the contemporary culture of childhood, family relationships, experiences with popular media, *and* the status and power differentials of gender, race, and social class) in their literacy productions at school. In doing so, Dyson's wonderful insights show the children to be extremely capable with language and literacy (see Dyson, 1997a, 1997b, 2003, for example).

Dyson's work may serve as a wakeup call to teachers who do not see these children for the capable people they are, and she does seem to intend that. But she confines her focus to the world as the children see it. Her work reveals the ways in which race, class, and gender are perceived by the children she studies, and enters into their views of the world. But Dyson does not connect the children's views to the world as it is seen by adults. She does not connect the children's views to larger critical political frames. Her readers are left to draw their own conclusions.

If we were to count Dyson as an advocacy researcher (because she studies the marginalized and issues wakeup calls), we could include her in the section of this chapter on "situated literacies." Or we could perhaps argue that, because she cites Vygotsky, and her work centers on writing as an activity, her work is in some ways related to activity theory and might be placed in the last section of this chapter. Dyson's work is clearly ethnographic, informed by anthropology, and she does study cultural constructs that are part of local literacies. But, with the greatest respect for her fine work, we are speaking of her only in this footnote. This is because Dyson's work does not come within the parameters of our definition of advocacy research. It is not explicitly political, or transformative in purpose; it does not explicitly stand with people to improve their social, material, and political circumstances, and to change the world. If it has such effects (and perhaps it does), that appears to be unintended.

6.  We have constructed a subcategory called *adolescent literacies* for two reasons. First, adolescence in contemporary global capitalist society is a context in which the study of literacy as social practice can be situated. Adolescence is a cultural construction (Lesko, 2001) that

positions and produces subjects in certain ways, and frames the types of literacies to which people of a certain age have access. Literacies (and human subjects) are situated within the frame of adolescence. Second, we have found a body of research on adolescent literacies that attempts to advocate *for the age group*, on the assumption that age is at times one of the categories that produce power inequities. We point to the fact that in North America publicly funded education is providing little financial and moral support for continuing attention to the acquisition of literacy in adolescence. Advocacy researchers who study adolescents are well aware of this.

Should we also have constructed a subcategory for this chapter called *early childhood literacies*? We could perhaps have done so. Perhaps we could have helped to undermine the hold that Piaget's theories and stages of cognitive development continue to have on early childhood research. We could have included Ferreiro (1984), Harste, Woodward, and Burke (1984), and Solsken (1993) in the history of such a category. We could have included Dyson, and Celia Genishi's (1999) work. We could have argued that early childhood too is a context for the study of situated literacies, and that young children too form a group in need of advocacy.

But we have not. At the risk of obscuring the achievements of researchers who study young children (and we do realize that the majority of them women), we have chosen not to form a subcategory for early childhood advocacy research in literacy education. This is because, unlike the adolescent literacy researchers we have included, many early childhood researchers take a psychological approach to understanding young children and their literacy "development." When early childhood researchers advocate, when they acknowledge social difference and social inequity, when they seek to unsettle the status quo and transform literacy education and the social world, we have tried to include them elsewhere in this book. See, in particular, chapter 1 in the section on critical literacy in primary and elementary education.

7. Activity theory may be our most controversial subcategory. We have asked our readers to consider this subcategory "a short speculation." We do acknowledge that it is small and narrow. There are many distinguished literacy researchers who frame their work with

cultural–historical activity theory, but they do not explicitly advocate, and we have not included them. The temptation when working with activity theory or cultural psychology (or any body of theory that attempts to place the human mind in society) is to focus on the "mind" of the individual subject, without making connections to history and culture in the construction of the individual's subjectivity. As with our other subcategories, we have included only the studies *we know of* that advocate and work openly for social transformation. If our readers know of others, we would like to hear about them.

8. We have given some thought to the links between cultural–historical activity theory and the "complexity sciences," which also focus on the human mind in society (neuroscience, neuropsychology, narrative psychology, and some reinterpretations of developmental psychology are among them). We are, of course, interested in theories that connect mind and body in literacy research, and we have included some in chapter 6, "The Literate Body." We acknowledge here that in this book about advocacy research we are turning away from many large conceptual literatures that link the phenomenological with the biological, and that link cultural psychology and many other nested systems of cognition to literary engagement and response to literature. This is because their link to advocacy is not yet clear to us.

We are, however, now beginning to appreciate the field of "complexity thinking," a field that is capturing the imaginations of many educational researchers. (See Davis & Sumara, in press-a; and Davis, Sumara, & Luce-Kapler, 2000; alyssa for excellent explanations and examples of complexity thinking in educational research.) Complexity thinking is useful to advocacy researchers in that it provides a theoretical umbrella under which researchers can note profound similarities across a diversity of phenomena. It encourages a research attitude of "mindful participation" with a community around matters of shared concern. By reminding us of the need to look at many systems at once, complexity thinking allows us to avoid a dualistic discourse of theories "in tension," or "this or that" solutions to complex problems (Davis & Sumara, in press-a). Importantly, complexity thinking provides advocacy researchers with insights into how social collectives work.

Davis and Sumara (1999) have already linked complexity thinking in education to possibilities for transformation. They explain that complexity thinking provides a discourse that offers researchers advice on how to bring together the self-interests of autonomous agents into greater collective possibilities (in press-b) to affect change. They realize that researchers' attempts at transformation are deeply ethical matters. We will continue to read about complexity thinking, as its links to literacy research and advocacy research continue to emerge.

## CHAPTER 5: LINGUISTIC STUDIES

1. It is not always easy to distinguish among these three subcategories of linguistic research. Separating them may seem artificial and the distinctions may seem forced. One might wonder why we engage in this category work at all, when the categories are so inclined to leak and bleed into each other, and to cause us such trouble. But categorizing is an exercise in analyzing and distinguishing, in examining and understanding their similarities and differences. Categorizing is both an act of construction and of deconstruction that may, if only provisionally, create meaning and insight into advocacy research.

2. *Ways With Words* by Shirley Brice Heath (1983) is an example of this kind of research. It is included it in chapter 3 as an example of *situated literacies* research that advocates. It *is* an anthropological study. It is also a *sociolinguistic* study that conforms to this definition. *Ways With Words,* we note, begins with a tribute to Dell Hymes.

3. See for example, the Web postings of internet activists who use psycholinguistic research studies to discredit the U.S. government's literacy education policies, and instructional practices that reduce reading to phonics, skills, and drills. They argue against blaming teachers and Whole Language approaches for low scores

on standardized tests. www.susanohanian.org, for example, points out that these policies serve conservative political purposes. Her Web site critiques news reporting in the mainstream media, posts "research that counts," editorializes, and posts letters from psycholinguistic researchers and from "resisting" teachers who refuse to limit their literacy instruction to phonics programs, in accordance with state law. Ohanian declares on her Web site, "We are making such materials available in our efforts to advance understanding of education issues vital to a democracy."

Consider too the lifelong record of psycholinguistic advocacy research produced by Ken and Yetta Goodman. It would be hard to overestimate their contributions to countering (with information, theoretical insight, practical strategies, and sheer determination) literacy policies that constrain teachers, disadvantage children, and serve the political purposes of the conservative Right. (See K. Goodman, 1998, and K. Goodman, Goodman, Rapoport, & Shannon, 2003, for examples.)

4. What label ought to be given to the advocacy research that grows out of the Critical Whole Language (CWL) movement? No one label is appropriate for all of it. It can be called *action research* when it involves repeated cycles of planning, action, and reflection. All the examples we have found are certainly instances of *teacher research*, intended to improve classroom practice, as our example studies make clear. Psycholinguistic research intended to improve classroom practice often draws university educators and classroom teachers together to do research, and then it may become *collaborative action research* (see Hudelson & Lindfors, 1993, for eight examples of collaborative action research projects grounded in psycholinguistic and sociolinguistic theory). Not all of the action research, teacher research, and collaborative action research informed by psycholinguistic theory advocates for justice, however, as our example studies do. See Edelsky, 2005 for more examples of "teacher resisters" and the ways in which their work contributes to social transformation and justice.

For the purposes of this book we accept as advocacy research the publications of teachers who teach literacy in ways consistent with psycholinguistic theories of reading and writing, *and* who at the same time work for justice with critical awareness of systems of privilege and power. We also accept as advocacy research the publications of others who work with these teachers or who write about their transformative work.

## CHAPTER SIX: WHY SOCIAL JUSTICE: ETHICS FOR ADVOCACY RESEARCH

1. Summary comments on each study are offered again in this chapter for the reader's convenience, and have been reshaped to emphasize their orientations to social justice. Gutiérrez et al. (1999) is reviewed under "Activity Theory" in chapter 4 on "Literacy as Social Practice." Hicks (2002) and Cherland (1994) are also mentioned in chapter 4 under "Situated Literacies." And Blackburn (2002) is discussed in chapter 2 in the subsection on "Queer Theory."
2. We use the word *unconceal* here to echo Heidegger's remark that, in intellectual projects intended to be transformative, "The first step is to unconceal."
3. Cherland (1994) has been chosen for discussion here because it provides a dramatic example of advocacy research in literacy education that makes use of feminist critical theory, and the idea that justice will require dismantling systems of privilege and dominance. It does not necessarily represent Cherland's views of power and privilege today, more than 10 years later. *All* the example studies in all our chapters are historically situated snapshots of the researchers, which imply their beliefs at one moment in time. Cherland (1994) is a person who no longer exists.

## CHAPTER SEVEN: THE LITERATE BODY

1. A comment made by Dr. Carol Schick, University of Regina, 1995.

# References

## Preface & Introduction

Allen, J. (Ed.). (1999). *Class actions: Teaching for social justice in elementary and middle school.* New York: Teachers College Press.

Ansell-Pearson, K. (1994). Introduction: Nietzsche's overcoming of morality. In F. Nietzsche (Ed.), *On the genealogy of morality* (pp. ix–xxiii). Cambridge, UK: Cambridge University Press.

Apple. M. W. (2002). Preface: The Freirean legacy. In J. J. Slater, S. M. Fain, & C. A. Rossato (Eds.), *The Freirean legacy: Educating for social justice* (pp. ix–xii). New York: Peter Lang.

Bogdan, R. C., & Biklen, S. K. (1982). *Qualitative research for education: An introduction to theory and methods.* Boston: Allyn & Bacon.

Britzman, D. (1998). Queer pedagogy and its strange techniques. In D. Britzman, *Lost subjects, contested objects: Toward a psychoanalytic inquiry of learning* (pp. 79–96). Albany: State University of New York.

Brodkey, L. (1991). Tropics of literacy. In C. Mitchell & K. Weiler (Eds.), *Rewriting literacy: Culture and the discourse of the other* (pp. 161–168). Toronto: OISE.

Caputo, J. D. (1993). *Against ethics: Contributions to a poetics of obligation with constant reference to deconstruction.* Bloomington: Indiana University Press.

Davis, B., & Sumara, D. (in press). *Complexity and education: Emergent thinking on learning, pedagogy, and research.*

Edelsky, C. (1994). Education for democracy. *Language Arts, 71,* 252–257.

Edelsky, C., & Cherland, M. R. (2005). A critical issue in critical literacy: The "popularity effect." In R. E. White & K. Cooper (Eds.), *The practical critical educator* (pp. 95–111). New York: Kluwer.

Ellsworth, E. (1992). Why doesn't this feel empowering? Working through the repressive myths of critical pedagogy. In C. Luke & J. Gore (Eds.), *Feminisms and critical pedagogy* (pp. 90–119). New York: Routledge.

Fine, M. (1986). Why urban adolescents drop into and out of public high school. *Teachers College Record, 87,* 393–409.

Foucault, M. (1988). An aesthetics of existence (A. Fontana, Interviewer; A. Sheridan, Trans.). In L. D. Kritzman (Ed.), *Politics, philosophy, culture: Interviews and other writings, 1977–1984* (pp. 47–53). New York: Routledge. (Interview conducted 1984)

Gore, J. (1992). What we can do for you! What can "we" do for "you"? Struggling over empowerment in critical and feminist pedagogy. In C. Luke & J. Gore (Eds.), *Feminisms and critical pedagogy* (pp 54–73). New York: Routledge.

Graff, H. J. (1987). *Legacies of literacy: Continuities and contradictions in western culture and society.* Bloomington: Indiana University Press.

Grant, L., & Fine, G. A. (1992). Sociology unleashed: Creative dimensions in classical ethnography. In M. D. Lecompte, W. L. Millroy, & J. Preissle (Eds.), *The handbook of qualitative research in education* (pp. 405–446). San Diego, CA: Academic Press.

Groome, T. (1998). Educating for life: A spiritual vision for every teacher and parent. Allen, TX: Thomas More.

Habermas, J. (1971). *Theory and practice.* Boston: Beacon.

Harding, S. (1996). Gendered ways of knowing and the "epistemological crisis" of the west. In N. Goldberger, J. Tarule, B. Clinchy, & M. Belenky (Eds.), *Knowledge, difference and power: Essays inspired by Women's Ways of Knowing* (pp. 431–454). New York: Basic Books.

Keenan, T. (1997). *Fables of responsibility: Aberrations and predicaments in ethics and politics.* Stanford, CA: Stanford University Press.

Kemmis, S., & McTaggart, R. (2000). Participatory action research. In N. K. Denzin & Y. S. Lincoln (Eds.), *Handbook of qualitative research* (2nd ed., pp. 567–606). Thousand Oaks, CA: Sage.

Kincheloe, J. L., & McLaren, P. (2000). Rethinking critical theory and qualitative research. In N. K. Denzin & Y. S. Lincoln (Eds.), *Handbook of qualitative research* (2nd ed., pp. 279–313). Thousand Oaks, CA: Sage.

Kumashiro, K. K. (1999). Reading queer Asian American masculinities and sexualities in elementary school. In W. J. Letts & J. T. Sears (Eds.), *Queering elementary education: Advancing the dialogue about sexualities and schooling* (pp. 61–70). Lanham, MD: Rowman & Littlefield.

Kumashiro, K. K. (2001). "Posts" perspectives on anti-oppressive education in Social Studies, English, Mathematics, and Science classrooms. *Educational Researcher, 30*(3), 3–12.

Kumashiro, K. K. (2003). *Against common sense: Teaching and learning toward social justice.* New York: Routledge Falmer.

Lather, P. (1991). *Getting smart: Feminist research and pedagogy with/in the postmodern.* New York: Routledge.

Lather, P. (1992). Critical frames in educational research: Feminist and poststructural perspectives. *Theory Into Practice, 31,* 87–99.

Lather, P. (1999). To be of use: The work of reviewing. *Review of Educational Research, 69*, 2–7.

McLaren, P., & Gutierrez, K. (1996). Global politics and local antagonisms: Research and practice as dissent and possibility. *Anuario de Educao (Brasil),* 27–60.

Moje, E., & O'Brien, D. (Eds.). (2001). *Constructions of literacy: Studies of teaching and learning in and out of secondary schools.* Mahwah, NJ: Lawrence Erlbaum Associates, Inc.

Nietzsche, F. (1994). "Guilt," "bad conscience" and related matters (C. Diethe, Trans.). In K. Ansell-Pearson (Ed.), *On the genealogy of morality* (pp. 38–71). Cambridge, UK: Cambridge University Press. (Original work published 1887)

Pennycook, A. (2001). *Critical applied linguistics: A critical introduction.* Mahwah, NJ: Lawrence Erlbaum Associates, Inc.

Richardson, L. (2000). Writing: A method of inquiry. In N. K. Denzin & Y. S. Lincoln (Eds.), *Handbook of qualitative research* (2nd ed., pp. 923–948). Thousand Oaks, CA: Sage.

Rikowski, G., & McLaren, P. (2002). Postmodernism in educational theory. In D. Hill, P. McLaren, M. Cole, & G. Rikowski (Eds.), *Marxism against postmodernism in educational theory* (pp. 3–13). Lanham, MD: Lexington Books.

Rist, R. C. (1970). Student social class and teacher expectations: The self-fulfilling prophecy in ghetto education. *Harvard Educational Review, 40*(3), 247–265.

Rist, R. C. (2000). Author's introduction: The enduring dilemmas of race and class and color in American education. *Harvard Educational Review, 70,* 257–265.

Schensul, J. J., & Schensul, S. L. (1992). Collaborative research: Methods of inquiry for social change. In M. D. Lecompte, W. L. Millroy, & J. Preissle (Eds.), *The handbook of qualitative research in education* (pp. 161–200). San Diego, CA: Academic Press.

Simon, R. (1992). *Teaching against the grain: Texts for a pedagogy of possibility.* Toronto: OISE.

Slater, J. J., Fain, S. M., & Rossato, C. A. (Eds.). (2002). *The Freirean legacy: Educating for social justice.* New York: Peter Lang.

Sumara, D., & Davis, B. (1999). Interrupting heteronormativity: Toward a queer curriculum theory. *Curriculum Inquiry, 29,* 191–208.

Tate, W. (1997). Critical race theory and education: History, theory, and implications. In M. W. Apple (Ed.), *Review of research in education* (Vol. 22, pp. 195–247). Washington, DC: AERA.

Williams, R. (1961). *The long revolution.* London: Chatto & Windus.

Wysocki, A. F., Johnson-Eilola, J. (1999). Blinded by the letter: Why are we using literacy as a metaphor for everything else? In G. Hawisher & C. Selfe (Eds.), *Passions, pedagogies and 21st century technologies* (pp. 349–368). Logan, UH: Utah State University Press.

## CHAPTER ONE: PAULO FREIRE AND CRITICAL LITERACY(IES)

Allen, R. L. (2002). *Whiteness as territoriality: An analysis of white identity politics in society, education and theory.* Doctoral dissertation, UCLA.

Alvermann, D. (2002). *Adolescents and literacies in a digital world.* New York: Peter Lang.

Altwerger, B., & Saavedra, E. (1999). Forward. In C. Edelsky (Ed.), *Making justice our project: Teachers working toward critical whole language practice* (pp. vii–xii). Urbana, IL: National Council of Teachers of English.

Apple. M. W. (2002) Preface: The Freirean legacy. In J. J. Slater, S. M. Fain, & C. A. Rossato, (Eds.), *The Freirean legacy: Educating for social justice* (pp. ix–xii). New York: Peter Lang.

Aronowitz, S. (1993). Paulo Freire's Radical Democratic Humanism. In P. McLaren & P. Leonard (Eds.), *Paulo Freire: A Critical Encounter* (pp. 8–24). New York: Routledge.

Baker, C. & Luke, A. (1991). *Towards a critical sociology of reading pedagogy: Papers of the XII World Congress on Reading.* Philadephia: J. Benjamins.

Boran, S., & Comber, B. (2001). *Critiquing whole language and classroom inquiry.* Urbana, IL: National Council of Teachers of English.

Church, S. (1999). Leadership as critical practice: A work-in-progress. In C. Edelsky (Ed.), *Making justice our project: Teachers working toward critical whole language practice* (pp. 286–302). Urbana, IL: National Council of Teachers of English.

Comber, B. (in press). Critical literacy educators at work: Dispositions, discursive resources and repertoires of practice. In R. White & K. Cooper (Eds.), *The Practical Critical Educator.* The Netherlands: Kluwer.

Comber, B., Nixon, H., Ashmore, L., Wells, M., & Trimboli, R. (2005, April). *Urban renewal from the inside out: Spatial and critical literacies in a low socioeconomic school community.* Paper presented at the American Educational Research Association, 2005 Annual Meeting, Montreal, Canada.

Comber, B., & Nixon, H. (2005). Children reread and rewrite their local neighborhoods: Critical literacies and identity work. In J. Evans (Ed.), *Literacy moves on: Popular culture, new technologies and critical literacy in the elementary classroom* (pp. 127–148). Portsmouth NH: Heinemann.

Comber, B., & Nixon, H. (1999). Literacy education as a site for social justice: What do our practices do? In C. Edelsky (Ed.), *Making justice our project: Teachers working toward critical whole language practice* (pp. 316–352). Urbana, IL: National Council of Teachers of English.

Comber, B., & Simpson, A. (2001). *Negotiating critical literacies in classrooms.* Mahwah, NJ: Lawrence Erlbaum Associates, Inc.

Darder, A. (2002). *Reinventing Paulo Freire: Pedagogy of love.* Boulder, Colorado: Westview.

Darder, A. (2003). Teaching as an act of love: Reflections on Paulo Freire and his contributions to our lives and our work. In A. Darder, M. Baltodano, & R. Torres

(Eds.) *The critical pedagogy reader*, (pp.497–510). New York: Routledge/Falmer.

Darder, A., Batodamo, M., & Torres, R. (2003). *The critical pedagogy reader*. New York: Routledge.

de Castell, S., Luke, A., & Egan, K. (1986). *Literacy, society and schooling*. Cambridge, UK: Cambridge University Press.

de Los Reyes, E., & Gozemba, P. A. (2002). *Pockets of hope: How students and teachers change the world*. Westport, CT: Bergin & Garvey.

Duncan-Andrade, J. (2004). Your best friend or your worst enemy: Youth popular culture, pedagogy, and curriculum in urban classrooms. *The Review of Education, Pedagogy and Cultural Studies, 26,* 313–337.

Duncan-Andrade, J., & Morrell, E. (2005). Turn up that radio, teacher: popular cultural pedagogy in new century urban schools. *Journal of School Leadership*, May, nd.

Edelsky, C. (1999). *Making justice our project: Teachers working toward critical whole language practice*. Urbana, IL: National Council of Teachers of English.

Endres, B. (2001). A critical read on critical literacy: From critique to dialogue as an ideal for literacy education. *Educational Theory, 51,* 401–414.

Evans, J. (2005). *Literacy moves on: Popular culture, new technologies and critical literacy in the elementary classroom*. Portsmouth, NH: Heinemann.

Fraser, J. (1997). Love and history in the work of Paulo Freire. In P. Freire, W. Fraser, D. Macedo, T. McKinnon & W. Stokes (Eds.) *Mentoring the Mentor: A critical dialogue with Paulo Freire* (pp.175–199). New York: Peter Lang.

Freire, P. (1978). *Pedagogy in Process: The letters to Guinea-Bissau*. New York: Seabury Press.

Freire, A., & Macedo, D. (Eds.). (1998). *The Paulo Freire reader*. New York: Continuum.

Freire, P. (1970). *Cultural action for freedom*. Harmondsworth, UK: Penguin.

Freire, P. (1970/2003). *Pedagogy of the oppressed*. New York: Continuum.

Freire, P. (1973). *Education for critical consciousness*. New York: Seabury.

Freire, P. (1978). *Pedagogy in Process: The Letters to Guinea-Bissau*. New York: Seabury.

Freire, P. (1993). *Pedagogy of the city*. New York: Continuum.

Freire, P. (1994). *Pedagogy of hope: Reliving "pedagogy of the oppressed."* New York: Continuum.

Freire, P. (1997). *Pedagogy of the heart*. New York: Continuum.

Freire, P. (1998a). *Pedagogy of freedom: Ethics, democracy, and civic courage*. Lanham, MD: Rowman and Littlefield.

Freire, P. (1998b; 2005). *Teachers as cultural workers: Letters to those who dare to teach*. Boulder, CO: Westview.

Freire, P., & Faundez, A. (1989). *Learning to question: A pedagogy of liberation*. New York: Continuum.

Freire, P., & Macedo, D. (1987). *Literacy: Reading the word and the world*. South Hadley, MA: Bergin and Garvey.

Freire, P., Fraser, J., Macedo, D. McKinnon, T., & Stokes, W. (Eds.). (1997). *Mentoring the Mentor*. New York: Peter Lang.

Gaztambide-Fernandez, R. (2003). Editor's review. *Harvard Educational Review,* *73*, 94–110.

Gee, J. (1997). Dilemmas of literacy: Plato and Freire. In P. Freire, W. Fraser, D. Macedo, T. McKinnon & W. Stokes (Eds.) *Mentoring the Mentor: A critical dialogue with Paulo Freire* (pp.229–242). New York: Peter Lang.

Gilbert, P. (1991). From voice to text: Reconsidering writing and reading in the English classroom. *English Education, 23,* 195–211.

Giroux, H. (1994). Doesn't anybody write in the Cultural Studies classroom? In H. Giroux (Ed.) *Disturbing pleasures: Learning popular culture*, (pp. 127–140). New York: Routledge.

Giroux, H. (1993). Paulo Freire and the politics of postcolonialism. In P. McLaren & P. Leonard (Eds.), *Paulo Freire: A critical encounter* (pp. 177–188). New York: Routledge.

Giroux, H., & McLaren, P. (1994). *Between the borders: Pedagogy and the politics of cultural studies.* New York: Routledge.

Giroux, H., & Shannon, P. (1997). *Education and cultural studies: Toward a performative practice.* New York: Routledge.

Giroux, H., Lankshear, C., McLaren, P., & Peters, M. (1996). *Counternarratives: Cultural studies and critical pedagogies in postmodern spaces.* New York: Routledge.

Graff, H. (1987). *The legacies of literacy: Continuities and contradictions in western culture and society.* Bloomington: Indiana University Press.

Grossberg, L. (1994). Introduction: Bringin' it all back home—Pedagogy and Cultural Studies. In H. Giroux & P. McLaren (Eds.), *Between borders: Pedagogy and the politics of cultural studies* (pp. 1–25). New York: Routledge.

Grossberg, L. (1997). *Bringing it all back home.* Durham, NC: Duke University Press.

Gruenewald, D. (2003). The best of both worlds: A critical pedagogy of place. *Educational Researcher, 32*(4), 3–12.

Hoechsmann, M. (2004). Reading youth writing: Grazing in the pastures of cultural studies and education. *The Review of Education, Pedagogy and Cultural Studies, 26,* 193–210.

hooks, b. (1988). *Talking back: Thinking feminist, thinking black.* Toronto: Between the Lines.

Huiskamp, G. (2002). Negotiating communities of meaning in theory and practice: Rereading pedagogy of the oppressed as direct dialogic encounter. In J. Slater, S. Fain, & C. Rossatto (Eds.), *The Freirean legacy: Educating for social justice* (pp. 73–94). New York: Peter Lang.

Janks, H. (2003). Domination, access, diversity and design: A synthesis for critical literacy education. *Educational Review, 52,* 175–186.

Kellner, D. (2000). Multiple literacies and critical pedagogies: New paradigms. In P. Trifonas (Ed.), *Revolutionary pedagogies* (pp. 196–221). New York: Routledge.

Knoblauch, C. H., & Brannon, L. (1993). *Critical teaching and the idea of literacy.* Portsmouth, NH: Boynton/Cook.

Knobel, M., & Healy, A. (1998). *Critical literacy in the primary classroom.* Newton, NSW, Australia: Primary English Teaching Association.

Lankshear, C. (1997). *Changing literacies*. Buckingham, UK: Open University Press.

Lankshear, C., & Knobel, M. (2003). *New literacy: Changing knowledge and classroom learning*. Buckingham, UK: Open University Press.

Lankshear, C., & McLaren, P. (1993). *Critical literacy: Politics, Praxis, and the postmodern*. Albany, NY: SUNY Press.

Lankshear, C., Peters, M., & Knobel, M. (1996). Critical pedagogy and cyberspace. In H. Giroux, C. Lankshear, P. McLaren, & M. Peters (Eds.), *Counternarratives: Cultural studies and critical pedagogies in postmodern spaces* (pp. 149–188). New York: Routledge.

Lensmire, T. (2001). Writing for critical democracy: Student voice and teacher practice in the writing workshop. In S. Boran & B. Comber (Eds.), *Critiquing whole language and classroom inquiry* (pp. 103–122). Urbana, IL: National Council of Teachers of English.

Leonard, P. (1993). Critical pedagogy and state welfare: Intellectual encounters with Freire and Gramsci, 1974–86. In P. McLaren & P. Leonard (Eds.) *Paulo Freire: A critical encounter,* (pp.155–168). New York: Routledge.

Luke, A. (2000). Critical literacy in Australia: A matter of context and standpoint. *Journal of Adolescent and Adult Literacy, 43,* 448–461.

Luke, A., & Freebody, P. (1997). The social practices of reading. In S. Muspratt, A. Luke, & P. Freebody (Eds.), *Constructing critical literacies* (pp. 185–226). Cresskill, NJ: Hampton.

Luke, A., & Luke, C. (2001). Adolescence lost/childhood regained: On early intervention and the emergence of the techno-subject. *Journal of Early Childhood Literacy, 1,* 91–120.

Mayo, P. (1997). Reflections on Freire's work: A Maltese contribution. *Taboo: The Journal of Culture and Education, 2,* 120–123.

Mayo, P. (1999). *Gramsci, Freire and adult education: Possibilities for transformative action*. London: Zed Books.

Mayo, P. (2004). *Liberation praxis: Paulo Freire's legacy for racial education and politics*. Westport, CT: Praeger.

McLaren, P. (1997). *Revolutionary multiculturalism: Pedagogies of dissent for the new millennium*. Boulder, CO: Westview.

McLaren, P. (2000a). Paulo Freire's pedagogy of possibility. In S. Steiner (Ed.), *Freirean pedagogy, praxis, and possibilities: Projects for the new millennium* (pp. 1–22). New York: Falmer.

McLaren, P. (2000b). *Che Guevara, Paulo Freire, and the pedagogy of revolution*. Lanham, MD: Rowman and Littlefield.

McLaren, P., & Farahmanpur, R. (2005). *Teaching against global capitalism and the new imperialism: A critical pedagogy*. Lanham, MD: Rowman and Littlefield.

McLaren, P., & Lankshear, C. (1994). *Politics of liberation: Paths from Freire*. New York: Routledge.

Morgan, W. (1997). *Critical literacy in the classroom: The art of the possible*. New York: Routledge.

Muspratt, S., Luke, A., & Freebody, P. (1997). *Constructing critical literacies*. Cresskill, NJ: Hampton.

O'Brien, J. (1994). Critical literacy in an early childhood classroom: A progress report. *The Australian Journal of Language and Literacy, 17,* 36–44.

O'Brien, J. (2001). I knew that already": How children's books limit inquiry. In S. Boran & B. Comber (Eds.), *Critiquing whole language and school inquiry* (pp. 142–168). Urbana, IL: NCTE.

O'Neill, M. (1992). Teaching literature as cultural criticism. *English Quarterly, 25,* 19–25.

Schugurensky, D. (1998). The legacy of Paulo Freire: A critical review of his contributions. *Convergence, XXI*(1&2), 17–29.

Searle, C. (1998). *None but our words: Critical literacy in the classroom.* Buckingham, UK: Open University Press.

Searle, C. (1993). Words to a life-land: Literacy, the imagination and Palestine. In C. Lankshear & P. McLaren (Eds.), *Critical literacy: Politics, praxis and the postmodern* (pp. 167–192). Albany, NY: State University of New York Press.

Shannon, P. (2001). Turn, turn, turn: Language education, politics and freedom at the turn of three centuries. In P. Shannon (Ed.) *Becoming political, too: New readings and writings on the politics of literacy education* (pp. 10–30). Portsmouth, NH: Heinemann.

Shannon, P. (2000). Imagine that: Literacy education for public democracy. In N. Padak, K. Roskos, T. Rosinski, and J. Peck (Eds.), *Distinguished Educators on Reading: Contributions that have shaped effective literacy instruction* (pp. 69–87). Newark, DE: The International Reading Association.

Shannon, P. (1990). *The struggle to continue: Progressive reading instruction in the United States.* Portsmouth, NH: Heinemann.

Shannon, T., & Shannon, P. (2001). Classrooms in community: From curriculum to pedagogy. In S. Boran & B. Comber (Eds.), *Critiquing whole language and classroom inquiry* (pp. 123–141). Urbana, IL: National Council of Teachers of English.

Shor, I. (Ed.). (1987). *Freire for the classroom: Sourcebook for liberatory teaching.* Portsmouth, NH: Heinemann.

Shor, I., & Pari, C. (Eds.). (1999). *Education is politics: Critical teaching across differences, K–12* Portsmouth, NH: Heinemann.

Shor I., & Pari, C. (Eds.). (2000). *Education is politics: Critical teaching across differences, PostSecondary.* Portsmouth, NH: Heinemann.

Steiner, S. (Ed.). (2000). *Freirean pedagogy, praxis and possibilities: Projects for the new millennium.* New York: Falmer.

Stokes, W. T. (1997). Progressive teacher education: Consciousness, identity, and knowledge. In P. Freire, J. Fraser, D. Maceod, T. McKinnon, & W. Stokes (Eds.) *Mentoring the mentor: A critical dialogue with Paulo Freire* (pp. 201–227). New York: Peter Lang.

Taxel, J. (2002). Children's literature at the turn of the century: Toward a political economy of the publishing industry. *Research in the Teaching of English, 37,* 145–197.

Torres, C. A. (1993). From the pedagogy of the oppressed to a Luta Continua—the political pedagogy of Paulo Freire. In P. McLaren & P. Leonard (Eds.), *Paulo Freire: A critical encounter* (pp. 119–145). London: Routledge.

Torres. C. A. (1998). *Democracy, education, and multiculturalism: Dilemmas of citizenship in a global world.* Lanham: Rowman & Littlefield.

Vasquez, V. (2004). *Negotiating critical literacies.* Mahwah, NJ: Lawrence Erlbaum Associates, Inc.

Vasquez, V. (2005). Creating opportunities for critical literacy with young children: Using everyday issues and everyday text. In J. Evans (Ed.), *Literacy moves on: Popular culture, new technologies and critical literacy in the elementary classroom* (pp. 83–105). Portsmouth NH: Heinemann.

Weiler, K. (1996). Myths of Paulo Freire. *Educational Theory, 46,* 353–371.

Weiler, K. (2001). Rereading Paulo Freire. In K. Weiler (Ed.) text *Feminist engagements: Reading, resisting and revisioning male theorists in education and cultural studies* (pp. 67–87).

Weiner, E. (2001). Beyond remediation: Toward ideological literacies of learning. *Journal of Adolescent and Adult Literacy, 46*(2), 150–168.

Weiner, E. (2003). Beyond "Doing:" Cultural studies: Toward a cultural studies of critical pedagogy. *The Review of Education, Pedagogy, and Cultural Studies, 25,* 55–73.

Weiner, E. (2005). *Private learning, public needs: The neoliberal assault on democratic education.* New York: Peter Lang.

Willis, P. (1977). *Learning to labor: How workingclass kids get workingclass jobs.* Westmead, UK: Saxon House.

## CHAPTER TWO: RADICAL COUNTERNARRATIVES I

### Feminist Theory and Research

AAUW Educational Foundation. (1995). *How schools shortchange girls.* New York: Marlowe.

Barnes, L. (1990). Gender bias in teachers' written comments. In S. Gabriel & I. Smithson (Eds.) *Gender in the classroom: Power and pedagogy,* (pp.128–140). Chicago, IL: University of Illinois.

Bean, T., & Harper, H. (in press). Reading men differently: Alternative portrayals of masculinity in contemporary young adult fiction. *Reading Psychology: An International Quarterly.*

Best, A. (2000). *Prom night: Youth, schools, and popular culture.* New York: Routledge.

Cameron, D. (1998). *The feminist critique of language: A reader,* 2nd ed. New York: Routledge.

Caywood, C. & Overing, G. (1987). *Teaching writing: Pedagogy, gender and equity.* Albany, NY: State University of New York.

Christian-Smith, L. (1993). *Texts of desire: Essays on fiction, femininity and schooling:* London: The Falmer Press.

Cherland, M. (1994). *Private practices: Girls reading fiction and constructing identity.* London: Taylor and Francis.

Davies, B. (1991). *Frogs and snails and feminist tales: Preschool children and gender.* Sydney, Australia: Allen & Unwin.

Davies, B. (2003). *Shards of glass: Children reading and writing beyond gendered identities,* 2nd edition. Sydney: Allen and Unwin.

Davies, B. & Banks (1992). The gender trap: A feminist poststructuralist analysis of primary school children's talk about gender. *Journal of Curriculum Studies, 24,* 1–25.

Dolby, N. (2003). Popular culture and democratic practice: *Harvard Educational Review, 73,* 258–284.

Faludi, S. (1991). *Backlash: The undeclared war against American women.* New York: Doubleday.

Fetterley, (1978). *The resisting reader.* Bloomington, IL.: Indiana University.

Finders, M. (1997). *Just girls: Hidden literacies and life in junior high.* New York: Teachers College Press.

Gilbert, P. (1989). Personally (and passively) yours: Girls, literacy and education. *Oxford Review of Education, 15,* 257–265.

Giroux, H. (1997). *Education and Cultural Studies: Toward a performative practice.* New York: Routledge.

Grossberg, L. Nelson, C., & Treichler, P. (1992). *Cultural studies.* New York: Routledge.

Guzzetti, B. (2002). Zines. In B. Guzzetti (Ed.), *Literacy in America: An encyclopedia of history, theory and practice, volume two.* Santa Barbara, CA: ABC Clio.

Harper, H. (2000). *Wild words/dangerous desires: High school girls and feminist avant-garde writing.* New York: Peter Lang.

Harper, H. (1998). Suffering femininity: The power and pleasure of young adolescent literature for girls. *Journal of Adolescent and Adult literacy,* 42, pp. 145–148.

Harper, H. (in press). Studying masculinity in books about girls. Special issue on boys, literacy and schooling in *Canadian Journal of Education.*

Horsman, J. (1990). *Something in My Mind Besides the Everyday.* Toronto: The Women's Press.

Horsman, J. (2000). *Too Scared to Learn:* Women, *violence and education.* Mahwah, NJ: Lawrence Erlbaum.

Innes, S. A. (1998a). *Millennium girls: today's girls around the world.* Lanham, MD: Rowman & Littlefield.

Innes, S. A. (1998b). *Delinquents and Debutantes: Twentieth-century American Girls' Cultures.* New York: New York University Press.

Kehler, M., & Martino, W. (Eds.). (in press). Boys, literacies and schooling [Special issue]. *Canadian Journal of Education.*

McRobbie, A. (2000). *Feminism and youth culture* (2nd ed.). New York: Routledge.

McRobbie, A. (1997). More! New sexualities in girls' and women's magazines. In A. McRobbie (Ed.) *Back to reality: Social experience and cultural studies* (pp.190–209). Manchester, UK: Manchester University.

McRobbie, A. (1994). *Postmodernism and popular culture.* New York: Routledge.

McRobbie, A. (1991). *Feminism and youth culture: From 'Jackie' to 'Just Seventeen.'* Boston: Unwin Hyman.

Mazzarella, S., & Pecora, N. (2001). *Growing up girls: Popular culture and the construction of identity.* New York: Peter Lang.

Radway, J. (1986). *Reading the romance: Women, patriarchy, and popular literature.* Chapel Hill: University of North Carolina Press.

Radway, J. (1984). *Reading the romance: Women, patriarchy, and popular literature.* Chapel Hill: University of North Carolina.

Rice, S. (2000). Gendered readings of a traditional 'feminist' folktale by sixth grade boys and girls. *Journal of Literacy Research, 32,* 211–236.

Rice, S. (2002). Creating spaces for boys and girls to expand their definitions of masculinity and femininity through children's literature. *Journal of Children's Literature,* fall, 33–42.

Rockhill, K. (1987). Gender, language and the politics of literacy. *British Journal of Sociology of Education, 8,* 153–167.

Rockhill, K. (1991). Literacy as threat/desire: Longing to be SOMEBODY. In J. Gaskell & A. McLaren (Eds.), *Women and education* (pp. 333–349). Calgary, Canada: Detselig.

Rockhill, K. (1993). Dis/connecting literacy and sexuality: Speaking the unspeakable in the classroom. In C. Lankshear & P. McLaren (Eds.), *Critical literacy: Politics, praxis and the postmodern* (pp. 335–366). Albany, NY: SUNY Press.

Sadker & Sadker (1994). *Failing at fairness: How America's schools cheat girls.* New York: C. Scribner's Sons.

Stone, L. (1994). *The education feminist reader.* New York: Routledge.

Walkerdine, V. (1987). Some day my prince will come. In A. McRobbie & M. Nava (Eds.).*Gender and Generation* (pp.162–168). London: Macmillan.

Walkerdine, V. (1990). *Schoolgirl Fictions.* London: Verso Press.

Wason-Ellam, L. (1997). 'If only I was like Barbie.' *Language Arts, 74,* 430–437.

Weiler, K. (2001). *Feminist engagements: Reading, resisting, and revisioning male theorists in education and cultural studies.* New York: Routledge.

## Queer Theory

Aronowitz, S., & Giroux, H. A. (1991). *Postmodern education: Politics, culture, and social criticism.* Minneapolis: University of Minnesota Press.

Blackburn, M. V. (2002). Disrupting the (hetero)normative: Exploring literacy performances and identity work with queer youth. *Journal of Adolescent and Adult Literacy, 46,* 312–324.

Blackburn, M. V. (2003a). Exploring literacy performances and power dynamics at The Loft: Queer youth reading the word and the world. *Research in the Teaching of English, 37,* 467–490.

Blackburn, M. V. (2003b). Losing, finding, and making space for activism through literacy performances and identity work. *Penn GSE Perspectives on Urban Education,* [online serial] *1*(3). Retrieved from http://www.urbanedjournal.org/archive/issues/articles/article0008.html

Blackburn, M. V. (2004). Understanding agency beyond school-sanctioned activities. *Theory Into Practice, 43*, 102–110.

Britzman, D. P. (1995a). Is there a queer pedagogy? Or, stop reading straight. *Educational Theory, 45*, 151–165.

Britzman, D. P. (1995b). What is this thing called love? *Taboo: The Journal of Cultural Studies in Education, 65–93.*

Britzman, D. P. (1996). On becoming a "little sex researcher": Some comments on a polymorphously perverse curriculum. *Journal of Curriculum Theorizing, 12*(2), 4–11.

Britzman, D. P. (1998a). On some psychical consequences of AIDS education. In W. F. Pinar ( Ed.), *Queer theory in education* (pp. 321–335). Mahwah, NJ: Lawrence Erlbaum Associates.

Britzman, D. P. (1998b). *Lost subjects, contested objects: Toward a psychoanalytic inquiry of learning.* Albany, NY: SUNY Press.

Butler, J. (1990). *Gender trouble: Feminism and the subversion of identity.* New York: Routledge.

Butler, J. (1999). Preface. *Gender trouble: Feminism and the subversion of identity* (10th anniversary ed., pp. vii–xxvi). New York: Routledge.

Carlson, D. (1998). Who am I? Gay identity and a democratic politics of the self. In W. F. Pinar (Ed.), *Queer theory in education* (pp. 107–119). Mahwah, NJ: Lawrence Erlbaum Associates.

de Castell, S., & Bryson, M. (1998). From the ridiculous to the sublime: On finding oneself in educational research. In W. F. Pinar (Ed.), *Queer theory in education* (pp. 245–250). Mahwah, NJ: Lawrence Erlbaum Associates.

Derrida, J. (1987). *The post card: From Socrates to Freud and beyond.* Chicago: University of Chicago Press.

Foucault, M. (1988). *The care of the self, volume three of the "History of sexuality."* New York: Vintage Books.

Foucault, M. (1978/1990). *The history of sexuality: An introduction. Volume I.* New York: Vintage.

Freud, A. (1979). *Psychoanalysis for teachers and parents.* New York: Norton.

Freud, S. (1968). *The standard edition of the complete psychological works of Sigmund Freud, Volume VII (1901–1905).* London: Hogarth.

Fuss, D. (1991). Inside/out. In D. Fuss (Ed.), *Inside/out: Lesbian theories, gay theories* (pp. 1–10). New York: Routledge.

Gamson, J. (2000). Sexualities, queer theory and qualitative research. In N. K. Denzin & Y. S. Lincoln (Eds.), *Handbook of qualitative research* (2nd ed., pp. 347–365). Thousand Oaks, CA: Sage.

Garber, L. (Ed.). (1994). *Tilting the tower: Lesbians teaching queer subjects.* New York: Routledge.

Gleitzman, M. (1996). *Two weeks with the queen.* Sydney, Australia: Pan Macmillan.

Gonzales, M. C. (1994). Cultural conflict: Introducing the queer in a Mexican-American literature class. In L. Garber (Ed.), *Tilting the tower* (pp. 56–62). New York: Routledge.

Hammett, R. F. (1992). A rationale and unit plan for introducing gay and lesbian literature into the Grade 12 curriculum. In P. Shannon (Ed.), *Becoming political: Readings and writings in the politics of literacy education* (pp. 250–262). Portsmouth, NH: Heinemann.

Haver, W. (1998). Of mad men who practice invention to the brink of intelligibility. In W. F. Pinar (Ed.), *Queer theory in education* (pp. 349–364). Mahwah, NJ: Lawrence Erlbaum Associates.

Honeychurch, K. G. (1998). Carnal knowledge: Re-searching (through) the sexual body. In W. F. Pinar (Ed.), *Queer theory in education* (pp. 251–273). Mahwah, NJ: Lawrence Erlbaum Associates.

Jarraway, D. R. (2002). Tales of the city: Marginality, community, and the problem of (gay) identity in Wallace Thurman's "Harlem" fiction. *College English, 65*, 36–52.

King, J. R., & Schneider, J. J. (1999). Locating a place for gay and lesbian themes in elementary reading, writing and talking. In W. J. Letts & J. T. Sears (Eds.), *Queering elementary education: Advancing the dialogue about sexualities and schooling* (pp. 125–136). Lanham, MD: Rowman & Littlefield.

Kinsey, A. C., Pomeroy, W. B., & Martin, C. E. (1948). *Sexual behavior in the human male*. Philadelphia: W. B. Saunders.

Kinsey, A. C., Pomeroy, W. B., Martin, C. E., & Gebhard, P. H. (1953). *Sexual behavior in the human female*. Philadelphia: W. B. Saunders.

Kopelson, K. (2002). Dis/integrating the gay/queer binary: "Reconstructed identity politics" for a performative pedagogy. *College English, 65*, 17–35.

Kumashiro, K. K. (2002). *Troubling education: "Queer" activism and anti-oppressive pedagogy*. New York: Routledge Falmer.

Kumashiro, K. K. (2003). *Against common sense: Teaching and learning toward social justice*. New York: Routledge Falmer.

Lacan, J. (1977). *The four fundamental concepts of psycho-analysis*. London: Hogarth.

Letts, W. J., & Sears, J. T. (Eds.). (1999). *Queering elementary education: Advancing the dialogue about sexualities and schooling*. Lanham, MD: Rowman & Littlefield.

Lorde, A. (1982). *Zami: A new spelling of my name*. Freedom, CA: The Crossing.

Lowry, L. (1993). *The giver*. New York: Bantam Doubleday.

Luhmann, S. (1998). Queering/querying pedagogy? Or, pedagogy is a pretty queer thing. In W. F. Pinar (Ed.), *Queer theory in education* (pp. 141–155). Mahwah, NJ: Lawrence Erlbaum Associates.

Lyotard, J. F. (1984). *The postmodern condition: A report on knowledge* (G. Bennington and B. Massumi, Trans.). Minneapolis: University of Minnesota Press.

Martino, W. (1999). "It's OK to be gay": Interrupting straight thinking in the English classroom. In W. J. Letts & J. T. Sears (Eds.), *Queering elementary education: Advancing the dialogue about sexualities and schooling* (pp. 137–149). Lanham, MD: Rowman & Littlefield.

Meiners, E. (1998). Remember when all the cars were Fords and all the lesbians were women? Some notes on identity, mobility, and capital. In W. F. Pinar (Ed.), *Queer theory in education* (pp. 121–140). Mahwah, NJ: Lawrence Erlbaum Associates.

Miller, J. L. (1998). Autobiography as a queer curriculum practice. In W. F. Pinar (Ed.), *Queer theory in education* (pp. 365–373). Mahwah, NJ: Lawrence Erlbaum Associates.

Morris, M. (1998). Unresting the curriculum: Queer projects, queer imaginings. In W. F. Pinar (Ed.), *Queer theory in education* (pp. 275–286). Mahwah, NJ: Lawrence Erlbaum Associates.

Ortner, S. B., & Whitehead, H. (Eds.). (1981). *Sexual meanings: The cultural construction of gender and sexuality.* Cambridge, UK: Cambridge University Press.

Pennycook, A. (2001). *Critical applied linguistics: A critical introduction.* Mahwah, NJ: Lawrence Erlbaum Associates, Inc.

Pinar, W. F. (Ed.). (1998). *Queer theory in education.* Mahwah, NJ: Lawrence Erlbaum Associates.

Rodriguez, N. (1998). (Queer) youth as political and pedagogical. In W. F. Pinar (Ed.), *Queer theory in education* (pp. 173–185). Mahwah, NJ: Lawrence Erlbaum Associates.

Schneider, J. L. (2002). Secret sins of the Orient: Creating a (Homo)textual context for reading Byron's *The Giaour. College English, 65,* 81–95.

Sears, J. T. (1988). Growing up gay: Is anyone there to listen? *American School Counselors Newsletter, 26,* 8–9.

Sears, J. T. (1990). *Growing up gay in the South.* New York: Haworth.

Sears, J. T. (Ed.). (1992). *Sexuality and the curriculum: The politics and practices of sexuality education.* New York: Teachers College Press.

Sears, J. T. (1997). Centering culture: Teaching for critical sexual literacy using the sexual diversity wheel. *Journal of Moral Education, 26,* 273–283.

Sears, J. T. (1998). A generational and theoretical analysis of culture and male (homo)sexuality. In W. F. Pinar (Ed.), *Queer theory in education* (pp. 73–105). Mahwah, NJ: Lawrence Erlbaum Associates.

Sears, J. T. (1999). Teaching queerly: Some elementary propositions. In W. J. Letts & J. T. Sears (Eds.), *Queering elementary education: Advancing the dialogue about sexualities and schooling* (pp. 3–14). Lanham, MD: Rowman & Littlefield.

Sears, J. T., with Carper, J. C. (1998). *Curriculum, religion, and public education: Conversations for an enlarging public square.* New York: Teachers College Press.

Sedgewick, E. K. (1990). *Epistemology of the closet.* Berkeley: University of California Press.

Spurlin, W. J. (2002). Theorizing queer pedagogy in English studies after the 1990s. *College English, 65,* 9–16.

Steinberg, S. R. (1998). Appropriating queerness: Hollywood sanitation. In W. F. Pinar (Ed.), *Queer theory in education* (pp. 187–195). Mahwah, NJ: Lawrence Erlbaum Associates.

Sumara D., & Davis, B. (1999). Interrupting heteronormativity: Toward a queer curriculum theory. *Curriculum Inquiry, 29,* 191–208.

Sumara, D., & Davis, B. (1998). Telling tales of surprise. In W. F. Pinar (Ed.), *Queer theory in education* (pp. 197–219). Mahwah, NJ: Lawrence Erlbaum Associates.

Sykes, H., & Goldstein, H. (2004). From performed to performing ethnography: Translating life history research into anti-homophobia curriculum for a teacher education program. *Teaching Education, 15*, 41–61.

Tierney, W. G., & Dilley, P. (1998). Constructing knowledge: Educational research and gay and lesbian studies. In W. F. Pinar (Ed.), *Queer theory in education* (pp. 49–71). Mahwah, NJ: Lawrence Erlbaum Associates, Inc.

Walcott, R. (1998). Queer texts and performativity: Zora, rap, and community. In W. F. Pinar (Ed.), *Queer theory in education* (pp. 157–171). Mahwah, NJ: Lawrence Erlbaum Associates.

Zeikowitz, R. E. (2002). Befriending the Medieval queer: A pedagogy for literature classes. *College English, 65*, 67–80.

## CHAPTER THREE:
## RADICAL COUNTERNARRATIVES IN LITERACY EDUCATION II
### Postcolonial Theory

Appiah, K. A. (1991). Is the post in postmodernism the post in postcolonial? *Critical Inquiry, 17*, 336–357.

Ashcroft, B., Griffiths, G., & Tiffin, H. (Eds.). (1989). *The empire writes back: Theory and practice in post-colonial literatures.* London: Routledge.

Ashcroft, B., Griffiths, G., & Tiffin, H. (Eds.). (1995). *The Post-colonial studies reader.* London: Routledge.

Bhabha, H. K. (1985). Signs taken for wonders: Questions of ambivalence and authority under a tree outside Delhi, May 1917. *Critical Inquiry, 12*, 144–165.

Canagarajah, S. (1999). *Resisting linguistic imperialism in English teaching.* Oxford, UK: Oxford University Press.

Delpit, L. (1988). The silenced dialogue: Power and pedagogy in educating other people's children. *Harvard Educational Review, 58*, 280–298.

Delpit, L. (1995). *Other people's children.* New York: The New Press.

Delpit, L., & Dowdy, J. K. (2002). *The skin that we speak: Thoughts on language and culture in the classroom.* New York: The New Press.

Fanon, F. (1952). *Black skin/white masks* (C. L. Markmann, Trans., 1968). London: MacGibbon and Kee.

Fanon, F. (1963). *The wretched of the earth* (C. Farrington, Trans.). New York: Grover.

Foucault, M. (1980). *Power/knowledge* (C. Gordon, Ed., C. Gordon, L. Marshall, J. Mepham, & K. Soper, Trans.). New York: Pantheon.

Greenlaw, J. (1995). Heterogeneous representations of Chinese women in young adult literature: A postcolonial reading. *Canadian Children's Literature, 21*(3), 26–38.

Gunderson, L. (2000). Voices of the teenage diasporas. *Journal of Adolescent and Adult Literacies, 43*, 692–706.

Gunderson, L. (2004). The language, literacy, achievement, and social consequences of English-only programs for immigrant students. In J. Hoffman & D. Schalhert (Eds.) The 53rd *National Reading Conference Yearbook* (pp. 1–27). Milwaukee, WI: NRC, Inc.

Harper, H. (2000). English Studies in the least harmful ways: Teaching identity and language. In B. R. C. Barrell & R. F. Hammett (Eds.), *Advocating change: Contemporary Issues in subject English* (pp. 90–101). Toronto, Canada: Irwin.

Hart, J., & Goldie, T. (1993). Post-colonial theory. In I. R. Makaryk (Ed.), *Encyclopedia of contemporary literary theory: Approaches, scholars, terms* (pp. 155–158). Toronto: University of Toronto Press.

hooks, b. (1994). *Teaching to transgress: Education as the practice of freedom.* New York and London: Routledge.

Lamming, G. (1960). *The pleasures of exile.* London: Michael Joseph.

Luke, A. (1997). Literacy and the Other: A sociological approach to literacy research and policy in multilingual societies. *Reading Research Quarterly, 35*, 132–141.

Luke, A., Nakata, M. Singh, M., & Smith, R. (1993). Policy and the politics of representation: Torres Strait Islanders and Aborigines at the margins. In R. Lingard, J. Knight & P. Porter (Eds.), *Schooling reform in hard times* (pp. 139–152). London: Falmer.

MacGillivray, L., Ardell, A. L., Curwen, M. S., & Palma, J. (2004). Colonized teachers: Examining the implementation of a scripted reading program. *Teaching Education, 15*(2), 131–144.

McCarthy, C., Giardin, M. D.,Harewood, S. J., & Park, J. K. (2003). Contesting culture: Identity and curriculum dilemmas in the age of globalization, postcolonialism, and multiplicity. *Harvard Educational Review, 73*(3), 449–465.

Mohanty, C. T. (1995). Under western eyes: Feminist scholarship and colonial discourses. In B. Ashcroft, G. Griffiths, & H. Tiffin (Eds.), *The post-colonial studies reader* (pp. 259–263). London: Routledge.

Ogbu, J. (1990). Literacy and schooling in subordinate cultures: The case of Black Americans. In K. Lomotey (Ed.), *Going to school: The African American experience* (pp. 113–131). Albany, NY: SUNY Press.

Ogbu, J. U. (1991). Low school performance as an adaptation: The case of Blacks in Stockton, California. In M. A. Gibson & J. U. Ogbu (Eds.), *Minority status and schooling: A comparative study of immigrant and involuntary minorities* (pp. 249–285). New York: Garland.

Pennycook, A. (2001). *Critical applied linguistics: A critical introduction.* Mahwah, NJ: Lawrence Erlbaum Associates, Inc.

Pennycook, A. (1998). *English and the discourses of colonialism.* London: Routledge.

Petersen, K. H. (1995). First things first: Problems of a feminist approach to African literature. In B. Ashcroft, G. Griffiths & H. Tiffin (Eds.), *The post-colonial studies reader* (pp. 251–254). London: Routledge.

Pratt, M. L. (1992). *Imperial eyes: Travel writing and transculturation.* New York: Routledge.

*Report of the Royal Commission on Aboriginal Peoples.* (1996). Ottawa, Ontario, Canada: Ministry of Supply and Services.

Said, E. (1978). *Orientalism.* London: Routledge and Kegan Paul.

Said, E. (1993). *Culture and imperialism.* New York: Vintage Books.

Semali, L., & Kinchloe, J. L. (1999). *What is indigenous knowledge? Voices from the academy.* New York: Falmer.

Singh, M. G. (1995). Edward Said's critique of Orientalism and Australia's "Asia literacy" curriculum. *Journal of Curriculum Studies, 27,* 599–620.

Singh, M. G. (1996). Studying Asia for the national economic interest: An analysis of the Australian Government's strategy for schools. *Discourse: Studies in the Cultural Politics of Education, 17,* 153–170.

Singh, M. G., & Greenlaw, J. (1998). Postcolonial theory in the literature classroom: Contrapuntal readings. *Theory Into Practice, 37*(3), 193–202.

Spivak, G. C. (1988). Can the subaltern speak? In C. Nelson & L. Grossberg (Eds.), *Marxism and the interpretation of culture.* London: Macmillan.

Spivak, G. C. (1995). Three women's texts and a critique of imperialism. In B. Ashcroft, G. Griffiths, & H. Tiffin (Eds.), *The post-colonial studies reader* (pp. 269–272). London: Routledge.

Tejeda, C., Espinoza, M., & Gutierrez, K. (2003). Toward a decolonizing pedagogy: Social justice reconsidered. In P. P. Tritons (Ed.), *Pedagogies of difference: Rethinking education for social change* (pp. 11–40). New York and London: Routledge Falmer.

Viswanathan, G. (1989). *Masks of conquest: Literary study in British rule in India.* New York: Columbia University Press.

Viswanathan, G. (1998). Milton, imperialism and education. *Modern Language Quarterly 59,* 345–361.

Willinsky, J. (1998). *Learning to divide the world: Education at empire's end.* Minneapolis: University of Minnesota Press.

Wright, H. K. (2004). *A prescience of African cultural studies: The future of literature in Africa is not what it was.* New York: Peter Lang.

## Critical Race Theory

Bell, D. A. (1979). *Bakke,* minority admissions, and the usual price of racial remedies. *California Law Review, 76,* 3–19.

Bell, D. A. (1987). *And we are not saved: The elusive quest for racial justice.* New York: Basic Books.

Bell, D. A. (1989). The final report: Harvard's affirmative action allegory. *Michigan Law Review, 87,* 2382–2410.

Bergerson, A. A. (2003). Critical race theory: Is there room for white scholars in fighting racism in education? *Qualitative Studies in Education, 16,* 51–63.

Blackburn, M. V. (2002). Disrupting the (hetero)normative: Exploring literacy performances and identity work with queer youth. *Journal of Adolescent and Adult Literacy, 46,* 312–324.

Blackburn, M. V. (2003a). Exploring literacy performances and power dynamics at The Loft: Queer youth reading the word and the world. *Research in the Teaching of English, 37,* 467–490.

Blackburn, M. V. (2003b). Losing, finding, and making space for activism through literacy performances and identity work. *Penn GSE Perspectives on Urban Education,* [online serial] *1*(3). Retrieved from http://www.urbanedjournal.org/archive/issues/articles/article0008.html

Blackburn, M. V. (2004). Understanding agency beyond school-sanctioned activities. *Theory Into Practice, 43*, 102–110.

Crenshaw, K. W. (1988). Race, reform and retrenchment: Transformation and legitimation in anti-discrimination law. *Harvard Law Review, 101*, 1331–1387.

Crenshaw, K. W. (1993). Beyond racism and misogyny: Black feminism and 2 Live Crew. In M. J. Matsuda, C. R. Lawrence, R. Delgado, & K. W. Crenshaw (Eds.), *Words that wound: Critical race theory, assaultive speech, and the First Amendment* (pp. 111–132). Boulder, CO: Westview.

Crenshaw, K., Gotanda, N., Peller, G., & Thomas, K. (Eds.). (1995). *Critical race theory: The key writings that formed the movement.* New York: The New Press.

Delgado, R. (1990). When a story is just a story: Does voice really matter? *Virginia Law Review, 76*, 95–111.

Fine, M., Weis, L., Pruitt, L. P., & Burns, A. (Eds.). (2004). *Off white: Readings on power, privilege, and resistance* (2nd ed.). New York and London: Routledge.

Graff, H. J. (1979). *The literacy myth: Literacy and social structure in the nineteenth century city.* New York: Academic Press.

Greene, S., & Abt-Perkins, D (Eds). (2003). Introduction: How can literacy research contribute to racial understanding? *Making Race Visible: Literacy Research for Cultural Understanding* (pp. 1–31). New York: Teachers College Press.

Gutierrez, K., Asasato, J., Santos, M., & Gotanda, N. (2002). Backlash pedagogy: Language and culture and the politics of reform. *Review of Education, Pedagogy and Cultural Studies, 24*, 335–351.

Heath, S. B. (1983). *Ways with words: Language, life and work in communities and classrooms.* Cambridge, MA: Cambridge University Press.

Herrnstein, R. J., & Murray, C. (1994). *The bell curve: Intelligence and class structure in American life.* New York: Free Press.

Hilliard, A. G. (1979). Standardization and cultural bias as impediments to the scientific study and validation of "intelligence." *Journal of Research and Development in Education, 12*, 47–58.

Jensen, A. R. (1969). How much can we boost IQ and scholastic achievement? *Harvard Educational Review, 39*, 1–123.

Kamin, L. (1974). *The science and politics of IQ.* New York: Wiley.

Kincheloe, J., Steinberg, S. R., Rodriguez, N. M., & Chennault, R. E. (Eds.). (2000). *White reign: Deploying whiteness in America.* New York: St. Martin's Press.

King, J. (1991). Dyconscious racism: Ideology, identity and the miseducation of teachers. *Journal of Negro Education, 60*, 133–146.

Ladson-Billings, G. J. (1999). Preparing teachers for diverse populations: A critical race theory perspective. *Review of Educational Research, 24*, 211–247.

Lali, R., & Hinchman, K. A. (2001). Critical issues: Examining constructions of race in literacy research. *Journal of Literacy Research, 33*, 529–561.

Lamos, S. (2000). Basic writing, CUNY, and "mainstreaming": (De)racialization reconsidered. *Journal of Basic Writing, 19*(2), 22–43.

Madaus, G. E. (1994). A technological and historical consideration of equity issues associated with proposals to change the nation's testing policy. *Harvard Educational Review, 64,* 76–95.

Monture-Angus, P. (2002). On being homeless: One Aboriginal woman's "conquest" of Canadian universities, 1989–89. In F. Valdes, J. M. Culp, & A. P. Harris (Eds.), *Crossroads, directions, and a new critical race theory* (pp. 274–287). Philadelphia: Temple University Press.

Morrison, T. (1992). *Playing in the dark: Whiteness and the literary imagination.* New York: Random House.

Nieto, S. (2003). Afterword. In S. Greene & D. Abt-Perkins (Eds.), *Making race visible: Literacy research for cultural understanding* (pp. 149–205). New York: Teachers College Press.

Prendergast, C. (2002). The economy of literacy: How the Supreme Court stalled the civil rights movement. *Harvard Educational Review, 72,* 206–229.

Prendergast, C. (2003). *Literacy and racial justice: The politics of learning after Brown versus Board of Education.* Carbondale, IL: Southern Illinois University Press.

Razack, S. H. (2002). "Simple logic:" Race, the Identity Documents Rule, and the story of a nation besieged and betrayed. In F. Valdes, J. McCristal Culp, & P. Harris (Eds.), *Crossroads, directions, and a new critical race theory* (pp. 199–220). Philadelphia: Temple University Press.

Schick, C. (2000). "By virtue of being White": Resistance in anti-racist pedagogy. *Race, Ethnicity and Education, 3,* 83–102.

Solórzano, D. G., & Delgado Bernal, D. (2001). Examining transformational resistance through a critical race and LatCrit theory framework: Chicana and Chicano students in an urban context. *Urban Education, 36,* 308–342.

Solórzano, D. G., & Yosso, T. J. (2001). Critical race and LatCrit theory and method: Counterstorytelling. *International Journal of Qualitative Studies in Education, 14,* 471–495.

Solórzano, D. G., & Yosso, T. J. (2002). Critical race methodology: Counter-storytelling as an analytical framework for education research. *Qualitative Inquiry, 8,* 23–44.

Tate, W. F. (1997). Critical race theory and education: History, theory and implications. In M. Apple (Ed.), *Review of educational research* (Vol. 22, pp. 195–247). Washington, DC: AERA.

Tate, W., & Ladson-Billings, G. (1995). Toward a critical race theory of education. *Teachers College Record, 97,* 47–68.

Tate, W. F., Ladson-Billings, G., & Grant, C. A. (1993). The *Brown* decision revisited: Mathematizing social problems. *Educational Policy, 7,* 255–275.

Valdes, F., McCristal Culp, J., & Harris, A. P. (Eds.). (2002). *Crossroads, directions, and a new critical race theory.* Philadelphia: Temple University Press.

West, C. (1995). Foreword. In K. Crenshaw, N. Gotanda, G. Peller, & K. Thomas (Eds.), *Critical race theory: The key writings that formed the movement.* New York: The New Press.

Willis, A. I. (2000). Keeping it real: Teaching and learning about culture, literacy, and respect. *English Education, 32*, 267–278.

Willis, A. I. (2003). Parallax: Addressing race in preservice literacy education. In S. Greene & D. Abt-Perkins (Eds.), *Making race visible: Literacy research for cultural understanding* (pp. 51–70). New York: Teachers College Press.

Yosso, T. J. (2002). Toward a critical race curriculum. *Equity & Excellence in Education, 35*, 93–107.


## CHAPTER FOUR: LITERACY AS SOCIAL PRACTICE


Alvermann, D. E., & Hagood, M. C. (2000). Critical media literacy: Research, theory, and practice in "New Times." *Journal of Educational Research, 93*, 193–205.

Alvermann, D. E., Moon, J. S., & Hagood, M. C. (1999). *Popular culture in the classroom: Teaching and researching critical media literacy.* Newark, DE: An IRA and NRC publication.

Au, K. H. (1980). Participation structures in reading lessons with Hawaiian children: Analysis of a culturally appropriate instructional event. *Anthropology and Education Quarterly, 11*(2), 91–115.

Barton, D. (1994). *Literacy: An introduction to the ecology of the written word.* Oxford: Basil Blackwell.

Barton, D., & Hamilton, M. (1998). *Local literacies: Reading and writing in one community.* New York and London: Routledge.

Barton, D., Hamilton, M., & Ivanic, R. (2000). *Situated literacies: Reading and writing in context.* London: Routledge.

Barton, D., & Ivanic, R. (Eds.). (1991). *Writing in the community.* Newbury Park, CA: Sage.

Barton, D., & Tusting, K. (Eds.). (2005). *Beyond communities of practice.* Cambridge, UK: Cambridge University Press.

Bean, T., & Harper, H. (in press). Exploring Notions of Freedom in and through young adult literature. *Journal of Adolescent & Adult Literacy.*

Blackburn, M. V. (2002). Disrupting the (hetero)normative: Exploring literacy performances and identity work with queer youth. *Journal of Adolescent & Adult Literacy, 46*, 312–324.

Blackburn, M. V. (2003a). Exploring literacy performances and power dynamics at The Loft: Queer youth reading the word and the world. *Research in the Teaching of English, 37*, 467–490.

Blackburn, M. V. (2003b). Losing, finding, and making space for activism through literacy performances and identity work. Penn GSE *Perspectives on Urban Education,* [online serial] *1*(3). Retrieved from http://www.urbanedjournal.org/archive/issues/articles/article0008.html

Blackburn, M. V. (2004). Understanding agency beyond school-sanctioned activities. *Theory Into Practice, 43*(2), 102–110.

Bledsoe, C. H., & Robey, K. M. (1993). Arabic literacy and secrecy among the Mende of Sierre Leone. In B. Street (Ed.), *Cross-cultural approaches to literacy* (pp. 110–134). Cambridge, UK: Cambridge University Press.

Bloch, M. (1993). The uses of schooling and literacy in a Zafimaniry village. In B. Street (Ed.), *Cross-cultural approaches to literacy* (pp. 87–109). Cambridge, UK: Cambridge University Press.

Bourdieu, P. (1984). *Distinction: A social critique of the judgment of taste* (R. Nice, Trans.). Cambridge, MA: Harvard University Press. (Original work published 1979)

Bruner, J. (1990). *Acts of meaning.* Cambridge, MA: Harvard University Press.

Camitta, M. (1993). Vernacular writing: Varieties of literacy among Philadelphia high school students. In B. Street (Ed.), *Cross-cultural approaches to literacy* (pp. 228–246). Cambridge, UK: Cambridge University Press.

Cazden, C. (1992). *Whole language plus: Essays on literacy, in the United States and New Zealand.* New York: Teachers College Press.

Cazden, C. (2000). Taking cultural differences into account. In Cope, B., & Kazalantis, M. (Eds.), *Multiliteracies: Literacy learning and the design of social futures* (pp. 249–266). London: Routledge.

Chandler-Olcott, K., & Mahar, D. (2003). Adolescents' anime-inspired "fanfictions": An exploration of multiliteracies. *Journal of Adolescent and Adult Literacy, 46,* 556–566.

Cherland, M. (1994). *Private practices: Girls reading fiction and constructing identity.* London: Taylor & Francis.

Cole, M. (1996). *Cultural psychology: A once and future discipline.* Cambridge, MA: Belknap Press of Harvard University Press.

Cope, B., & Kazalantis, M. (Eds.). (2000). *Multiliteracies: Literacy learning and the design of social futures.* London: Routledge.

Davis, B., & Sumara, D. (in press-a). *Complexity and education: Emergent thinking on learning, pedagogy, and research.*

Davis, B., & Sumara, D. (in press-b). Complexity science and educational action research: Toward a pragmatics of transformation. *International Journal of Educational Action Research.*

Davis, B., & Sumara, D. (1999). From complexity to complicity: Reading complexity theory as a moral and ethical imperative. *Journal of Curriculum Theorizing, 15*(2), 19–38.

Davis, B., Sumara, D., & Luce-Kapler, R. (2000). *Engaging minds: Learning and teaching in a complex world.* Mahwah, NJ: Lawrence Erlbaum Associates.

Delpit, L. (1988). The silenced dialogue: Power and pedagogy in educating other people's children. *Harvard Educational Review, 58,* 280–298.

Dyson, A. H. (1997a). *What difference does difference make? Teacher reflections on diversity, literacy and the urban primary school.* Urbana, IL: NCTE.

Dyson, A. H. (1997b). *Writing superheroes: Contemporary childhood, popular culture, and classroom literacy.* New York: Teachers College Press.

Dyson, A. H. (2003). "Welcome to the jam": Popular culture, school literacy, and the making of childhoods. *Harvard Educational Review, 73,* 328–361.

Fairclough, N. (1992). *Discourse and social power.* London: Polity.

Fecho, B. (1998). Crossing boundaries of race in a critical literacy classroom. In D. E. Alvermann, K. A. Hinchman, D. W. Moore, S. F. Phelps, & D. R. Waff (Eds.),

*Reconceptualizing the literacies in adolescents' lives* (pp. 75–101). Mahwah, NJ: Lawrence Erlbaum Associates.

Ferreiro, E. (1984). The underlying logic of literacy development. In H. Goelman, A. Oberg, & F. Smith (Eds.), *Awakening to literacy* (pp. 154–173). Portsmouth, NH: Heinemann.

Finders, M. (1997). *Just girls: Hidden literacies and life in junior high.* New York: Teachers College Press.

Fishman, A. (1988). *Amish literacy: What and how it means.* Portsmouth, NH: Heinemann.

Freire, P. (1970). *Pedagogy of the oppressed.* New York: Continuum.

Freire, P. (1998). *Pedagogy of freedom.* New York: Rowman and Littlefield.

Gee, J. P. (1992). What is literacy? In P. Shannon (Ed.), *Becoming political: Readings and writings in the politics of literacy education* (pp. 21–28). Portsmouth NH: Heinemann.

Gee, J. P. (1999). Reading and the new literacy studies: Reframing the National Academy of Science Report on Reading. *Journal of Literacy Research, 31,* 355–368.

Gee, J. P. (2000). Teenagers in new times: A new literacy studies perspective. *Journal of Adolescent and Adult Literacy, 43*(5), 15–23.

Gee, J. P., & Crawford, V. M. (1998). Two kinds of teenagers: Language, identity and social class. In D. E. Alvermann, K. A. Hinchman, D. W. Moore, S. F. Phelps, & D. R. Waff (Eds.), *Reconceptualizing the literacies in adolescents' lives* (pp. 225–245). Mahwah, NJ: Lawrence Erlbaum Associates.

Genishi, C. (1999). Between psychology and poststructuralism: Where is L2 learning located? *TESOL Quarterly, 33,* 287–291.

Giovanni, N. (1971). Beautiful Black men. In D. Randall (Ed.), *The Black poets* (pp. 320–321). New York: Bantam.

Giroux, H. (1999). Doing cultural studies: Youth and the challenge of pedagogy. *Harvard Educational Review, 6,* 278–308.

Grabill, J. T., & Hicks, T. (2005). Multiliteracies meet methods: The case for digital writing in English Education. *English Education, 37,* 301–311.

Green, B., & Kostogriz, A. (2002). Learning difficulties and the new literacy studies. In J. Soler, J. Wearmouth, & G. Reid (Eds.), *Contextualizing difficulties in literacy development: Exploring politics, culture, ethnicity, and ethics.* (pp. 102–114). New York: Routledge/Falmer.

Gregory, E., & Williams, A. (2000). *City literacies: Learning to read across generations and cultures.* London & New York: Routledge.

Gunderson, L., & Anderson, J. (2003). Multicultural views of literacy learning and teaching. In A. I. Willis, G. E. Garcia, R. B/ Barrere, & V. J. Harris (Eds.), *Multicultural issues in literacy research and practice* (pp. 123–142). Mahwah, NJ: Lawrence Erlbaum Associates.

Gutiérrez, K. D., Baquedano-López, P., & Tejeda, C. (1999). Rethinking diversity: Hybridity and hybrid language practices in the third space. *Mind, Culture and Activity, 6,* 286–303.

Gutiérrez, K. D., Baquedano-López, P., Alvarez, H. H., & Chiu, M. M. (1999). Building a culture of collaboration through hybrid language practices. *Theory Into Practice, 38,* 87–93.

Hall, S. (1996). The meaning of New Times. In D. Morley & K. Chen (Eds.), *Stuart Hall: Critical dialogues in cultural studies* (pp. 223–238). London: Routledge.

Hall, S. & Jacques, M. (Eds.). (1990). *New Times.* New York: Verso.

Harper, H., & Bean, T. (2006). Fallen angels: Finding adolescents and adolescent literacy(ies) in a renewed project of democratic citizenship. In D. Alvermann, K. Hinchman, D. Moore, S. Phelps, & D. Wolf (Eds.), *Reconceptualizing the literacies in adolescents' lives* (2nd ed.). Mahwah, NJ: Lawrence Erlbaum Associates.

Harste, J., Woodward, V., & Burke, C. (1984). *Language stories and literacy lessons.* Portsmouth, NH: Heinemann.

Heath, S. B. (1983). *Ways with words: Language, life, and work in communities and classrooms.* Cambridge, UK: Cambridge University Press.

Hicks, D. (2002). *Reading lives: Working-class children and literacy learning.* New York: Teachers College Press.

Hull, G., & Schulz, K. (2001). Literacy and learning out of school: A review of theory and research. *Review of Educational Research, 71,* 575–611.

Katz, M. (1971). *Class, bureaucracy, and schools: The illusion of educational change in America.* New York: Praeger.

Kress, G. (2000). Design and transformation: New theories of meaning. In B. Cope & M. Kazalantis (Eds.), *Multiliteracies: Literacy learning and the design of social futures* (pp. 153–161). London: Routledge.

Lalik, R., Dellinger, L., & Druggish, R. (2003). Fostering collaboration between home and school through curriculum development: Perspectives of three Appalachian children. In A. I. Willis, G. E. Garcia, R. B. Barrere & V. J. Harris (Eds.), *Multicultural issues in literacy research and practice* (pp. 69–99). Mahwah, NJ: Lawrence Erlbaum Associates.

Lesko, N. (2001). *Act your age! A cultural construction of adolescence.* New York: Routledge Falmer.

Lewis, C. (2001). *Literacy practices as social acts: Power, status and cultural norms in the classroom.* Mahwah, NJ: Lawrence Erlbaum Associates.

Lewis, I. M. (1993). Literacy and cultural identity in the Horn of Africa: The Somali case. In B. Street (Ed.), *Cross-cultural approaches to literacy* (143–156). Cambridge, UK: Cambridge University Press.

Luke, A. (2000). Critical literacy in Australia: A matter of context and standpoint. *Journal of Adolescent and Adult Literacy, 43*(5), 47–60.

Luke, A., & Elkins, J. (1998). Redefining literacy in "New Times." *Journal of Adolescent and Adult Literacy, 42,* 4–7.

Luke, A., & Elkins, J. (2000). Special themed issue: Re/mediating adolescent literacies. *Journal of Adolescent and Adult Literacies, 43,* 396–398.

Luke, C. (2000). Cyber-schooling and technological change: Multiliteracies for new times. In B. Cope & M. Kazalantis (Eds.), *Multiliteracies: Literacy learning and the design of social futures* (pp. 69–91). London: Routledge.

Luria, A. R. (1979). *The making of mind.* Cambridge, MA: Harvard University Press.

Majors, Y. (2003). Shoptalk: Teaching and learning in an African American hair salon. *Mind, Culture and Activity, 10,* 289–310.

Martino, W. (1999). "It's OK to be gay": Interrupting straight thinking in the English classroom. In W. J. Letts & J. T. Sears (Eds.), *Queering elementary education: Advancing the dialogue about sexualities and schooling* (pp. 137–149). Lanham, MD: Rowman & Littlefield.

Moje, E. B. (2000a). "To be part of the story": The literacy practices of gangsta adolescents. *Teachers College Record, 102,* 651–690.

Moje, E. B. (2000b). *All the stories that we have: Adolescents' insights about literacy and learning in secondary schools.* Newark, DE: IRA.

Moje, E. B., Young, J. P., Readence, J. E., & Moore, D. (2000). Reinventing adolescent literacies for new times: Perennial and millennial issues. *Journal of Adolescent and Adult Literacies, 43,* 400–410.

Moje, E. B., Willes, D. J., & Fassio, K. (2001). Constructing and negotiating literacy in a writer's workshop: Literacy teaching and learning in the seventh grade. In E. B. Moje & D. G. O'Brien (Eds.), *Constructions of literacy: Studies of teaching and learning in and out of secondary schools.* (pp. 193–212). Mahwah, NJ: Lawrence Erlbaum Associates.

Moll, L., & Diaz, R. (1987). Teaching writing as communication: The use of ethnographic findings in classroom practice. In Bloome, D. (Ed.), *Literacy and Schooling* (pp. 193–221). Norwood, NJ: Ablex.

Moore, D. W., Bean, T. W., Birdyshaw, D., & Rycik, J. A. (1999). Adolescent literacy: A position statement for the Commission on Adolescent Literacy of the International Reading Association. *Journal of Adolescent and Adult Literacy, 43,* 97–112.

Moore, D. W., & Readence, J. E. (2001). Situating secondary school literacy research. In E. Moje & D. G. O'Brien (Eds.), *Constructions of literacy: Studies of teaching and learning in and out of secondary schools.* Mahwah, NJ: Lawrence Erlbaum Associates, Inc.

Moore, D., Alvermann, D., & Hinchman, K. A. (2000). *Struggling adolescent readers: A collection of teaching strategies.* Newark, DE: IRA.

New London Group. (1996). A pedagogy of multiliteracies. *Harvard Educational Review, 66,* 60–92.

Newman, M. (2002). *The designs of academic literacy: A multiliteracies examination of school achievement.* Westport, CT: Bergin & Garvey.

Nieto, S. (2000). Language, literacy and culture: Intersections and implications. In T. Shanahan & F. V. Rodriguez-Brown (Eds.), *49th Yearbook of the National Reading Conference* (pp. 41–60). Chicago: NRC, Inc.

Prendergast, C. (2003). *Literacy and racial justice: The politics of learning after Brown versus Board of Education.* Carbondale, IL: Southern Illinois University Press.

Rockhill, K. (1993). Gender, language and the politics of literacy. In B. Street (Ed.), *Cross-cultural approaches to literacy* (pp. 156–175). Cambridge, UK: Cambridge University Press.

Russell, D. R. (1997). Writing and genre in higher education and workplaces: A review of studies that use cultural-historical activity theory. *Mind, Culture, and Activity, 4,* 224–237.

Rycik, J. A., & Irvin, J. (2001). *What adolescents deserve: A commitment to students' literacy learning.* Newark. DE: IRA.

Scribner, S., & Cole, M. (1981). *The psychology of literacy.* Cambridge, MA: Harvard University Press.

Simon, R. (1992). *Teaching against the grain: Texts for a pedagogy of possibility.* South Hadley, MA: Bergin & Garvey.

Solsken, J. W. (1993). *Literacy, gender, and work in families and at school.* Norwood, NJ: Ablex.

Sperling, M. (1996). Revisiting the writing-speaking connection: Challenges for research on writing and writing instruction. *Review of Educational Research, 66,* 53–86.

Street, B. (Ed.). (1993). *Cross-cultural approaches to literacy.* Cambridge, UK: Cambridge University Press.

Street, B. V. (1984). *Literacy in theory and practice.* Cambridge, UK: Cambridge University Press.

Street, B. V. (1995). *Social literacies: Critical approaches to literacy in development, ethnography and education.* London: Longman.

Sturtevant, E., Boyd, F., Hinchman, K., Brozo, W., Alvermann, D., & Moore, D. (Eds.). (2006). *Principled practices for adolescent literacy: A framework for instruction and policy.* Mahwah, NJ: Lawrence Erlbaum Associates, Inc.

Taylor, D., & Dorsey-Gaines, C. (1988). *Growing up literate: Learning from inner-city families.* Portsmouth, NH: Heinemann.

Vygotsky, L. S. (1978). *Mind in society.* Cambridge, MA: Harvard University Press.

Vygotsky, L. S. (1981). The genesis of higher mental functions. In J. V. Wertsch (Ed.), *The concept of activity in Soviet psychology.* Armonk, NY: M. E. Sharpe.

Weiner, E. (2002). Beyond remediation: Ideological literacies of learning in developmental classrooms. *Journal of Adolescent and Adult Literacies, 46,* 150–168.

Weinstein-Shr, G. (1993). Literacy and social process: A community in transition. In B. Street (Ed.), *Cross-cultural approaches to literacy* (pp. 272–294). Cambridge, UK: Cambridge University Press.

Wertsch, J. V. (1985). *Vygotsky and the social formation of mind.* Cambridge, MA: Harvard University Press.

Willis, A. I. (2002). Literacy at Calhoun Colored School, 1892–1945. *Reading Research Quarterly, 37,* 8–38.

## CHAPTER FIVE: LINGUISTIC STUDIES

Allen, J. (Ed.). (1999). *Class actions: Teaching for social justice in elementary and middle school.* New York: Teachers College Press.

Altwerger, B. (2005). The push of the pendulum. In L. Poynor & P. M. Wolfe (Eds.), *Marketing fear in America's public schools: The real war on literacy.* (pp. 31–49). Mahwah, NJ: Lawrence Erlbaum Associates.

Altwerger, B., & Saavedra, E. R. (1999). Foreword. In C. Edelsky (Ed.), *Making justice our project: Teachers working toward critical whole language practice* (pp. vii–xii). Urbana, IL: NCTE.

Altwerger, B., & Strauss, S. L. (2002). The business behind testing. *Language Arts, 79,* 256–262.

Apple, M. W. (1993). *Official knowledge: Democratic education in a conservative age.* London: Routledge.

Aronowitz, R. (1984). Reading tests as texts. In D. Tannen (Ed.), *Coherence in spoken and written discourse* (pp. 245–265). Norwood, NJ: Ablex.

Ashton-Warner, S. (1963). *Teacher.* New York: Simon & Schuster.

Au, K. (1980). Participant structures in a reading lesson with Hawaiian children. *Anthropology and Education Quarterly, 11,* 91–115.

Au, K., & Jordan, C. (1981). Teaching reading to Hawaiian children: Finding a culturally appropriate solution. In H. Trueba, G. P. Guthrie, & K. Au (Eds.), *Culture and the bilingual classroom: Studies in classroom ethnography* (pp. 139–152). Rowley, MA: Newbury House Publishers.

Auerbach, E. (1991). Literacy and ideology. In W. Grabe (Ed.), *Annual review of applied linguistics* (pp. 71–85). New York: Cambridge University Press.

Baker, C. D., & Freebody, P. (1986). Representations of questioning and answering in children's first school books. *Language in Society, 15,* 451–484.

Baker, C. D., & Freebody, P. (1989). *Children's first schoolbooks: Introductions to the culture of literacy.* Oxford, UK: Basil Blackwell.

Baker, C. D., & A. Luke (Eds.). (1991). *Towards a critical sociology of reading pedagogy.* Amsterdam, The Netherlands: John Benjamins.

Bernstein, B. (1972). A sociolinguistic approach to education with some reference to educability. In J. J. Gumperz & D. Hymes (Eds.), *Directions in Sociolinguistics* (pp. 465–497). New York: Holt.

Bloome, D. (1987). Introduction. In D. Bloome (Ed.), *Literacy and schooling* (pp. xiii–xxiii). Norwood, NJ: Ablex.

Bloome, D. (2001). Boundaries on the construction of literacy in secondary classrooms: Envisioning reading and writing in a democratic and just society. In E. Moje & D. G. O'Brien (Eds.), *Constructions of literacy: Studies of teaching and learning in and out of secondary schools* (pp. 287–304). Mahwah, NJ: Lawrence Erlbaum Associates.

Bloome, D., & Katz, L. (1997). Literacy as social practice and classroom chronotopes. *Reading and Writing Quarterly: Overcoming Learning Difficulties, 13,* 205–225.

Bloome, D., Katz, L., & Champion, T. (2003). Young children's narratives and ideologies of language in classrooms. *Reading and Writing Quarterly: Overcoming Learning Difficulties, 19,* 205–223.

Bourdieu, P. (1977). Symbolic power. In D. Gleeson (Ed.), *Identity and structure* (pp. 112–119). Driffield, UK: Nafferton.

Bourdieu, P. (1991). *Language and symbolic power* (J. B. Thompson, Ed., G. Raymond & M. Adamson, Trans.). Cambridge, UK: Polity.

Christian, B., & Bloome, D. (2004). Learning to read is who you are. *Reading and Writing Quarterly: Overcoming Learning Difficulties, 20,* 365–384.

Collins, J. (1986). Differential instruction in reading groups. In J. Cook-Gumperz (Ed.), *The social construction of literacy* (pp. 117–137). Cambridge, UK: Cambridge University Press.

Collins, J. (1987). Using cohesion analysis to understand access to knowledge. In D. Bloome (Ed.), *Literacy and schooling* (pp. 67–97). Norwood, NJ: Ablex.

Collins, J. (1991). Hegemonic practice: Literacy and standard language in public education. In C. Mitchell & K. Weiler (Eds.), *Rewriting literacy: Culture and the discourse of the Other* (pp. 229–254). Toronto, Canada: OISE.

Collins, J., & Michaels, S. (1986). Speaking and writing: Discourse strategies and the acquisition of literacy. In J. Cook-Gumperz (Ed.), *The social construction of literacy* (pp. 207–222). Cambridge, UK: Cambridge University Press.

Connell, R. (1993). *Schools and social justice.* Philadelphia: Temple University Press.

Cook-Gumperz, J. (Ed.). (1986). *The social construction of literacy.* Cambridge, UK: Cambridge University Press.

Comber, B. (1994). Critical literacy: An introduction to Australian debates and perspectives. *Journal of Curriculum Studies, 26,* 655–668.

Delpit, L. (1988). The silenced dialogue: Power and pedagogy in educating other people's children. *Harvard Educational Review, 58,* 280–298.

Derrida, J. (1980). *Writing and difference.* Chicago: University of Chicago Press.

Dworin, J. (2003). Examining children's biliteracy in the classroom. In A. I. Willis, G. E. Garcia, R. B. Barrere, & V. J. Harris (Eds.), *Multicultural issues in literacy research and practice* (pp. 29–48). Mahwah, NJ: Lawrence Erlbaum Associates.

Edelsky, C. (1984). *Writing in a bilingual program: Habia una vez.* Norwood, NJ: Ablex.

Edelsky, C. (1994). Education for democracy. *Language Arts, 71,* 252–257.

Edelsky, C. (2005). *With literacy and justice for all: Rethinking the social in language and in education.* (4th ed.). Mahwah, NJ: Lawrence Erlbaum Associates.

Edelsky, C. (2005). Relatively speaking: McCarthyism and teacher-resisters. In L. Poynor & P. Wolfe (Eds.), *Marketing fear in America's public schools.* (pp. 11–28). Mahwah, NJ: Lawrence Erlbaum Associates.

Edelsky, C., Altwerger, B., & Flores, B. (1991). *Whole language: What's the difference?* Portsmouth, NH: Heinemann.

Espinoza, C. M., & Moore, K. J. (1999). Understanding and transforming the meaning of our lives through poetry, biographies, and songs. In C. Edelsky (Ed.), *Making justice our project: Teachers working toward critical whole language practice* (pp. 37–54). Urbana, IL: NCTE.

Fairclough, N. (Ed.). (1992). *Critical language awareness.* UK: Longman Group.

Fairclough, N. (1989). *Language and power.* London: Longman.

Fairclough, N. (1992). *Discourse and social change.* Cambridge, UK: Polity.

Fecho, B. (1998). Crossing boundaries of race in a critical literacy classroom. In D. E. Alvermann, K. A. Hinchman, D. W. Moore, S. F. Phelps, & D. R. Waff (Eds.), *Reconceptualizing the literacies in adolescents' lives* (pp. 75–101). Mahwah, NJ: Lawrence Erlbaum Associates.

Ferreiro, E. (2003). *Past and present of the verbs to read and to write: Essays on literacy.* Trans. Mark Fried. Toronto, Canada: Douglas & McIntyre.

Ferreiro, E., & Teberosky, A. (1982). *Literacy before schooling.* (K. Goodman Castro, Trans.). Exeter, NH: Heinemann.

Fishman, J. A. (1978). *Language and ethnicity in minority sociolinguistic perspective.* Clevedon, England: Multilingual Matters Ltd.

Fordham, S. (1991). Racelessness in private schools: Should we deconstruct the racial and cultural identity of African American adolescents? *Teachers College Record, 92,* 470–484.

Foss, A. (2002). Peeling the onion: Teaching critical literacy with students of privilege. *Language Arts, 79,* 393–403.

Foucault, M. (1972). *The archeology of knowledge.* (A. Sheridan-Smith, Trans.). New York: Harper & Row.

Foucault, M. (1979). *Discipline and punish* (A. Sheridan, Trans.). New York: Harper.

Foucault, M. (1980). *Power/knowledge* (C. Gordon, Ed., and C. Gordon, L. Marshall, J. Mepham, & K. Soper, Trans.). New York: Pantheon.

Foucault, M. (1988). *Technologies of the self* (L. H. Martin, H. Gutman, & P. H. Hutton, Eds.). London: Tavistock.

Freebody, P. (1991). Reading and social class. In A. Luke & P. Gilbert (Eds.), *Literacy in contexts* (pp. 68–84). Sydney: Allen & Unwin.

Freebody, P., Luke, A., & Gilbert, P. (1991). Reading positions and practices in the classroom. *Curriculum Inquiry, 21,* 435–457.

Freire, P., & Macedo, D. (1987). *Literacy: Reading the word and the world.* South Hadley, MA: Bergin & Garvey.

Garfinkle, H. (1967). *Studies in ethnomethodology.* Englewood Cliffs, NJ: Prentice-Hall.

Gee, J. P. (2001). Foreword. In C. Lewis (Ed.), *Literary practices as social acts: Power, status and cultural norms in the classroom.* (pp. xv–xix). Mahwah, NJ: Lawrence Erlbaum Associates.

Gee, J. P. (1999). *An introduction to discourse analysis: Theory and method.* London: Routledge.

Gee, J. P. (1996). *Sociolinguistics and literacies: Ideology in discourses* (2nd ed.). London: Taylor and Francis.

Gee, J. P. (2000). Teenagers in new times: A new literacy studies perspective. *Journal of Adolescent and Adult Literacy, 43,* 412–420.

Gee, J. P. (1992). What is literacy? In P. Shannon (Ed.), *Becoming political: Readings and writings in the politics of literacy education* (pp. 21–28). Portsmouth, NH: Heinemann.

Gee, J. P. (2003). *What video games have to teach us about learning and literacy.* New York: Palgrave Macmillan.

Gee, J. P., & Crawford, V. (1998). Two kinds of teenagers: Language, identity and social class. In D. Alverman, K. Hinchman, D. Moore, S. Phelps, & D. Waff (Eds.), *Reconceptualizing the literacies in adolescents' lives* (pp. 225–245). Hillsdale, NJ: Lawrence Erlbaum Associates.

Gee, J. P., Hull, G., & Lankshear, C. (1996). *The new work order: Behind the language of the new capitalism.* Boulder, CO: Westview.

Gilbert, P. (1992). The story so far: Gender, literacy and social regulation. *Gender and Education, 4,* 185–199.

Gilmore, P. (1985). Sulking, stepping and tracking: The effects of attitude assessment on access to literacy. In D. Bloome (Ed.), *Literacy and schooling* (pp. 98–120). Norwood, NJ: Ablex.

Goffman, E. (1961). *Asylums: Essays on the social situation of mental patients and other inmates.* New York: Anchor.

Goodman, K. (1968). The psycholinguistic nature of the reading process. In K. Goodman (Ed.), *The psycholinguistic nature of the reading process* (pp. 13–26). Detroit, MI: Wayne State University Press.

Goodman, K. (1973). *Miscue analysis: Applications to reading instruction.* Urbana, IL: Eric Clearinghouse and NCTE.

Goodman, K. (1982). *Language and literacy: The selected writings of Kenneth S. Goodman.* London: Routledge & Kegan Paul.

Goodman, K. (1996). *On reading.* Richmond Hill, Ontario: Scholastic Canada.

Goodman, K. (1998). *In defense of good teaching: What teachers need to know about the "reading wars."* Portland, ME: Stenhouse.

Goodman, K., Goodman, Y., Rapoport, R., & Shannon, P. (2003). *Saving our schools: The case for public education in America.* Oakland, CA: RDR Books.

Goodman, K. S., Shannon, P. Freeman, Y. S., & Murphy, S. (1988). *Report card on basal readers.* Katonah, NY: R. C. Owen.

Goodman, Y. (1985). Kidwatching: Observing the language learner in the classroom. In A. Jaggar & M. Smith-Burke (Eds.), *Observing the language learner* (pp. 9–19). Newark, DE: International Reading Association.

Goodman, Y., Watson, D., & Burke, C. L. (1987). *Reading miscue inventory: Alternative procedures.* New York: R. C. Owen.

Goodman, Y., Watson, D., & Burke, C. L. (1996). *Reading strategies: Focus on comprehension.* Katonah, NY: R. C. Owen.

Gumperz, J. J. (1968). The speech community. in D. Sills (Ed.), *International encyclopedia of the social sciences* (pp. 381–386). New York: Macmillan.

Gutiérrez, K., & Larson, J. (1994). Language borders: Recitation as hegemonic discourse. *International Journal of Educational Reform, 3,* 22–36.

Gutiérrez, K., Rymes, B., & Larson, J. (1995). Script, counterscript, and underlife in the classroom: James Brown versus *Brown v. Board of Education. Harvard Educational Review, 65,* 445–471.

Habermas, J. (1979). *Communications and the evolution of society* (T. McCarthy, Trans.). London: Heinemann.

Hall, S. (1996). The meaning of New Times. In D. Morley & K. Chen (Eds.), *Stuart Hall: Critical dialogues in cultural studies* (pp. 223–238). London: Routledge.

Halliday, M. (1973). Language as a social semiotic: Towards a general sociolinguistic theory. In M. Makkaai & L. Heilman (Eds.), *Linguistics at the crossroads.* The Hague: Mouton.

Harste, J. C., Short, K. G., with Burke, C. (1988). *Creating classrooms for authors: The reading-writing connection.* Portsmouth, NH: Heinemann.

Heap, J. (1977). Toward a phenomenology of reading. *Journal of Phenomenological Psychology, 8,* 103–114.

Heap, J. (1982). Understanding classroom events: A critique of Durkin, with an alternative. *Journal of Reading Behavior, 14,* 391–412.

Heath, S. B. (1983). *Ways with words: Language, life, and work in communities and classrooms.* Cambridge, UK: Cambridge University Press.

Hudelson, S. J., & Lindfors, J. W. (1993). *Delicate balances: Collaborative research in language education.* Urbana, IL: NCTE.

Hymes, D. (1962). The ethnography of speaking. In T. Gladwin & W. C. Sturtevant (Eds.), *Anthropology and Human Behavior* (pp. 13–53). Washington, DC: Anthropological Society of Washington.

Hymes, D. (1973). The scope of sociolinguistics. In R. Shuy (Ed.), *23rd Annual Monograph Series on Languages and Linguistics* (pp. 313–333). Washington, DC: Georgetown University Press.

Janks, H. (2001). Identity and conflict in the critical literacy classroom. In B. Comber & A. Simpson (Eds.), *Negotiating critical literacies in classrooms* (pp. 137–150). Mahwah, NJ: Lawrence Erlbaum Associates.

Kress, G. (1989). Linguistic processes in sociocultural practice. Oxford, UK: Oxford University Press.

Kress, G. (2003). *Literacy in the new media age.* London: Routledge.

Labov, W. (1966). *The social stratification of English in New York City.* Washington, DC: Center for Applied Linguistics.

Larson, J. (1995). Talk matters: The role of pivot in the distribution of literacy knowledge among novice writers. *Linguistics and Education, 7,* 277–302.

Lemke, J. (1995). *Textual politics.* London: Taylor & Francis.

Lewis, C. (2001). *Literary practices as social acts: Power, status and cultural norms in the classroom.* Mahwah, NJ: Lawrence Erlbaum Associates, Inc.

Luke, A. (1988). *Literacy, textbooks and ideology.* London: Falmer.

Luke, A. (1991). The political economy of reading instruction. In C. D. Baker & A. Luke (Eds.), *Towards a critical sociology of reading pedagogy* (pp. 3–25). Amsterdam, The Netherlands: John Benjamins.

Luke, A. (1992). The body literate: Discourse and inscription in early literacy instruction. *Linguistics and Education, 4,* 107–129.

Luke, A. (1993). Stories of social regulation: The micropolitics of classroom narratives. In B. Green (Ed.), *The insistence of the letter: Literacy and curriculum theorizing* (pp. 137–153). London: Falmer.

Luke, A. (1995). Text and discourse in education: An introduction to critical discourse analysis. In M. Apple (Ed.), *Review of research in education* (Vol. 21, pp. 3–48). Washington, DC: AERA.

Luke, A. (2002). Beyond science and ideology critique: Developments in critical discourse analysis. *Annual Review of Applied Linguistics, 22,* 96–110.

MacIntosh, P. (1998). White privilege: Unpacking the invisible knapsack. In P. S. Rothenberg (Ed.), *Race, class, and gender in the United States: An integrated study* (4th ed., pp. 165–169). New York: St. Martin's.

Martin, J. (1984). Types of writing in infants and primary school. In L. Unsworth (Ed.), *Reading writing and spelling.* Proceedings of the 5th Macarthur Reading and Language Symposium. Sydney, Australia: Macarthur Institute of Higher Education.

Martin, J. (1991). *Technology, technicality and discourses of uncommon sense.* Paper presented to the 16th Australian Reading Association Annual Conference, Adelaide, South Australia.

McDermott, R. P., & Gospodinoff, K. (1981). Social contexts for ethnic borders and school failure. In H. Trueba, G. P. Guthrie & K. Au (Eds.), *Culture and the bilingual classroom: Studies in classroom ethnography* (pp. 212–230). Rowley, MA: Newbury House.

Mehan. H. (1979). *Learning lessons: Social organization in the classroom.* Cambridge, MA: Harvard University Press.

Mellor, B., Patterson, A., & O'Neill, M. (2000). *Reading fictions.* Urbana, IL: NCTE. (First published by Chalkface Press, 1991)

Michaels, S. (1981). "Sharing time": Children's narrative styles and differential access to literacy. *Language in Society, 10,* 423–442.

Michaels, S. (1991). Hearing the connections in children's oral and written discourse. In C. Mitchell & K. Weiler (Eds.), *Rewriting literacy: Culture and the discourse of the Other* (pp. 103–122). Toronto, Canada: OISE.

Moll, L., & Diaz, R. (1987). Teaching writing as communication: The use of ethnographic findings in classroom practice. In D. Bloome (Ed.), *Literacy and schooling* (pp. 193–222). Norwood, NJ: Ablex.

Pennycook, A. (2001). *Critical applied linguistics: A critical introduction.* Mahwah, NJ: Lawrence Erlbaum Associates.

Peterson, B. (1994). Teaching for social justice: One teacher's journey. In B. Bigelow, L. Christiansen, S. Karp, B. Miner, & B. Peterson (Eds.), *Rethinking our classrooms: Teaching for equity and justice* (pp. 30–38). Milwaukee, WI: Rethinking Schools.

Rizvi, F., & Lingard, B. (1996). Foreword. In J. P. Gee, G. Hull, & C. Lankshear (Eds.), *The new work order: Behind the language of the new capitalism* (pp. vii–ix). Boulder, CO: Westview.

Rogers, R. (2002). Between contexts: A critical analysis of family literacy, discursive practices, and literate subjectivities. *Reading Research Quarterly, 37,* 249–277.

Rogers, R. (Ed.). (2004). *An introduction to critical discourse analysis in education.* Mahwah, NJ: Lawrence Erlbaum Associates.

Rymes, B. (2001). *Conversational borderlands: Language and identity in an urban high school.* New York: Teachers College Press.

St. Pierre, E. A. (2000). Poststructural feminism in education: An overview. *Qualitative Studies in Education, 13,* 477–515.

Schegloff, E. A. (1972). Sequencing and conversational opening. In J. Gumperz & D. Hymes (Eds.), *Directions in sociolinguistics* (pp. 346–380). New York: Holt, Rinehart, Winston.

Simpson, A. (1996). Fictions and facts: An investigation of the reading practices of girls and boys. *English Education, 28,* 268–279.

Skilton-Sylvester, E. (1997). *Inside, outside and in-between: Identities, literacies and educational policies in the lives of Cambodian women and girls in Philadelphia.* Unpublished doctoral dissertation, University of Pennsylvania, Philadelphia.

Skilton-Sylvester, E. (2002). Literate at home but not at school: A Cambodian girl's journey from playwright to struggling writer. In G. Hull & K. Schultz (Eds.), *School's out! Bridging out-of-school literacies with classroom practice* (pp. 61–92). New York: Teachers College Press.

Smith, F. (1971). *Understanding reading.* New York: Holt.

Smith, F. (1986). *Understanding reading* (3rd ed.). Hillsdale, NJ: Lawrence Erlbaum Associates.

Solsken, J. (1993). *Literacy, gender, and work in families and in school.* Norwood, NJ: Ablex.

Strauss, S. (2003). *Silent "e" speaks out*. Mahwah, NJ: Lawrence Erlbaum Associates.
Wilkinson, L., & Janks, H. (1998). Teaching direct and reported speech from a Critical Language Awareness perspective. *Educational Review, 50*, 181–190.
Williams, G. (1992). *Sociolinguistics: A sociological critique*. London: Routledge.
Research that counts. Retrieved July 6, 2004 from www.susanohanian.org

**CHAPTER SIX:**
**WHY SOCIAL JUSTICE ETHICS FOR ADVOCACY RESEARCH?**

Artiles, A. J. (2003). Special education's changing identity: Paradoxes and dilemmas in views of culture and space. *Harvard Educational Review, 73*, 164–202.
Bahktin, M. M. (1993). *Toward a philosophy of the act* (V. Liapunov & M. Holquist, Eds., and V. Liapunov, Trans.). Austin: University of Texas Press.
Blackburn, M. V. (2002). Disrupting the (hetero)normative: Exploring literacy performances and identity work with queer youth. *Journal of Adolescent and Adult Literacy, 46*, 312–324.
Boler, M. (1999). *Feeling power: Emotions and education*. New York: Routledge.
Bourdieu, P. (1991). *Language and symbolic power*. Cambridge, MA: Harvard University Press.
Butler, J. (1990). *Gender trouble: Feminism and the subversion of identity*. New York: Routledge.
Carini, P. (1982). *The school lives of seven children: A five year study*. Grand Forks: The University of North Dakota Press.
Cherland, M. R. (1994). *Private practices: Girls reading fiction and constructing identity*. London: Taylor & Francis.
Connell, R. (1993). *Schools and social justice*. Philadelphia: Temple University Press.
Denzin, N. K. (1997). The sixth moment. In N. K. Denzin (Ed.), *Interpretive ethnography: Ethnographic practices for the 21st century* (pp. 250–289). Thousand Oaks, CA: Sage.
Derrida, J. (1980). *Writing and difference*. Chicago: University of Chicago Press.
Fine, M., Weis, L., Weseen, S., & Wong, L. (2000). For whom? Qualitative research, representations, and social responsibilities. In N. K. Denzin & Y. S. Lincoln (Eds.), *Handbook of qualitative research* (2nd ed., pp. 107–131). Thousand Oaks, CA: Sage.
Foucault, M. (1979). *Discipline and punish: The birth of the prison* (A. Sheridan, Trans.). New York: Vintage Books.
Foucault, M. (1997). The ethics of concern of the self as a practice of freedom (R. Fornet-Betancourt, H. Becker, & A. Gomez-Muller, Interviewers. P. Aranov & D. McGrawth, Trans.). In P. Rabinow (Ed.), *Ethics: Subjectivity and truth* (pp. 281–301). New York: The New Press.
Freire, P. (1998). *Pedagogy of freedom: Ethics, democracy, and civic courage*. Lanham, MD: Rowman and Littlefield.
Freire, P. (1999). *Pedagogy of the oppressed* (Rev. ed.). New York: Continuum.

Gamson, J. (2000). Sexualities, queer theory, and qualitative research. In N. K. Denzin & Y. S. Lincoln (Eds.), *Handbook of qualitative research* (2nd ed., pp. 347–365). Thousand Oaks, CA: Sage.

Greene, M. (1995). *Releasing the imagination.* San Francisco: Jossey-Bass.

Greene, M. (1998). Introduction. In W. Ayers, J. A. Hunt, & T. Quinn (Eds.), *Teaching for social justice.* (pp. xxvii–xlvi). New York: The New Press.

Gutiérrez, K. D., Baquedano-Lopez, P., Alvarez, H. H., & Chiu, M. M. (1999). Building a culture of collaboration through hybrid language practices. *Theory Into Practice, 38,* 87–93.

Hall, S. (1996). The meaning of "New Times." In D. Morley & K. Chen (Eds.), *Stuart Hall: Critical dialogues in cultural studies* (pp. 223–238). London: Routledge.

Heath, S. B. (1983). *Ways with words: Language, life, and work in communities and classrooms.* New York: Cambridge University Press.

Hicks, D. (2002). *Reading lives: Working-class children and literacy learning.* New York: Teachers College Press.

Kant, I. (1959). *Foundations of the metaphysics of morals* (L. Beck, Trans.). New York: Bobbs-Merrill.

Keenan, T. (1997). *Fables of responsibility: Aberrations and predicaments in ethics and politics.* Stanford, CA: Stanford University Press.

Luke, A. (2002). Curriculum, ethics, metanarrative: Teaching and learning beyond the nation. *Curriculum Perspectives, 22,* 49–55.

Lyotard, J. (1984). *The postmodern condition: A report on knowledge* (G. Bennington & B. Massumi, Trans.). Minneapolis: University of Minnesota Press.

Miller, J. (1990). *Seductions: Studies in reading and culture.* London: Virago.

Miller, J. (1996). *School for women.* London: Virago.

Murdoch, I. (1991). *The sovereignty of good.* New York: Routledge. (Original work published 1970)

Noddings, N. (1984). *Caring: A feminine approach to ethics and moral education.* Berkeley, CA: University of California Press.

Nussbaum, M. (1990). *Love's knowledge: Essays on philosophy and literature.* New York: Oxford University Press.

Olthuis, J. H. (1997). Introduction: Love/knowledge: Sojourning with others, meeting with differences. In J. H. Olthuis (Ed.), *Knowing other-wise: Philosophy at the threshold of spirituality.* New York: Fordham University Press.

Popkewitz, T. (1995). Foreword. In P. L. McLaren & J. M. Giarelli (Eds.), *Critical theory and educational research* (pp. xi–xxii). Albany, NY: SUNY Press.

Powell, R. (1999). *Literacy as a moral imperative: Facing the challenges of a pluralistic society.* Lanham, MD: Rowman & Littlefield.

Quinby, L. (2002). Just discourse: The limits of truth for the discourse of social justice. *The Review of Education, Pedagogy, & Cultural Studies, 24,* 235–249.

Rawls, J. (1971). *A theory of justice.* Cambridge, MA: Harvard University Press.

Rorty, A. (1988). Communication as the context of character. Part 4 in *Mind in action: Essays in the philosophy of mind.* Boston: Beacon.

Ryan, K. E. (1995). Evaluation ethics and issues of social justice: Contributions from female moral thinking. *Studies in Symbolic Interaction, 19,* 141–151.

St. Pierre, E. A. (2000). Poststructural feminism in education: An overview. *Qualitative Studies in Education, 13,* 477–515.

St. Pierre, E. A. (2001, April 10–14). *Ethics under deconstruction.* A paper presented at the Annual Meeting of the American Educational Research Association, Seattle, Washington.

Stanley, L., & Wise, S. (1993). *Breaking out again: Feminist ontology and epistemology.* London: Routledge.

Vygotsky, L. S. (1978). *Mind in society: The development of higher psychological processes.* Cambridge, MA: Harvard University Press.

Vygotsky, L. S. (1986). *Thought and language* (Rev. ed.; A. Kozulin, Ed. and Trans.). Cambridge, MA: MIT. (Original work published 1934)

Walkerdine, V. (1988). *The mastery of reason: Cognitive development and the production of rationality.* London: Routledge.

Walkerdine, V. (1990). *Schoolgirl fictions.* New York: Verso.

West, C., & Zimmerman, D. H. (1987). Doing gender. *Gender and Society, 1,* 125–151.

William, R. (1977). *Marxism and literature.* New York: Oxford University Press.

Young, I. M. (1993). Justice and communicative democracy. In R. Gottlieb (Ed.), *Radical philosophy: Tradition, counter-tradition, politics.* (pp. 123–143). Philadelphia: Temple University Press.

## CHAPTER SEVEN: THE LITERATE BODY

Apple, M. (1986). *Teachers and texts: A political economy of class and gender relations in education.* New York: Routledge.

Blount, J. (2005). *Fit to teach: Same-sex desire, gender, and school work in the twentieth century.* Albany, NY: SUNY Press.

Britzman, D. (1991). Decentering discourses in teacher education: Or, the unleashing of unpopular things. *Journal of Education, 173,* 60–80.

Britzman, D. (1995). What is this thing called love? *Taboo: The Journal of Culture and Education, 1,* 65–93.

Cavanagh, S. (2005). Female teacher gender and sexuality in twentieth century Ontario Canada. In R. Coulter & H. Harper (Eds.), *History is hers: Women educators in twentieth century Ontario* (pp. 111–134). Calgary, Alberta, Canada: Detselig.

Cavanagh, S. (2003). The gender of professionalism and occupational closure: The Management of tenure-related disputes by the Federation of Women Teachers' Associations of Ontario' 1918–1949. *Gender and Education 15,* 39–57.

Conboy, K., Medina, N., & Stanbury, S. (1997). *Writing on the body: Female embodiment and feminist theory.* New York: Columbia University.

Cyles, P. (2000). The Kama Sutra as curriculum. In C. O'Farrell, D. Meadmore, E. McWilliam, & C. Symes (Eds.), *Taught Bodies* (pp. 17–26). New York: Peter Lang.

Davies, B., & Sumara, D. (in press). *Complexity and education: Emergent thinking on learning, pedagogy, and research.* Mahwah, NJ: Lawrence Erlbaum Associates.

De Fabrizio, L. (2004). Transgressing the curricular body. *Journal of Curriculum Theorizing, 20*(2), 3–5.

Deleuze, G. (1992). "Ethology: Spinoza and us." In S. Lotringer (Ed.), *Incorporations.* New York: Zone.

Dillabough, J. (1999). Gender politics and conceptions of the modern teacher: women, identity and professionalism. *British Journal of Sociology of Education, 20,* 373–394.

Eagleton, T. (2003). Peter Books on bodies. In T. Eagleton (Ed.) *Figures of dissent: Critical essays on Fish, Spivak, Zizek and others* (pp. 129–135). London: Verso.

Foucault, M. (1979). *Discipline and punish: The birth of the prison.* New York: Vintage Books.

Foucault, M. (1981). *The history of sexuality* (Vol. 1). Harmondsworth, Middlesex, UK: Pelican.

Gallop, J. (1988). *Thinking through the body.* New York: Columbia University.

Gallop, J. (1995). *Pedagogy: The question of impersonation.* Bloomington: Indiana University.

Gallop, J. (1997). *Feminist accused of sexual harassment.* Durham, NC: Duke University.

Grosz, E. (1994). *Volatile bodies: Toward a Corporeal Feminism.* Bloomington, IL: University of Indiana.

Grosz E. (1995). *Space, time and perversion: Essays on the politics of the body.* New York: Routledge.

Grumet, M. (1988). *Bitter milk: Women and teaching.* Amherst: University of Massachusetts.

Harbeck, K. (1997). *Gay and Lesbian Educators: Personal freedoms, public constraints.* Madlen, MA: Amethyst.

Harper, H. (2004). Personal and professional freedom in the hinterlands: Women teachers in Northern Ontario. *Oral History Forum/d'histore orale, 24,* 46–66.

Jones, A. (2000). Surveillance and student handwriting: tracing the body. In C. O'Farrell, D. Meadmore, E. McWilliam, & C. Symes (Eds.), *Taught bodies* (pp. 151–164). New York: Peter Lang.

Kelly, U. (1997). *Schooling desire.* New York: Routledge.

Khatt, D. (1992). *Lesbian teacher: An invisible presence.* Albany, NY: SUNY Press.

Kirkpatrick, D., & Thorpe, S. (2000). Iconic (pre)occupations: Pedagogy and the body in the Australian awards for university teaching. In C. O'Farrell, D. Meadmore, E. McWilliam, & C. Symes (Eds.), *Taught bodies* (pp. 165–179). New York: Peter Lang.

Lankshear, C., Peters, M., & Knobel, M. (1996). Critical pedagogy and cyberspace. In H. Giroux, C. Lankshear, P. McLaren, & M. Peters (Eds.), *Counternarratives* (pp. 149–185). New York: Routledge.

Luke, A., & Elkins, J. (1998). Reinventing literacy in "New Times." *Journal of Adolescent & Adult Literacy, 42,* 4–7.

Luke, C. (1996). Feminist pedagogy theory: Reflections on power and authority. *Educational Theory, 46,* 283–302.

Macrine, S. L. (2002). Pedagogical bondage: Body bound and gagged in a techno-rational world. In S. Shapiro & S. Shapiro (Eds.), *Body movements: Pedagogy, politics and social change* (pp.133–146). Cresskill, NJ: Hampton.

McLaren, P. (1990). Schooling the postmodern body: Critical pedagogy and the politics of enfleshment. In H. Giroux (Ed.), *Postmodernism, feminism and cultural politics.* Albany, NY: SUNY Press.

McWilliam, E. (2000). Stuck in the missionary position? Pedagogy and desire in new times. In C. O'Farrell, D. Meadmore, E. McWilliam & C. Symes (Eds.) *Taught Bodies,* (pp.27–37). New York: Peter Lang.

McWilliam, E. (1999). *Pedagogical pleasures.* New York: Peter Lang.

McWilliam, E. (1996). Introduction: Pedagogies, technologies, bodies. In E.McWilliam, P. Taylor (Eds.) *Pedagogy, Technology and the Body* (pp.1–22). New York: Peter Lang.

McWilliam, E., & Jones, A. (1996). Eros and pedagogical bodies: The state of (non)affairs. In E. McWilliam & P. G. Taylor (Eds.). *Pedagogy, technology and the body* (pp. 127–136). New York: Peter Lang.

Middleton, S. (2002). Sitting in rows and teaching on-line: Life histories, technology and pedagogy. In S. Shapiro & S. Shapiro (Eds.), *Body movements: Pedagogy, politics and social change* (pp.209–236). Cresskill, NJ: Hampton.

Mission, R., & Morgan, W. (2000). Teaching an aesthetic body: Towards a different practice of English. In C. O'Farrell, D. Meadmore, E. McWilliam, & C. Symes (Eds.), *Taught bodies* (pp. 91–104). New York: Peter Lang.

Morrison, T. (1992). *Playing in the dark: Whiteness and the literary imagination.* Cambridge, MA: Harvard University.

O'Brien, S. (2000). The lecherous professor: "An explosive thriller about naked lust, perverted justice and obsession beyond control." In C. O'Farrell et al. (Eds.), *Taught bodies* (pp. 39–55). New York: Peter Lang.

O'Farrell, C., Meadmore, D., McWilliam, E., & Symes, C. (Eds.). (2000). *Taught bodies.* New York: Peter Lang.

Pillow, W. (2002). Exposed methodology: The body as a deconstructive practice. In E. St. Pierre & W. Pillow (Eds.), *Working the ruins: Feminist poststructural theory and methods in education* (pp. 199–219). New York: Routledge.

Probyn, E. (2004). Teaching bodies: Affects in the classroom. *Body & Society, 10*(4), 21–43.

Rofes, E. (1985). *Socrates, Plato, and guys like me.* Boston: Alyson.

Shapiro, S. (1994). Re-membering the body in critical pedagogy. *Education and Society, 12,* 61–79.

Shapiro, S., & Shapiro, S. (2002). *Body movements: Pedagogy, politics and social change.* Cresskill, NJ: Hampton.

Simon, R. (1992). *Teaching against the grain. Texts for a pedagogy of possibility.* Toronto, Canada: OISE.

Strathern, A. J. (1996). *Body thoughts.* Anne Arbor, MI: University of Michigan.

Vick, M. (1996). Fixing the body: Prescriptions for pedagogy, 1850–1950. In E. McWilliam & P. G. Taylor (Eds.), *Pedagogy, technology and the body* (pp. 113–126). New York: Peter Lang.

## CHAPTER EIGHT: LITERACY, DEMOCRACY AND FREEDOM

Apple, M. (2000). *Official knowledge: Democratic education in a conservative age* (2nd ed.). New York: Routledge.

Baecler, J. (1995). *Democracy: An analytical survey*. Paris: UNESCO.

Berlin, I. (1958/1970). *Two concepts of liberty: An inaugural lecture delivered before the University of Oxford*. Oxford, England: Clarendon.

Boler, M. (2004). *Democratic dialogue in education: Troubling speech, disturbing silence*. New York: Peter Lang.

Bowles, H., & Gintis (1986). *Democracy and capitalism*. New York: Basic Books.

Carlson, D. (2002). *Leaving safe harbors: Toward a new progressivism in American education and public life*. New York: RoutledgeFalmer.

Carlson, D. & Dimitriadis, G. (2003). Introduction. In G. Dimitriadis & D. Carlson (Eds.) *Promises to keep: Cultural Studies, democratic education and public life,* (pp.1–38). New York: RoutledgeFalmer.

Chomsky, N. (2000). Democracy and education. In his text *Chomsky on Miseducation* (pp. 37–55). New York: Rowman & Littlefield.

Cunningham, F. (2002). *Theory of democracy: A critical introduction*. New York: Routledge.

Darling-Hammond, L. (1998). Education for democracy. In W. Ayers & J. Miller (Eds.), *A light in dark times: Maxine Greene and the unfinished conversation* (pp. 78–92). New York: Teachers College Press.

Davies, L. (2000). The civil school and civil society: Gender, democracy and development. In M. Arnot & J. Dillabough (Eds.), *Challenging democracy: International perspectives on gender, education and citizenship* (pp. 278–296). New York: RoutledgeFalmer.

Dewey, J. (1916). *Education and democracy*. New York: MacMillan.

Dewey, J. (1938). *Experience and education*. New York; Collier.

Dillabough, J. & Arnot, M.(2000). Feminist political frameworks: New approaches to the study of gender, citizenship and education. In M. Arnot & J. Dillabough (Eds.) *Challenging democracy: International perspectives on gender, education and citizenship* (pp.21–40). New York: Routledge/Falmer.

Dimitriadis, G., & Carlson, D. (2003). *Promises to keep: Cultural Studies, democratic education and public life*. New York: RoutledgeFalmer.

Dolby, N. (2003). Popular culture and democratic practice. *Harvard Education Review, 73,* 258–284.

Edelsky, C. (2004). Democracy in the balance. *Language Arts, 82,* 8–15.

Engel, M. (2000). *The struggle for control of public education*. Philadelphia: Temple University.

Freire, P. (1997). *Pedagogy of the heart*. New York: Continuum.

Freire, P., & Macedo, D. (1987). *Literacy: Reading the word and the world*. South Hadley, MA: Bergin & Garvey.

Giroux, H. (1993). *Living dangerously: Multiculturalism and the politics of difference*.

Giroux, H. (2003). *The abandoned generation: Democracy beyond the culture of fear*. New York: Palgrave-MacMillan.

Graff, H. (1987). *The legacies of literacy*. Bloomington: Indiana University Press.

Greene, M. (1988). *The dialectic of freedom*. New York: Teachers College Press.

Greene, (1984). *Education, freedom, and possibility*. Inaugural lecture at Teachers College, Columbia University, New York.

Hasbrook, M. (2002). Re-viewing multicultural sites: An inquiry of transcultural between ness. In J. Harmon (Ed.), *Just literacy: Promoting justice through language and learning* (pp. 58–87). New York: New York State English Council.

Hernandez, A. (1997). *Pedagogy, democracy and feminism: Rethinking the public sphere*. Albany, NY: State University of New York Press.

Hirschmann, N. (2003). *The subject of literacy: Toward a feminist theory of freedom*. Princeton, NJ: Princeton University Press.

Houston, B. (2004). Democratic Dialogue: Who takes responsibility? In M. Boler (Ed.), *Democratic dialogue in education: Troubling speech, disturbing silence* (pp. 105–120). New York: Peter Lang.

Jones, A. (2004). Talking cure: The desire for dialogue. In M. Boler (Ed.), *Democratic dialogue in education: Troubling speech, disturbing silence* (pp. 57–67). New York: Peter Lang.

Kahne, J., & Westheimer, J. (2003). Teaching democracy. *Phi Delta Kappan, 85*, 34–40.

Lankshear C. (1997). *Changing literacies*. Buckingham, UK: Open University Press.

Luke, A., & Elkins, J. (1998). Reinventing literacy in "New Times." *Journal of Adolescent & Adult Literacy, 42*, 4–7.

Miron, L., & Dhillon, P. (2004). Liberal-democratic theory, education, and the state. *Educational Researcher, 33*(5), 32–37.

Morris, M. (2000). Existential and phenomenological influences on Maxine Greene. In William Pinar (Ed.), *The passionate mind of Maxine Green: "I am—not yet"* (pp. 124–1236). London: Falmer.

Mouffe, C. (1992). Feminism, citizenship, and radical democratic politics. In J. Butler & J. Scott (Eds.), *Feminist theorize the political* (pp. 369–384). New York: Routledge.

Noddings, N. (1999). Renewing democracy in schools. *Phi Delta Kappan, 80*, 579–584.

Osborne, K. (2001). Democracy, democratic citizenship, and education. In J. Portelli & P. Solomon (Eds.), *The erosion of democracy in education: From critique to possibilities* (pp. 29–61). Calgary, Canada: Detselig.

Powell, R. (1999). *Literacy as a moral imperative*: Facing the challenges of a pluralistic society. New York: Rowman & Littlefield.

Riley, P., & Welchman, J. (2003). Rousseau, Dewey, and democracy. In R. Curan (Ed.), *A companion to the philosophy of education* (pp. 94–112). Oxford, UK: Blackwell.

Rosenblatt, L. (1938/1995). *Literature as exploration*. New York: Modern Language Association of America.

Rosenblatt, L. (1990). In E. J. Farrell & J. R. Squire (Eds.), *Transactions with literature: A fifty-year perspective.* (pp. 100–107). Urbana, IL: NCTE.

Shannon, P. (2001). Turn, turn, turn: Language education, politics and freedom at the turn of three centuries. In his edited text, *Becoming Political, too: New readings and writing on the politics of literacy education* (pp. 10–30). Portsmouth, NH: Heinemann.

Simon, R. (1992). *Teaching Against the Grain: Texts for a pedagogy of possibility.* Toronto, Canada: OISE.

Simon, R. (2001). Empowerment as a pedagogy of possibility. In P. Shannon (Ed.), *Becoming political, too: New readings and writing on the politics of literacy education* (pp. 142–155). Portsmouth, NH: Heinemann.

Spring, J. (1998). *The American School, 1642–1990.* New York: Longman.

Taylor, C. (1985). *Hegel and modern society.* Cambridge, UK: Cambridge University Press.

Westheimer, J., & Kahne J. (2004). What kind of citizen? The politics of educating for democracy. *American Educational Research Journal, 41*, 237–269.

Westheimer, J. & Kahne, J. (2003). Democracy and civic engagement. *Phi Delta Kappan, 85*, pp.63–66.

Willinsky, J. (2000*). If only we knew: Increasing the public value of Social-Science research.* New York: Routledge.

Willinsky, J. (1991). *The triumph of literature/the fate of literacy.* New York: Teachers College Press.

# Author Index

# Subject Index

## A

Aboriginal languages, 101–102
absences, in discourse, 196
academic literacy study, 133
access/gatekeeping study, 162–163
action research, 284n4
    collaborative, 144, 178, 179–181, 284n4
    critical *vs.* participatory, 6
    defining, 4, 5
    *see also* advocacy research
activity theory, 20, 280n5
    after-school activities and, 148
    bilingual community writing and, 148–149
    characteristics of, 146–147
    context and, 148
    contributions of, 151
    criticisms of, 151–152
    cultural–historical, 20, 149,
        281n7–282nn7–8
    example studies, 149–151
    history of, 147–149
    hybrid activities study, 150–151
    joint activity after-school projects study,
        149–150
    labeling study, 152
    literacy in workplace and, 148
    situated literacies and, 118
adolescent literacies, 19, 280n6–281n6

Black English study, 140
    challenges/critical responses, 144–145
    critical media literacy study, 143–144
    defining, 137
    example studies, 140–144
    fans of alternative popular culture texts
        study, 145–146
    gangsta literacy practices study, 140–142
    history of, 138–140
    identity work study, 143
    individual freedom/collective responsi-
        bility and, 140
    other studies of note, 145–146
    power relations in education and, 138–139
    race/class and, 139
    radical democratic citizenship and, 139
    social class study, 142–143
    systemic privilege and, 139
    unequal school achievement and, 138
adult literacy program, gender and access
    to, 61–62
advocacy planning. *see* advocacy research
advocacy research
    advocacy research paradigm, 5–6
    as collaborative, 4–5
    history of, 3–7
    in literacy education, 16–18